Jerusalem

HISTORY OF A GLOBAL CITY

Under the direction of Vincent
Lemire, with Katell Berthelot,
Julien Loiseau, and Yann Potin

Translated by Juliana Froggatt

UNIVERSITY OF CALIFORNIA PRESS

University of California Press
Oakland, California

© 2022 by the Regents of the University of California

Originally published as *Jérusalem: Histoire d'une ville-monde* © 2016 by
Flammarion

Library of Congress Cataloging-in-Publication Data

Names: Lemire, Vincent, 1973– editor. | Berthelot, Katell, contributor. |
  Loiseau, Julien, contributor. | Potin, Yann, contributor. | Froggatt,
  Juliana, 1981– translator.
Title: Jerusalem : history of a global city / under the direction of Vincent
  Lemire ; with Katell Berthelot, Julien Loiseau, and Yann Potin ;
  translated by Juliana Froggatt.
Description: Oakland, California : University of California Press, [2022] |
  "Originally published as Jérusalem: histoire d'une ville-monde ©2016
  by Flammarion"—Title page verso. | Includes bibliographical references
  and index.
Identifiers: LCCN 2021042865 (print) | LCCN 2021042866 (ebook) |
  ISBN 9780520299900 (hardback) | ISBN 9780520971523 (ebook)
Subjects: LCSH: Jerusalem—History.
Classification: LCC DS109.9 J4574513 (print) | LCC DS109.9 (ebook) |
  DDC 956.94/42—dc23
LC record available at https://lccn.loc.gov/2021042865
LC ebook record available at https://lccn.loc.gov/2021042866

31 30 29 28 27 26 25 24 23 22
10 9 8 7 6 5 4 3 2 1

*Publication supported by a grant from
The Community Foundation for Greater New Haven
as part of the Urban Haven Project.*

Contents

Conclusion. The Memory of the Dead, the History
of the Living   254

Maps

Introduction

Jerusalem, historical comet whose history is reduced
almost to a long burning wake, placed on its scorched hill
like a rocket on its launchpad—so much fury of eternity in
such a small body—Pythian city, epileptic city, gasping
ceaselessly at the trance of the future.

Julien Gracq, *Lettrines*, March 1967

How to write the history of an "epileptic city"? How to calmly tell the story of a city crushed by memories, exhausted by identities, compacted under the pressure of projections and projects, ground down by speeches and strategies, dismembered by claims and appropriations? Jerusalem doesn't belong to itself, Jerusalem isn't in Jerusalem, Jerusalem is a global city, a city where the whole world meets periodically, to face up to, to confront, to size up each other.

The shared cradle of three monotheistic narratives, Jerusalem is observed by the whole world as the laboratory of living together or of civil war, of urbanity or of hatred of the other. In recent years, at the mercy of the combats and confrontations that periodically run through the city, Jerusalem has become the favored stage on which to project dangerous fantasies of evildoers forging a clash of civilizations.

Julien Gracq, in March 1967, perfectly translated the overwhelming impression that grabs every reasonable historian in approaching Jerusalem as one approaches a molten crater: "historical comet," "long burning wake," prophetic or "Pythian city," which exhausts itself in preserving the most ancient past and auguring the most distant future, held

1

under pressure in an almost infinite chronological arc, from Genesis to the Apocalypse. In these conditions, how to offer a new history of Jerusalem, how to construct a renewed history of a city recounted a thousand times, overexposed, worn out by the conjunction of reputedly incompatible narratives and by the weave of superimposed identities?

We say it straightaway: the four authors assembled here refuse to consider Jerusalem the coatrack of false identities; they oppose head-on the nebulous doctrine of the clash of civilizations; they wager that the history of Jerusalem can be told without resorting to anachronistic reductions that make all of its inhabitants into passive puppets, bearers despite themselves of crude identities that today carry the simplistic names of "Jews," "Christians," and "Muslims." A ground-level history, respectful of ambivalences and ambiguities, closer to the fractures of time and the spirits of places: that, on the contrary, is what is offered in the following pages.

To meet this challenge, we must start first of all with this surprising paradox: *Jerusalem is a city without history.* Heritage is omnipresent, archaeological remains are everywhere, memories are thundering, identities are deafening, but history, in the middle of this crazy cacophony, is absent. History as a human and social science, as a scientific discipline, as an attempt to confront the sources and the association of points of view. . . . History is absent from Jerusalem, or rather it has absented itself and let itself be buried under the pile of memories. Rigorous historians work, of course, they do their best, but they are inaudible, invisible, confined among their peers in scholarly meetings and specialized academic exchanges, because this pointillistic approach is less risky for them, but also because the dominant political and social demand is for something else: Jerusalem is a store of memory, not a place of history. Universal black box, world conservatory of ancient traditions—we turn toward it to search for lost memories of a forgetful West, to reinforce the leached identities of our modern disenchantment, but rarely to truly know its history.

Is it a coincidence that up to now there has been no "History of Jerusalem from Its Origins to the Present Day" available on the book market, in either French or English? This simple fact is in itself disconcerting: although the Holy City fascinates the whole world, no serious synthesis has been offered to the public until now that attempts a global understanding of the history

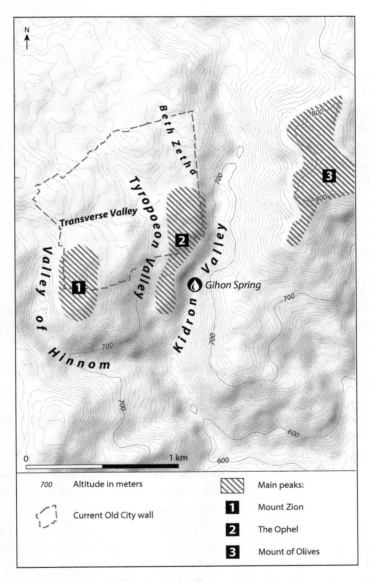

N

Beth Zetha

Tyropoeon Valley

Transverse Valley

Valley of Hinnom

Kidron Valley

1

2

Gihon Spring

700

700

700

700

700

700

800

800

3

600

600

0   1 km

700   Altitude in meters

Current Old City wall

Main peaks:

1   Mount Zion

2   The Ophel

3   Mount of Olives

Map 1. Topography of Jerusalem

of this city, which is always called "extraordinary" or "exceptional," the better to exclude it from any rational approach.[1]

A city without history, therefore, asphyxiated by memories that short-circuit and scramble its chronology: in the logic of memory, time is compacted, compressed, folded in on itself. As in a César Baldaccini "Compression," the very structure of passing time, the succession of epochs and sequences of events disappears to give place to "eternal" identities, to "perpetual" conflicts, and to "immutable" communities. One encounters so many expressions in all the pages of the books devoted to the Holy City and offered to the general public. To counter this indigestible salmagundi, to make Jerusalem a true object of history, we will thus commence by respecting its chronology—we will attempt to identify distinct historical sequences of events to show that Jerusalem is not a city more "eternal" than any other and that each of its epochs tells a singular story. Of course, moving back and forth in the chronology and overlap between chapters aren't forbidden in the pages you will read, but we will abstain from too much ruffling of calendar pages, because the succession of generations, of regimes, and of contexts is an essential safeguard against the illusion of identity permanence. At the end of this volume, a new time line gives the public, for the first time, a chronological synthesis of reference, complete and detailed.

Second paradox, perhaps less noticeable to nonspecialists: *Jerusalem is a city without geography.* Geopolitics is summoned all the time there to explain everything, borders seem to stripe its territory in every direction, maps are systematically exhibited to illustrate the great episodes of its military history, but geography as attention to topography, to elevation, to the constraints of site and the potentials of location, to climate and soils, to the layout of urban districts, to their peopling, to their activities and interactions . . . geography is absent, masked by the omnipresence of geopolitical analysis. The history of Jerusalem is generally recounted without the places (streets, monuments, hills, valleys, springs, rocks, caves, walls, cemeteries) having to be anything other than a map of a general staff or a simple setting for folkloric or patrimonial use.

In this logic, the history of Jerusalem generally ends up disembodied, as if evaporated, developing at several meters from the urban area, simple layout of ideas and actors moving in an abstract and inarticulate space.

The altitude of the city, perched at almost eight hundred meters (half a mile) at the summit of a narrow crest line; its severe climate, at once Mediterranean and mountainous; its dominant hills and deep ravines, which have forever oriented its main axes of circulation (see map 1); its position on the threshold between the rich coastal plains that border the Mediterranean to the west and the desert that plunges toward the Jordan Rift Valley and the stifling banks of the Dead Sea to the east—all of these basic facts are generally passed over in silence, as if geography had little weight in explaining the history of the Holy City. To offer a history that is incarnate, concrete, and situated in Jerusalem, we will therefore respect its geography—we will try to always refer to the places that order and shape this history, that give it their potentialities and constraints. To illustrate and accompany this "geographical requirement," ten original maps over the course of the book will permit readers to not lose sight of the terrain and to not get lost themselves.

To construct a new history of Jerusalem, we have thus chosen to rely on the most proved methods and to renew the marriage of two old academic disciplines, history and geography, whose long complicity is one of the happy original features of French universities. Starting from these two solid bases, it is possible to construct a history at once contextualized and situated, diachronic and geographic.

To escape from the abstract developments of immutable identities that pollute most of the accounts consecrated to the Holy City, a third and final principle has guided the writing of this new history of Jerusalem: starting from the observation that the Holy City is the site of the emergence and meeting of the three monotheisms, we have not wanted to consider the boundaries between these three traditions as impassable limits that have remained immobile over the centuries. Quite on the contrary, the porousness, the movements, the exchanges, and the hybridizations between these traditions have been the subject of very particular attention. Not from a fetishism of multiculturalism, but because Jerusalem itself imposes this approach: because the thrice-holy city magnetizes the foundational monotheistic traditions and concentrates them within a restricted perimeter and on a few recurrent focal points, its history is precisely that of the intense interaction among these traditions, giving rise to a large number of exchanges and transfers.

By focusing our attention on the emblematic segments that structure the urban space—on the Temple Mount / Haram al-Sharif (also called the Esplanade of the Mosques), on the walls that have often moved but whose topographical structure has remained almost unchanged, on the gates and the axes of circulation that order the city and set it in motion, on the valleys that surround Jerusalem and each preserve a particular bundle of religious traditions—we can show that the spirit of these places traverses ruptures in time and preestablished identity categories by effecting surprising transfers of sacredness. Finally, the attention paid to Jerusalem's religious places and geography makes it possible to restore the coherence and dynamics of this world city's urban history, a history at once organic and connected, local and global, anchored in its territory and open to the four winds, because Jerusalem rightfully deserves, perhaps more than any other city on the planet, to benefit from these new horizons of history.

1 The Birth of a Holy City

4000 BCE TO SECOND CENTURY CE

The paradox of Jerusalem can be summed up in a few words: a town of no major strategic importance, lacking desirable natural resources, has become the nerve center of a regional conflict with global repercussions, and its name, today pronounced by millions of people in their weekly liturgical assemblies, symbolizes a universal eschatological hope.

Jerusalem's setting has, however, many handicaps (see map 1 in the introduction). At the heart of a mountainous zone, it is away from the region's major trade routes; the main road linking Transjordan to the coastal plain passes north of Jerusalem. The first urban cluster entirely covered a rocky spur at the site today called the City of David. This hill is situated below a rise that slightly dominates it—the Temple Mount, to the north, the current Esplanade of the Mosques—which was further raised later to create a vast platform capable of containing the whole cult complex erected by that great builder King Herod. Between the Temple Mount and the rocky spur with the first urban cluster, we can moreover distinguish an intermediary space, the Ophel, which housed a specific quarter during the city's development in biblical times. The hills to the west (the current Mount Zion) and to the east (the Mount of Olives) also overlook the rocky spur.

This spur nevertheless dominates three valleys: the Kidron Valley to the east (which crosses the Judaean Desert to the Dead Sea), the Valley of Hinnom (or Gehenna) to the west, and that of Tyropoeon, which passes through approximately the middle of the present Old City from north to south. The curious word *Tyropoeon* comes from *The Jewish War* by the first-century historian Flavius Josephus[1] and literally means "Cheesemakers," but it must in fact be a corrupted form of a lost original Semitic name. Whatever the case, since at least the first century BCE, this third valley has divided the city into eastern and western parts before joining the Kidron Valley at the current Pool of Siloam, a bit north of the latter valley's junction with the Valley of Hinnom. Still another valley, less known and named Beth Zetha, runs almost in parallel with the Kidron Valley; its starting point is at the famous American Colony Hotel north of the present Old City, and it joins the Kidron Valley at the foot of the northeast end of the Temple's esplanade. It quite naturally formed the north edge of the esplanade and of the city itself in the Israelite period. This valley carries abundant water in winter, hence the presence in this area of basins like the Pool of Bethesda and the Pool of Israel (Birket Israel). Finally, the western part of the current Old City is divided by the Transverse Valley—also called the Cross Valley— the only one with a clear east-west orientation. It starts from the Citadel (near the Jaffa Gate) and joins the Tyropoeon to the north of the Western Wall (or Wailing Wall). This valley corresponded to the northern limit of the city in the Hasmonean period (see map 3). Some of these valleys are no longer visible today, as they have been partly filled in over time, but the height differences of the past have been measured during archeological digs.[2]

The main reason for the settlement of a human group on Jerusalem's site in the Bronze Age doubtless lies in the presence of a fountainhead, known as the Gihon Spring, below the rocky spur. This permitted the development of farming on the valley floor from the earliest era, despite very steep slopes and a very dry climate, in a region at the crossroads of two climatic zones, the Judaean Desert and the Mediterranean coast. The rainfall pattern, typical of a mountainous region, did not guarantee regular showers throughout the year; the rains, often violent and sudden, were concentrated from November to April. Additionally, precipitation was quite unequal from one year to the next, resulting in serious water-supply

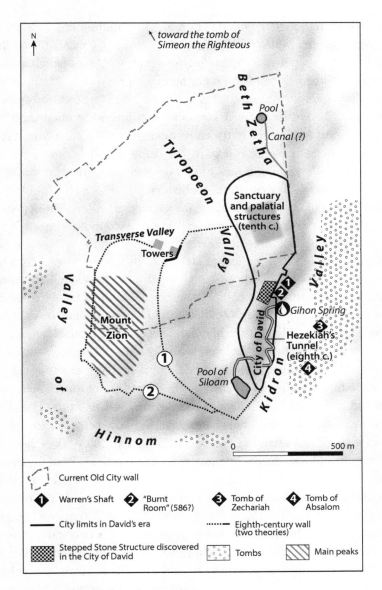

N
↑

toward the tomb of
Simeon the Righteous

Pool

Canal (?)

Beth Zetha

Tyropoeon

**Sanctuary
and palatial
structures
(tenth c.)**

Transverse Valley

Towers

Valley

Valley

**Mount
Zion**

City of David

Gihon Spring

**Hezekiah's
Tunnel
(eighth c.)**

Kidron

①

②

*Pool of
Siloam*

Valley   of

Hinnom

0   500 m

❶ ❷ ❸ ❹

⌐⌐ Current Old City wall

❶ Warren's Shaft   ❷ "Burnt
                          Room" (586?)

❸ Tomb of
    Zechariah

❹ Tomb of
    Absalom

───── City limits in David's era   ·········· Eighth-century wall
                                                        (two theories)

▨ Stepped Stone Structure discovered
    in the City of David

▫ Tombs   ▨ Main peaks

Map 2. Biblical Jerusalem

problems, even though the median rainfall (500 millimeters, or 20 inches, per year) is comparable to that of certain European areas (580 millimeters, or 23 inches, per year in London, for example). Another constraint of the site, the steep slope of the rocky spur with the first settlement area, forced the inhabitants, from the beginning, to build terraces and embankments, on which successive urban constructions were piled atop each other (see map 2). This led to the continuous reuse of materials and foundations of preceding eras and partly explains why it is difficult to find traces of certain strata and thus of certain periods—a recurrent problem for those who wish to write the city's history.

The history of ancient Jerusalem, for a long time essentially dependent on biblical sources, has nevertheless been profoundly revised by the archaeological excavations that have been conducted there since the nineteenth century, but also by those at other Middle Eastern sites, which have helped to put into our hands evidence (Moabite or Assyrian, for example) invalidating or confirming certain elements of biblical tales.[3] Indeed, at the heart of the historiography of Jerusalem and of ancient Israel in general resides the problem of the historical accuracy of biblical information and of its often conflicting dialogue with the material remains unearthed by archaeological digs.[4] This methodological problem arises equally for the postbiblical period—Flavius Josephus's testimony must similarly be corrected in the light of archaeological data on Judaea in the Hellenistic and Roman eras, for example—but it is particularly acute for the biblical era, in view of the sacred character of the text in the eyes of Jews and Christians, as well as the contemporary political issues around the State of Israel. Modern Israel's founding fathers indeed considered the biblical tales of the ancient Kingdoms of Israel and Judah as one of the pillars of the new state's legitimacy, and today the Bible still remains the great founding story of Israeli national identity—hence the particular intensity of the debate on the reigns of David and Solomon, from whom the Israelite and Judaean monarchies ensued. Yet, as we will see, from the point of view of Jerusalem's urban history, David's reign seems not to have represented a real break but is, rather, in keeping with the Canaanite occupation of the site. Without necessarily rejecting the testimony of the biblical sources, which can contain useful information if read critically, the historian must be freed from the theological interpretation of history that characterizes the Deuteronomistic corpus, all the biblical books called "historical," from Joshua to Second Kings.

In antiquity, as in later periods, politics and religion were closely mingled. Without artificially disassociating what should be thought of jointly, we must nevertheless emphasize the strictly political, geostrategic, urban, economic, and social aspects of this history. It is furthermore necessary to grasp the fundamental role, at once social, political, and religious, of the Temple of Jerusalem, a role that escalated from around the tenth century BCE until its destruction in 70 CE (in spite of its destruction and reconstruction during the sixth century BCE) and conferred on the city, little by little, its specificity and its greatness. Alongside the chronology based on the empires that successively dominated the Middle East (Assyria, Babylonia, Persia, Hellenistic kingdoms, Rome) appears a Jewish chronology which for its part describes a "period of the First Temple" (tenth century–586 BCE) and a "period of the Second Temple" (c. 539 BCE–70 CE), interrupted by the Babylonian interval—that is, a chronology centered on the construction and destruction of sanctuaries.

In a manner altogether ordinary for antiquity, Jerusalem's history is, in fact, punctuated by wars, destruction, and reconstruction: the Assyrian siege of 701 BCE, Babylonian destruction of 586 BCE, punitive expedition and profanation of the Temple by Antiochus IV in 167 BCE, capture by Antiochus VII in 134–133 BCE, capture by Pompey in 63 BCE, capture by Herod in 37 BCE, and destruction by the Romans in 70 CE, to mention only the most prominent events of the city's ancient history. Constantly, in the sources relating to these episodes, the question of the sanctuary menaced, profaned, or saved in extremis appears in the foreground. The alternation of destructions and reconstructions concerns above all the walls of the city, indispensable protection and guarantee of independence. Once again, looking past the episodes of destruction, we observe throughout the first millennium BCE a crescendo, up to the apogee represented by the construction of the third wall by Herod Agrippa I in the first century CE, followed by the radical destruction in 70 (see map 3). As we will see, the defeat in 70 followed by the foundation of the Roman colony Aelia Capitolina in the second century CE represents the deepest and most enduring rupture that ancient Jerusalem experienced. But we must first of all return to the modest beginnings of the little urban cluster that would become the thrice-holy city.

THE BRONZE AGE: A FORTRESS AROUND A SPRING

The very first proof of the presence of even slightly sedentary humans, dating back to the end of the fourth millennium BCE, is hardly impressive: it was at best an unfortified farming village, situated near the Gihon Spring. Graves began to appear at that time on the southwest slope of the Mount of Olives, the eastern slope of the Kidron Valley (see map 2). They continued to be used, it appears, during the phase when the site was abandoned in the middle of the third millennium BCE. This abandonment isn't unique to Jerusalem, as the surface excavations conducted in the West Bank by Israel Finkelstein, an archaeologist at Tel Aviv University, revealed the existence of recurrent cycles of occupation in the "highlands" (Judaea-Samaria, the current West Bank) from the fourth millennium until the beginning of the Iron Age, in the twelfth century. According to the archaeologist's observations, the same sites were inhabited, abandoned, and then reoccupied on three occasions: around 3000, around 1800, and finally around 1200.[5] Jerusalem fits well in this general pattern, but during the second occupation cycle, in the Middle Bronze Age, it had already emerged as a regional power, despite its unusual character. Indeed, the remains of a fortress with imposing walls, dating to the eighteenth century BCE, have been uncovered, notably near the Gihon Spring; the perimeter wall must have been around three meters (ten feet) wide. Comparable fortifications have been identified at Tel Rumeida, now part of Hebron, and at Tell Balata, ancient Shechem (modern-day Nablus).

Jerusalem thus very probably represented one of the principal city-states that developed during the second urbanization phase in Canaan. This hypothesis is corroborated by the mention of Jerusalem in an execration text (that is, a text consisting of a curse) discovered on a nineteenth-century BCE Egyptian figurine, as well as in eighteenth-century BCE Egyptian documents. Jerusalem is designated in these as R-Sh-L-M-M, which should perhaps be pronounced as Rushalimum, and two names of chiefs are associated with it, Shas'an and Y'qar'am. The statuette is broken, which symbolically represents the desire to break the city's political resistance in the face of Egyptian power, in the framework of a quasi-magical performative rite.

The hydraulic system might equally constitute a sign of Jerusalem's development at this period. According to the archaeologist Ronny Reich, who brought to light the existence of a tower next to the Gihon Spring, the water-supply structure known as Warren's Shaft (named for the archaeologist who discovered it in the nineteenth century) dates at least in part to this era, and not to the tenth century BCE, as presumed by Yigal Shiloh, who excavated the City of David in the 1980s (see map 2). Also according to Reich, there was a similar water-supply structure inside Gezer, an important city-state on the coastal plain, in the same period. The importance of these constructions indirectly testifies to the demographic importance of the city, because these projects required the ability to draw on a substantial workforce. Finally, one last indication of Jerusalem's development in the eighteenth century BCE lies in the presence of decorated bone plaques, probably from finely worked furniture or boxes.[6]

Following biblical chronology, and provided that one equates the Salem of Genesis 14:18 with Jerusalem, the latter was governed in the eighteenth century BCE by a king named Melchizedek ("King of righteousness" or "My king is justice"), a priest of God Most High, to whom Abraham gave "one-tenth of everything."[7] Genesis was likely redacted very late (sixth century BCE or after), and its historicity is strongly subject to caution, but it remains significant that this text depicts a king at Jerusalem at such an early stage. Perhaps this is the echo of an earlier period, in the fourteenth century BCE, when we know from a reliable source, thanks to Egyptian evidence, that a king reigned at Jerusalem.

But between the nineteenth and eighteenth centuries BCE, we observe first and foremost a phase of decline, again characteristic of the region's highlands as a whole throughout the Late Bronze Age (1550–1200 BCE). The settlements near Jerusalem were depopulated, and Jerusalem itself also seems to have declined. Moreover, we know that at the end of the sixteenth century BCE, Canaan fell into the orbit of the Egyptian Empire. The Canaanite city-states, governed by kinglets, retained a limited autonomy under strict Egyptian control, exercised through governors installed at Gaza and Bet She'an. This was the time of the Eighteenth Dynasty.

FOURTEENTH CENTURY BCE: THE CAPITAL OF KING ABDI-HEBA, UNDER EGYPTIAN CONTROL

A chance archaeological discovery in Egypt, at El Amarna (the capital of the pharaoh Akhenaton, considered a precursor of monotheistic religions), brought to light evidence unexpectedly related to fourteenth-century BCE Jerusalem, while excavations in that city itself have found hardly any vestiges of the era besides a few shards. There was nothing from Jerusalem itself, therefore, to suggest that it was the residence of a local governor or kinglet. However, the diplomatic correspondence found at El Amarna is definite: of the 382 inventoried letters, six or even seven tablets were sent by the king of Jerusalem Abdi-Heba (or Abdi-Hepa), "Servant of Heba" (a Hurrian goddess); two other tablets, sent by a sovereign named Shuwardata, in turn invoke Jerusalem, called Urushalim, "The city founded by Shalim," a Canaanite divinity.

The content of these letters, written in Akkadian by a scribe of "Syrian" origin, reveals that Abdi-Heba must have been educated at the Egyptian court, where, like other Canaanite princes, he was likely sent as a hostage. It was the pharaoh himself who named Abdi-Heba the king of Jerusalem, which seems to have been a city of modest size then. An Egyptian garrison of probably fifty men was stationed there, meant to protect the city against attacks by the Habiru (or ʿApiru), more or less nomadic groups that sometimes allowed themselves to be recruited as mercenaries and sometimes gave themselves up to pillaging herds (let us recall in passing that the theory of an assimilation between the Habiru and the ancient Hebrews is now largely abandoned). But, in fact, the Egyptian garrison posed a problem for Abdi-Heba, perhaps because he was not able to pay the salary he owed it, in the form of food, drink, and so forth. The garrison ended up leaving the city, and the Canaanite king then sent repeated appeals to the pharaoh for new troops. During this period, Abdi-Heba was struggling with the kings of the Shephelah (the coastal plain), alongside the sovereign of Akko (now Acre) and Shuwardata, who probably governed what later became southern Judaea. Later evidence shows that the political configuration subsequently changed: Abdi-Heba then allied with Milkilu, the king of Gezer, and fought Shuwardata, whom he opposed in a territorial dispute.

Two letters mention the "territory of Jerusalem," which apparently extended from the Idumean hills in the south and from the area of Gezer in the southwest to an undetermined point in the direction of Shechem to the north.[8] Does this mean Jerusalem was fortified at that time? Seemingly no, as we have found no vestige of this in the field, but it is difficult to imagine that the imposing walls of the eighteenth-century BCE fortress had completely disappeared. Perhaps part of these fortifications remained in use.

In any event, a continuity can be observed in burial places: we find tombs from the fourteenth century BCE on the western slope of the Mount of Olives, just like those of an earlier age. In the western part of modern Jerusalem, a Canaanite tomb from that period has also been discovered, which contained vases imported from Cyprus and Mycenaean Greece. But considering the distance that separates this site from the City of David, its link with Abdi-Heba's city remains uncertain (see map 2).

Fourteenth-century Jerusalem has not left significant archaeological traces, with the exception of a discovery made in July 2010 that throws further light on this period. The excavations conducted by Eilat Mazar in the Ophel area unearthed a small fragment (2.8 by 2 centimeters, or 1.1 by 0.79 inches) of a clay tablet inscribed in Akkadian and dating to the fourteenth century. This is the most ancient written document ever found in Jerusalem, almost six centuries older than the inscription in what is known as Hezekiah's Tunnel. Analysis of its clay seems to indicate that this tablet was made in Jerusalem. Although only a few words can be deciphered, the quality of the writing is so remarkable that it must be the work of an experienced scribe. According to Wayne Horowitz, an Assyriologist at the Hebrew University of Jerusalem, this tablet alone confirms the existence of a royal court where scribes were charged with writing diplomatic letters and administrative documents requiring advanced skills.[9] In 2013, a second fragment of cuneiform tablet was found in the Ophel area, but it has only a few letters. It is from a different tablet than fragment 1: it might be slightly older and Egyptian in origin.[10]

We wish to emphasize the fact that if the chance discovery in Egypt had not put into our hands the above-described correspondence in Akkadian (to which we must now add the two tablet fragments found in Jerusalem itself), we could have thought that fourteenth-century BCE Jerusalem was deserted or at most barely more than a hamlet. Although the absence of archaeological traces is a problem for the historian, it does not therefore permit definitive conclusions, particularly concerning a site where continuous erosion and occupation have played a large role in the effacement of remains. It will be useful to remember this in evaluating current debates about tenth-century BCE Jerusalem, the time when, according to the Bible, David and then Solomon reigned over Jerusalem: the gap between relatively abundant textual documentation and lacunary archaeological evidence is still the principal source of debate among historians today.

TWELFTH TO ELEVENTH CENTURIES BCE: A "JEBUSITE," "HITTITE," OR "CANAANITE" CITY?

The biblical texts make no secret of Jerusalem's existence prior to the emergence of the Kingdoms of Israel and Judah, which formed between the tenth and ninth centuries BCE. The book of Joshua, which records the conquest of the promised land by the children of Israel, supposed to have taken place from the end of the thirteenth through the twelfth century BCE, presents Jerusalem as a city of the Jebusites, one of the peoples whom the Bible describes as settled in Canaan at that time.

These Jebusites are known only through the biblical tradition. According to the archaeologist Benjamin Mazar and the Bible scholar Moshe Weinfeld, who both taught at the Hebrew University of Jerusalem, one from the 1940s to the 1970s and the other from the 1970s to the 1990s, the Jebusites were one of the peoples who migrated south after the collapse of the Hittite Empire at the end of the thirteenth century BCE. The Hittites, whose territory stretched from Anatolia (in modern-day Turkey) to northern Syria and Mesopotamia, are counted among the great kingdoms of the Bronze Age, alongside Egypt, Mycenae, and Assyria, the last then a rising power. The Jebusites might have formed a subgroup within the Hittites. A biblical text such as Ezekiel 16:3 (or 16:45), where God tells Jerusalem, "Your father was an Amorite, and your mother a Hittite," might contain, according to Weinfeld, the echo of a distant historical reality, relating to the Canaanite and Hittite origin of the city's non-Israelite population. The question of the connection between the Anatolian Hittites and the "Hittites" mentioned in the Bible among the seven peoples of

Canaan is still debated, but Weinfeld has pointed out that Hittite documents have rites very similar to those of the Bible's priestly code: for example, after giving birth, a woman must be purified by the sacrifice of a lamb and a pigeon or turtledove, as in Leviticus 12:6.[11] These similarities seem to corroborate the theory of real contacts between the Hittite Empire and the southern Levant. For other archaeologists and historians, however, the "Jebusites" cannot be distinguished from the Canaanites. The arguments drawn from biblical texts, of uncertain date, are indeed tenuous, to say the least.

According to Joshua 10, Jerusalem was governed by a king named Adoni-zedek, "My lord is justice," a name which cannot fail to recall that of Melchizedek, "My king is justice," in Genesis 14. This sovereign was placed at the head of a coalition of Canaanite city-states, all of which Joshua defeated. However, while the book of Joshua evokes a total and brilliant conquest of the country of Canaan—which archaeologists today agree has almost no historical truth—Jerusalem itself is presented as remaining in the hands of its Canaanite inhabitants (Jo 15:63). The book of Judges, which immediately follows Joshua, relays a contradictory narrative: according to Judges 1:8, Jerusalem was taken and burned by the Tribe of Judah, but a few verses later (Jgs 1:21), the text reproduces the book of Joshua's version. In fact, most biblical accounts instead argue that David took the city some two centuries after the supposed time of the conquest, when, according to the second book of Samuel (5:1–10), he had already been king at Hebron for seven years.

Outside the Bible, Jerusalem's history between the fourteenth century and the start of the period called Israelite, in the tenth or even ninth century, is documented only by archaeological vestiges whose interpretation is fiercely disputed. Thus, the famous "Stepped Stone Structure" on the east side of the City of David, consisting of terraces abutting a main retaining wall (the most monumental part of the current archaeological park), goes back a priori to the twelfth or eleventh century—that is, the period of Jebusite or Canaanite occupation (see map 2). Although of small extent, the city already would have constituted a substantial urban conglomeration, probably fortified, and endowed, as in earlier times, with a water-supply system accessible from inside the walls. Numerous questions remain, like that of the possible relations that Jerusalem maintained with the hinterland and the new villages that multiplied in the twelfth and eleventh centuries in the highlands, villages that are agreed, on account of several centuries of continuous occupation, to qualify as "proto-Israelite."

FROM JEBUS TO ZION, THE CITY OF DAVID: RUPTURE OR CONTINUITY?

According to the Bible, at the very end of the eleventh and the start of the tenth century BCE began the period of the so-called United Monarchy, David and his son Solomon reigning from Jerusalem over a kingdom that certain biblical passages describe as extending from Egypt to the Euphrates. For many years, the reality and scope of the rupture represented by David's era in the history of Jerusalem has been one of the most heated historiographical debates in ancient Middle East archaeology. This debate, moreover, relates to another controversy, concerning the low or high (also called "conventional" and then "modified conventional," following some revision) chronology that must be applied to the sites of ancient Israel. Without entering into the technical details of this quarrel between specialists, let us simply remember that proponents of the low chronology tend to shift the dating of archaeological vestiges forward forty to seventy years, thus situating at the end of the tenth or even the beginning of the ninth century the remains that some archaeologists, however, associate with David's reign, traditionally dated to the beginning of the tenth century. The debate's other element remains the biblical narrative, which has long been the object of an uncritical reading. Its degree of historicity has received very different assessments: Israel Finkelstein, for instance, believes that the accounts of David and Solomon are historically unreliable and in reality reflect later preoccupations, dating to the eighth and seventh centuries, notably linked to the reigns of Manasseh and Josiah. For his part, Amnon Ben-Tor, of the Hebrew University of Jerusalem, denounces what he judges to be an ideological preconception and objects to depriving ourselves of an essential resource by refusing to use the accounts in the books of Samuel and of Kings to reconstruct the history of the United Monarchy.

In these complex debates, the most convincing position ultimately occupies the middle ground. We can assume that the extent and the influence of David's kingdom were idealized by the redactors of the biblical texts, whose goal was not historical exactitude: David often takes on the traits of a legendary hero in these books. But the hypercritical exegetes and extreme minimalist historians such as Thomas L. Thompson and Niels Peter Lemche, for whom the entire saga of David and Solomon boils down to a myth, pure and simple, obviously go to the other extreme. The Tel Dan victory stele, which must undoubtedly be attributed to the king of Damascus Hazael, and that of the Moabite king Mesha—both dated to the ninth century BCE—make reference, for example, to the triumphs of foreign kings against the kings of Israel and Judah and present these latter as "of David's dynasty." The concordance of these attestations, scarcely a century after the period associated with David's reign, makes extremely likely his historical existence, as well as his role in founding a "dynasty" that reigned over the Kingdom of Judah. However, it remains difficult to determine the extent of the territory included in the Davidic kingdom.

Archaeological excavations conducted in the 1960s and 1980s and again today in the Arab neighborhood of Silwan in the City of David (a biblical designation going back to 2 Samuel 5:7, which also refers to the village as "the stronghold of Zion") confirm the site's occupation in the tenth century BCE, during the period traditionally called the United Monarchy. But as we have seen, the dating of some remains that would enable us to evaluate the importance of constructions from that era poses problems, as they go back in part to the twelfth and eleventh centuries BCE—that is, the period of Canaanite occupation. According to most archaeologists, the Stepped Stone Structure on the City of David's east side already supported the Canaanite city's acropolis, located on top of the hill. The Israelite city retained this structure, reinforced many times over. The excavations directed by Eilat Mazar in 2005, moreover, uncovered vestiges of a building that was constructed *on* the Stepped Stone Structure and whose thick walls led to its identification as a fortress of an exceptional importance for the period and the region—and this at a time when Jerusalem itself was smaller than many cities of the coast or the highlands (see map 2). Mazar saw these as remains of David's palace (2 Samuel 5:11), but most archaeologists dispute this conclusion.[12] Amihai Mazar (Eilat's cousin) for his part concluded, based on the dating of pottery associated with these walls, that they belong to the twelfth or eleventh century—that is, before the Israelite period.[13] This interpretation of the archaeological remains is not incompatible with the account of 2 Samuel 5:7–9, according to which David conquered a city that already had a fortress.[14] But other interpretations have been proposed: For Ronny Reich, the construction of the Stepped Stone Structure cannot be precisely dated (he places it between the thirteenth and seventh centuries), and the tenth century, after all, has left very few archaeological traces.[15] As for Israel Finkelstein, he believes that the Stepped Stone Structure postdates the era of David and Solomon by at least a century, arguing that ceramic debris found between the steps dates to the ninth or even the eighth century BCE.[16]

The debates among archaeologists are thus steaming right along. Insofar as the technical arguments relating to stratigraphy (the identification and dating of an archaeological site's layers) and the dating of pottery, which the nonspecialist would have a hard time verifying, have been handled with authority by both sides and delivered to the reader as so many decisive proofs of very divergent theories, it is difficult to disentangle the true from the false, or at least the accurate from the inaccurate, and the raw data from their interpretation. Nonetheless, it seems clear that tenth-century BCE Jerusalem was not the capital of a great empire, but it was possibly an important regional center under the aegis of a charismatic and enterprising chief, protected by an imposing citadel. In comparison, remember that no archaeological find in situ (except the two tablet fragments discussed above) documents the period of Abdi-Heba's reign in the fourteenth century, yet we know that Jerusalem at that time was the capital of a small, localized kingdom (even if it was under Egyptian control). We must thus guard against drawing hasty conclusions from the silence of the sources, even archaeological, if only because archaeological discoveries keep coming and are often complementary but sometimes contradict one another.

To identify the developments of the tenth century BCE and the historicity of the biblical account of Davidic kingship, data other than those concerning Jerusalem alone must be taken into account. The discovery in 2008 of a fortified city on the southwest border of the territory identified as the Kingdom of Judah, at Khirbet Qeiyafa, seems to corroborate the theory that a centralized political entity formed in Judah in the tenth century, at least according to the archaeologist in charge of the excavation,

Joseph Garfinkel. He emphasizes that the type of fortifications identified at Khirbet Qeiyafa corresponds to what is known of later Kingdom of Judah sites, for example at Beit Shemesh or Beersheba. He also asserts that an ostracon (a fragment of pottery) was found there bearing traces of writing, unfortunately very difficult to decipher, which might refer to legal matters or even social justice issues. The use of writing and the existence of administrative documents, and thus of scribes, might be a clue to the formation of the Kingdom of Judah at the end of the eleventh or beginning of the tenth century—that is, in the era that the Bible associates with David.[17] But it is still necessary to demonstrate with certainty that the writing is Hebrew and that the city should be linked to the Israelite camp and not to that of the Philistines on the coastal plain. The absence of pork bones tips the balance in favor of the former, without closing the debate. Finally, two portable altars found at the Khirbet Qeiyafa site have decorated columns that recall the biblical description of Solomon's Temple (see below), which some researchers have seen as an additional clue in favor of the site's identification as an Israelite city. Remember, however, that portable altars framed by columns had already been discovered at non-Israelite sites in the past, for example at Tell el-Far'ah in Samaria. To summarize, no piece of evidence taken in isolation is entirely conclusive, but their joint presence tends to give weight to the theory of the politico-military organization of the Kingdom of Judah beginning at the end of the eleventh century BCE. The question of altars and of worship, moreover, brings us to the debate around Solomon's Temple and takes us back to Jerusalem.

EXTENSION TOWARD THE TEMPLE MOUNT: A NEW CENTER?

According to the traditional chronology, the tenth century BCE saw a fundamental step in Jerusalem's development: its extension to the north, onto the hill that later became the Temple Mount, with the construction, attributed to Solomon by the first book of Kings, of an architectural ensemble comprising a sanctuary, its annexes, and a palace—or more exactly, a palatial ensemble consisting of several buildings, perhaps including a court of justice and an arsenal (see 1 Kgs 7; see map 2). This extension gave the city a new center, still very much alive today. If the description given is reliable, the extension to the north, accompanied by the enlargement of the Israelite acropolis over the entire area between the City of David's summit and the Temple Mount, must have doubled the city's size, which probably then reached between twelve and sixteen hectares (thirty to forty acres). Moshe Weinfeld stresses how revolutionary an event in the history of ancient Israel the transformation of Jerusalem into a royal sanctuary was, because of the resulting centralization of worship and progressive rejection of other Israelite places of worship—for example Bethel, which Amos 7:13 refers to as "the king's sanctuary." But from the point of view of Jerusalem's history, the status of royal city was part of an already ancient tradition; as for the place of worship, many have wondered about a possible continuity of occupation at the site, with the Israelite sanctuary succeeding a Canaanite sanctuary earlier situated on the Temple Mount. However, this hypothesis, linked to the question of the rupture or continuity between the Canaanite period and that of the Israelite monarchy, remains unprovable. A late biblical tradition, attested for the first time in the second book of Chronicles (2 Chr 3:1), composed in the era of the Second Temple, associates the Temple Mount with the Mount Moriah on which Abraham almost sacrificed his son Isaac, according to Genesis 22:2. This quasi sacrifice, generally interpreted as a proof of Abraham's faith but also (in Second Temple and Rabbinic Judaism) as a merit of Abraham's and Isaac's that expiated the sins of all the generations of the people of Israel, was thus associated with the Israelite Temple's atoning and purifying function. But it must be emphasized that this mythical narrative and its rereadings are largely subsequent to the construction of the sanctuary itself.

Temple-palace complexes are well attested in the ancient Middle East at that time, and the detailed description of the Temple's architecture and internal organization found in 1 Kings 6–7, even if it contains some a posteriori idealization, overlaps in many ways with the data of sites known elsewhere in the Levant, such as Ain Dara in northern Syria or Tell Tayinat in southern Turkey. We find at these sites a tripartite division of the temple among the porch (*ulam* in Hebrew), the sanctuary proper (*heikhal*), and the "Holy of Holies" (*devir*), where, according to the biblical tradition, was found not a statue of the divinity but the Ark of the Covenant containing the Tablets of the Law, crowned by two cherubim representing the throne of God. Two pillars often appear at the entrance of these sanctuaries, perhaps symbolizing the threshold of the divine dwelling; the Bible describes those of the Temple as richly decorated and gives them the names Jachin and Boaz (1 Kgs 7:21). Insofar as these Middle East architectural traditions predate the Assyrian invasion of the eighth century BCE and disappear thereafter, it seems that the biblical stories convey a memory of historical facts going back to a period before the end of the eighth century.

The exact location of the buildings on the Temple Mount and an assessment of the architectural complex's importance remain, however, hypothetical, because, according to all the archaeologists, no trace of the First Temple or of Solomon's palace can be found. Two factors can help to explain this absence of archaeological remains: first, the rocky character of the Temple Mount, but more importantly the later constructions, which contributed to the disappearance of any trace of the first edifices. Added to this is the impossibility (since the birth of modern archaeology, in the middle of the nineteenth century) of excavating on the esplanade itself, which complicates the archaeologists' task even more. In any case, the degree of continuity between the eras of the First Temple (tenth century to 586 BCE) and the Second Temple (end of the sixth century BCE to 70 CE) is large enough that the location of the First Temple on the esplanade is beyond doubt. In fact, according to the traditional chronology, the construction of the Second Temple began at the very start of the Persian period—that is, about fifty years after the destruction of the first (see below). It is highly doubtful that in just two generations the memory of the First Temple's site could have been lost, especially since the theory of a Jerusalem completely emptied of its inhabitants after the destruction of 586 BCE is today strongly called into question. To summarize, the relatively short amount of time elapsed between destruction and reconstruction, added to the permanent Judaean presence in the region of Jerusalem during this period, permits the very likely conclusion that the Second Temple was built on the site of the first. As to the location of the Second Temple, there is no doubt about it, thanks to monumental remains of the Herodian era still visible today.

EIGHTH CENTURY BCE: AN UNPRECEDENTED
PHASE OF URBAN DEVELOPMENT

According to archaeological sources, Jerusalem's true urban boom did not happen until the end of the ninth century BCE and reached its peak at the end of the eighth or the very beginning of the seventh century, the era of King Hezekiah and his immediate successors, whose historical existence is corroborated by a great many documents outside the Bible. Seemingly insignificant findings have furnished invaluable information on the inhabitants' standard of living and on the commercial exchanges that then connected Jerusalem to the coastal plain and the Phoenician cities there. During their excavations in the City of David, Ronny Reich and Eli Shukron found both quite large numbers of bones from Mediterranean fish and *bullae* (small round pieces of clay bearing the impression of a stone seal) used to seal the packages in which goods were transported, at least one of which depicts a Phoenician ship. Such a massive import of fish evinces, according to the archaeologists, an elevated standard of living and consequently the presence of a significant urban elite, which could not exist except in a developed and prosperous city. Proto-Aeolian capitals discovered in the 1960s by Kathleen Kenyon on the east side of the City of David testify to a certain architectural refinement and to developed regional exchanges. These capitals are comparable to those found in the great northern centers such as Hazor, Megiddo, and Samaria in the eighth century BCE, with palmate motifs recalling the decoration of Phoenician ivory objects. Just a few kilometers south of the City of David, archaeological excavations in the Ramat Rachel kibbutz have moreover brought to light the remains of a Judaean royal palace also containing architectural characteristics inspired by the Northern Kingdom and by Phoenicia. Eighth-century BCE Jerusalem, the capital of the Kingdom of Judah, was thus in all likelihood integrated into a network of exchanges made as much with the Kingdom of Israel to the north as with the Phoenician cities of the Mediterranean coast.[18]

But the eighth century was also under the shadow of the growing threat of the Neo-Assyrian Empire (911–609 BCE), which was then asserting itself as the dominant Middle Eastern power, going so far as to conquer Egyptian cities in the seventh century BCE. In the service of an expansionist policy, the Assyrian army won victory after victory, frequently followed by massacres and deportations. The annals of the Assyrian kings and the bas-reliefs of their palaces testify abundantly, but perhaps also with exaggeration (like all propaganda), to the cruelty of the abuse inflicted on the populations that refused to submit to the Assyrian yoke. In 722 BCE, Shalmaneser V took Samaria, the capital of the Kingdom of Israel, which was annexed by his successor, Sargon II; the Assyrian armies then menaced the south, which they invaded in 701 BCE. A bas-relief from Sennacherib's palace at Nineveh (today displayed at the British Museum in London) documents, in an exceptional manner, the siege of Lachish, the Kingdom of Judah's second city (after Jerusalem), and portrays the surrender and deportation of the conquered Judaeans. Jerusalem held out against an Assyrian siege in 701 and escaped the fate of Samaria and Lachish, as testify not only the second book of Kings but also cylinders from the Assyrian royal archive, such as the Taylor Prism, found at Nineveh, which refers to "Hezekiah the Judahite, who did not submit to" Sennacherib's "yoke."[19] The Assyrian retreat doubtless increased the prestige of the deity residing in the temple at Jerusalem and consequently of the sanctuary itself, according to the belief, widespread at the time, that it is the gods who award victory.

In any case, the influx of refugees from the north and from the areas of the Kingdom of Judah devastated by the Assyrians was without doubt the principal factor in Jerusalem's exceptional urban development at the end of the eighth and beginning of the seventh centuries, even if some scholars, such as Nadav Na'aman, defend the theory of a more gradual increase, linked instead to a socioeconomic development supported by the hinterland.[20]

Reich and Shukron's excavations in the area around the Gihon Spring revealed the remains of the City of David's eighth-century eastern wall, as well as dwellings that demonstrate population density (see map 2). Faced with demographic pressure, Jerusalem expanded to the north and to the west, across what is today Mount Zion. In 2013, in the area around Gihon, figurines and a ceramic bowl shard with a partially preserved Hebrew inscription (comprising two names) were also found, which date to the eighth or seventh century.[21]

In the Old City's Jewish Quarter, Nahman Avigad's excavations have revealed the existence of an enormous wall (seven meters, or twenty-three feet, wide) also going back to the eighth century. Remains found around the Citadel at the Jaffa Gate indicate that the city's western limit had already reached this area at that time. Cemeteries also multiplied over the course of the eighth and seventh centuries: that period saw the development of the northern cemetery, beyond the present Damascus Gate, and the Valley of Hinnom also welcomed a large number of burials, while the east slope of the Kidron Valley housed the tombs of the richest families. Some of these tombs, partly cut into the rock, are small monuments (like that commonly called the Tomb of Pharaoh's Daughter) and have Hebrew inscriptions, for example ". . . yahu, master of the household," which doubtless refers to a high royal functionary; we see here a possible connection with the king's steward Shebna(yahu) mentioned in Isaiah 22:15–16. Finally, it was also during this period that the water-supply system became more complex, with the creation of the Siloam Channel (or Channel II), associated with an irrigation system, and with what is called the Siloam or Hezekiah's Tunnel (although nothing allows its certain attribution to him, beyond the hypothesis of works undertaken with a view to resisting an Assyrian siege, and the testimony of 2 Kgs 20:20). The tunnel, 533 meters (1,749 feet) long, carved into rock, permitted the flow of the Gihon Spring's water to what is called the Pool of Siloam, located south of the City of David, inside the walls (see map 2). A six-line Hebrew inscription, found in 1880 at the southern end of the tunnel, reports how the two teams of workers that dug it—one from the north, the other from the south—succeeded in joining up the two parts at the halfway point.

In the eighth and seventh centuries, Jerusalem was thus an extensive, developed, and prosperous city, a true religious and administrative center of the Kingdom of Judah. According to Yigal Shiloh, in the seventh century, Jerusalem stretched across sixty hectares (148 acres), an area ten times larger than that of the Canaanite city that David conquered.[22] In the same era, Lachish, about fifty kilometers (thirty miles) southwest of Jerusalem and considered Judah's second city, covered only eight hectares (twenty acres). Moreover, Shiloh's excavations on the City of David's east side, in a neighborhood that may have contained public buildings adjacent to the residences of notables of the court, brought to light a significant number of bullae revealing the existence of administrative archives. These bullae generally carry the name of the stamp's owner, according to the usual formula: "Belongs to X, son of Y." More than 60 percent of the names include a theophoric component such as *yahu* (e.g., Hilqiyahu) or

El (e.g., Elishama). On one of the bullae, we read the name of "Gemaryahu son of Shaphan," who might have been the scribe active under King Jehoiakim, son of Josiah, referred to in the book of Jeremiah (36:9–13). Other clay bullae bearing the names of Judaean cities in Paleo-Hebrew evince the existence of a tax system in the seventh century BCE, probably under the reign of Manasseh, the son of Hezekiah. A fiscal bulla recently discovered in situ during excavations around the Temple Mount by Reich and Shukron bears an inscription that can be translated as "The seventh [regnal year] / Bethlehem / for the king."[23] This type of fiscal stamp was affixed to the commodities sent to Jerusalem as royal taxes in kind.

On the religious side, we observe that the animal statuettes and fertility figurines (representing women supporting an abundant bosom with their hands) found in the archaeological layers corresponding to the seventh century are all broken and disappear completely thereafter, in the layers dated to the Persian and Hellenistic eras. Many see this as a confirmation of the historicity of "Josiah's reformation," which would have imposed a strict monotheism (2 Kgs 23:1–20).

A number of texts from the prophetic biblical books, whose first redaction may be reasonably dated to the eighth and seventh centuries, bear witness to an evolution in the representation of Jerusalem, at least within certain elite groups. Perhaps in connection with the growing centralization of worship, they describe Jerusalem as the center of the world, toward which the nations rush to venerate the God of Israel; the city supplants Mount Sinai, the place of revelation, in becoming the place from which the revelation will be communicated to all humanity. In the book of Isaiah, this vision is accompanied by an ideal of universal peace:

In days to come
the mountain of the Lord's house
shall be established as the highest of the mountains,
and shall be raised above the hills;
all the nations shall stream to it.
Many peoples shall come and say,
"Come, let us go up to the mountain of the Lord. . . . "
. . . .
They shall beat their swords into plowshares,
and their spears into pruning hooks;

nation shall not lift up sword against nation,
neither shall they learn war any more.

(Is 2:2–4; cf. Mi 4:1–4)

This vision of the city-temple as the center of the world is rooted in Mesopotamian traditions going back to the end of the third millennium, which also evoked a central sanctuary on which people converged from the ends of the earth to bring offerings to and prostrate themselves before the sanctuary's god. Nippur and Babylon, in particular, gave birth to such ideologies.

For Moshe Weinfeld, five elements characterize the biblical or immediately postbiblical traditions concerning the city-temple Jerusalem, largely attributable to the Mesopotamian background: First of all, the Temple is presented as located on the highest mountain in the world—hardly credible in Jerusalem's case but nevertheless echoing the Songs of Ascents and texts that describe Mount Zion. The second element concerns the connection between the earthly temple and the celestial temple, the former representing the gate of heaven; this aspect is present in chapter 6 of the book of Isaiah. The third element matches the notion of *tabbur ha-aretz*, "center" or "navel of the world," which also applied to the sanctuary at Delphi; it is found especially throughout the postexilic book of Ezekiel. The fourth element, which again characterizes the book of Ezekiel, sees in the Temple the source of cosmic life and fertility (see Ez 47:1–12, where water gushes from under the Temple). Finally, the Temple is perceived as the starting point for the creation of the world; this aspect is later still, insofar as it is clearly attested only in traditions dating to the period of the Second Temple. Beyond the biblical and postbiblical period, this conception of Jerusalem as city-temple and center of the world, partly born from the encounter with Mesopotamian culture, marked and inspired not only the entire Jewish tradition but also the Christian one.

THE END OF "BIBLICAL GRANDEUR"?

Far from the glorious visions of the books of Isaiah and Micah, the first phase of Jerusalem's grandeur ended in 586 BCE with the Babylonian invasion and the destruction of the First Temple, along with part of the city, by the Neo-Babylonian king Nebuchadnezzar, following a first seizure of the city in 597 BCE. The Judaean king Jehoiakim rebelled against the Babylonian Empire, says the second book of Kings (24:1), which also gives the event a theological reading: God wanted to punish the Kingdom of Judah because of King Manasseh's sins. Nebuchadnezzar exiled the Judaean elites to Babylon but still accorded some autonomy to Jerusalem, whose government he entrusted to Zedekiah (2 Kgs 24:17). The latter in turn committed the error of also revolting against the Babylonian sovereign, dragging the city into one of the blackest episodes in its history, at least in both Jewish and Christian biblical memory. The Temple and the kingship, the two constituent elements of Jerusalem's special status, disappeared. Even though the Temple was reconstructed starting at the end of the sixth century BCE, the city did not recover true political autonomy, like the rest of Judaea, until the Hasmonean period, from 141 to 63 BCE (see below).

Traces of destruction by the Babylonian armies have been preserved under the archaeological layers of the Hellenistic and Roman eras, notably in Area G of Yigal Shiloh's excavations, on the City of David's east side, with the well-known "Burnt Room" (see map 2). Stone and bone objects, as well as arrowheads, doubtless going back to the time of the siege, have also been found in this zone. The walls of Jerusalem were destroyed, but probably not the city as a whole.

The catastrophe of 586 BCE left lasting marks on what became the Hebrew Bible, notably in the book of Psalms, destined for a wide reception and an intensive liturgical use in the Christian world, as among the Jews. Lamentations about the exile mix with promises of restoration and the jubilation that accompanies them. The famous verses of Psalm 137— "If I forget you, O Jerusalem, / let my right hand wither! / Let my tongue cling to the roof of my mouth, / if I do not remember you, / if I do not set Jerusalem / above my highest joy"—are today still inscribed on the walls of synagogues around the world. The Temple's destruction in 586 also permanently marked Jewish historiography: its presumed date, the ninth of the month of Av (Tisha B'Av), became in Rabbinic and modern Judaism a fast day, which was associated with other catastrophes in Jewish history, such as the Second Temple's destruction (see below). For Judaism and

Christianity, proponents of a typological vision of history—according to which events from different epochs, sometimes very far apart in time, echo and superimpose themselves on one another—the catastrophe of 586 is in some way the archetype of all the destructions that later struck Jerusalem, traditionally perceived as divine punishments.

THE PERSIAN RENAISSANCE

The history of biblical Jerusalem did not, however, end with the destruction of the sixth century BCE; after the Neo-Babylonian period (586–539 BCE), marked by devastation, the Persian period (539–333 BCE) saw the beginning of Jerusalem's rebirth. Certainly, the Kingdom of Judah had ceased to exist; it took shape again only as the province of Judaea (Yehud in Aramaic) within the Achaemenid Persian Empire, during the second half of the sixth century BCE. Cyrus II, the Great, after seizing Babylon in 539/538—with the support of the god Marduk's Babylonian clergy (and perhaps also certain exiles from Judah)—authorized the return of the exiles to Jerusalem and Judaea, as well as the reconstruction of the Temple. According to the historian Joseph Blenkinsopp, in view of Achaemenid practices, we can even consider that the reconstruction of the Temple was not just authorized but well and truly mandated by the Persians.[24] The Cyrus Cylinder testifies to the Persian policy of reconstructing sanctuaries in various places in the empire, often accompanied by a policy of financing cults (including, later on, in Egypt, where antagonism toward the Persians was nonetheless particularly strong). Under the Achaemenid Empire, Jerusalem thus regained its status as a city-temple, even if the reconstruction was laborious and the new sanctuary remained modest.

According to the book of Ezra, Zerubbabel returned to Jerusalem in 521 BCE as governor, accompanied by some of the exiles, and undertook the work of rebuilding the Temple in the second year after his arrival (Ezr 3:8–10). This reconstruction enterprise encountered opposition from the part of the population "of the land," identified with the descendants of peoples displaced by the Assyrians—that is, the ancestors of the Samaritans (Ezr 4). Despite this opposition, the biblical book describes the reconstruction as carried out in Zerubbabel's own time. The rest of the book of Ezra describes a religious reform, while the book of Nehemiah reports how its namesake, who also came from Babylonia after having been named governor, in 445 BCE, under Artaxerxes I, succeeded in raising the city's walls in fifty-two days (Neh 3:1–32). According to Nehemiah 7:2, Jerusalem had a citadel (*birah*) in the fifth century, which should probably be identified as the governor's residence. The book of Nehemiah gives unrealistic population numbers (42,360 people [7:66]) while otherwise alluding to the fact that the city was sparsely inhabited (7:4). In chapter 11, the author even describes how lots were drawn in the cities of Judaea to decide who would repopulate Jerusalem (one person in ten having to go), as if the state of the city had not given rise to voluntary settlement there!

Archaeology, for its part, struggles to make Persian Jerusalem emerge from the rubble. Very few traces of buildings survive, and we count only small discoveries: pottery remains, the impressions of seals on jar handles (where the name Yehud recurs, as well as the names of satraps—governors—such as Ahazai and Hananiah), a seal with a standing animal, a fifth-century BCE silver Lycian coin, and so forth. Considering the modesty of the material traces relating to this period, there is lively controversy among archaeologists regarding the city's extent in the Persian era and the exact placement of "Nehemiah's wall." The small community of the Persian epoch doubtless repaired the ancient wall and sealed the breaches instead of constructing new fortifications. It seems that Jerusalem had a very reduced urban area then, quite far from the glory of the eighth and seventh centuries. The City of David again constituted the core of the urbanized space, the heart from which it later unfurled to the north and the west, as in the Iron Age II. Ronny Reich says that only the ridge of the City of David, to the Pool of Siloam below, was inhabited. Indeed, the Gihon Spring was blocked up during this period (hence the total absence of archaeological traces relating to it then), which led the locals to resettle near the other available source of potable water, namely the Pool of Siloam. Israel Finkelstein estimates Jerusalem's population at one thousand inhabitants at most, although other researchers put the number of people at fifteen hundred.[25] Emblematically, the massive Israelite fortifications destroyed in 586 remained abandoned until the Hasmoneans rebuilt the western rampart. Finkelstein goes so far as to propose dating to the Hasmonean era the book of Nehemiah's description of the wall's reconstruction. In other words, the biblical narrative in this case would reflect not the reality of the Persian epoch but that of the second century BCE.

Whatever the exact dating of the final redaction of the biblical books relating to this period, the fact remains that Jerusalem, deprived of the political role that had characterized it in both the Bronze Age and the time of the First Temple, became a city-temple in the Persian era in a new way. The priestly elites from then on assumed the function of intermediaries between the Judaeans and the empire, in connection with an appointed governor, generally dropped in from Persia. It was in the Persian era that the high priest imposed himself as the true leader of the Judaean population, not only in the province of Judaea but also in the diaspora, as documentation from the Jewish community in Elephantine in Egypt testifies. Paradoxically, in light of biblical literature that advocates the centralization of worship at Jerusalem, the Elephantine Jews or Judaeans wrote at the end of the fifth century BCE to Jerusalem's high priest, Johanan, to obtain his support for the reconstruction of the local Jewish sanctuary. Faced with his reserved reaction, they turned to Bagohi, the satrap then ruling over Judaea. This permits the contextualization to some extent of the uniqueness of the Jerusalem temple, which was not so absolute as is generally presented; widening the investigation to include the Hellenistic era, we could also point to the fact that in the second century BCE, another Jewish temple was founded in Egypt, in Leontopolis, by the high priest Onias IV, removed from the Hierosolymitan cult by a rival.[26] Finally, we must stress that the importance of the Jerusalem temple was not exclusively religious but also fiscal, because the taxes sent to the Achaemenid (and later the Ptolemaic and the Seleucid) authorities passed through it. This dual cultic and financial role of the sanctuary and the priests who officiated there explains many events that affected Jerusalem's destiny in the Hellenistic age, when the Temple's riches aroused the envy of certain sovereigns, such as Antiochus IV.

THE BEGINNING OF THE HELLENISTIC ERA: IN THE SHADOW OF THE PTOLEMIES

With regard to the beginning of the Hellenistic age, the evidence is particularly lacking, as much archaeologically as textually. Flavius Josephus, in his *Jewish Antiquities*, mentions a visit by Alexander the Great to Jerusalem, after the capture of Gaza in 332 BCE.[27] According to the first-century CE Jewish historian, the Macedonian conqueror prostrated himself before the name of God written on the miter of the high priest, who came to meet him in great pomp, surrounded by the priests of the Temple and the inhabitants of the city, all dressed in white. To those in his entourage who expressed astonishment at such a display of servility, Alexander responded that he prostrated himself not before the high priest, Jaddūs, but before the God whom Jaddūs served, and that he had dreamed that Jaddūs told him God would give him victory over Darius III and deliver the Persian Empire into his hands. Again according to Josephus's account, Alexander then went to the Temple, where he offered sacrifices to the God of Israel, scrupulously following the high priest's instructions. Finally, he granted Jews throughout the empire the right to live according to their ancestral customs and invited those who wished to join his troops and accompany him on his campaigns.

This tale is obviously legendary and apologetic: on the way to conquer Egypt, Alexander had no reason to turn from the route that led straight there from Gaza, to pay homage to the God of the Judaeans; he doubtless went directly from Gaza to Pelusium, at the northeast end of the Nile delta, along the coast. Josephus's text in reality reflects the thinking of numerous Jewish authors in the Hellenistic and Roman eras on what the behavior of a pious and just sovereign should be vis-à-vis the Jews: he should on the one hand respect Jerusalem's Temple and contribute to worship there through offerings or tax cuts and on the other hand guarantee Jews the possibility to live according to the Law of Moses, often referred to as "the ancestral constitution" of the Jews (or Judaeans).

After Alexander's death, Judaea and Jerusalem first fell to the Ptolemies (at the end of four military campaigns, staggered from 320 to 301 BCE). According to Agatharchides of Cnidos (cited by Josephus in *Against Apion*), Ptolemy I Soter took the city in 302, on a Shabbat day. The sources are lacking, but it seems that afterward the relations between Jerusalem's priestly elite and the Ptolemaic sovereigns were peaceful and the city enjoyed a period of prosperity, even if Judaea, located between the Ptolemaic and Seleucid spheres of influence, suffered no fewer than five wars in the third century BCE. But these clashes took place along the

Mediterranean coast rather than in Judaea proper. According to the third book of Maccabees, after his victory at Raphia in 217, Ptolemy IV tried to penetrate the Jerusalem temple's Holy of Holies and did not agree to renounce this fatal project until a divine intervention struck him down to the ground. But there is probably nothing historical about this episode, and the fiction recounted by 3 Maccabees instead represents a response of the Jewish community in Egypt to events relating to the profanation of the Temple by Antiochus IV Epiphanes, which we will discuss later.

The testimony of Hecataeus of Abdera, an early third-century BCE Greek ethnographer, cited two centuries later by Diodorus Siculus, probably indirectly reflects certain aspects of Judaea under Ptolemaic control: according to this text that relates the origin of the Jews and how they settled in Judaea, Moses founded Jerusalem and built the Temple (*sic*) there, then installed priests at the head of the ethnos, as judges and as guardians of laws and morals. "The Jews [Judaeans] have never had any king," Hecataeus wrote. "The leadership of the people has always been entrusted to a priest, who excels all the rest in prudence and virtue. They call him the chief priest, and they regard him as the messenger and interpreter of the mind and commands of God."[28] This political role of the priests, and the high priest in particular, characterized both the Hellenistic and the Persian eras until the emergence of the Hasmonean dynasty, itself of priestly origin.

The Sirach, or Wisdom of Ben Sira, a notable early second-century BCE Judaean, contains a number of sociological observations and also testifies to the importance of the priestly class. It describes the high priest Simon II (died circa 196 BCE) in dithyrambic terms, evoking in particular his role as builder:

[It] was the high priest, Simon son of Onias,
who in his life repaired the house [the temple's central structure],
and in his time fortified the temple.
He laid the foundations for the high double walls,
the high retaining walls for the temple enclosure.
In his days a water cistern was dug,
a reservoir like the sea in circumference.
He considered how to save his people from ruin,
and fortified the city against siege.[29]

In both the writings of Hecataeus of Abdera and the Wisdom of Ben Sira, which are of very different natures, the recurring element is the central place of priests in Judaean society in the Hellenistic era, and through it, the Temple's centrality and Jerusalem's role as city-sanctuary.

In 200 BCE, Judaea's domination passed from the Ptolemies to the Seleucids, who then reigned over Asia. Jerusalem was taken in 198 BCE and seems to have suffered in the wars between Antiochus III and Ptolemy IV. However, according to Josephus, the inhabitants rallied to Antiochus III and opened the city's gates to him, so that the Seleucid sovereign would show them benevolence. In the *Jewish Antiquities,* Josephus cites, in particular, a letter from Antiochus III granting Jerusalem a number of benefits (*philanthrōpa*), including offerings for the Temple, exemption from taxes on the wood used in the Temple's embellishment, and exemption from taxation for three years for all those who lived in the city or came to repopulate it;[30] finally, the Seleucid sovereign freed slaves and confirmed the right of the Jews to live according to their ancestral laws. Since the great historian of the Seleucid world Elias Bickerman analyzed this document in 1935, its historicity has not been in doubt.[31] It seems in particular that the Seleucid sovereign well and truly adopted a policy that respected the sanctuary, explicitly prohibiting any (non-Jewish) stranger from entering the precinct reserved for Jews in a state of ritual purity.

According to Josephus's account, the text of the royal programma was as follows:

> It is unlawful for any foreigner to enter the enclosure of the temple which is forbidden to the Jews, except to those of them who are accustomed to enter after purifying themselves in accordance with the law of the country. Nor shall anyone bring into the city the flesh of horses or of mules or of wild or tame asses, or of leopards, foxes or hares or, in general, of any animals forbidden to the Jews. Nor is it lawful to bring in their skins or even to breed any of these animals in the city. But only the sacrificial animals known to their ancestors and necessary for the propitiation of God shall they be permitted to use. And the person who violates any of these statutes shall pay to the priests a fine of three thousand drachmas of silver.[32]

This prohibition of horses and asses seems extreme and should perhaps be understood as aimed at the Temple and its outbuildings, as Victor Tcherikover suggested. But it also reflects a tendency to extend the

Temple's sanctity to the whole city, attested as an ideal in second-century BCE literary sources, such as the Temple Scroll, found at Qumran (see below). In any case, the image emerges of a religiously conservative city where the priestly class played a prominent role.

For all that, Jerusalem did not remain untouched by Greek cultural influence during the first part of the Hellenistic era. Coins also testify to the city's integration into the Ptolemaic world: several minted in Jerusalem and dated to the beginning of the third century BCE reproduce the images of Ptolemy I and II and their spouses, or the eagle, symbol of Ptolemaic power. Furthermore, almost a thousand handles from Rhodian-type wine jars have been found in the City of David, with stamps indicating their origin, testifying to important economic exchanges with the Hellenistic world (particularly the islands: Cnidos, Chios, etc.). This wine was imported mostly between the middle of the third and the middle of the second century BCE. Then there was a sharp decline, probably linked to the new political circumstances after the foundation of the Hasmonean dynasty. The Zenon papyri (named for the Greek agent of Ptolemy II's "finance minister" who was sent on a mission to Judaea in 259 BCE) bear witness to the Ptolemies' heavy involvement in the trade of wine, oil, and slaves in this region, a business that seems to have been quite prosperous and also concerned Jerusalem, which Zenon mentions on several occasions.

The (grecized) names of many Judaean characters mentioned in the books of Maccabees and other sources (Jason, Menelaus, Alcimus, Eupolemus, etc.) reveal a considerable openness to the Greek world under the Seleucids. This was so much the case that at the request of part of Jerusalem's population, a Greek polis was even founded there under Antiochus IV, the Seleucid city Antiochia in Jerusalem, peopled by Hellenized Judaeans, Greek settlers, and probably Syrophoenicians. As the historian John Ma has rightly emphasized, this was not, however, a *refoundation* of Jerusalem in the form of a polis but rather the creation of a Greek city *alongside* the Judaean priestly state, permitting its citizens to form a *politeuma*, to acquire Greek laws and institutions, to build a gymnasium, and so forth.[33] The first book of Maccabees, written toward the end of the second century BCE by a historian close to the Hasmonean dynasty, violently denounces the city's Hellenization, particularly the construction of the gymnasium (1 Mc 1:14–15), responsibility for which the second book of Maccabees, also written in the second century BCE, attributes to the high priest Jason.

It was similarly at the beginning of the second century BCE, in all likelihood, that the city again began to extend across the western hill (corresponding to the present Jewish Quarter and Mount Zion). According to the archaeologist Dan Bahat, this neighborhood, known as the Upper City, developed in response to the nobles' growing demand for buildings conforming to the standards of the Hellenistic world; it later became the district of Jerusalem's Hasmonean and Herodian elites (see map 3).[34]

169–164 BCE, BETWEEN FISCAL CRISIS AND PROFANATION OF THE SANCTUARY

Following Elias Bickerman, the books of Maccabees are often read as presenting a conflict between Hellenized Jews and pious Jews attached to the Mosaic law and the "traditions of the fathers."[35] In reality, it was likely a question of divergent interpretations of these laws. Moreover, the root of the conflict with the Seleucid government, which was the primary factor in what is known as the Maccabean Revolt, apparently related to fiscal policy and the refusal to cooperate with a tax increase demanded by Antiochus IV, which led him to intervene in an authoritarian manner, to despoil the Temple, and to appoint officials who were more complacent. Finally, it is probable that the Seleucid sovereign interpreted the divisions and power struggles among (and even within) priestly families as an attempt to rebel, resulting in his offensive against Jerusalem in 168 BCE. But as Claude Orrieux and Édouard Will aptly write, "[Antiochus IV] doubtless could have done without having the Judaean question on his hands, because his real political agenda lay elsewhere—basically in the recovery of his empire, compromised by the downfall of his father and menaced by Ptolemaic retribution."[36]

In any case, on his return from Egypt in 168 BCE, Antiochus IV, perhaps frustrated by the thwarting of his Egyptian ambitions by Roman intervention, perhaps genuinely convinced that a revolt had been fomented at Jerusalem, abandoned himself to bloody reprisals. According to the books of Maccabees, this military intervention was accompanied by massacres, pillaging of the Temple, and a terrible religious persecution involving the prohibition of practices fundamental to Judaism—such as circumcision, the observance of Shabbat, and compliance with food laws—as well as the obligation to sacrifice to the Greek gods. Antiochus himself sacrificed a pig in the Jerusalem temple, which the book of Daniel calls "the abomination that desolates" (9:27, 12:11; cf. 8:13, 11:31). The first book of Maccabees depicts a devastated, burned Jerusalem, its houses and its walls laid low; the Seleucid army then rebuilt the City of David, fortifying it and transforming it into a citadel and a food and weapon depot for the garrison that was stationed there, and Jerusalem was emptied of its Jewish inhabitants (1 Mc 1:31–39). This description is undoubtedly exaggerated, but the archaeological data to determine how are lacking. The first book of Maccabees next reports how a priestly family from Modein, led by its patriarch, Mattathias, revolted against the royal orders, killing the king's soldiers and impious Jews at the same time. According to chapter 4, Judas Maccabaeus, one of Mattathias's sons, retook control of Jerusalem and purified the sanctuary, in the month of Kislev in the year 164 BCE—an event that gave birth to the Jewish holiday Hanukkah, which the Rabbinic tradition, however, associates with later legendary incidents, such as the miracle of the oil flask that sustained the Temple's candelabrum. The first book of Maccabees also reports that Judas's brothers Jonathan and Simon rebuilt Jerusalem's walls.

There remains the problem of the Akra, the Seleucid citadel constructed under Antiochus IV, base of the Antiochians in Jerusalem (citizens of the polis of Antiochia)—whose location is debated, even if the southeast angle of the Temple Mount or the area south of the esplanade, just beyond the Huldah Gates (at the Ophel), today seem the two most probable hypotheses in view of both written sources and archaeological traces. In November 2015, the discovery of a tower's foundation in the Givati Parking Lot excavation, in the City of David's upper part, led Doron Ben-Ami to locate the Akra at that very spot, but this identification is still under discussion (see map 3). The Seleucid citadel was finally conquered in 141 BCE by Simon, Judas's brother, who expelled the garrison, purified the site,[37] and celebrated Jerusalem's restored integrity with great pomp (1 Mc 13:50–51).

HASMONEAN JERUSALEM: JEWISH CITY
OR GREEK CITY? (141–63 BCE)

Thus opened a period of exceptional political autonomy, under the Hasmonean dynasty, which was gradually devoted (starting with Simon's high priesthood but especially during that of his son John Hyrcanus, between 135 and 104 BCE) to wars of expansion that led to the considerable extension of Judaean territory. At the time of Hyrcanus's son Alexander Jannaeus (103–76 BCE), this included the entire coastal plain from Gaza to Mount Carmel, Idumea and the Negev, Samaria, Galilee, and a good portion of Transjordan. These conquests enabled the enrichment of the Hasmoneans and their partisans, attested by numerous literary sources, including sources hostile to the dynasty. The accumulated riches also benefited Jerusalem, which experienced significant urban development. According to Lee Levine, Jerusalem's population multiplied fivefold between the end of the Persian epoch and the Hasmonean era, growing from around 5,000 to 25,000 or even 30,000 inhabitants.[38] Moreover, the Hasmoneans financed several large-scale works: a fortress (Baris) was constructed northwest of the Temple Mount, doubtless on the remains of the building there dating back to the Persian era (the Birah of Nehemiah 2:8), and a palace was erected in the Upper City's northern part. A passage was installed between the Upper City and the Temple Mount (Aristobulus II later burned this structure as he fled from Pompey in 63 BCE).

Jerusalem presented contrasting faces in this era. On the one hand, several elements made it a city marked by the practice of Judaism (the Greek word *ioudaismos,* generally translated as "Judaism," first appeared precisely at this time), quite different from the Hellenistic cities of the Levant: it contained only a single temple, which, without yet having assumed the monumental character that it would later acquire under Herod, was already attracting pilgrims. According to Josephus, the Greek historian Polybius (second century BCE) spoke of the "renown" of Jerusalem's sanctuary, identifying the city with the Temple.[39] Furthermore, Jewish literary sources—first and foremost the Dead Sea Scrolls—testify to the centrality of the Temple and the worship that took place there in the issues that divided Judaean society. For instance, the Qumran text titled *Miqtzat Ma'ase ha-Torah* ("Some precepts of the Law," also known as

4QMMT), which goes back to the second century BCE, echoes the polemics of one group against the ritual practices of another, which had not respected the laws concerning the festival calendar, purity, sacrifices, or priestly matrimonial prohibitions. According to this text, dogs must be excluded from Jerusalem (and not just the Temple precinct), for example, so as to avoid any risk of profanation (dogs might indeed gnaw on the bones of ritual sacrifices, which would constitute a profanation of the sacred). Another document of religious legislation (*halakhah*) found at Qumran, the Temple Scroll, whose main copy also dates to the second century BCE, stipulates that it is forbidden to bring to Jerusalem the skins of animals slaughtered elsewhere, as these are impure, and the only ones that must be allowed are those of beasts sacrificed directly at the Temple (the only place where sacrifices are supposed to happen). The Temple Scroll moreover extends the interdiction on disabled priests serving in the Temple (Lv 21:17–23) to all Israel (rather than just priests) and to all Jerusalem (rather than just the Temple): the blind, for example, therefore did not have the right to enter the city, where they could be vectors of impurity because they do not see what they touch. These texts remain largely theoretical and utopian, but they reflect the near obsessive concern with ritual purity that prevailed in certain priestly milieus, most particularly with regard to the Holy City, Jerusalem.

A text from the Jewish diaspora in Egypt also evinces, over the course of a paragraph, this concern for purity. The *Letter of Aristeas*, the work of a Jew well established at the Ptolemaic court, written in Greek and most probably dating to the second century BCE, contains an almost thirty-paragraph description of Jerusalem, not a self-evident part of a work mainly dedicated to the translation of the Torah into Greek at Alexandria. Largely fictitious and idealized, this portrait reproduces the geographic topoi of Hellenistic literature but is also a continuation of biblical descriptions, themselves inspired by the Mesopotamian tradition of the city-temple located on a very high mountain. It is the sanctuary and the worship that took place there that primarily hold the attention of the author of the *Letter of Aristeas*, but not exclusively. He also quickly mentions the size of Jerusalem, with an enclosure of forty stades (about six and a half kilometers, or four miles), a quite exaggerated number that nonetheless leads him to describe the city as of medium size. According to him,

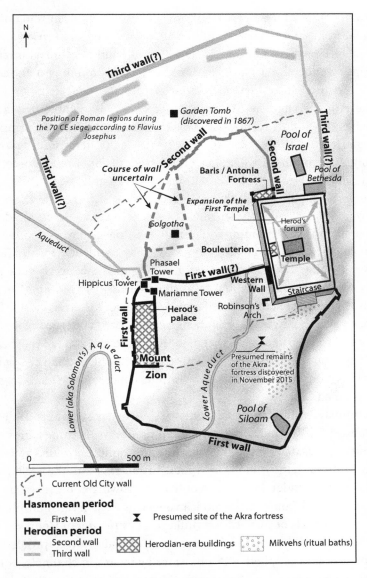

N

Third wall(?)

Garden Tomb
(discovered in 1867)

Position of Roman legions during
the 70 CE siege, according to Flavius
Josephus

Third wall(?)

Pool of
Israel

Third wall(?)

Course of wall
uncertain

Second wall

Second wall

Pool of
Bethesda

Baris / Antonia
Fortress

Expansion of the
First Temple

Herod's
forum

Golgotha

Bouleuterion

Temple

Aqueduct

Phasael
Tower

First wall(?)

Hippicus Tower

Western
Wall

Staircase

Mariamne Tower

Herod's
palace

Robinson's
Arch

First wall

Lower (aka Solomon's) Aqueduct

Mount
Zion

Presumed remains
of the Akra
fortress discovered
in November 2015

Lower Aqueduct

Pool of
Siloam

First wall

0   500 m

Current Old City wall

Hasmonean period

First wall   ✗ Presumed site of the Akra fortress

Herodian period

Second wall   ▨ Herodian-era buildings   ⬚ Mikvehs (ritual baths)

Third wall

*Map 3. Hasmonean and Herodian epochs (second century BCE to
70 CE)*

Jerusalem realized the Aristotelian ideal of a town that, in remaining of limited extent, preserved the equilibrium between city and *chōra*, or agricultural territory. We can thus measure the amount of idealization in this description and the role played in it by the Hellenistic culture of the author and of the implicitly targeted Alexandrian public.

The emphasis on the Temple's water supply is notable: the author describes this inflow as inexhaustible, thanks to the Gihon Spring, and makes reference to the existence of "marvelous underground reservoirs passing description, to a distance of five stades [about one kilometer, or half a mile], . . . round the foundations of the Temple; of these each had innumerable pipes, so that the various channels converged at the several reservoirs."[40] Beyond its lyricism, this description is no doubt alluding to the aqueduct that, beginning in Hasmonean times, conveyed water from the so-called Solomon's Pools (near present-day Bethlehem) to the Temple Mount. Finally, the *Letter of Aristeas* refers to the concern with ritual purity of Jerusalem's inhabitants in the context of describing the city's streets: "There are stairs to the [upper and lower] thoroughfares. Some persons make their way at the higher level and some underneath, and they are careful to keep apart as they go, so that those in a state of purification may touch nothing improper."[41] Contrasting with the utopian character of the description as a whole, this observation's concrete tone tends to give it a certain credibility.

Examination of the material evidence shows that beginning in the second century BCE, human and animal representation became almost nonexistent in Jerusalem; Hasmonean coins, for example, avoided any representation other than symbolic or vegetal, in contrast with the period when Jerusalem was under Ptolemaic control. A growing concern with ritual purity is attested from the Hasmonean epoch as well, in the multiplication of baths for rituals or purification (mikvehs, or *miqvaot* in Hebrew). They were often carved into the rock of the floors of houses, waterproofed with gray plaster, and supplied with rainwater by means of channels. For this period, we have found no fewer than thirty mikvehs in the City of David and the Tyropoeon Valley, in the houses of the Lower City (see map 3). The presence of significant quantities of stoneware among these archaeological remains also testifies to the increasing concern with ritual purity, because stone, as opposed to materials such as ceramic (which is considered porous), does not carry impurity. Hasmonean-era Jerusalem thus presents the face of a city that respected the precepts of the Law of Moses more strictly than it did at other times.

But simultaneously, the process of Hellenization continued on other fronts, less apparent perhaps in the city itself. Under John Hyrcanus, the Hasmoneans began to employ mercenaries, who did not worship the God of Israel; admittedly, they probably did not reside in Jerusalem. The Hasmonean palace at Jericho has numerous Greek architectural features, including porticoes, Dorian columns, and mosaics. Aristobulus I, son of Hyrcanus, was nicknamed Philhellene (Friend of the Greeks). Moreover, Greek symbols appeared on Hasmonean coins, such as the anchor, a Seleucid symbol, or the laurel wreath, associated with Apollo and Zeus. Finally, Alexander Jannaeus was the first to use his Greek name (Alexandros) accompanied by his royal title in Greek (*basileus*) on his coinage. We note, therefore, that the Hasmonean dynasty practiced a mix of fidelity to ancestral customs and integration of foreign elements. In Jerusalem, Jason's Tomb and the Tomb of Benei Hezir (still visible today in the Kidron Valley), which then belonged to priestly families, constitute a sign of the permanence of the city's elites' openness to Hellenistic culture in the Hasmonean era. Intensified observance of Mosaic religious law and cultural Hellenization were finally less antagonistic than they might at first appear—on the condition, however, that Greek culture's polytheistic cultic aspects be set aside.

From 163 to 63 BCE, Jerusalem was neither conquered nor occupied by foreign armies, although it was threatened on several occasions and suffered a particularly difficult siege conducted by Antiochus VII Sidetes around 134–133. John Hyrcanus succeeded in surrendering under honorable conditions, in such a way that the city itself was not taken and only part of the walls needed to be destroyed.[42] During the rule of Alexander Jannaeus, Ptolemy Lathyrus invaded Judaea but did not manage to reach Jerusalem. Also in the time of Jannaeus, the expeditions of Antiochus XII Dionysus, the last of the Seleucids, and of Aretas III, king of the Nabataeans, which invaded Judaea as well, caused no damage to Jerusalem.[43] But this break in sieges and incursions by foreign armies ended in 63 BCE, when Pompey conquered the city. Judaea had gradually but irremediably fallen into the increasingly direct grip of Rome, which would prove fatal for Jerusalem. But first the Herodian dynasty gave it an unequaled luster.

HEROD THE BUILDER: JERUSALEM AT THE HEIGHT OF ITS GLORY

According to Flavius Josephus, whom we must doubtless follow on this point, the siege and defeat by Pompey in 63 BCE and the ensuing disastrous consequences for Judaea (notably its division into three distinct regions by Gabinius, the Roman governor of Syria) were directly linked to the rivalry between Jannaeus's sons, Aristobulus II and Hyrcanus II. In any case, Pompey penetrated the Holy of Holies, thus profaning the Temple. He did not plunder it, however, and he had the sanctuary purified and worship there restored. Marcus Licinius Crassus (who was part of the first triumvirate with Caesar and Pompey in 60 BCE) did not show such scruples when, in 54 BCE, he helped himself to the Temple's treasure to finance his campaign against the Parthians. Between 48 and 44, Caesar published a decree confirming Hyrcanus II as high priest, but with the simple title of *ethnarch* (literally, "ruler of the people") and no longer *king*. Hyrcanus nonetheless obtained the authorization to rebuild the walls that Pompey had destroyed in 63 and to refortify Jerusalem.

The struggle between Hyrcanus and Aristobulus also benefited Antipater and his son Herod, whose influence kept growing and who succeeded in supplanting the last Hasmoneans. In 40 BCE, the Roman Senate proclaimed Herod the king of Judaea. But it was not until 37 BCE that he managed to settle in Jerusalem, after defeating Antigonus II Mattathias, grandson of Alexander Jannaeus and Salome Alexandra, who took refuge in the Temple during Herod's siege. Following his victory at Actium in 31 BCE, Octavian (later called Augustus) confirmed Herod's royal title and added new territories to his kingdom; in return, Herod demonstrated unfailing loyalty to the emperor, constructing cities, monuments, and sanctuaries in his honor and choosing to bear the epithet Philokaisar (Friend of Caesar). He consequently benefited from Augustus's good graces, and under his reign, Jerusalem enjoyed a period of great prosperity and urban development unequaled in its history, which continued with some of his descendants, particularly his grandson Herod Agrippa I (who reigned from 37 to 44 CE). It would not be until the nineteenth century that Jerusalem would regain such a level of urban and demographic development.

Archaeology concretely illustrates Jerusalem's prosperity at the beginning of the first century CE. While studies devoted to this period often contrast the Lower City to the Upper City in terms of the inhabitants' standard of living, to the point of describing the former as "poor," it seems that in reality most neighborhoods were home to diverse population types and that Jerusalem as a whole benefited from a relatively elevated standard of living, even though the Upper City gathered together the vast majority of the nobles and the priestly aristocracy. The archaeological excavations in the upper part of the Old City's Jewish Quarter have revealed a luxurious residential neighborhood, of mansions decorated in a sober but refined manner, with murals and nonfigurative mosaics with geometric motifs, as well as ritual baths and numerous pieces of furniture and other objects made of stone (see map 3). One of these dwellings extended over approximately six hundred square meters (6,458 square feet), divided into two floors because of the slope of the land—a significant size in such a densely populated city.

In the first century CE, Pliny the Elder invoked Jerusalem, "by far the most famous city of the East and not of Judaea only."[44] In the Roman era, this reputation was due almost entirely to the activities of Herod, the great builder and architecture enthusiast, as the work of the archaeologist Ehud Netzer has shown.[45] In (re)constructing palace and temple, Herod arose as a new Solomon and thereby sought to increase his royal legitimacy. All Judaea (and far beyond) remains marked to this day by Herod's builder's zeal, be it the palaces of Jericho, Massada, and Herodion, the walls of the Temple Mount in Jerusalem, or the Herodian tower of which elements can still be seen in the Citadel, near the present Jaffa Gate. Under Herod, this part of the city became monumental and imposing.

Indeed, building on architectural elements dating back to the Hasmoneans, Herod constructed two towers at the citadel, named Phasael (after his brother) and Mariamne (after his favorite wife)—and added a third, Hippicus (still partially visible today)—and erected a palace a bit to the south, in what is now the Armenian Quarter (see map 3). He also restored the fortress (rebaptized Antonia in honor of Mark Antony) northwest of the Temple Mount, as well as Jerusalem's first wall, and built a second wall, which began at the Antonia and joined the first wall a little farther northwest, perhaps at the Mariamne Tower, thus including within the fortifications an entire zone north of the first wall. Herod Agrippa I, the last king of Judaea, began building Jerusalem's third wall around 41–42 CE; its route extended even farther north and west, maybe beyond the present Damascus Gate, encircling the quarter then called Bezetha (see map 3).

It was, however, the renovation and enlargement of the Temple, accompanied by the redesign of the esplanade (which was raised for the occasion and surrounded by a perimeter wall incorporating stones weighing up to 400 metric tons, or 441 tons), that represented the culmination of Herod's architectural work. "He who had not seen the new Temple of Herod had not, in all his life, seen a fine building," says the Babylonian Talmud,[46] which otherwise paints a very negative portrait of this parvenu king and client of Rome. According to Josephus, "[the Temple] being covered on all sides with massive plates of gold, the sun was no sooner up than it radiated so fiery a flash that persons straining to look at it were compelled to avert their eyes, as from the solar rays. To approaching strangers it appeared from a distance like a snow-clad mountain; for all that was not overlaid with gold was of purest white."[47]

Besides the works undertaken in the sanctuary itself, monumental gates and staircases offering access from the south and west were installed, Corinthian-style porticoes erected around the esplanade's perimeter, and new buildings constructed near the southern portico (the Royal Stoa, where commercial transactions took place—such as money changing and the purchase of animals for sacrifice—and which also housed a court). The Temple's esplanade thus looked like a Roman forum in many ways. According to Josephus, several courts of justice held their assemblies on the esplanade, and the Sanhedrin sat in an adjacent building to the southwest. The construction work began in 19 BCE, and—still following Josephus, who is echoed later on in the Babylonian Talmud—during the year and a half when the sanctuary was being enlarged, miraculously it rained only at night, so the laborers would not be hindered in their jobs.[48] Eight more years were needed to build the porticoes. But the works were still ongoing under Herod Agrippa II, great-grandson of Herod the Great, with the result that their completion just preceded the outbreak of the war against Rome.

A city-temple enjoying its influence on the whole diaspora, Jerusalem was also at that time a city of pilgrimage, to a degree never before reached in its history. During the three major Jewish holidays that prescribe a visit to the Temple, Pesah (Passover), Shavuot (Pentecost), and Sukkot (the Feast of Booths or of Tabernacles), thousands of pilgrims flocked to Jerusalem; some even suggest the figure of twenty thousand extra people in the city on these occasions at the end of the first century CE. While Jerusalem under Herod the Great counted around forty thousand inhabitants in an area of about one square kilometer (0.4 square miles), toward 44–45 CE the population reached eighty to ninety thousand and the city extended over 1.8 square kilometers (0.69 square miles), a considerable size in the Roman world. This influx of people during the pilgrimages necessitated substantial urban development, some traces of which are still visible. For instance, a group of buildings serving as a hostel for well-to-do pilgrims, with private ritual baths and a synagogue, has been found. Ronny Reich further believes that tents were raised in the Kidron and Hinnom Valleys and that some pilgrims stayed in the surrounding villages. With the Kidron Valley currently too densely populated for excavation (at least near the City of David), this theory cannot be verified, but traces of pilgrims have been found in the surrounding area (at Mamilla, for example), in the form of pots, bought and then left on the spot. Reich relates these pots on the city's periphery to the biblical obligation to consume in Jerusalem the second tithe on agricultural products (*ma'aser sheni*), an obligation that concerns the Jews living in the land of Israel but not those in the diaspora (just like the obligation about the first fruits of the harvest [*bikkurim*], which the biblical law says must be brought to the Temple so they can be given to the priests). Another possible sign of the city's organization for pilgrimages, a sort of garbage dump has been identified east of the city, containing crockery debris, animal bones, bits from brick ovens, and so forth. This type of deposit does not exist in other districts, and its proximity to the Temple and the City of David might be linked to the intense activity brought about by worship and by the presence of pilgrims in this part of town.[49]

The development of pilgrimages also meant increased water needs, both for consumption and for supplying ritual baths. The Gihon Spring, again accessible in the first century BCE at the latest, was not sufficient to provide the city with water, and numerous cisterns permitting the collection of rainwater have been found during excavations. Moreover, Herod renovated the Pool of Siloam below the City of David and the so-called Solomon's Pools near Bethlehem; in fact, he also constructed new ones: the Struthion

Pool, the Pool of Bethesda, the Birket Israel (all three north of the Temple Mount), and the Serpent's Pool (in the Valley of Hinnom, west of the city). Among these many pools, it seems that the pilgrims mainly used that of Siloam and one of those north of the Temple esplanade. The Pool of Siloam, for instance, had plaster steps, like the mikvehs; these were later redone in stone, undoubtedly because of wear and the need for a more resistant material. A bathing complex probably intended for the purification of pilgrims has likewise been discovered south of the Temple Mount, perhaps mixing public baths and ritual mikvehs sensu stricto. Two aqueducts were built to bring water from the region of Hebron and Bethlehem. In particular, Herod added an "upper" aqueduct, which supplied the Upper City (around the Mamilla Pool) by means of a system of siphons and Roman-style elevation on arches, to the Hasmonean or "lower" aqueduct, which was devoid of arches and since the second century BCE had carried water from Solomon's Pools to the Temple to fill the basins needed for ritual purification and the cleansing of the altar (see map 3).

It is thanks to its renowned, unique Temple that Jerusalem enjoyed such a central place in Judaism at the turn of the Common Era. Certainly, competing sanctuaries had existed or still existed, such as the temple of Leontopolis in Egypt that Onias IV founded in the second century BCE and which did not disappear until 73 CE. The Samaritans continued to contest Jerusalem's supremacy and dreamed of restoring the sanctuary on Mount Gerizim, destroyed by the Hasmoneans at the end of the second century BCE. Furthermore, the institution of the synagogue, which first appeared in Egypt in the third century BCE and is attested at Jerusalem itself in an inscription (known as the Theodotus inscription) from the end of the first century BCE, already filled liturgical and study functions, which later permitted it to take over for the vanished Temple as the setting of the collective religious life of the Jews throughout the empire. However, the role of the Temple and its sacrificial system in the Judaism of the time should not be underestimated. As testimony we have the half-shekel tax, sent to the Temple each year by every adult Jewish man in Judaea (obligatorily) but also in the diaspora (as a voluntary contribution), to support the needs of daily worship and the maintenance of buildings and hydraulic installations.

Royal city (because of its palaces and fortresses) and city-temple, Herodian Jerusalem was also in certain respects a Hellenistic polis. Indeed, it was undoubtedly endowed with a boule (an assembly, a sort of municipal council) that brought together magistrates from the aristocracy, such as the *agoranomos* (the person in charge of the markets); this assembly sat in a bouleuterion, which should perhaps be identified as located on the Temple esplanade's west side, not far from the gymnasium (see map 3). Herod modernized the city's streets and markets and provided it with infrastructure similar to that of numerous cities of the Hellenized Roman East: a forum on the Temple esplanade, a gymnasium, a theater, a hippodrome, and an amphitheater—all major innovations for Jerusalem, except the gymnasium. Behaving in the classic manner of a Hellenistic *euergetēs* (public benefactor, necessarily a notable), Herod not only constructed many kinds of public buildings but also celebrated the quinquennial games in honor of Augustus, in which Greek athletes and musicians participated; he likewise organized gladiatorial combats, the first of their kind in Judaea. Archaeologists have had trouble in locating the theater and the hippodrome, of which no trace has been found, but the testimony of Josephus, who was himself from Jerusalem, can hardly be questioned on this point.

In many respects, Jerusalem at the end of the first century BCE must have appeared to the traveler as quite similar to the other great cities of the Greco-Roman world, particularly as the Herodian architecture was inspired by Hellenistic and Roman models; it even seems that Herod brought in craftsmen especially from Rome. However, just as in the Hasmonean era, Jerusalem was simultaneously a Jewish city with a very particular character, owing to its unique sanctuary (more massive and sumptuous than ever), its religious institutions and liturgical calendar, its rejection of anthropomorphic representation and particularly of statues, and its observance of the rules of ritual purity and more generally of religious laws. This is evidenced by a Greek inscription, two fragments of which were found during archaeological digs, which attests the existence of the *soreg*, the barrier forbidding non-Jews access to the forecourt of the Jews and warning foreigners that they will incur the death penalty in the case of infraction. The inscription specifies: "No foreigner [*allogenēs*] is to enter within the balustrade and forecourt around the sacred precinct. Whoever is caught will himself be responsible for (his) consequent death."[50] Moreover, according to Josephus, "Persons afflicted with gonorrhea or leprosy were excluded from the city altogether; the temple was closed to women during their menstruation."[51] Indeed, the Temple should in no way be rendered impure or desecrated, as that would compromise the worship conducted there. Lee Levine sums up the situation of Herodian Jerusalem well in writing that it was "the most Jewish of cities" in the Roman world and "the most cosmopolitan of Jewish cities."[52]

FROM APOGEE TO DESTRUCTION: WAR WITH ROME

On the death of Herod the Great in 4 BCE, trouble broke out; the governor of Syria intervened to restore order, but not without taking some of the Temple's treasure, which constituted a double sacrilege and triggered new riots. Following the division of Herod's kingdom among his sons, Judaea and Jerusalem fell to Archelaus. Judged incompetent by the Romans, he was rapidly removed from power and exiled, and Judaea came under the direct control of Rome in 6 CE. At that time, Jerusalem lost its status as capital, the Romans having decided to transfer the seat of government to Caesarea, the city that Herod built in honor of Augustus. From then on, Jerusalem was attached to the province of Syria while being administered by a prefect, who became the procurator of Judaea after 44.

Another new element was the stationing of foreign troops in the city. This presence was the source of numerous incidents, and the relations between the Roman authorities and the people of Jerusalem were often quite tense. Thus when Pilate, the prefect from 26 to 36, took funds from the Temple's treasury to construct an additional aqueduct intended to meet the city's growing water needs, the locals, viewing this as a profanation, gathered to protest, and the resulting repression caused many deaths.[53] In comparison, the crucifixion of Jesus during Pilate's prefecture was just a detail in the city's story, an ordinary measure whose consequences for human history no one could have predicted. If the Romans did not hesitate to violently put down all forms of opposition to their empire, all the more reason to eliminate agitators or those who were thought to be so. . . . The city ran a new and serious risk when Caligula, in 40–41, decided to erect a statue of himself in the Jerusalem temple. War could have broken out, but the governor of Syria, Petronius, reacted with prudence, and the emperor's assassination in 41 resolved the problem.

Generally speaking, the Roman authorities respected the Jews' desire to live according to their ancestral laws, but the Romans understood neither Jewish monotheism nor the rejection of representation, particularly when it came to Roman army standards or imperial images. Finally, beyond the incompetence or negligence of certain prefects or procurators, we must recall the roles played by individuals, often simple soldiers. For instance, Josephus reports that in the time of the procurator Cumanus (48–52), at Passover, a Roman soldier indulged in a gratuitous provocation before the crowd: "Raising his robe, [he] stooped in an indecent attitude, so as to turn his backside to the Jews, and made a noise in keeping with his posture."[54] The result was a riot that was suppressed in blood.

The outbreak of the war of 66–73 was a continuation of these multiple incidents, which occurred in the context of messianic expectation and an aspiration to liberation from the Roman yoke, resulting in, among other things, the development of the Zealot movement, which emerged at the beginning of the first century CE. Starting in the 50s, a quasi-terrorist group raged in Judaea, the Sicarii, whose name comes from the Latin *sica*, which refers to a dagger. These fierce independence fighters, even more radical than the Zealots, assassinated Jews close to the Romans (rather than Romans themselves), usually within a crowd. What finally sparked an explosion was nothing other than the cupidity of the procurator Gessius Florus (62–66), who seized seventeen talents from the Temple's treasury. Some inhabitants derided Florus by organizing a collection for him, and when the notables refused to give up the names of the mockers, Florus ordered his soldiers to pillage the upper market with impunity, triggering a massacre.[55] Afterward he sent two cohorts to march through Jerusalem and, according to Josephus, instructed them to provoke the crowd; new confrontations did not fail to occur, so a revolt broke out. Florus withdrew to Caesarea, while the insurgents occupied the Temple's esplanade and decided to interrupt the daily sacrifices in the emperor's honor, a very serious political gesture.

First led by moderates, including Flavius Josephus, who was responsible for military operations in Galilee, the revolt fell little by little into the hands of extremist groups, which Josephus qualifies, not without bias, as "brigands." The general Vespasian, who became the legate of Judaea in 67, progressively curbed the insurrection; when he was proclaimed emperor in 69, he left his son Titus to complete the siege of Jerusalem, now overpopulated and worn out. As the Romans regained control of the country, Jews had in fact flocked to Jerusalem; the city thus confronted supply problems of all kinds, which the siege dramatically exacerbated. Josephus describes horrible scenes, such as when a mother roasted her infant, ate one half, and then offered the other half to rebels attracted by the suspicious smell.[56] At this stage of the war, the rebels were constantly denigrated by Josephus, who also called them "tyrants" and assigned them the real responsibility for the city's fate, thus attempting to whitewash Titus, his protector. He describes Jerusalem as prey to rival rebel groups, which had taken the population hostage, were killing each other, and had committed grave strategic errors in their reciprocal desire to do the other harm (such as setting fire to warehouses where provisions were stored).

The city was completely surrounded: the Tenth Legion held the Mount of Olives, while the Fifth, Twelfth, and Fifteenth Legions were spread out in front of the north and west ramparts (see map 3). Titus's camp was first located northwest of the city, facing the tower Psephinus erected on the third rampart, which Josephus asserts with emphasis was "seventy cubits high, [and] afforded from sunrise a prospect embracing both Arabia [i.e., Jordan] and the utmost limits of Hebrew territory as far as the sea";[57] later, Titus moved his camp to "the camp of the Assyrians," probably on Mount Scopus. Despite its three walls and its towers so vaunted by Josephus, Jerusalem finally fell: on July 24, 70, the Antonia Fortress was taken; Titus had it razed and a ramp built on its site to access the Temple, on which he concentrated his attacks. On August 10, the insurgents set fire to the part of the northwest portico that was connected to the Antonia; in the days that followed, the Romans burned the neighboring portico, and other fires followed, devastating the entirety of the esplanade's north portico. The sanctuary's destruction loomed on the horizon. Yet, according to Josephus, Titus wished to spare the Temple, because of its great beauty. Cassius Dio, a third-century historian, for his part evokes Roman "superstition." But when a soldier threw a torch into the sanctuary and everything caught on fire, the die was cast. Josephus speaks of "destiny," conceived of as an instrument of divine will. According to him and the Rabbinic tradition, the sanctuary was destroyed on the ninth of Av (August 30, 70)—that is (following the Jewish sources, which elaborate a cyclical and typological vision of history), the same Hebraic date as that of the First Temple's destruction, six centuries earlier.

The fire in the sanctuary was followed by the looting of the city, accompanied by a veritable slaughter:

> And then the din—nothing more deafening or appalling could be conceived than that. There were the war-cries of the Roman legions sweeping onward in mass, the howls of the rebels encircled by fire and sword, the rush of the people who, cut off above, fled panic-stricken only to fall into the arms of the foe, and their shrieks as they met their fate. . . . You would indeed have thought that the temple-hill was boiling over from its base, being everywhere one mass of flame, but yet that the stream of blood was more copious than the flames and the slain more numerous than the slayers. For the ground was nowhere visible through the corpses; but the soldiers had to clamber over heaps of bodies in pursuit of the fugitives.[58]

Before leaving the devastated Jerusalem for Caesarea, Titus ordered that what remained of the city and the Temple be razed and the ramparts pulled down, with the exception of the three Herodian towers at what is now the Citadel, which were to serve later as headquarters for Roman troops. Of the Temple, only some religious implements were conserved and transported to Rome, as the Arch of Titus shows, representing the triumph with, among other things, the seven-branched candelabrum carried high. The scope of the devastation indicates that the Romans wanted to be done with insurrections in Judaea once and for all. Furthermore, the Flavian dynasty largely instrumentalized the victory against Judaea, using this to establish its imperial legitimacy.

A PARADOXICAL REBIRTH: THE AELIA CAPITOLINA EPISODE

After the catastrophe in 70 CE, the center of Judaism in Palestine moved to the coast (to Jamnia, now Yavne) and to Galilee. From 70 to around 130, Jerusalem was not really repopulated: an examination of the graves that surrounded the city at the end of the Second Temple period, nearly a thousand rock-cut tombs, shows that their usage almost entirely ceased after 70, and in any case no more were created; at most, some families continued to bury their dead in the old ancestral vault, perhaps even illegally.

During this period, Jerusalem was placed under the care of the Tenth Legion, the Legio X Fretensis, whose first mission was to keep order in a region given over to endemic banditry. Originally, the legion probably set up camp on Mount Zion, south of the citadel, but it was a camp of wood, which has left few archaeological traces, besides numerous clay bricks and tiles depicting the legion's emblems (a boat, a dolphin, and a boar) and its abbreviation, LEG.X.F. It is possible that the camp later moved to the Tyropoeon Valley, southwest of the destroyed Temple's esplanade (see map 4 in chapter 2). In any case, bricks and tiles stamped with the legion's emblems have been found throughout the city. They were made in potters' workshops that used Roman techniques, located outside the city, on Romema's hill, where West Jerusalem's Central Bus Station now stands, but work stopped there in the third century CE. Other traces of the presence of the Legio X Fretensis: in the esplanade's southwest corner, not far from the vestiges of Robinson's Arch, which supported one of the monumental staircases leading to the Temple Mount, a bakery linked to the legion and baths and latrines for soldiers have been identified. Finally, column pieces with inscriptions commemorating the victory of Titus and the legion have been found at the Temple esplanade's south; perhaps these columns were erected at one of the city's gates. The Legio X Fretensis remained in Jerusalem until the end of the third century, when it was transferred to Ayla (now Eilat), on the Red Sea. It was then replaced by a small detachment of Moorish cavalry from the First Legion, Legio I Illyricorum.

In 132–35 the last great Jewish revolt against Rome took place, led by a charismatic commander named Simeon bar Kosba (Bar Kokhba), in whom some Jews recognized the Messiah. It was fought in Judaea but did not directly affect Jerusalem, because the insurgents did not manage to seize the city. Hope for its liberation and restoration was nonetheless alive among them, as evidenced by the legends on some coins struck during this period, which state, "For the liberty of Jerusalem." In fact, it seems that the revolt's principal cause was the emperor Hadrian's decision to rebuild Jerusalem by founding a Roman colony there—not from hostility toward the Jews, incidentally, but on the contrary in the name of Jerusalem's reputation and prestige before its destruction in 70.[59] Simply, the emperor planned to establish a Roman colony with veterans of the Fifth Legion, called Macedonica, and their families, next to the Tenth Legion.

Furthermore, this foundation, which probably took place around 130, during Hadrian's visit to the eastern provinces, had a marked pagan dimension, if only in its rite of *circumductio*, consisting of tracing a furrow representing the colony's sacred boundary with the aid of a plow harnessed to two oxen, led by the founding magistrate, who was accompanied by priests—the city's coins show Hadrian himself carrying out the rite, the plow at his hand. But Bar Kokhba's revolt failed after three years, and this new defeat resulted in an even greater de-Judaization of Jerusalem.

The city's change of status meant that it was rebuilt according to a Roman plan and received a new name, Aelia Capitolina, after Hadrian's nomen (family name), Aelius, and in honor of Jupiter Capitolinus. Around 200, the emperor Septimius Severus visited and rebaptized the city Aelia Capitolina Commodiana Pia Felix. Use of the name Jerusalem timidly returned only in the fourth century, at the time of the city's first Christianization, after the conversion of Constantine. Aelia Capitolina was a "Rome in miniature," in the words of Aulus Gellius; it is represented as such in the images that depict it, for example the coins struck in the colony, some of which show the she-wolf surmounted by the legionary eagle or by an allegory of Rome. It differed from other cities of Palestine, including Caesarea, in a lesser presence of Hellenistic cultural traits. These were not, however, completely absent: Aelia's first mintage also depicted the goddess Tyche (Fortune), although instead of being associated with the Greco-Palestinian Astarte or the Dionysus-Demeter couple, as on Caesarea's civic coins, there she was represented sacrificing alongside a legionary eagle. Nicole Belayche explains that Aelia Capitolina had the character of a Roman enclave because Jerusalem was razed and its population replaced; any kind of continuity with the local culture, Jewish or Greco-Palestinian, was thereby made impossible.[60]

After the rebellion's failure, Hadrian indeed forbade Jews from staying in Jerusalem (and its district), with the exception of the ninth of Av, when they were allowed to go and lament the destroyed Temple, whose stones were now used for the construction of other buildings. The Bordeaux Pilgrim, who left one of the earliest Christian accounts of a journey in Palestine (333), wrote of the esplanade that there were two statues of Hadrian there, "and not far from the statues there is a perforated stone [*lapis pertusus*], to which the Jews come every year and anoint it, bewail themselves with groans, rend their garments, and so depart."[61] The description of Jerusalem that the Bordeaux Pilgrim gives us is rich in references to the Old Testament (Solomon, Hezekiah, David), but with the exception of the scene around the perforated stone, Jews themselves are largely absent from the city. The Pilgrim notes that at Mount Zion, "Of seven synagogues which once were there, one alone remains; the rest are plowed over and sown upon, as said Isaiah the prophet." Eusebius of Caesarea and Cyril of Jerusalem, third- and fourth-century Church Fathers, attest, moreover, that the grounds of the esplanade were cultivated and that gourds were grown there.[62] Shimon Gibson and David Jacobson, in their work on the area under the Haram al-Sharif, conclude for their part that the esplanade was completely abandoned between 135 and 638.[63] In any event, Roman Jerusalem was thus paradoxically the only city in the empire off-limits to Jews in the second century. They rebuilt a small community there, however, at the beginning of the third century, under Caracalla; perhaps they used the only synagogue still remaining mentioned by the Bordeaux Pilgrim in the fourth century. A Christian community is also attested, which in 134, Eusebius tells us, chose a bishop named Mark, who was not of Jewish origin, but on the whole this community left hardly any trace in the patristic literature. Christian Jerusalem did not yet exist, and as Belayche reminds us, the question of Jerusalem's theological status did not concern the second- and third-century Church Fathers.

In the Roman colony from the second to the fourth century, public and private pagan cults proliferated: army cults, the imperial cult, cults of various deities of the Greco-Roman pantheon, sometimes orientalized. A temple dedicated to Jupiter Capitolinus was built, perhaps at the site of Golgotha, on the north side of the colony's forum, corresponding to the modern-day Muristan; behind the Capitol a cult statue of Venus-Aphrodite-Tyche was erected, doubtless accompanied by an altar (see map 4 in chapter 2). According to an alternative theory, for the most part based on Cassius Dio's testimony,[64] Golgotha hosted only a temple dedicated to Venus, while the temple of Jupiter was erected on the site of the old Jewish Temple or at least on the esplanade, thus illustrating Rome's replacement of Israel.[65] According to some evidence, the esplanade featured two monumental imperial statues, and a statue of Hadrian was put up at the entrance to the city's north gate (the current Damascus Gate). There was a sanctuary dedicated to Serapis, the healer god, north of the current Church of Saint Anne, next to the ancient Probatic (Sheep) Pool (or Pool of Bethesda), where the evangelical tradition (John 5) situates the healing of the paralytic man (see map 4 in chapter 2)—a beautiful illustration of the fact that beyond the transfers of sovereignty and political reappropriations of places, their cult and cultural functions persist.

Several monumental arches were built in the city, particularly that of the Damascus Gate, the main passage and checkpoint but also an emblem of the colony going back to its foundation; the so-called Ecce Homo Arch, also dating from the second century, was for its part connected to a military area.[66] The city contained many other elements typical of Roman towns: a theater, baths, two forums, two colonnaded *cardines* (major north-south streets; singular *cardo*), and so on. The legionary soldiers rebuilt the upper aqueduct, dating back to Herod, in 195, but Aelia Capitolina remained devoid of walls. The city was also smaller than in the time of the Second Temple, generally deemed to no longer include the ancient City of David, and the Pool of Siloam was apparently covered with earth. The recent excavation of the Givati Parking Lot in the City of David's upper part has, however, brought to light the remains of a beautiful Roman dwelling constructed in the third century CE, which shows that the city later experienced new development in this area.

Aelia Capitolina's urban plan is still very noticeable in the Old City. We can thus easily find the route of the two *cardines*, which left from the city's north gate: the first, the more easterly, followed the Tyropoeon Valley (the current Al-Wad, or Hagai, Street), while the other, also called the *cardo maximus*, followed a north-south axis to the *decumanus maximus*, the current King David Street (see map 4 in chapter 2); it was extended farther south in the Byzantine era, under Justinian, and the columns that can be seen in the Jewish Quarter today in fact correspond to the Byzantine part. The Roman city plan is also apparent in the differing street organization of the Old City's north, which still reflects the right-angled routes of Aelia Capitolina's roads, and south (the Jewish and Armenian Quarters), which was originally built beginning in the fourth century, after the legion's departure, and whose streets follow much more sinuous paths.

The Old City's street plan thus still rests largely on the morphology of the Roman city. As the archaeologist Guy Stiebel pointed out, not without a trace of irony, "Aelia Capitolina effectively saved Jerusalem. It raised her once again onto the stage of history. She returned like a phoenix from the ashes."[67] But beginning in the fourth century, the Roman Empire's progressive Christianization and the development of Christian pilgrimages changed the face of the city, once again "Jerusalem," condemning Aelia Capitolina to appear as only a historical parenthesis.

.   .   .   .   .

THE PRESENCE OF THE ABSENT TEMPLE

The destruction of the Temple and the city in 70 CE and the foundation of Aelia Capitolina mark a real break in Jerusalem's history. The end of the Second Temple period reconfigured the political role of Jerusalem, this ancient royal city that was sometimes modest (under the king Abdi-Heba, for example) and sometimes resplendent (notably under Herod and his descendants). Indeed, it was now dethroned from its role as regional capital: Caesarea, founded by Herod, then Ramla, founded by the Umayyads on the coastal plan, took over in the following centuries. Certainly, the Zionist project and the creation of the modern State of Israel placed Jerusalem back in the heart of the regional and global political scene, but the continuity with the royal city of antiquity that was imagined by certain political actors is a clearly anachronistic optical illusion, even if it is maintained by the permanence of the remains of the Herodian temple's enclosure.

This absent Temple is what haunts the city in the eyes of later Jewish traditions, which commemorate this destruction indefinitely. The Christian and then Muslim sanctuaries installed in place of the Jewish Temple (whether on the esplanade or in other parts of the city) reactivated this tradition, but they certainly did not confer on Jerusalem a city-temple status comparable to that observed for the first millennium BCE. The Holy Sepulchre certainly aroused Christianity's passions during the Crusades, but it was also neglected in favor of other key Christian spots. The first Christian centuries, until the fourth-century invention of the Constantinian holy places, were moreover indifferent to earthly Jerusalem, immediately rivaled by Rome, Constantinople, Alexandria, Antioch, and so forth. Similarly, in Muslim culture, although the direction of prayer (qibla) was originally toward Jerusalem, Mecca and Medina very quickly supplanted it. Even Jewish communities in the Middle Ages and at the start of the modern era neglected the concrete Jerusalem in favor of "new Jerusalems" such as Toledo, Thessaloníki, Prague, and Vilnius.[68] Even if a Jewish community existed in Jerusalem from the end of antiquity to the first aliyot (immigration movements) at the end of the nineteenth and beginning of the twentieth century, it was ultimately the twentieth-century destruction of the European Jewish communities and the creation of the State of Israel, combined with the development of modern means of transport, that reestablished a concrete and continuous link between Jews and terrestrial Jerusalem, which once again is inhabited and visited by massive numbers of Jews from around the world.

2 Roman Pantheon, Christian Reliquary, and Jewish Traditions

SECOND TO SEVENTH CENTURIES

"No human heart / changes half so fast as a city's face," Baudelaire wrote in the middle of the nineteenth century about the disappearance of old Paris.[1] Concerning Jerusalem at the end of antiquity, between the destruction of the Second Temple (70) and the Arab conquest (635–38), one might add that not only the city's face but also its very name changed drastically several times. Yerushalayim, Aelia Capitolina, al-Quds: in just a few hundred years, the Holy City was repeatedly renamed, following the rhythm of conquests, destructions, refoundations, and, it should be said, the functions successively assigned to it. These morphological upheavals and toponymic variations oblige us to ask a simple but striking preliminary question: are we really talking about the same city? Are the site's continuity and relative topographical permanence sufficient to suppose that we are looking, throughout these five centuries, at the same historical object? Shouldn't the chronological breaks, not to say disjunctions, lead us to think that the ruptures outweigh the continuities during this particularly troubled sequence in the city's history? After all, between the destruction of the Second Temple (70) and the foundation of the Roman colony Aelia Capitolina (135), wasn't the city officially wiped off the map?

These questions deserve to be asked because they prevent us from reconstructing a smooth and falsely linear history of Jerusalem in this period; however, they must not lead us into a deconstructivist abyss to the point of denying a historical—if not a permanent—existence to this little city richly endowed with monotheistic holy sites, perched at the top of the Palestinian range. Indeed, if the coherence of this historical sequence is problematic, it is no less incontestable: it is what links, no more and no less, the three monotheistic religions together. From the New Testament tradition that situates the death of the young Jew Jesus of Nazareth in the 30s CE through the destruction of Herod's Temple in 70 to the construction of the Dome of the Rock in 691, the inextricable topographical, historical, and textual imbrication of the three monotheisms is obvious. Between these two end dates, and in particular between Emperor Constantine's conversion to Christianity (312) and the city's Islamic conquest (635–38), the question that arises is that of a first and uncertain "Christianization" of Jerusalem, which happened through both a reappropriation of Jewish traditions and a property transfer of certain Roman monuments. In short, the history of Jerusalem between the second and seventh centuries can well and truly be treated as a coherent chronological sequence: this is the era when it was the privileged theater of the long genesis and refinement of the three monotheisms. Before retracing this fragmentary history as best we can by dwelling on a few documentary sources that mark its chronology, let us first recall its topographical and symbolic setting, then its political and territorial context.

A TOPOGRAPHICAL AND SYMBOLIC SETTING: THE TEMPLE AND THE PALACE

If one gallops through the planimetric reconstructions of the city between the second and seventh centuries, its face seems to have an eternally similar profile: a topographical inertia seems to have overcome the successive phases of destruction and reconstruction of the buildings themselves (see map 4). Despite the mobility of the supposed lines of the surrounding wall, between the time of Herod and that of Byzantine dominion, the age-old silhouette materialized a quadrangular mole that is immediately

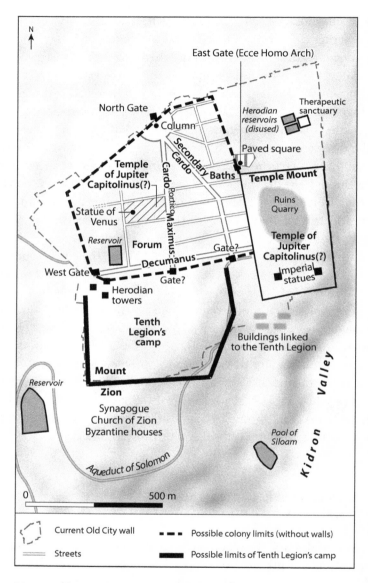

N

East Gate (Ecce Homo Arch)

North Gate

Column

Herodian
reservoirs
(disused)

Therapeutic
sanctuary

Paved square

Temple
of Jupiter
Capitolinus(?)

Secondary
Cardo

Cardo
Maximus

Portico

Baths

Temple Mount

Ruins
Quarry

Statue of
Venus

Temple of
Jupiter
Capitolinus(?)

Reservoir

Forum

Gate?

Decumanus

Imperial
statues

West Gate

Gate?

Herodian
towers

Tenth
Legion's
camp

Buildings linked
to the Tenth Legion

Mount

Valley

Zion

Reservoir

Synagogue
Church of Zion
Byzantine houses

Pool of
Siloam

Kidron

Aqueduct of Solomon

0   500 m

╭ ╮
╰ ╯ Current Old City wall   ■ ■ ■ Possible colony limits (without walls)

═══ Streets   ▬▬▬ Possible limits of Tenth Legion's camp

Map 4. Aelia Capitolina (c. 130–325)

recognizable because it is composed of two more or less interlocking rectangles that simply correspond to the mission imposed on the wall: enclose the two main elevations, Mount Zion to the west and the Temple Mount to the east, separated by the central Tyropoeon Valley, which commands the incision of the principal northern entrance, the present Damascus Gate. These two key ridges, generally oriented meridionally, are cut through the middle by two sills, which overlook the openings toward the west (the present Jaffa Gate, Hebron Gate, or Bab al-Khalil) and the east (today's Lions' Gate, Saint Stephen's Gate, or Bab Sitti Maryam; see map 1 in the introduction). This geometric equation of the city seems all the more immutable given that textual descriptions have never ceased to highlight the two hills (Mount Zion and the Temple Mount), even after the Roman destructions in 70 CE. This structuring symmetry reveals the division of the city's political and sacred functions, just as the Old Testament and the books of Kings constantly illustrate: between union and rivalry, the temple and the palace, priestly and royal power, are associated in a foundational but problematic solidarity. If the precise location of the ancient Mount Zion has long posed a problem for archaeologists, it is certain that the splitting of the topographical eminences reveals an essential narrative function in the city's history, incarnating the intermittent overlaying of the political by the sacred, of civil by religious space, and thus of the city by its sanctuary.

The function of the walls seems to be to articulate these two spaces: each of the city's inner poles embodied the seat of one of the two powers that commanded its center—the temple and the palace—and welcomed the two populations that already roamed it in biblical times, pilgrims and courtiers (see map 2 in chapter 1).

When beginning the history of Jerusalem's first Christianization, a question arises: how did Christianity—both rupture from and continuity with Judaism of the first (Abrahamic) covenant—adapt to this topographical and symbolic setting, to its apparently immutable structures? We can see that Christianity introduced into Jerusalem a third fundamental space, which broke the symmetric duality inherited from biblical times: the sanctuary that concentrates attention on the memory of the death and resurrection of Christ, not exactly a king (but a descendant of King David) and not exactly a priest (but at least a rabbi for his circle of disciples). Strangely, a change of toponym did not accompany this break; although individual conversion in Christianity is accompanied by baptism, literally and figuratively a name change—Simon becomes Peter, Saul becomes Paul—the city of the revelation was not renamed at the moment of its first Christianization (325) but rather rebaptized, in the strict meaning of the term: Constantine and his mother, Helena, intended to find the Jewish "Jerusalem" under the Roman "Aelia Capitolina," even if the Roman toponym remained in use for a long time.

To understand the topographical logic that underlay the city's first Byzantine Christianization (325–638), we must thus take a close look at the preceding Roman sequence (135–325), because that is what transmitted the patrimonial and urban framework within which the first Christian monuments were later erected. Curiously, for lack of available sources and sometimes for lack of interest, most historians have not lingered over the two centuries of this so-called Roman or pagan period, during which the capital of the kings of Judah was named Aelia Capitolina, echoing the name of the family from which Emperor Hadrian issued. This falsely intermediate moment is nevertheless not a parenthesis in the city's history: the shadow it cast largely determined the dynamic of imperial Christianization, begun by Constantine, from the fourth century onward.

THE POLITICAL AND TERRITORIAL CONTEXT: JERUSALEM "DECAPITALIZED"

The five centuries that separate the foundation of Colonia Aelia Capitolina around 130 and the Arab conquest of the city by Caliph 'Umar's troops in 635–38 are without doubt the least well documented period in Jerusalem's history. To understand the era despite this, one must first grasp its new political and territorial context.

Hadrian's Romanization of the city began a double administrative evolution: on attaining the status of imperial colony, consecrated to the cult of the Capitoline triad (Jupiter, Juno, Minerva) under the personal tutelage of the emperor, who gave the city the name of his lineage, it found itself "decapitalized"; it became a provincial city, in the strict sense of the term. Until the Muslim conquest, it thus remained firmly within the network of the empire's diocesan districts. An imperial functionary, the "over-

seer" (*episcopus* in Latin, "bishop" in English) only slowly gained autonomy from the governor of the Roman province of Palestine, who was based
at Caesarea. For the Christian empire's officials, the colony that was the
ex-capital of Judaea was not called anything other than Aelia or Helia.
The testimony of the pilgrim Arculf records the still common usage of this
term around 680, and Islamic sources continue to use the name Iliya
beyond the seventh century before "al-Quds" became usual, beginning in
the eleventh century. Within the eastern Christian empire, whose capital
was Constantinople, Jerusalem could not become a political capital again
and so had to content itself with being a city of pilgrimage.

The best indication of this Romanization remains the official name of
Jerusalem's diocese: it was not until late, at the end of the Council of
Chalcedon (451), owing to the theological debates then running through
the imperial church, that the bishop of Helia obtained the honorific title
of patriarch of Jerusalem. Helia's see claimed patriarchal dignity as the
memorial site of ancient Jerusalem: at that time, Rome, Constantinople,
and the two other evangelical capitals—Antioch (in memory of Luke) and
Alexandria (in memory of Mark)—had already enjoyed patriarchal dignity
for more than half a century. Beginning in 451, the patriarchal "Pentarchy"
corresponded in principle to the government of the church. It should be
noted that historically, Jerusalem was the last to join the directory of five
patriarchs, more than four hundred years after the death of Christ.

It so happens that this span of Byzantine Jerusalem's history exactly
coincides with a brief period of the city's political empowerment. The
acquisition of the patriarchal title, at the end of the episcopate of Juvenal
(422–58), was in fact contemporaneous with the exile in the Holy City of
Empress Eudocia, the disgraced wife of Theodosius II, between 443 and
her death in 460. It is moreover attested that this period corresponds to a
phase of investment and construction throughout the city, which Eudocia's
long-term presence no doubt explains. The political rhythm of this decapitalized city's history thus resonates with the successive phases of crisis
and consolidation of Byzantine central authority. From 530 onward, for
example, Jerusalem benefited fully from the investments of Emperor
Justinian (527–65), while at the beginning of the seventh century, faced
with growing Persian and Arab threats, Jerusalem soon found itself
directly endangered by its marginal position at the empire's eastern limit.

The city's Byzantine history should not, however, be excessively desecrated: Jerusalem's loss of political importance in fact clearly resonates
with the theological chronology of Christianity's first centuries. Thus, it
was doubtless not a coincidence that the bishop of Jerusalem had to wait
until 451 and the Council of Chalcedon, which reformulated the orthodox
faith in the dual human *and* divine nature of Christ, to finally succeed in
having his see recognized as one of the five patriarchates of the Christian
world. First of all, it was necessary to stave off the Arian and Nestorian
heresies—which accorded a major place to Christ's human, historical, and
thus potentially political dimension—so that Jerusalem could again
become one of the Christian world's capitals, at least spiritually. As long as
Christ, a descendant of King David, was considered primarily in his
human and historical dimension, there was indeed a certain political risk
in granting a prominent position to the bishop of the ancient City of
David. From a Jewish political capital humiliated by its defeat at the hands
of the Roman imperial power in 70, Jerusalem became just one of the
empire's numerous "capitol" cities in the second century. It must therefore
be emphasized that Constantine's conversion (312) did not call into question the enduring submission of the Holy City to an outside imperial
power; with the exception of brief spans in the Ayyubid and Mamluk eras,
Jerusalem did not become a truly sovereign—even if disputed—center of
political command again until the creation of the State of Israel in 1948.

JERUSALEM "CAPITOLIZED"? (135–325)

Medieval chroniclers, following Eusebius of Caesarea, long presented
Hadrian's foundation of the colony of Aelia Capitolina on the ruins of the
biblical Jerusalem as the Roman Empire's response to the last great Jewish
rebellion, called the Bar Kokhba revolt, which took place between 132 and
135. However, the detailed time line of events and a meticulous reading of
the sources today tend to show that Eusebius reversed the chronology and
took the effect for the cause. In fact, it was during his last long voyage in
the east, between 128 and 131, that Hadrian founded Aelia Capitolina,
shortly before the outbreak of the revolt, as this passage of Cassius Dio
suggests: "At Jerusalem he founded a city in place of the one which had

been razed to the ground, naming it Aelia Capitolina, and on the site of the temple of the god he raised a new temple to Jupiter. This brought on a war of no slight importance nor of brief duration."

Cassius Dio precisely recounts the revolt of 132–35, notably describing the rebels' guerilla tactics and tricks:

> So long, indeed, as Hadrian was close by in Egypt and again in Syria, they remained quiet, save in so far as they purposely made of poor quality such weapons as they were called upon to furnish, in order that the Romans might reject them and they themselves might thus have the use of them; but when he went farther away, they openly revolted. To be sure, they did not dare try conclusions with the Romans in the open field, but they occupied the advantageous positions in the country and strengthened them with mines and walls, in order that they might have places of refuge whenever they should be hard pressed.

In fact, the rebellion was definitively broken in 135, as reported by Cassius Dio, who specifies that following the Roman repression, "nearly the whole of Judaea was made desolate."[2]

The city of Jerusalem, destroyed by Titus in 70, was thus refounded as a Roman colony. However, it would be a mistake to contrast Titus's destruction with Hadrian's decision to reconstruct, enacted sixty years later. In reality, the two imperial decisions must be interpreted as the two poles of one and the same political sequence: namely, putting an end to the Jewish presence in Jerusalem, first by annihilating it, then by covering the ancient biblical city with the new Roman colony. The consistency of this imperial policy toward Jerusalem translated in particular into the transfer of the Jewish Temple's sacredness to the pantheon of Roman divinities.[3] Still, it must be noted that this transfer does not date only to the new pagan temples that were built in Jerusalem after its refoundation as a Roman colony: in actuality, it originates in the very time of the destruction of the Temple in 70. Flavius Josephus, in *The Jewish War*, written at the beginning of the 80s to explain the Jewish revolt of 66–70, thus reports that "on all Jews, wheresoever they be, [Vespasian] placed a tax, ordering each to pay two drachmas every year to the Capitol [Temple of Jupiter Capitolinus] as before they contributed to the Temple at Jerusalem."[4] The consistency of Rome's imperial policy toward the Jewish city of Jerusalem is evident here as well. It must be clarified, moreover, that the porosity between the various currents of Judaism and those that constituted what we now call proto-Christianity was then quite high, as shown by this passage of the *Ecclesiastical History*, composed by Eusebius of Caesarea at the beginning of the fourth century: "I have gathered from documents this much—that up to the siege of the Jews by Hadrian the succession of bishops [at Jerusalem] were fifteen in number. It is said that they were all Hebrews by origin who had nobly accepted the knowledge of Christ.... For their whole church at that time consisted of Hebrews who had continued Christian.... Such were the bishops in the city of Jerusalem, from the Apostles down to the time mentioned, and they were all Jews."[5] The Roman imperial policy thus aimed at both Judaism and Judeo-Christianity, if this subtle distinction established a posteriori was even perceptible to the Roman administrators at the time.

The textual sources that permit a precise description of the colony that Hadrian founded around 130 are rare and incomplete. In particular, on the basis of current knowledge we cannot place with any certainty the Temple of Jupiter Capitolinus constructed by Hadrian (see map 4). A literal reading of Cassius Dio might suggest a position at the very location of the ancient Jewish Temple ("and on the site of the temple of the god he raised a new temple to Jupiter"), and a passage by the Bordeaux Pilgrim describing a statue of Hadrian on the ancient esplanade around 333 might equally support this hypothesis. Other historians take up the later Christian interpretation that puts the new Roman temple near the supposed site of Christ's crucifixion (Golgotha), thus providing a base of legitimacy to the place that Helena, Constantine's mother, chose for the Holy Sepulchre in the fourth century: Roman monuments seem to be located in reverse, according to their potential to substantiate subsequent Christian monuments.

The *Chronicon Paschale*, a Byzantine chronicle that was compiled in the seventh century but includes some passages dating back to the third, lists the new, typically Roman city's main buildings, without, however, locating them in the urban space: "[Hadrian], having obliterated the temple of the Jews that existed in Jerusalem, founded the two public baths, the theater, the Capitol, the nymphaeum with four porticoes, the dodecapylon, and the quadrangular esplanade. He partitioned the city into seven districts and appointed special men as *amphodarchs* (district heads), to each of whom he assigned a district, and to this day each one is named for its *amphodarch*. On the city itself he imposed his own name, having called it Aelia."[6] Note that the "quadrangular esplanade," which can be identified with the Temple's ancient esplanade, is described separately from the Capitol, which argues for two different locations. . . . But it is particularly necessary to acknowledge that the sources which we have are vague and that besides the two major roads today well attested by archaeology (the *cardo maximus* and the *decumanus maximus*), the real appearance of Aelia Capitolina before Constantine largely escapes us.[7] The only certainty—established by the aboveground archaeological collection of quite numerous brick and tile fragments—is the lasting presence, undoubtedly until the end of the third century, of the Legio X Fretensis. If Aelia became a garrison camp, it is also true that in the function of its Capitol—regardless of the building's location in the city—it henceforth exalted the imperial cult through the figure of Jupiter or one of his auxiliary deities.

THE HOLY SEPULCHRE OF HELENA AND CONSTANTINE: A ROMANO-CHRISTIAN HYBRIDIZATION

Western historiography has long considered Constantine's conversion a decisive rupture symbolizing the Christian rebirth, if not refoundation, of the Holy City. Indeed, almost three hundred years after the death of Jesus of Nazareth, the first of Christianity's memorial sites appeared in Jerusalem, on the initiative of the Roman emperor Constantine (converted to the Christian faith in 312) and his mother, Helena, whom tradition reports stayed there between 325 and 327. However, this limited view of the chronology, which radically seals off a new "Christian" period from an old Roman or "pagan" period in Jerusalem's history, is doubly misleading. First of all, it makes it difficult to see the numerous continuities between Roman imperial ideology and Christianity as the new state religion. Second, it conceals the fragility and ambiguity of this first phase of the Holy City's Christianization. The historian Yvon Thébert, in attempting to deconstruct the myth of a "triumph of Christianity" over the

Roman Empire, in 1988 reversed the perspective normally used in addressing the connections between Roman imperialism and Christian ideology: "Like every religion, Christianity is fundamentally linked to politics. Only the decision by power to use this religious current allowed the latter a great expansion."[8] From this perspective, Constantine's conversion no longer appears as an essential historical issue, because it arose from a simple "individual trajectory." The real issue is rather Christianity's ideological capacity to strengthen the political and administrative efficacy of imperial structures. It is for this reason, Thébert continues, that "official Christianity faithfully reflected the structures of the empire, in its internal hierarchy, in the nature of the tasks entrusted to it, in its organization, copied from that of the civil power. . . . The idea of an organized religion winning the empire as part of an immense conversion movement is a myth. Catholicism did not conquer the society of the late empire but was secreted by it."[9] According to this interpretive framework, the year 325 was therefore not a break in the history of Jerusalem but, on the contrary, a new stage in the history of its *Romanization,* which now relied on the ideological potential of the new state religion, Christianity.

As paradoxical as it may seem, this new perspective allows a better understanding of the text that Eusebius of Caesarea dedicates to the first Christian foundations in Jerusalem, quoting a letter that Constantine is said to have addressed to Bishop Makarios (Macarius) of Jerusalem to ask him to build around the "sacred cave" (Christ's tomb) a "house of prayer worthy of the worship of God."[10] Beyond the wording that may confuse the modern reader, the terms employed testify to the Romano-Christian hybridization typical of Jerusalem in the Constantinian era.

The emperor, to bridge the three centuries separating his conversion from the life of Jesus, began by presenting the burial and the rediscovery of the Cross as a metaphor for oblivion and revelation: "For, that the monument of his most holy Passion, so long ago buried beneath the ground, should have remained unknown for so long a series of years, until its reappearance to his servants now set free through the removal of him who was the common enemy of all, is a fact which truly surpasses all admiration."[11] The material trace of biblical times was concealed underground, and it was a question of revealing it again in plain sight: from the fourth century, the rhetorical groundwork of religious archaeology was thus laid. In the narrative sequence that links the discovery of the Cross by the emperor's mother to the sanctuary's foundation by her son, the Helena-Constantine couple symbolically echoes the evangelical couple formed by the Virgin Mary and her son Jesus. The foregrounding of Helena's role, which reinforced the parallel between the emperor and Christ that became structural in the Byzantine tradition, is particularly clear in the narrative offered by Socrates of Constantinople: "Helena, the emperor's mother . . . , being divinely directed by dreams went to Jerusalem. Finding that which was once Jerusalem, desolate 'as a Preserve for autumnal fruits,' according to the prophet, she sought carefully the sepulchre of Christ, from which he arose after his burial; and after much difficulty, by God's help she discovered it."[12] There follows an account that is rather confused but in which it emerges that—by what is only seemingly a paradox—it was indeed the presence of the Roman temple built there to abolish its memory that allowed Helena to finally locate "the sepulchre of Christ." The transition between the classical Roman pantheon and the imperial conversion here becomes a mise en abyme in the subtle game of concealment-revelation that links the ancient Roman temple to the new Christian sanctuary: it is precisely because the Roman temple would have been built *in order to* hide the tomb that it then attested to the latter's location (see maps 4 and 5).

Constantine's letter to Bishop Makarios also testifies to the Roman imperial administration's strong imprint on this foundational building, even in the choice of decision-making authorities: "with respect to the erection and decoration of the walls, this is to inform you that our friend Dracilianus, the deputy of the Prætorian Præfects, and the governor of the province, have received a charge from us. . . . For the rest, your Holiness will give information as early as possible to the before-mentioned magistrates how many laborers and artificers, and what expenditure of money is required."[13] The new sanctuary was thus quite Roman, from the point of view of its administrative and material genesis and in terms of the building's religious symbolism, which explicitly took up certain salient features of Constantine's previous worship of the God of the Unconquered Sun (Sol Invictus), as this last passage from Eusebius shows: "Three gates, placed exactly east, were intended to receive the multitudes who entered the church. Opposite these gates the crowning part of the whole was the hemisphere, which rose to the very summit of the church. This was

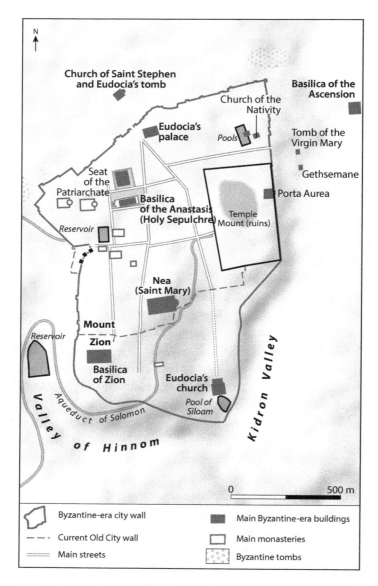

Map 5. *Byzantine Jerusalem (325–638)*

Church of Saint Stephen
and Eudocia's tomb

Basilica of the
Ascension

Church of the
Nativity

Eudocia's
palace

Pools

Tomb of the
Virgin Mary

Seat
of the
Patriarchate

Gethsemane

Basilica
of the Anastasis
(Holy Sepulchre)

Temple
Mount (ruins)

Porta Aurea

Reservoir

Nea
(Saint Mary)

Mount

Reservoir

Zion

Kidron Valley

Basilica
of Zion

Eudocia's
church

Pool of
Siloam

Valley

Aqueduct of Solomon

of Hinnom

0   500 m

Byzantine-era city wall

Main Byzantine-era buildings

Current Old City wall

Main monasteries

Main streets

Byzantine tombs

encircled by twelve columns (according to the number of the apostles of
our Saviour), having their capitals embellished with silver bowls of great
size, which the emperor himself presented as a splendid offering to his
God."[14] Even if historians lack clues to describe what this "hemisphere"
and these "bowls" really were, the strong ambiguity of this text by Eusebius
(himself a Christian bishop) testifies to the circulations that united the
Jewish, Roman, and Christian religious traditions, and it is undoubtedly
in this singularly equivocal ambiance that Jerusalem's fourth century
must be placed, rather than on a strictly "Christian" horizon, reconstructed
a posteriori from our current categories.

SEPTEMBER 13: JERUSALEM'S CITY FESTIVAL

The same polyphonic reading key must be used to interpret the date traditionally assigned to the new Basilica of the Holy Sepulchre's official dedication: September 13, 335, according to the Liturgy of Jerusalem.[15]
September 13 is in fact the date reserved in the Roman calendar for commemorating the dedication of the first Temple of Jupiter Capitolinus, in
Rome, in 509 BCE, the year of the Roman Republic's foundation. Here
again, there is no reason to be surprised: we know that the new sanctuary
erected by Constantine to celebrate Christ's Passion and resurrection was
supposedly located on the same spot where the Temple of Jupiter
Capitolinus built by Hadrian two centuries earlier had stood.

September 13 seems to have gradually established itself, over the
course of the Byzantine era, as a pivotal date in the calendar of Jerusalem's
city festivals. During her pilgrimage to Jerusalem from 381 to 384, Egeria
set on that day not only the commemoration of the Holy Sepulchre's dedication ("the holy church which is in Golgotha, and which they call the
martyrium") but also the remembrance of Helena's discovery of the Cross
ten years earlier, as well as the celebration of the First Temple's dedication
by King Solomon himself: "It was so ordained that, when the holy churches
above mentioned were first consecrated, that should be the day when the
Cross of the Lord had been found, in order that the whole celebration
should be made together, with all rejoicing, on the self-same day. Moreover,
it appears from the Holy Scriptures that this is also the day of dedication,

when holy Solomon, having finished the House of God which he had built, stood before the altar of God and prayed."[16] It is impossible to grasp all the richness and complexity of these memorial circulations if one refuses to acknowledge the fundamentally hybrid atmosphere in which the monotheistic traditions were slowly forged in the Roman Empire of the first centuries CE, particularly in Jerusalem.

The pilgrim Egeria gives a quite clear idea of these festivities: "When these days of dedication are come, they are kept for eight days. And people begin to assemble from all parts many days before; not only monks and *apotactitae* [members of certain early Christian sects that renounced worldly belongings] from various provinces, from Mesopotamia and Syria, from Egypt and the Thebaid (where there are very many monks), and from every different place and province . . . but lay people too in like manner, both men and women, with faithful minds, gather together in Jerusalem from every province on those days, for the sake of the holy day. And the bishops, even when they have been few, are present to the number of forty or fifty in Jerusalem on these days. . . . Now on these days of the dedication the adornment of all the churches is the same as at Easter and at Epiphany, also on each day the procession is made to the several holy places."[17] Reading this extremely vivid testimony leaves no doubt possible: September 13, by a sort of fusion of local traditions, became a major date in the "city time" of Jerusalem and its region during this first phase of Christianization.

The account of Bishop Arculf's pilgrimage circa 680, three hundred years after Egeria, confirms the convergence of local traditions around the date of September 13, beyond the geopolitical vicissitudes generally presented as clean breaks in the Holy City's history. While Jerusalem had been under Islamic dominion since 638, the great city festival described by Egeria in fact seems to have been maintained in the form of a vast urban fair that took place on the same date, "anniversario" (annually), Arculf tells us, without further precision:

On the twelfth day of the month of September yearly, an almost countless multitude of various nations is in the habit of gathering from all sides to Jerusalem for the purposes of commerce by mutual sale and purchase. Whence it necessarily happens that crowds of various nations stay in that hospitable city for some days, while the very great number of their camels and horses and asses, not to speak of mules and oxen, for their varied baggage, strews the streets of the city here and there with the abominations of their excrements. . . . Wonderful to say, on the night after the above-mentioned day of departure with the various beasts of burden of the crowds, an immense abundance of rain falls from the clouds on that city, which washes all the abominable filths from the streets, and cleanses it from the uncleanness.[18]

To summarize: September 13—whose importance originated in the long-ago dedication of the first Temple of Jupiter Capitolinus at the foundation of the Roman Republic in 509 BCE and which Egeria connected with the remembrance of not only the dedication of the first church of the Holy Sepulchre in 335 and Helena's discovery of the Cross in 325 but also the consecration of the Jewish First Temple, constructed by King Solomon—thus became the date of Jerusalem's major annual fair by the end of the seventh century, even though the city had passed under Islamic dominion by then. It was also when Jerusalem's "baptism" was renewed, as Arculf explicitly underlined: "After having thus baptized Jerusalem,[19] this overabundance of rain always ceases. Hence therefore we must in no negligent manner note in what honor this chosen and glorious city is held in the sight of the Eternal Sire, Who does not permit it to remain longer filthy, but because of the honour of His Only Begotten cleanses it so quickly, since it has within the circuit of its walls the honoured sites of His sacred Cross and Resurrection." Recognition of the interactions throughout Jerusalem's history between the Roman pantheons and the three monotheisms is therefore not a matter of historical reconstruction a posteriori or of an obsession with cultural mixing. Quite the contrary: these forms of hybridization appear to be the only means of grasping the simultaneous transfers of sacredness that weave through the city's history. Cutting Jerusalem's past into successive religious slices, as is too often done, not only dangerously essentializes the monotheist traditions but also precludes an understanding of the unsettling singularity of the Holy City's history.

SOLOMON'S MEMORY REACTIVATED

Jerusalem's religious appearance in the fourth century was due not only to its overlapping chronology, which associated the ending Roman pantheon and the emerging Christian monotheism ultimately quite simply: thanks to this first and fledgling Christianization, elements of the Jewish tradition that were dismantled when the Temple was destroyed in 70 also rose to the surface. Here too the paradox is only apparent: by embracing a Christian religion still largely dependent on its Jewish support, Constantine and his successors reactivated the memories of David, Solomon, Zechariah, and other Old Testament figures specifically attached to the memory of Jerusalem. The city's new religious landscape that emerged in the fourth century was thus woven with many threads: to the Romano-Christian horizon was added a Judeo-Christian one, no doubt particularly vibrant in the Kingdom of Israel's ancient capital.

The intertwining of Jewish, Roman, and Christian religious traditions is illustrated in the figure of the emperor Julian the Apostate (361–63), raised in the Christian religion and then fervent defender of a return to Roman polytheism before planning the reconstruction of Jerusalem's Jewish temple, as his hagiographer Ammianus Marcellinus reported a few years later: "Turning his activity to every part, and eager to extend the memory of his reign by great works, he planned at vast cost to restore the once splendid temple at Jerusalem, which after many mortal combats during the siege by Vespasian and later by Titus, had barely been stormed. He had entrusted the speedy performance of this work to Alypius of Antioch, who had once been vice-prefect of Britain. . . . Alypius pushed the work on with vigour, aided by the governor of the province."[20] The precision of the description and its setting in the account of Julian's campaign against the Persians, which did indeed bring him to Antioch in spring 363, leave little doubt about the project's actuality or the beginning of its realization. As the narrative continues, it mentions an eruption of "terrifying balls of flame," perhaps referring to an earthquake; in any case, they led to the project's abandonment, thus bringing to a close this surprising but significant historical digression.

The description transmitted by the Bordeaux Pilgrim during his voyage to Jerusalem in 333, a few years after the trip (325–27) by Constantine's mother, Helena, and two years before the first church of the Holy Sepulchre's dedication (335), clearly shows the extent to which Old Testament references still dominated the Christian imaginary. As the sociologist Maurice Halbwachs emphasizes in his *Legendary Topography of the Gospels in the Holy Land* about the Bordeaux Pilgrim's *Itinerary*,

"What strikes us is the preponderant and almost exclusive share given to the Old Testament. This seems quite natural, considering that Christian traditions had not yet had time to take root and spread throughout the country."[21] The Bordeaux Pilgrim thus describes, on the Temple's ancient esplanade, "many rooms, and here was Solomon's palace. There also is the chamber in which he [sat] and wrote the (Book of) Wisdom."[22] Later, when he describes "the building . . . itself, where stood the temple which Solomon built," he reinforces in passing the theory that the Temple of Jupiter Capitolinus (constructed by Hadrian) was located on the ancient esplanade itself.[23]

In any case, his testimony attests that Jews were granted permission to come pray on the site of the old Temple once a year: "The blood of Zacharias . . . was shed upon the stone pavement before the altar. . . . There are two statues of Hadrian, and not far from the statues there is a perforated stone, to which the Jews come every year and anoint it, bewail themselves with groans, rend their garments, and so depart."[24] It is impossible to locate this "perforated stone" with certainty, because it might be identified with the rock of Abraham—which is currently under the Dome of the Rock and indeed has a cavity that tunnels underground—or with one of the masonry elements of the ancient Herodian structure of which we have lost track (see map 4). What is at any rate quite significant is again the omission—or nonexistence—of memories of the Gospels in this description, as Halbwachs highlights: "Solomon, Zechariah, the Jews. But the presentation at the Temple is not located. It seems to be forgotten that as a child, Jesus once sat in the sanctuary among the teachers, whom he listened to and questioned."[25]

When he went to the Pool of Siloam, below the Temple's esplanade, the Bordeaux Pilgrim again testified to the vividness of Jewish memories in the collective imagination of Jerusalem's inhabitants: "This spring runs for six days and nights, but on the seventh day, which is the Sabbath, it does not run at all, either by day or by night."[26] From his reading of the Bordeaux Pilgrim, Halbwachs finally delivers a crucial interpretive key for understanding the arrangement of monotheistic imaginaries in the Holy City: "Thanks to what he notes and what he doesn't mention . . . , we know the essentials of what was shown to Christians then, in Jerusalem and in Palestine. What else the pilgrims who came after him would talk about . . .

possibly had not yet appeared and were matters of later localizations."[27] The
Christian remembrance of Jerusalem, far from being erased with time, to
the contrary developed as it slowly extricated itself from its Jewish substra-
tum. When the Bordeaux Pilgrim described Jerusalem in 333, he had before
his eyes a city that was largely impregnated with its Jewish and Roman heritage and whose Christianization was still very fragile and incomplete.

Other witnesses confirm this impression of entangled religious traditions in fourth-century Jerusalem. When Egeria, in the account of her visit
in 381–84, goes to the Temple's ancient esplanade, the omnipresence and
the precision of the memories connected to the former worship are striking: "In the middle of the Temple, there is a great mountain encircled by
walls that held the tabernacle; the ark of the covenant was also there."[28]
Egeria clearly describes a masonry edifice, which must therefore be interpreted as either a surviving element from the Temple destroyed in 70 or a
part of the Roman Temple of Jupiter Capitolinus constructed by Hadrian,
based on the theory that it was erected on the ancient sanctuary's site. In
her description of the Liturgy of Jerusalem, Egeria further states that "there
is never fasting on any Sabbath here throughout the year,"[29] echoing the
Bordeaux Pilgrim's description of the Pool of Siloam, which did not flow
during the Sabbath: it was thus not only Jerusalem's *space* but also its *time*
that was still impregnated with the old covenant. Saint Jerome (347–420),
in his account of Paula's pilgrimage to Jerusalem (386), also often refers to
the Old Testament, for example when describing the top of the Mount of
Olives, where "each year a red cow was burned in sacrifice to the lord."[30] If
we want to identify the reality of Jerusalem's religious physiognomy in the
decades following the first Constantinian foundations, it is indeed the
enshrining of Jewish, Roman, and Christian traditions that we must accentuate, without trying to flatten the chronology at any cost to make the
fourth century the first "all-Christian" period in the Holy City's history.

JUVENAL, EUDOCIA, AND MELANIA THE YOUNGER: THE NEW SOLDIERS OF CHRIST

In the fifth century, the Christian presence in Jerusalem grew. Under the
influence notably of Juvenal, the bishop of Jerusalem for more than three

decades (422–58), the Holy City rose to the rank of patriarchate, Christian convents and monasteries multiplied, relics proliferated, reception facilities for pilgrims were set up, and the worship of local saints, such as Stephen, was firmly planted in the landscape and the calendar. The pilgrimage accounts from this period are unequivocal from this perspective: as the cult of the Cross and the "Cave of Salvation" grew in credibility and visibility, the silhouette of the Jewish Temple seemed to fade, until it practically disappears in some descriptions. Thus Peter the Iberian, in the voice of John Rufus, provides this striking panorama during his first pilgrimage, in 437–38: "They saw from atop a hill about five stadia away, like the flashing of the sunrise, the high roof of the holy and worshipful churches, that of the saving and worshipful Cross, of the holy Anastasis, and again the worshipful Ascension, which [is] on the mountain opposite it."[31] However hard you look, Peter the Iberian's description doesn't mention the old Jewish Temple anywhere, although it is omnipresent in the accounts of Christian pilgrims from the previous century. Later, when he describes the Holy City's interior, he focuses on the memory of Stephen, the first Christian martyr, who was stoned to death in Jerusalem on the order of the Sanhedrin, according to the Christian tradition, and whose figure occupies a fundamental position in primitive Christianity's de-Judaization process: "[Peter the Iberian] first entered the *martyrion* of the holy Stephen, upon which he happened [to come] first. And when he went down to the cave, he venerated his sarcophagus."[32] A few years later, under the impetus of Empress Eudocia and Bishop Juvenal, the first chapel dedicated to Stephen's memory was constructed, north of the present Damascus Gate, where the École biblique et archéologique française currently stands (see map 5).[33] Christianity's de-Judaization in the Holy Land was under way: specifically Christian memories, which up to the previous century had still needed the guardianship of Old Testament memories, now gained in authority, and therefore in autonomy. Jerusalem's Christianization in the fifth century can also be explained by the long presence in the Holy City of the fallen empress Eudocia, the Byzantine emperor Theodosius II's ex-wife, who stayed there from 437 to 439 and then definitively from 443 until her death in 460. Even deprived of her title of *augusta*, she was followed to Jerusalem by part of her imperial retinue, giving her prestige and wealth. On her arrival, she was welcomed by

Melania the Younger, a rich patrician who had herself been living in the Holy City since 417 and dedicated her fortune to founding Christian monasteries and convents, especially on the Mount of Olives. It is not surprising that in Jerusalem, as elsewhere in the Roman world, the increase in female religious figures and monastic structures for women was a decisive step in Christianity's extension.

In any case, this rise in the power of monasticism had two major consequences: on the one hand, it allowed Juvenal to strengthen his autonomy with respect to both the imperial civil power and Caesarea's governor, by leaning heavily on the new "soldiers of Christ," the monks; on the other hand, the multiplication of monasteries offered new reception facilities to pilgrims and allowed Jerusalem, after a break of more than four hundred years, to become a pilgrimage center again. The elevation of Jerusalem's episcopal see to the rank of patriarchate in 451, at the end of the Council of Chalcedon, must be analyzed as the logical conclusion of these processes.

The reconstruction of the walls is another essential proof of Jerusalem's new urban core in the fifth century. Pulled down at the same time as the Temple by Titus's legionnaires in 70 CE, the walls of the Holy City seem not to have been rebuilt until four centuries later, under the auspices of Eudocia and Juvenal (see map 5). Indeed, the very first description of the new enclosure dates to the 450s, from the pen of Eucherius, the bishop of Lyon, a compiler of his contemporaries' travel accounts: "Jerusalem is called Ælia from Ælius Hadrianus; for, after its destruction by Titus, it received the name together with the works of its founder, Ælius. The place, they say, is naturally lofty, so that one has to ascend to it from every side; it rises by a long yet gentle slope. The site of the city itself is almost circular, enclosed within a circuit of walls of no small extent, whereby it now receives within itself Mount Sion, which was once outside."[34]

In addition, Eucherius describes numerous "cells of monks" outside the walls, confirming the idea that Christian foundations were multiplying in the Holy City's immediate vicinity. Finally, he states that "the most frequented gates (of the city) are three in number; one on the west [the current Jaffa Gate], another on the east [the current Lions' Gate], and the third on the north side of the city [the current Damascus Gate]."[35] A few decades later, at the beginning of the sixth century, Theodosius's descrip-

tion confirmed Eucherius's and showed that Jerusalem's core had continued to grow: Theodosius counts "six main gates" and systematically indicates the directions of the roads that were organized in a star around
Jerusalem, specifying the distances toward, among others, Jericho to the
east, Hebron to the south, Neapolis (Nablus) to the north, and Gaza to the
west.[36] In mentioning what is now the Damascus Gate, he did not forget
to honor the memories of Saints Stephen and Eudocia: "S. Stephen was
stoned outside the Galilaean Gate; and there is his church, which was
built by S. Eudocia, the wife of the emperor Theodosius."[37] At the end of
the fifth century, almost two hundred years after Constantine's conversion, Jerusalem was well on its way to becoming a Christian city.

THE TEMPLE AT GOLGOTHA: JERUSALEM DE-JUDAIZED

The Christianization of Jerusalem's holy sites reached a decisive stage in
the sixth century: the outline of the old Jewish Temple was erased and the
memories hitherto linked to it were henceforth located in Golgotha and
the Church of the Resurrection (the present Church of the Holy Sepulchre),
as if the new Christian pivot of the city's sacred geography were now able to
attract and organize all of the threads of remembrance accumulated up to
then. This was a complete reversal of the prevailing situation two centuries
earlier, at the time of Constantine's conversion, when the first fledging
Christian traditions were connected to the last visible traces of the old covenant. From this point on, in the imagination of Christian pilgrims in
Jerusalem, the hill of Golgotha took the place of the Temple's hill, focusing
gazes and rearranging stories. From this point of view, the description
offered by Theodosius's early sixth-century pilgrimage guide is particularly
enlightening: "In the city of Jerusalem at the Lord's Sepulchre is the place
of Calvary, where Abraham offered up his son *for a burnt-offering;* and
because the mountain is rocky, Abraham made the altar in the mountain
itself, *i.e.,* at its foot. Above the altar the mountain towers and the ascent of
the mountain is made by steps. There the Lord was crucified. From the
Lord's Sepulchre to the place of Calvary it is 15 paces; it is all under one
roof."[38] The foundational event of the monotheistic religions—which saw
the patriarch Abraham offer his son as a sacrifice to Yahweh—until then

located at the top of the Temple Mount or of Mount Moriah, was thereafter situated on the hill of Golgotha, the place of Christ's calvary, in an obvious play on the echoes between the two sacrifices. This displacement of sacredness from one topographical eminence to another materially expresses the slow but progressive autonomization of the Christian tradition from its ancient Jewish support.

Theodosius's guide is not the only account to document this surprising *translatio sacra:* the *Breviary of Jerusalem*, another pilgrimage guide dating to the beginning of the sixth century, amasses inside the Holy Sepulchre a number of Old Testament remembrances: "From hence you enter into Golgotha. . . . Here also is the charger wherein the head of St. John was carried [Mark 6:25–28]; and here is the horn with which David and Solomon were anointed; and in this place, too, is the ring with which Solomon sealed his writings, which ring is of amber. Here Adam was formed out of clay; here Abraham offered his own son Isaac [Genesis 22:1–14] in the very place where our Lord Jesus Christ was crucified."[39] The Church of the Holy Sepulchre, which Constantine founded in 325, thus became the reliquary of the kings of Israel, strengthening Christ's bond of filiation to the line of David, the first king of Israel, chosen by Samuel in Bethlehem from among the sons of Jesse (1 Samuel 16). Even more astonishing, Solomon's memory, until then exclusively located around the First Temple, which he himself built, was likewise moved to the Holy Sepulchre, in a process of memorial concentration and magnetization magnificently formulated by Maurice Halbwachs as concerning "cases in which several acts have been situated in the same place, without there being any necessary connections between them, as if a location already consecrated by some memory had attracted others, as if memories too obeyed a kind of herd instinct."[40] The memory of Adam and Abraham, the two founding figures of the Genesis story, was also magnetized by this new polarity and thereafter solidly anchored to the Holy Sepulchre, which today still records this association, with the "Chapel of Adam" that pilgrims visit under the Rock of Calvary.

This process of aggregating remembrances around the Holy Sepulchre finally stripped the old Jewish Temple of its last rags of memories, which completed its topographical erasure from the minds of pilgrims, as this laconic mention in the *Breviary of Jerusalem* attests: "From there you go to the Temple that Solomon built; nothing remains but a crypt. From there you go to the pinnacle where Satan deposited the Lord [Matthew 4:5]." If we acknowledge that a heritage element is as much an elaboration of memory as a physical construction, we must recognize that nothing of the old Jewish Temple remained in the minds of sixth-century Christian pilgrims, nothing "but a crypt," underground: the final memories of the old Temple were henceforth invisible, buried in the subterranean dark, and even the "pinnacle" that was until then described as the last visible vestige of the old Temple was thereafter covered up by an evangelical story, that of Satan's temptation of Christ.

The Piacenza Pilgrim's travel account, dating to the 560s or 570s, may be considered as a conclusion of this first phase of Jerusalem's Christianization. Reception facilities were then well in place, regularly distributed along the pilgrimage route: "Ascending the rising ground in the neighbourhood of Jerusalem, ... looking down into the valleys and visiting many monasteries and places where miracles had been performed, we beheld a multitude of men and women living as recluses upon the Mount of Olives."[41] On arriving in Jerusalem he described its walls, "because the Empress Eudocia herself added these walls to the city."[42] His depiction of the Holy Sepulchre repeats all the traditions accumulated by his predecessors and adds an astonishing note, again borrowed from the Temple hill's ancient stock of memories: "At one side is the altar of Abraham, whither he went to offer up Isaac.... Beside the altar is an aperture where, if you place your ear, you will hear the rushing of waters; and if you throw into it an apple, fruit, or anything else that will swim, and then go to the fountain of Siloam, you will find it again there."[43] If today it is proved that no spring nor stream passes near the Holy Sepulchre, it is interesting that this description of a watery underground connection between the Holy Sepulchre and the miraculous Pool of Siloam exactly reproduces the older tradition—which resurfaced in the nineteenth century—of the "four rivers of Paradise" said to flow under the Temple esplanade.[44] At the end of the sixth century, Christian pilgrims well and truly considered the Holy Sepulchre to be Jerusalem's new temple. Another sign of a first phase of Christianization completed in that period: the techniques for multiplying *eulogia* (relics of contact) seem to have been well developed and almost commonplace, as the Piacenza Pilgrim indicates in relating his visit to the Holy Sepulchre: "Into the tomb earth is carried from without, and those who enter it bear away a blessing with them from it when they depart."[45] A veritable economy of Christian pilgrimage was thus set up to increase and regulate *eulogia* production: one could then "carry Jerusalem," in the form of a handful of dirt, to any Christian home or monastery in the West.

Moreover, in every place of sacred Christian memory, relics proliferated, with progressively more detail, as if the supply was adapting to an ever-increasing need for remembrance. This was the case on Mount Zion (south of the city), which at that time concentrated all the traditions relating to Christ's condemnation and flagellation (traditions today assembled in the city's west, at the starting point of the current Via Dolorosa): "Thence we come to the Basilica of the Holy (Mount) Sion. . . . In that very church is the pillar upon which our Lord was scourged, upon which pillar is the following mark: when He embraced it, His breast imprinted itself upon the very stone; and His two hands with both their palms and fingers are to be seen upon the stone. . . . There is likewise the crown of thorns with which our Lord was crowned, and the spear which was thrust into His side, and many stones with which Stephen was stoned. There is also a pillar upon which the cross of the blessed Peter, upon which he was crucified at Rome, was placed. There, too, is the chalice of the Apostles, with which, after our Lord's resurrection, they used to celebrate mass; and many other relics which I have forgotten."[46] Relics abounded, gaining in detail and effectiveness; sometimes coming from Rome, they accentuated every single episode of Christ's life and death, to the point that such abundance seems to have overwhelmed the Piacenza Pilgrim.

The extraordinary proliferation of relics in the sixth-century Christianized Holy City testifies to this truth that is key to understanding the appearance and arrangement of Jerusalem's sacred sites: collective memory is not a trace of the past but "essentially a reconstruction of the past. . . . It adapts the image of ancient matters to the beliefs and spiritual needs of the *present*," to quote Halbwachs.[47] We must remember this while analyzing the later sequences of religious incorporation into the Holy City's cultural heritage—first Islamic (starting in the seventh century), then Christian again (during the Crusades and from the nineteenth century onward), and finally Jewish (from 1948 to the present).

THE MADABA MAP, THE CITY'S OLDEST
REPRESENTATION

The mosaic discovered at the end of the nineteenth century in Madaba (in present-day Jordan) is thought to be the oldest cartographic representation of Jerusalem. Produced at the end of the seventh century for Christian pilgrims who crisscrossed the Holy Land, it shows the city's morphology just before the Persian (614) and Arab (635–38) conquests. Here we see Jerusalem surrounded by a continuous wall with five visible gates: the Gate of the Pillar or Damascus Gate to the north, the Lions' Gate and the Golden Gate to the east, the Zion Gate to the south, and the Jaffa or Hebron Gate to the west. To the east, although the southeast corner of the mosaic map is now destroyed, it is impossible to distinguish the old Jewish Temple or even its esplanade. If we acknowledge that cartographic descriptions, like textual ones, attest an era's representations as much as its reality, the Madaba Map testifies well to the topographical and symbolic effacement of the old Jewish Temple in late sixth-century Jerusalem: it is an all-Roman and all-Christian city that we find here. The column-framed *cardo maximus*, which crosses the city from north to south, is the structuring element: Coming from the north, it first leads to the Constantinian basilica the Martyrium (the present-day Church of the Holy Sepulchre), clearly visible with its three east-facing monumental doors. Then, farther south, the *cardo* gives access to the Nea Ekklesia (the New Church of Saint Mary), built at the request of Emperor Justinian (527–65) and dedicated in 543. This church's construction may be considered the culmination of the Holy City's first Christianization phase. The Piacenza Pilgrim, circa 560–70, described it as follows: "From Sion we came to the Basilica of the Blessed Mary, where is a large congregation of monks, and where are also hospices (for strangers, both) for men and women. There I was received as a pilgrim; there were countless tables, and more than three thousand beds for sick persons."[48] Even if the numerical exaggeration is obvious, this makes clear the increasing power of facilities for receiving and aiding Christian pilgrims, who were ever more numerous in the late sixth century.

.   .   .   .   .

This is one of the many paradoxes that dot Jerusalem's long chronology: the de-Judaization, de-Romanization, and Byzantine Christianization of the city's holy sites was completed in the sixth century . . . just a few decades before Jerusalem came under Muslim control, after 635. Again, this new sequence should not be interpreted as a seamless chronological break, a Year Zero in the Holy City's chaotic history. In reality, Jerusalem's earliest Islamization was first marked by a fresh reactivation of its Jewish history. From 614, when the Persians conquered the Holy City, Jews were again allowed to settle there. Expelled once more by Emperor Heraclius in 630, at the start of the brief Byzantine reconquest, they were explicitly authorized to return after the Arabs captured Jerusalem. It was the same in 1187, when Saladin definitively retook the city from the Crusaders. In Jerusalem—until the early twentieth century's historic reversal—it was indeed Islam that permitted Jews to maintain their presence, while the city's Christian sequences were more often synonymous with expulsion and exclusion.

After 638, the new Islamic sovereignty not only had demographic consequences but was also accompanied by a decisive topographical change: the Temple's old esplanade was turned into a sanctuary. With the construction of the mosque on the esplanade's south side in the middle of the seventh century, then of the Dome of the Rock in the esplanade's center in 691–92, the Holy City's sacred geography, until then drawn to the Christian Holy Sepulchre as to a magnet, rotated again, toward the east and the Temple Mount. However, the Roman and Christian city did not disappear: the toponym Aelia was still commonly used, and the Christian inhabitants remained the majority in the following centuries, as Muslim chroniclers indicate. So goes the history of Jerusalem: the different segments that constitute the city continue their journeys, often discreetly, sometimes secretly, beyond or below the most apparent and most shattering historical ruptures.

3 In the Empire of the Caliphs

SEVENTH TO ELEVENTH CENTURIES

At the end of the nineteenth century, on the road from Jerusalem to Jericho and on the one that leads to Ramla, archaeologists found several lime and marble milestones bearing similar inscriptions. The one now in the Louvre indicates that Caliph 'Abd al-Malik (r. 685–705) "ordered the construction of this route and the manufacture of milestones" and that "from Iliya to this milestone is eight *mil*s." *Iliya* is the Arabic transcription of *Aelia*, the name that the Romans had given Jerusalem around 130. The Arabic *mil* took its name from the Roman unit of length *mille* and has roughly its value (2,285 meters [1.4 miles] instead of 1,842 meters [1.1 miles]). But what is most significant here is the decision to mark off the roads and measure the distances, a thoroughly imperial gesture of appropriating space which a Roman emperor could have performed.[1]

Continuity thus seems to prevail, at least in the practice of power, over the ruptures that punctuated Jerusalem's history throughout the seventh century. Certainly, the emperor who now reigned over Aelia/Iliya was no longer the basileus of Constantinople but instead the caliph of Damascus. Certainly, the faith that legitimized his power was no longer belief in the incarnation of Christ-God but rather in Muhammad's prophetic mission. Certainly, provincial Palestine's administrative language was no longer

87

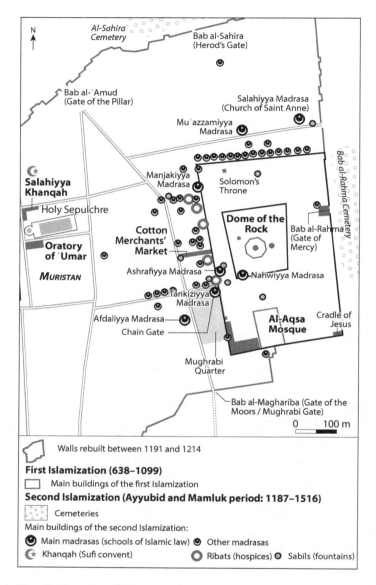

N

Al-Sahira Cemetery

Bab al-Sahira (Herod's Gate)

Bab al-'Amud (Gate of the Pillar)

Salahiyya Madrasa (Church of Saint Anne)

Mu'azzamiyya Madrasa

Salahiyya Khanqah

Manjakiyya Madrasa

Solomon's Throne

Bab al-Rahma Cemetery

Holy Sepulchre

Dome of the Rock

Bab al-Rahma (Gate of Mercy)

Oratory of 'Umar

Cotton Merchants' Market

Muristan

Ashrafiyya Madrasa

Nahwiyya Madrasa

Tankiziyya Madrasa

Afdaliyya Madrasa

Al-Aqsa Mosque

Cradle of Jesus

Chain Gate

Mughrabi Quarter

Bab al-Maghariba (Gate of the Moors / Mughrabi Gate)

0   100 m

Walls rebuilt between 1191 and 1214

First Islamization (638–1099)

Main buildings of the first Islamization

Second Islamization (Ayyubid and Mamluk period: 1187–1516)

Cemeteries

Main buildings of the second Islamization:

Main madrasas (schools of Islamic law)   Other madrasas

Khanqah (Sufi convent)   Ribats (hospices)   Sabils (fountains)

Map 6. From Temple Mount to Haram al-Sharif

only Greek but increasingly Arabic. Jerusalem, however, had not yet changed its face, although it changed hands three times in the first half of the seventh century: from Byzantines to Persians (614), from Persians to Byzantines (628), and from Byzantines to Arabs (between 635 and 638). The city and its inhabitants changed masters but, once peace returned, did not change daily life.

What today appears as one of the major breaks in Jerusalem's millennia-old history, the Arab conquest of the seventh century, was initially only a simple shift of imperial power. Let us go further: the military episode that delivered the city to the Arabs was in reality so minor, so secondary to the century's events, that historians are in a position neither to fix the date with certainty nor even to give the victor's name. The history of seventh-century Jerusalem is doubly veiled from our view. The collapse of Constantinople's empire, if not as all-encompassing as that of the Persian Empire under the Arabs' blows, was nonetheless so sudden as to rend extremely conjectural the chronology of events in the provinces that it lost. As for the Arab Empire, it was still too young and too unsure of its destiny to write its own history: Arabic historiography essentially dates to after the mid-eighth century. Between two histories, one withdrawing and one advancing, there was room for only two types of writing: that of the end of the world, on the one hand, particularly the Jewish apocalyptic, which saw in the arrival of the Sons of Ishmael (the Arabs) the sign of the Messiah's imminent advent, and, on the other hand, that of legendary origins, particularly Jerusalem's Muslim mythology, which made the city an essential link in the chain of prophets, from Abraham to Muhammad. The deciphering of the future and the rewriting of the past have blurred the reference points. The sequence of Jerusalem's history that we are about to enter is thus as decisive as it is uncertain.

JERUSALEM IMPERILED BY EMPIRES

The war had resumed at the beginning of the seventh century. Another war between the Persian Sassanid Empire and the Eastern Roman (Byzantine) Empire, but this time to the death, aiming at the adversary's definitive elimination. In this conflict, Jerusalem occupied a symbolic place out of all proportion to its military importance.

The Persian Interlude

The Persians took the city in 614, during the great offensive that also made them masters of Syria and Egypt, probably in May, if the Georgian Lectionary, which commemorates "the burning of Jerusalem" on May 17, is to be believed. They held it until 628 without seeing fit to settle there, preferring Caesarea, the capital of the Byzantine province of Palestine. Jerusalem lost a large part of its population, to the massacres that followed its capture (without accepting the improbable number of 66,509 victims advanced with an obviously polemical aim by the monk Strategikos) and to the Mesopotamian exile of some of its inhabitants. The destruction caused by the siege, the sacking, and the burning was no doubt quite extensive—even if the destruction of only the city's main churches (the Anastasis, the Martyrium, the Church of Zion) is known to us. Jerusalem's Christians, under the leadership of a simple priest, Modestus, in the absence of their patriarch Zacharias, exiled in 614, appealed to other churches (that of Armenia and perhaps also Alexandria) for financial aid to rebuild their sanctuaries.[2]

If they neglected to restore Jerusalem, the Persians, who counted among their ranks influential Nestorian Christians hostile to the Byzantine Church, did not fail to exploit the symbolic significance of their conquest. In 614, not content to exile the city's notables to Ctesiphon (south of present-day Baghdad), they also brought back to this winter capital of the Sassanian emperors the most prestigious of relics, the "True Cross" which Emperor Constantine's mother had miraculously discovered in Jerusalem in 326 and for which the Basilica of the Anastasis (also called the Church of the Holy Sepulchre) had been built (see map 5 in chapter 2). Another of the Persians' decisions must be viewed as likely having the same aim of symbolically dispossessing the defeated: entrusting the government of Jerusalem to a community that had been excluded from it, in principle, since Emperor Hadrian's time—the Jews. They had provided crucial support to the attackers in 614, convinced that the imminent collapse of the Kingdom of Edom (as Jewish apocalyptic thought designated the Byzantine Empire) heralded the coming of the Messiah. The Byzantine sources accuse them of having played a leading role in the massacres that followed the city's capture and of having forcibly converted a good number of survivors to Judaism. In any case, for a brief period before the Persians changed their minds for reasons that are unclear, the Jews got to return to Jerusalem.[3]

The Persians had made Jerusalem a symbol of their pending triumph over the Eastern Roman Empire. The Roman emperor Heraclius (r. 610–41) made it the central reference point of his project of reconquest. The military victory that he obtained in 627 near Nineveh was only a step toward the Persian Empire's conversion to Christianity, itself a prelude to the universal gathering under the banner of Christ. Furthermore, this era's holy hero, celebrated from the end of the conflict by the Byzantine Church, was not a Roman but a Persian, the son of a Zoroastrian priest, said to have been converted in Jerusalem in 620 by the grace of the True Cross and been martyred for his faith: Saint Anastasius (literally "Resurrected"). Heraclius also revived, after his victory over the Persians, the policy of forced baptism of the empire's Jews, already implemented by some of his predecessors despite the reticence of part of the church. Universal conversion could no longer wait, now that the True Cross had returned to its proper place. The famous relic triumphantly returned to Jerusalem in 630. Like a new Constantine refounding the Christian Empire, Heraclius personally brought it into the city on March 21, the day of the vernal equinox, which in the Byzantine calendar marked the creation of the celestial lights and the beginning of time.

Oddly, the Byzantine sources say nothing about the route that the imperial procession took to the Basilica of the Anastasis, to which the relic was restored. Two centuries later, Rabanus Maurus, the abbot of Fulda (Germany), recounted how the city gate, the same one through which Christ had entered Jerusalem on Palm Sunday, collapsed to block the passage of the emperor, who had no choice but to dismount from his horse and leave behind his imperial insignia so that the angel of the Lord would open the way for him. At the beginning of the ninth century, in Rabanus Maurus's time, the Beautiful Gate used by Christ was no longer identified with Benjamin's (or Saint Stephen's) Gate but rather with the Golden Gate (Porta Aurea), located a little farther south, in front of the Mount of Olives. The abbot of Fulda's edifying account thus explains why this monumental gate was already walled up in his era, as it still is today. However, the construction of the Golden Gate, built on the foundations of a Herodian gate, is still debated by specialists, who place it between the late sixth and late seventh centuries (see map 5 in chapter 2). Its perfect alignment on an east-west axis with the Basilica of the Anastasis, though, argues for a project contemporaneous with the True Cross's return to Jerusalem, intended to offer Heraclius a setting commensurate with his triumphal entry.[4] Whatever the case, the triumph was short lived; in the face of the threat posed by Arab incursions into the region, the relic was rushed off to Constantinople in 636 at the latest, presaging the empire's collapse.

The events of 614–30, by overexposing Jerusalem in the great history of the confrontation between the two empires which then dominated the Middle East, have to some extent put in the shadows, and certainly prompted a degree of indifference toward, the vicissitudes that affected the region over the following decade. Thus we do not know the exact year when Jerusalem passed into the hands of the Arabs. Indeed, the same uncertainty weighs on many episodes of the Arab conquests, that set of forays and sieges, as well as rare battles, which felled in quite a short period the two old empires exhausted by their centuries-old war. In the days of the Prophet Muhammad (c. 570–632), the raids of his partisans had already pushed from the Hejaz to south of Byzantine Palestine, to Mu'ta (in present-day Jordan) in 629, then to Yibna (north of Gaza) in 630 or 631. On Muhammad's death, his first successor (*khalifa*, "caliph") had to contend with the rebellion and apostasy of a large number of Arab tribes that had submitted to the Prophet. Conquests outside the peninsula did not really start until 634, under 'Umar's caliphate (634–44), with the Arabs' victory over the Byzantines at Gaza and then at Ajnadayn, between Gaza and Jerusalem.[5]

The Arab Conquest of Jerusalem

The ninth-century Arab historiographers who set out to establish the conquest's course of events, from material transmitted by the oral tradition, advanced three possible dates (636, 637, or 638) for the taking of Jerusalem, and a greater number of divergent narratives, which they refused to decide among, in accordance with their method. It is on the basis of a Byzantine chronicle, that of Theophanes the Confessor (d. 817), himself dependent on the information of Arab authors, that modern historians are in the habit of fixing Jerusalem's surrender in 638, at the end of a two-year siege and in the presence of Caliph 'Umar himself, who had come to negotiate the guarantees requested by the inhabitants. Precursor of the pilgrimage to Mecca and founder of Islamic law, pious figure who borrowed some of his features from Christ himself (he is likewise described as *faruq*, "savior" or "redeemer"), 'Umar thus gradually became the conqueror of Jerusalem in the Muslim tradition.

However, a critical reexamination of historical sources recently showed that no contemporaneous text mentions 'Umar's name in connection with Jerusalem's Arab conquest, that he visited Ayla/Eilat on the Gulf of Aqaba but never Aelia/Iliya, and that the account of his meeting with Jerusalem's patriarch Sophronios, as Theophanes staged it more than two centuries later, is only an alteration of the tradition in Arab authors of his audience with the bishop of Eilat. 'Umar went to Syria only once, in all likelihood after the Arabs' decisive victory over the Byzantines in the battle of Yarmuk, near Tiberias, in 636, but he never "visited" Jerusalem. The traditions relating to his coming to the city belong to another context, that of Jerusalem's sacralization as Islam's third holy city in the first decades of the eighth century. We will therefore find 'Umar in Jerusalem, as his presence haunts the city's very topography, but only on account of the pious legend.[6]

In this uncertain chronology, the only sure indication is furnished by the sermon that Jerusalem's patriarch delivered in the New Church of Saint Mary (Nea) on Christmas Day 634 (see map 5 in chapter 2). In it, Sophronios deplored that the faithful could not, as was their custom, celebrate the birth of Christ in Bethlehem, due to the menacing presence at Jerusalem's gates of the "Hagarenes" (the descendants of Hagar, Abraham's servant), whose "barbaric and savage sword" was like that of the angel who denied Adam access to Paradise. In the winter of 634–35, Arab cavalrymen made camp between Bethlehem and Jerusalem and raided the surrounding villages.[7] It is thus quite possible that the city's conquest occurred well before 638, perhaps in spring 635, especially because few traditions refer to a real siege of Jerusalem. The surrender was probably negotiated while the Arabs camped under the walls of the city, whose defenses the Persian siege of 614 had weakened. Except for the inhabitants themselves and their chief magistrate, Patriarch Sophronios,

Jerusalem's conquest by the Arabs was only a secondary event at a time when more significant cities, such as Damascus, were threatened in turn and the empire was losing one of its richest provinces. Its immediate consequences were nothing in comparison with the destruction and massacres perpetrated by the Persians in 614. The only notable, and lasting, change was the authorization given to the Jews, expelled by Heraclius in 630, to resettle in Jerusalem.

The Saracens' First Mosque

Little is known about the city's history during the first half century of Arab dominion. A single large project is attested, not only by later Arab authors but also by several Christian sources of the time, which mourn it: the construction by the "Saracens" ("Arabs of the tents," *Arabes skēnitai* in Greek) of a *midzghita* (per the Jerusalem monk Theodore's Georgian text, from the Arabic *masjid*, "place of prostration," the source of *mosque*). The development of a site of worship, symbol of the triumph of their new faith and gathering place for their community, was in many cases the first urban gesture of the conquering Arabs. When they did not decide to settle away from the old cities in a new garrison town, they requisitioned a church to transform into a mosque, as in Damascus, where the cathedral of Saint John the Baptist was first shared and then demolished to make room for a new edifice. In Jerusalem, the Arabs made a different choice: they built their mosque in an abandoned space, a field filled with ruins or garbage, according to diverging traditions—"in the place called the Capitol," the monk Theodore asserted; "in that renowned place where once the Temple had been magnificently constructed," specified Bishop Arculf, who arrived on pilgrimage from Gaul around 680.[8]

There is no doubt that a first Islamic place of worship was erected, and perhaps already rebuilt several times, between the late 630s and the early 670s, on the site of the mosque now known as Al-Aqsa (which Muslim tradition attributes to 'Umar; see map 6). The quadrangular edifice, which according to Arculf could accommodate three thousand people, probably reused in its foundation blocks from the Temple of Jupiter Capitolinus, which was erected by Emperor Hadrian and which some late antique Christian chroniclers situate at the Herodian esplanade's southern end. No precise date can be given, therefore, for the construction of Jerusalem's first mosque. However, a late (tenth-century) tradition credits Caliph Mu'awiya (r. 661–80) with building Al-Aqsa Mosque (whose name, as discussed below, is an anachronism for the seventh century). An apocalyptic Jewish midrash that makes this same Mu'awiya the builder of the Temple Mount walls could well confirm this attribution in its own way.[9]

The location of this first mosque, apart from the city, in the abandoned space of the former Herodian Temple, amid ruins of bad omen, is more surprising than one might think in retrospect. It may have been suggested by some of the Jewish converts to Islam who had swelled the ranks of the victors: according to an old (early eighth-century) tradition, 'Umar had entered Jerusalem in the company of a converted Yemeni rabbi, Ka'b al-Ahbar (Glory of the rabbis). Unless this choice was the consequence of a first dispute between the country's new masters and the Jews of the region who had helped them in their conquest and in return had gotten permission to settle in Jerusalem. The chronicle (composed around 660) by Sebeos, a Christian source hostile to both sides, claims that the Jews sought the site of the "Holy of Holies" after the conquest and wanted to build "a place for their prayers" there.[10] But the Arabs chased them away and turned it into a mosque.

In any event, according to the same chronicle, the development of the first synagogue in Jerusalem, this time "at the base of the Temple" and no longer on its very spot, closely followed the construction of the first mosque. This is the synagogue believed to have been identified in a seventh-century building discovered in the 1970s near the southwest corner of the Herodian esplanade (see map 6), with a stone lintel decorated with two menorahs, seven-branched candelabra.[11] This identification is contradicted, however, by the layout of the premises, that of a simple house.

THE IMPERIAL STAGE: THE UMAYYADS IN JERUSALEM

After the first wave of the Arab conquests, stopped short by the strife of the first *fitna* (civil war), which between 656 and 661 tore apart the community founded by Muhammad, Jerusalem took on a new importance with the rise of the Umayyad dynasty (660–750). Damascus replaced

Medina as the nominal capital at that time. But it was on the Syrian area as a whole (the Bilad al-Sham of Arabic sources), the home of the forces faithful to the dynasty, that the empire refocused itself, as it turned toward the conquest of Constantinople then. In 661, Mu'awiya had himself pro-claimed caliph in Jerusalem. In 685, if an isolated tradition is to be believed, Caliph 'Abd al-Malik made a choice identical to that of the dynasty's founder. Jerusalem, the Umayyad coronation site? The image is undoubtedly excessive, especially as the city was not picked as the capital of the military district (*jund*) of Palestine—Ludd (Lod) and then Ramla were. But the itinerant court of the Umayyads, whose sovereigns liked to get away from Damascus and move with the seasons, regularly came to the region. Around 710, Egyptian craftsmen are known to have been called to Jerusalem to work on the caliph's palace.[12] Moreover, now that the Persian Empire had collapsed, the conquering effort was concentrated on the Byzantine Empire. In the competition for universal dominion, the caliph had only the basileus as a worthy opponent, and as a political model. One part of this mirrored struggle played out in Jerusalem.

The Dome of the Rock, the Three Religions, and the End Times

Jerusalem's most famous monument is also the most enigmatic of all Islamic architecture. It is neither mosque nor mausoleum, and its mean-ing largely escaped the pilgrims of the Middle Ages, whether Muslims, Jews, or Christians, who willingly took it for Solomon's Temple. The meaning still partly escapes us today, at least if we want to grasp what it was at the end of the seventh century, just before Jerusalem's sacralization as Islam's third holy city covered it up and invested it with a new sense.[13]

From the outside, the building appears as an octagon 54 meters (177 feet) wide, with four symmetrical doors and a dome in the center, 20 meters (55 feet) wide and 25 meters (82 feet) high (see map 6). Inside, it consists of two concentric ambulatories, separated by arches, the first octagonal, the second circular, surrounding a central area under the dome, of almost equal diameter and height. Of the original decoration, the col-umns and capitals (mostly Corinthian) of the two arcades are still extant. Above all, there remains the extraordinary mosaic, with a gold back-ground, that covers the interior walls with motifs of plants and jewelry

(Byzantine and Persian crowns and breastplates), like trophies taken from the two vanquished empires. A mosaic also originally covered the upper part of the octagon's exterior walls, but it was replaced with polychrome ceramic tiles in the sixteenth century. Probably begun in 69 AH (688–89 CE), construction was completed within four years, in 72 (691–92), by order of Caliph ʿAbd al-Malik, as attested by the large mosaic foundation inscription that runs along the central arcade's outer and inner colonnades. The building, which this inscription refers to simply as "this dome" (*hadhihi l-qubba*), without giving it a name, is therefore the oldest Islamic monument still in place today.[14]

The cupola and the mosaic are emblematic elements of Byzantine architecture, which also features octagonal buildings. In the fifth and sixth centuries, many Christian martyria were constructed on this plan, above the graves of figures from sacred history. In Jerusalem, Emperor Maurice (r. 582–602), for example, had an octagonal sanctuary built over the tomb of the Virgin Mary, in the Kidron Valley (see map 5 in chapter 2). No tomb, however, is found under the *qubba* ordered by Caliph ʿAbd al-Malik, but instead a rock of around 18 by 13 meters (59 by 43 feet), not reaching more than 1.5 meters (5 feet) above the ground. This is what gave the edifice its common name, the Dome of the Rock (Qubbat al-Sakhra). It is undoubtedly the key to the mystery.

In the Jewish talmudic tradition, which still permeated seventh-century Islam, the stone that protrudes from the summit of Mont Moriah is both the omphalos (navel) of the world, the place where the first man was created, and, due to confusion with the land of Moriah referred to in the book of Genesis, the rock on which Abraham was prepared to sacrifice his son. But Abraham/Ibrahim also occupies a central place in the Qurʾan (he appears in 25 of the 114 suras), which presents him as not only "God's intimate friend" (*Khalil Allah*), the first monotheist (*hanif*), whose faith precedes the Law of Moses (Judaism) as well as the preaching of Jesus (Christianity), but also the ancestor of the Arabs.[15]

The Muslim tradition, which began to develop at the end of the seventh century, sets a good number of episodes from Abraham's life in Mecca or its environs. But it is quite likely that in the 680s, faced with the rebellion of Ibn Zubayr, who proclaimed himself caliph in Mecca, the Umayyad caliphs in Damascus encouraged the symbolic association between "the

Friend of God" and the city of Jerusalem, located in the heart of their domain. The construction of the Dome of the Rock, finished a few months before the siege of Mecca and the final assault on Ibn Zubayr resulted in the destruction of the Ka'ba, was probably not intended to offer Muslims an alternative to their canonical pilgrimage (the hajj), as later Shi'ite authors allege, eager to blacken the Umayyads' reputation by attributing this heresy to them.[16] But the new monument affirmed the singular prestige of Jerusalem and Palestine, "land of the prophets' emigration," against the historic claim of the old Meccan families that had been marginalized since the rise of the Umayyads.

The Islamic Empire's symbolic recentering was not, however, the only thing at stake here. As the geographer al-Muqaddasi, a native of Jerusalem, was pleased to recall at the end of the tenth century, of Caliph al-Walid (r. 705–15), who built the Great Mosque of Damascus:

> He beheld Syria to be a country that had long been occupied by the Christians, and he noted herein the beautiful churches still belonging to them, so enchantingly fair, and so renowned for their splendour. . . . So he built for the Muslims a mosque, by which he diverted them from these, for he made it one of the wonders of the world! Do you not see how 'Abdu-l-Malik, noting the greatness of the Dome of the Qumāmah [Jerusalem's Church of the Holy Sepulchre] and its magnificence, was moved lest it should dazzle the minds of the Muslims, and hence erected, above the Rock, the dome which now is seen there?[17]

The Dome of the Rock was thus at the end of the seventh century a central part of the affirmation of Islam's superiority over the two old Religions of the Book, respectable witnesses of the laws previously revealed to humankind but now obsolete and outdated. The Islamization of a major place of remembrance associated with Abraham, ancestor of the three monotheisms, in the same city as the Basilica of the Anastasis (Church of the Holy Sepulchre) meant not only the appropriation of the Holy Land by but also a conclusion of sacred history favoring its sole legitimate heirs, the Muslims.

The Dome's construction was contemporaneous with another major project, that of establishing a Qur'anic vulgate, which later Muslim tradition retrospectively attributed to the third caliph, 'Uthman (r. 644–56), so as not to give the impious Umayyads too much credit. Although the oldest known copies of the Qur'an go back to the late seventh century (they cannot be dated with certainty), the Dome of the Rock's large mosaic inscription (240 meters [787 feet] long) offers the oldest dated example (691–92) of some assertions of Muslim dogma.[18] Thus, here one reads for the first time of the oneness of God, which is found on gold coins struck by Caliph 'Abd al-Malik in 697–98 and in the Qur'an's famous sura 112:

> Say, 'He is God the One, God the eternal. He begot no one nor was He begotten. No one is comparable to Him.'[19]

This reminder is aimed not at polytheists but rather at Christians, who see Jesus as the son of God and whom the Qur'an denounces on this account as "associators" (*mushrikun*), guilty of placing other deities alongside the unique God. Several passages of the inscription, arranged around the Rock and attested in the Qur'anic text, repeatedly stress the unparalleled role of Jesus the son of Mary, at once prophet and word of God, as well as spirit emanating from him (Qur'an 4:171), while enjoining believers to deny the dogma of the incarnation and of the Trinity: "Say not, 'Three.'" The Dome's mosaic inscription thus bears a double message. To Muslims seduced by the gold of the Anastasis and tempted by convergence with, if not conversion to, Christianity, it forcefully recalls the monotheistic dogma established by Abraham, which was damaged by Christian "associators" and reestablished by Muhammad. To Christians, it tells of the continuity of the prophetic chain, from Abraham to Muhammad by way of Jesus, which makes their conversion to Islam the logical conclusion of sacred history.

Furthermore, the Dome of the Rock preserves two other inscriptions engraved during its construction, inside the building, above its north and east entrance doors. These texts complement the large mosaic inscription—which is, let us remember, older than the oldest extant copies of the Qur'an.[20] For the first time in the young religion's history, almost sixty years after Muhammad's death, he is presented as the Messenger of God. The Dome of the Rock thus offers the oldest example of the Islamic declaration of faith, affirming both God's oneness and Muhammad's prophetic mission. But its inscriptions add a further meaning, absent from the Qur'an, by making Muhammad his community's intercessor with God in the End Times. The Dome of the Rock's construction is therefore inseparable from the eschatological expectation that has agitated Middle Eastern societies since the sixth century and also characterizes Muhammad's original preaching. The Qur'an announces the Last Hour; the Dome of the Rock prepares it in Jerusalem, inscribing Islam in the heritage of Jewish and especially Christian eschatologies.

The Dome of the Rock's designers clearly invested it with several distinct messages. It is therefore all the more remarkable that when the monument was completed in 691–92, it bore no trace of the story that would contribute the most to making Jerusalem Islam's third holy city: that of the Prophet Muhammad's Night Journey.

The Great Mosque of Jerusalem and Its Successive Avatars

The Dome of the Rock, it must be remembered, is not a mosque. Certainly, the arrangement of several mihrabs, the little ornamented niches that indicate the direction (qibla) of prayer—which in Jerusalem is to the south (toward Mecca)—shows that the monument readily welcomed the prayers (salat), daily and individual, of Muslim believers. But, in words that the Muslim tradition attributes to the Prophet, "the whole world is an oratory [masjid], except the cemeteries and public baths." Individual prayer may be accomplished anywhere except the most unclean places, as long as the supplicants have washed their bodies of impurities and pray in the right direction. By contrast, the Friday congregational prayer, on the day when believers gather together (jum'a), can be lawfully held only in a Friday mosque (jami'), which for this purpose must be equipped with a pulpit (minbar) from which the preacher delivers the weekly sermon. In principle—and in Jerusalem there was no deviation from this until the fourteenth century—each city had just one Friday mosque, a symbol of the Muslim community's unity. It is this edifice alone that is conventionally called the "great mosque" or the "cathedral mosque," to distinguish it from simple neighborhood oratories (masjid). In the time of Caliph 'Abd al-Malik, the Dome of the Rock, which he built, opened its doors to the public only on Mondays and Thursdays, not on Fridays—proof, if any were needed, that it was not a mosque. The other days of the week, none but the servants of the sanctuary were authorized to enter, after having purified themselves and changed their clothes, to burn incense and perfume the Rock.[21]

From an unknown date, Jerusalem's new masters, the Arab conquerors and their converted clients (mawali; sing. mawla), had at their disposal, as noted above, an established place of prayer south of the old Herodian esplanade, probably on the ruins of the Roman Temple of Jupiter Capitolinus. The oldest sources do not give it any particular name. For example, the papyrus letters by the governor of Egypt Qurra ibn Sharik (r. 709–14), whom the caliph had solicited for craftsmen from his province, simply mention the construction site of "the mosque in Jerusalem."[22] It was rare, in Islam's first centuries, for a Friday mosque, a unique building in a city, to have a specific name. In Fustat, Islamic Egypt's first capital, "the mosque of ʿAmr," named for the country's conqueror and city's founder, was an exception, but it was also called, more simply, "the old mosque." In Jerusalem at the beginning of the eighth century, the Great Mosque was still not called either the Mosque of ʿUmar or Al-Aqsa Mosque.

If it did not bear its founder's name, this was also because no one could claim to have built it alone. The mosque described by Bishop Arculf around 680, of imposing dimensions, was likely already constructed in Muʿawiya's reign to replace a first, temporary edifice. According to a tradition whose first transmitters were none other than the two men charged by Caliph ʿAbd al-Malik to supervise his work sites in Jerusalem, the Dome of the Rock's builder also wanted to (re)construct the Great Mosque facing it, plus two of the doors controlling access to the esplanade. It is true that only the rich can get credit! ʿAbd al-Malik's mosque, perhaps because of weaknesses in the foundation under the Herodian esplanade's southern end, was partly destroyed by a series of earthquakes in 713–14. Following these tremors, the craftsmen were called from Egypt to participate in the building's reconstruction. It is therefore understandable that later Arabic historians hesitate to attribute to Caliph al-Walid, ʿAbd al-Malik's son and successor, the paternity of Jerusalem's Great Mosque. In fact, al-Walid has remained famous for having rebuilt, in monumental proportions, the Prophet's Mosque in Medina, entirely remade since, and that of Damascus, which has remained largely in the same state and is now known as the Umayyad Mosque. In Jerusalem, by contrast, his work was doubtless limited to a simple restoration. Whatever the case, one tradition attributes to this caliph the sumptuous decoration that would then have adorned the walls of the Great Mosque—like those of Medina and Damascus, at the latter of which entire mosaic panels can still be admired today.[23]

Of the Great Mosque restored and decorated by al-Walid, nothing now remains. Nor, moreover, of the one rebuilt in 758 by al-Mansur, the second caliph of the Abbasid dynasty, which had eliminated that of the Umayyads eight years earlier. Repeated earthquakes, in 747–48 and then in the 770s, overcame successive buildings. Following the Abbasid victory over the Umayyads, the transfer of the Islamic Empire's center, from Syria to Iraq (where al-Mansur founded Baghdad in 762), would make Jerusalem gradually lose its imperial luster. In the second half of the eighth century, however, two Abbasid caliphs went there in person, on the way back from their pilgrimages to Mecca—a sign that a very strong symbolic bond had started to be forged between the sanctuaries of the two cities. In 758, al-Mansur stayed in Jerusalem for a month and supervised the Great Mosque's reconstruction; he would return twelve years later. As for his son and successor, al-Mahdi, he visited in 780; it was doubtless during this trip that he restored the edifice rebuilt by his father.

Their successors hardly made themselves known in Jerusalem—it is true that, after the reign of Harun al-Rashid (786–809), the caliphs in Baghdad renounced the pilgrimage to Mecca and, more generally, locked themselves away in their palaces. Only al-Ma'mun ordered, in 831, interventions on the two great Jerusalem monuments—of a wholly symbolic kind and without visiting in person. At the Dome of the Rock, he had his name substituted for that of Caliph 'Abd al-Malik in the large inscription on the central arcade and over the entrance doors, to appropriate before history itself the foundation of this one-of-a-kind building. At the mosque, he had a huge bronze door installed, specially conveyed from Baghdad and decorated with his name inlaid in silver.[24] In the absence of a major building program, the Great Mosque described around 990 by the geographer and Jerusalem native al-Muqaddasi must have been the one that was rebuilt two centuries earlier: twenty-six doors allowed access, eleven on the east side and fifteen at the front, on the north side, with a main door of bronze—said to have once belonged to the Persian emperor—in the middle, on an axis with the mihrab.[25] Nothing remains of this mosque either, because it was destroyed by another earthquake, in 1033, which damaged many buildings across Palestine, from Gaza to Hebron and from Ascalon to Nablus.

By contrast, the project that began the next year, in 1034, laid the foundations of the current mosque, smaller and wider than the previous edifice, with seven naves perpendicular to the qibla wall—the central nave, in the mihrab's axis, twice as wide as the others (see map 6).[26] A new dynasty of caliphs then presided over Jerusalem's destiny: the Fatimids, Isma'ili Shi'ites whose empire centered on Egypt and extended from the Maghreb to southern Syria. In their struggle against the Baghdad-based Abbasids, Jerusalem recovered a long-lost importance. Caliph al-Zahir also took care that the beautiful mosaic inscription commemorating the restoration of the mosque's cupola, in 1035, mentioned his name and blessed those of his ancestors and descendants. This is the oldest text found in situ in this building—except for the one that adorns the door given two centuries earlier by Caliph al-Ma'mun. The words deployed in the mosaic open with a Qur'anic quotation whose choice owes nothing to chance—the first verse of sura 17, called *Al-Isra'* (The Night Journey):

> Glory to Him who made His servant travel by night from the sacred place of worship [*al-masjid al-haram*] to the furthest place of worship [*al-masjid al-aqsa*], whose surroundings We have blessed, to show him some of Our signs: He alone is the All Hearing, the All Seeing.

Thus, four centuries after the foundation of the city's first mosque, an unbreakable link had been established in the Muslim imaginary between Jerusalem and the Qur'anic account of the Prophet Muhammad's Night Journey (*Isra'*). The edifice reconstructed by the Cairo-based Shi'ite caliph al-Zahir had ceased to be simply the Great Mosque of Jerusalem and had become in the eyes of all "the furthest place of worship," Al-Aqsa Mosque. We must thus return to the traditions that increasingly defined, from the eighth century onward, Jerusalem's sanctity in Islam and gave birth to "the Noble Sanctuary" (al-Haram al-Sharif).

GENESIS OF THE HARAM AL-SHARIF

The concept of "tradition" has already been used here several times. In the progressive formation of Islamic knowledge, it includes a specific technical meaning that must be borne in mind. A tradition (hadith) is a word of authority whose genealogy goes back to the Prophet Muhammad himself, to one of his wives, or to one of his companions (of whom there are precise lists). Tens of thousands of traditions thus circulated among Islam's first generations and were scrupulously collected by scholars who made them a specialty: this tradition made it possible to illuminate an obscure Qur'anic verse; that one, to base a legal rule on a decision by the Prophet; another, to establish an account of a historical episode in the community's early days of existence; yet another, to justify a particular devotion, a ritual gesture, a pious practice.

The hadith's authority also made them remarkable tools for legitimizing innovations, whether legal, religious, or even political. So the traditionists who systematically collected and classified these traditions, beginning in the ninth century (that is, two centuries after the Prophet's death), established validation rules to distinguish authentic ones from forgeries. It is a hadith's chain of transmission (*isnad*), the list of those who relayed it since the Prophet's generation, that allows its credibility to be measured—a tradition is trustworthy insofar as its transmission chain reaches far back in time and those who have handed it down are reliable. Jerusalem's sacredness in Islam, under its different aspects, emerged from this abundant material, whose authenticity is an unimportant question. It matters little whether the Prophet well and truly uttered a certain word but rather at what time and in which milieu each hadith began to circulate.

Birth of a Literary Genre: The Spiritual Merits
of Jerusalem (Fada'il al-Quds)

It was undeniably one of the great literary successes of the Middle Ages, a genre in which any scholar of any renown could be tempted to distinguish themselves. *Fada'il al-Quds,* or *The Merits of Jerusalem* (we will come back to the name al-Quds, which was gradually applied to the city), has in fact been the subject of many collections, which differ in their choices of traditions, versions, classifications, perspectives. Formerly attested traditions could thus go missing in these compilations, only to reappear in other works centuries later. The oldest surviving collections date to only the eleventh century: al-Wasiti's *The Spiritual Merits of the Holy House [Jerusalem] (Fada'il al-Bayt al-Muqqadas)* and Ibn al-Murajja's *The Spiritual Merits of the Holy House [Jerusalem] and Hebron and the Spiritual Merits of Syria (Fada'il Bayt al-Maqdis wa-al-Khalil wa-Fada'il al-Sham)*. New treatises were composed in the second half of the twelfth century, in the very specific context of the fight against the Franks, the city's masters since 1099—a success that Saladin's reconquest of 1187 did not interrupt. No fewer than thirty new *Fada'il al-Quds* collections were compiled between the late thirteenth and early sixteenth centuries, in the time of the Mamluk sultans.[27]

The late chronology of the treatises on Jerusalem's "spiritual merits" should not, however, make us forget the much earlier genealogy of these traditions. Study of the chains of transmission shows that the oldest of their first disseminators lived in the first half of the eighth century: therefore, they were part of the generation not of the companions but of those called the successors, or of the successors of successors. Beginning in the Umayyad era, traditions circulated in Muslim milieus on the particular sanctity of Syria (Bilad al-Sham), land of the prophets, to which Jerusalem brought all the prestige of its "spiritual merits." It was therefore not surprising that these first disseminators had lived, for the most part, in Palestine or the cities of southern Syria. A few families in Jerusalem, like that of Salama ibn Qaysar, even produced entire chains of transmitters by themselves alone. Some of their members served the Umayyad caliphs: the best-known case is that of Raja ibn Haywa (d. 730), whom Caliph 'Abd al-Malik charged with supervising the Dome of the Rock's construction and to whom important traditions about Jerusalem date back.[28]

It is thus quite tempting to see in this bountiful literature the scholarly side of Umayyad propaganda—of which the Dome of the Rock would be the architectural side—in the service of this dynasty of caliphs who had made Syria the heart of the Islamic Empire. But that would be misleading, because the exaltation of Jerusalem's "spiritual merits" cut both ways. By rooting the city's sacredness in a mythology, or even a cosmology, it deprived the political discourse likely to be deployed there of any topicality. The emergence of these traditions and, more broadly, Jerusalem's sacralization in Islam, to which they bear witness, could help as well as harm the plans of the Umayyad authorities. At a time (the first half of the eighth century) when, in the name of defending the interests of the House of the Prophet (of which the Umayyads had initially been the adversaries), opposition to Damascus's power was rising dangerously and when the desire of hadith specialists for autonomy from political power was beginning to assert itself, Jerusalem's "spiritual merits" ultimately offered an alternative to the city's official history.

'Umar in Jerusalem, or How to Integrate the City into the Islamic Order

The second successor (caliph) of the Prophet, 'Umar ibn al-Khattab, under whose reign the first conquests outside the Arabian Peninsula were made, occupies a central place in Islamic tradition. He is considered the inventor of the pilgrimage to Mecca, whose pre-Islamic rites he had the intuition to resume even before a verse revealed to Muhammad instructed him to do so. 'Umar was the one who set the rules, regulated the rituals, settled the disputes: the numerous hadith that refer to him portray him as the veritable founder of Islamic law (like the apostle John for Christian dogma). By gradually developing the legend of 'Umar in Jerusalem to better integrate the city into the Islamic order, traditionists chose to call up its central figure, that of a guarantor of the orthodoxy of gestures and practices.[29]

Several late accounts, as discussed above, make the caliph's arrival a major episode in Jerusalem's conquest. The places where 'Umar stopped there thus delineate the city's first Islamic topography. According to the transmitter Raja ibn Haywa, 'Umar, having left from Jabiyah, came to Jerusalem from the west. The first building he visited was "David's Hall" (Mihrab Dawud). Before referring to a decorated niche that indicates the direction of prayer, the word *mihrab* in fact meant "palace, hall, or room." Located near the Hebron Gate (Bab al-Khalil, the current Jaffa Gate), this ancient structure, a tower constructed by Herod for his brother Phasael (according to the historian Flavius Josephus),[30] had housed monks since the end of the fifth century. The Christian tradition saw it as the "Tower of David," where the holy king recited the Psalms. The Islamic tradition recounts how 'Umar entered it at night, prayed there until dawn, and led the first prayer of the day on the spot. The sura (Qur'an 38) he recited to his companions at that time narrates David's story exactly, his transgression and his repentance, then describes him arbitrating a dispute in his audience hall.

'Umar's visit to Jerusalem thus enabled the second caliph to be portrayed as a new David, in the very space where the latter had dispensed justice in God's name. It also justified the Islamization of a Christian sanctuary of secondary importance, situated at an entrance to the city. The Mihrab Dawud was perhaps the first Muslim place of worship in Jerusalem, even before the Arabs settled on the Herodian esplanade. Indeed, it ceased to be frequented by Christian pilgrims and entered the circuit of pious tours of Muslim pilgrims. This episode in 'Umar's legend helped to perpetuate David's memory at this precise spot in the city. Before the Herodian tower was destroyed in 1239, the mosque installed at its top was certainly dismantled by the Crusaders and then reestablished after the reconquest in 1187. But in the citadel rebuilt on its site, which was quickly seen as the ancient "David's abode" (Maqam Dawud), a new mosque polarized the old toponym. It is this structure's minaret, erected in 1310–11, which is still visible and is today called "the Tower of David" (see map 7 in chapter 4).[31]

The tradition relates how 'Umar then met the civic authority, in the person of Patriarch Sophronios. Unsurprisingly, it is near the Basilica of the Anastasis (Church of the Holy Sepulchre), the city's most famous Christian sanctuary, that the story places the encounter between the two men. The caliph uttered the Muslim prayer, for the first time in Jerusalem *intra muros,* on a flight of steps leading to the basilica. The gesture, performed on "the blessed staircase" (*al-daraja al-mubarraka*) whose location would be pointed out to pilgrims, was both recognition and restriction. First, recognition of the existence of the Christian sanctuary whose antiquity and legality could not be questioned under the law of Islam. Second, restriction of the liberty thus granted by the victor to the vanquished, which could not thenceforth grow beyond the existing places of worship of a religion that was respectable, certainly, but obsolete.

The story of 'Umar's prayer before the Basilica of the Anastasis summed up in a single action what the pragmatic choice of the Arab conquerors had been and what the Islamic law had progressively codified: the right left to the "People of the Book" (Jews and Christians, but also Sabaeans and Zoroastrians) to follow their religion and keep their places of worship, on the condition that they avoid building new ones and refrain from proselytizing. It is definitely not by chance that later Arabic historians attribute authorship of the "pact of protection" (*dhimma*) to Caliph 'Umar and associate its drafting with the negotiations that led to Jerusalem's surrender. Certainly, all of the new empire's cities were by definition peopled by non-Muslim subjects: the question posed by their places of worship was raised as much in Persia as in Egypt. But in the first half of the eighth century, when 'Umar's legend was developed, the only "protected people" (*dhimmi*) whose number and influence still represented a political issue were the Christians. 'Umar the Legislator needed to have come to Jerusalem for the law to legitimately both recognize and restrict their freedom of worship.

In 1193, six years after Saladin reconquered Jerusalem, he ordered the construction of an oratory (*masjid*) on the site of "the blessed staircase," on the southern side of the Church of the Holy Sepulchre, and placed it under 'Umar's protection. Since that date, the Oratory of 'Umar has preserved the memory of Islam's second caliph in the very heart of Christian Jerusalem (see map 6).[32]

However, another locale polarized, with substantially more force, the legend of 'Umar in Jerusalem: the ensemble formed by "the Rock" (al-Sakhra) and "the Temple" (Bayt al-Maqdis), both on Herod's esplanade. When the traditions about 'Umar's visit to Jerusalem were established, in the first half of the eighth century, the Dome of the Rock already exalted this focal point of Abrahamic memory. It is thus hardly surprising that 'Umar's visit to the Rock, in the company of the converted Jew Ka'b al-Ahbar, has been described in detail. By contrast, the disagreement that then arose between the two is quite revealing of the legend's role. Against Ka'b, who wanted the Muslim prayer to be delivered from the Rock in the direction of Mecca—to unite the two qiblas (directions of prayer), that of Moses and that of Muhammad; in other words, to join Judaism and Islam—'Umar pitted the tradition according to which the Prophet fixed the qibla in "the front part" of mosques; thus he went "in front of the Rock" to pray. The Rock, here a symbol of Judaism, should therefore not be associated with the Ka'ba, a symbol of Islam, in the direction adopted for prayer. Jerusalem's particular sacredness was not to eclipse that of Mecca, Islam having succeeded Judaism—who better than 'Umar could make this reminder with authority?

The legend of 'Umar in Jerusalem is also an opportunity to evoke the history of the Temple of the Jews, destroyed twice as punishment for their sins, as sura 17, recited by 'Umar on his arrival in the city, teaches. After having prayed "in front of the Rock," 'Umar went "toward a waste dump under which the Byzantines had buried the Temple dated to the time of the children of Israel." The ancient Temple Mount abandoned and even given over to garbage as a sign of the Christian prophecy's fulfillment is a good illustration of its likely state in the seventh century. But let 'Umar clear part of the former site of the Temple of the Jews, and the continuity of sacred history is restored. According to another tradition, 'Umar decided to erect Jerusalem's first mosque on this very spot. As we know, such an edifice was indeed constructed on the Herodian esplanade's southern end, on the probable site of the ruins of the Temple of Jupiter Capitolinus, which some local traditions identified with those of the Jewish Temple. The Mosque of 'Umar, as it was long called, marked not the old Temple's restoration but the arrival of the true temple of God, oriented toward the Ka'ba.[33]

Muhammad in Jerusalem, or How to Assemble the Chain of Prophets

The new religion that had emerged in Arabia in the first decades of the seventh century, Islam, was formed from a continuum of texts and beliefs shared wholly or partly with Judaism, Christianity, and, to a lesser extent, Zoroastrianism (the Persian Empire's official religion). Indeed, significant Jewish and Christian communities lived in Arabia—for example, the Jews in the oasis of Medina and the Christians in that of Najran. Furthermore, regular contact united Arabia's small sedentary settlements and the Fertile Crescent's cities, such as Hira, an important Monophysite monastic center, in what is now southwestern Iraq. There was no lack of intermediaries, therefore, which explains the porosity between the texts of the Bible and the Qur'an and the close proximity of Jewish, Christian, and Muslim dogmas. The Muslim story of the End Times, the herald role of Dajjal (the false messiah), and the resurrection of the dead for the Day of Judgment do not much deviate from Christian eschatology. As for the twenty-six prophets mentioned in the Qur'an, besides Muhammad, their names and stories sometimes repeat the biblical text word for word, from Adam to Jesus by way of Noah, Abraham, Moses, and John the Baptist. The Qur'an presents Muhammad as the "Seal of the Prophets," God's last apostle, who came to close and complete revelation. Islam arrived to reap the legacy of its predecessors.[34]

So it is not surprising that Muslim tradition attributes an initiatory experience to Muhammad, a journey into the celestial realm like those taken by biblical figures such as Enoch or Ezra according to Jewish apocalyptic literature of the first centuries CE. Traditionists have collected many such stories.[35] Some relate how the Prophet Muhammad ascended to the heavens—with the aid of a ladder (*mi'raj*), by the hand of an angel, or thanks to his winged mount (the famous Buraq)—visited paradise, and got a glimpse of hell before being taken to Mecca. Others recount how he traveled from Mecca, step by step, until reaching a heavenly sanctuary most often called Bayt al-Maqdis (Holy House, or Temple). In either case, Ascension (*Mi'raj*) or Journey (*Isra'*), which are sometimes combined in a single narrative, Muhammad met the prophets who had preceded him, from whom he received knowledge of the Last Days and the signs of Islam's superiority.

A short version, however, acquired a particular authority by being integrated in the Qur'an itself, in one of those back-and-forths between Qur'an and hadith characteristic of the initial formation of Islam's scriptural corpora. It is the famous first verse of sura 17, called *Al-Isra'* (The Night Journey):

> Glory to Him who made His servant travel by night from the sacred place of worship [*al-masjid al-haram*] to the furthest place of worship [*al-masjid al-aqsa*], whose surroundings We have blessed, to show him some of Our signs: He alone is the All Hearing, the All Seeing.

Beginning in the eighth century, traditionists and exegetes set about reconciling the different versions of this initiatory experience with the one mentioned briefly in the Qur'an. Since Mecca was Muhammad's starting point in most of the narratives, "the sacred place of worship" could be only the mosque of the Ka'ba. As for "the furthest place of worship," it was the celestial counterpart of the terrestrial sanctuary, that "House of God" in paradise to which some accounts also give the name Bayt al-Maqdis. However, the combination of the two sets of traditions—the Journey and the Ascension—in a single unified narrative suggested another interpretation: this "furthest place of worship" was not a heavenly but rather an earthly place, the Journey's end and Ascension's beginning.

Since the construction of the two great Umayyad monuments on the Herodian esplanade, the site of the Rock and of the ancient Solomon's Temple, Jerusalem could legitimately claim this title. The prophetic link between Mecca and Jerusalem established by the story of Abraham (who built the Ka'ba, according to the Qur'anic narrative) supplies additional evidence for this identification. Therefore, the Prophet had traveled from Mecca to Jerusalem before being raised into the heavens, like other prophets before him, from "the furthest place of worship" (al-masjid al-aqsa). At the beginning of the ninth century, however, as in the well-known *Life of the Prophet (Sirat al-Nabi)* by Ibn Ishaq (d. 768), known only through the revised version transmitted by Ibn Hisham (d. 833), it appears to have still been necessary to explain that "the furthest place of worship" was none other than "the temple [*bayt al-maqdis*] of Iliya" (the Arabic version of Jerusalem's Roman name).

From then on, the appellation *al-masjid al-aqsa* (the furthest place of worship) was alternatively given either to the Great Mosque, completed in 715, at the Herodian esplanade's southern end or to the whole esplanade itself, whose walls were long more visible and detached from the rest of the city than they have been since the urban expansion of the fourteenth century. The most striking episodes of the Journey and the Ascension came to leave their marks on place-names and stones alike. The Haram Gate, located under Al-Aqsa Mosque, to the esplanade's south, known today as the Double Gate, was formerly called the Gate of the Prophet (Bab al-Nabi)—the one through which the archangel brought Muhammad into "the furthest place of worship." Also shown here is the ring, or the hole in the stone, to which Muhammad, like the other prophets before him, attached his mount before entering the sanctuary.

As for the precise place from which the Prophet rose to heaven, it is the object of contradictory traditions. Some argue that the Rock, under the Dome, was the very spot of his ascension, citing the print of his foot or that of his mount which was left there and is shown to pilgrims. But others make the Rock the navel of the world and the location where God himself ascended after the Creation. Therefore, the site of Muhammad's *mi'raj* is preferably placed outside the Dome of the Rock, on the terrace's west side, where a small memorial structure, the Dome of the Ascension (Qubbat al-Mi'raj), has stood since at least the end of the eighth century. A Dome of the Prophet (Qubbat al-Nabi) was built nearby, to commemorate Muhammad's prayer before the angels and the prophets; destroyed by the Franks and then restored after 1187, it was replaced, probably in the fourteenth century, by the little mihrab of the Prophet that can be seen today.[36]

Haram al-Sharif, Islam's Third-Holiest Site and the Recovered Temple

'Umar's legend had integrated Jerusalem into the new Islamic order and made Solomon's Temple, rediscovered by his efforts, a milestone on the road to Islam's advent. As for the story of the Prophet's Journey and Ascension, it had established the continuity of the prophetic chain and of divine revelation, from Jerusalem to Mecca and back. The conditions were thus right for making "the furthest place of worship," the name given alternatively to the Great Mosque and to the whole Herodian esplanade, Islam's third sanctuary (*haram*), after those of Mecca and Medina. The reuse of an ancient site with still visible elements of pagan decoration (such as the sun and moon that adorned the entrance known as the Gate of the Prophet) was in no way an obstacle. In fact, as elsewhere in the Islamic Empire (Egypt, for example), the might of the vestiges of the "age of ignorance" (*jahiliyya*) testified to both the vanity of human endeavors and the historical destiny of Islam, the universal heir of extinct civilizations.

"The Noble Sanctuary" (al-Haram al-Sharif) thus constituted, in Muslim devotion and mysticism, a place both plural and unified. Many were the marks left on the esplanade by the prophets of the past. Believers could pray before Solomon's Throne (where this prophet sat after building the Temple), Mary's mihrab (the room where—according to Qur'an 3:37–39—Zakariyya, the father of John the Baptist, provided subsistence to the mother of Jesus), or the cradle of Jesus (where he whom Qur'an 3:45 calls the Word of God spoke as soon as he was born). These traces, noted by pilgrimage guides and monumentalized in the form of a dome or a small oratory, changed location over the course of centuries and were sometimes mixed up with others. In the eleventh century, the mihrabs of Mary and of Zakariyya were moved to the esplanade's southeast corner and identified with a small underground mosque also associated with the cradle of Jesus. Moreover, this is where Christian tradition places the "pinnacle," the tower where Christ was tempted by the devil.

In addition to the traces of the prophets, the Haram was marked with harbingers of the End Times. The Dome of the Rock's inscriptions already underlined, at the end of the seventh century, the intercessory role that Muhammad was to play for his community during the Last Judgment. Later Muslim tradition sowed other clues linking the Haram's space to the narrative of the End of Days. One esplanade access point, on the west side, was called Hell's Gate. Of the Dome of the Rock's four doors, the eastern one was associated with the angel Israfil, identified as the "caller" who will announce the Last Judgment (Qur'an 50:41). Under the Dome, the black marble slab on which the faithful pray was considered one of the gates to heaven, establishing an additional parallel between the *harams* of Jerusalem and of Mecca: for Muslims, the Black Stone in the Ka'ba is a piece of paradise.[37]

But the Noble Sanctuary's ruptured, fragmentary, and changing topography in no way weakened its unity. Through a constant metonymic usage, the Haram was simultaneously the site of Solomon's Temple (often identified as the Dome of the Rock) and, as a whole, the Temple itself; the site of "the furthest place of worship" (Al-Aqsa Mosque, located on the esplanade's southern end) and in its totality itself "the furthest place of worship"; the site where Judgment Day will be announced and the place where resurrected humanity will assemble; one of the entrances to paradise and the very location of paradise and of hell, to the Rock's right and left, respectively. Thus the Haram housed a multitude of indoor oratories and outdoor mihrabs associated with raised prayer areas (*musalla*)—but it was also a vast mosque in itself.

The Haram owes this particular property—a mosque containing multiple mosques—to its architectural attributes identical to those of the Great Mosques of Damascus and Medina: four minarets, ablution sites near the doors, a paved court surrounded by porticoes, and a covered building (in the Haram, Al-Aqsa Mosque) for the Friday congregational prayer.[38] The Haram's unity was also underlined by the strict demarcation of its entrances, whose number was limited. The sanctuary's doors, thresholds that no one can cross without purifying themselves, defined a forbidden and sacred space (a *haram* properly speaking). Identifying the number, names, and locations of these doors in Islam's first centuries has posed important problems, however, as the Frankish conquest of 1099 and the Islamic reconquest of 1187 upset the Haram's toponymy.[39] Yet several door names have remained, even as their location has often changed: names of prophets (Bab al-Khalil, "of Abraham"; Bab Dawud, "of David"; Bab al-Nabi, "of the Prophet") and mystical names (Bab al-Sakina, "of the Divine Presence"; Bab Hitta, "of Absolution"; Bab al-Tawba, "of Repentance"). The particular sanctity of the sanctuary's boundaries makes these doors suitable places to engage in mystic contemplation or await the Last Judgment. In the 960s, several princes of the Ikhshidid family, who had ruled and died in Egypt, were taken to Jerusalem in their coffins and buried inside the Gate of the Tribes (of Israel; Bab al-Asbat), a monumental entrance at the Haram's northeastern corner. In the 1090s, during his stay in Jerusalem, the great theologian and mystic al-Ghazali resided in a *zawiya* above the Gate of Mercy (Bab al-Rahma, the ancient Porta Aurea to the sanctuary's east; see map 6).[40]

Clearly demarcated by the ancient western Herodian wall then still visible on that side of the city, strictly defined by the limited number of its entrances, and sacralized by the innumerable traditions associated with its topography, the Haram al-Sharif had become, in the eyes of all, the Temple itself—as if it had never been destroyed. For Christian pilgrims, such as the abbot of Fulda Rabanus Maurus, who allegedly went to Jerusalem in the early ninth century, the Noble Sanctuary, viewable only from the outside, was none other than Solomon's Temple—and the Dome of the Rock, the Holy of Holies. The Islamic monuments' singular beauty was, paradoxically, only further proof of this. Moreover, the same identification was at work in the devotions of the Jews, who prayed in the direction of the Rock, which had been assimilated to the "Foundation Stone" (*Even ha-Shetiyah*), where the Ark of the Covenant rested before the angels carried it off. During Jewish festivals such as Sukkot, the Feast of Tabernacles, a procession went to each of the Haram's entrances, starting at the southwestern Huldah Gate (perhaps the David's Gate of the Muslims), named for the woman prophet, before reaching the Mount of Olives, from whose height the faithful could contemplate the inaccessible Temple. In fact, Jews were allowed to pray at the doors but not to enter the Haram. In the eleventh century, the Fatimid authorities granted them the use of a sanctuary built into one of the gates of the Haram's western wall (within the sacred space of the precincts): the Cave (Ha-Me'arah) was the center of Jerusalem's Jewish community, where the Torah scrolls were deposited. Pious foundations established by members of the diaspora, as the letters of the Cairo Geniza attest, contributed to the maintenance of this synagogue.[41]

The Holy House (Bayt al-Maqdis), the Holy (al-Quds): On Jerusalem's Names

Iliya (Aelia), Jerusalem's old Roman name, remained in use long after the Arab conquest, still attested at the end of the Middle Ages. But ninth- and tenth-century historians and traditionists already specified for their readers "Iliya, the Holy House [*Bayt al-Maqdis*]." The Holy House, the Temple—that of Solomon, which, as we have seen, in that period existed again for all in the guise of the Noble Sanctuary—thus gradually gave its name to the city. The same metonymic shift occurred in favor of what became Jerusalem's common appellation, al-Quds (literally "the Holy"). This expression, employed in Islam's traditions of its first centuries as a synonym for "the furthest place of worship" (extended to the whole esplanade), came to designate the city itself. At the end of the tenth century, the geographer al-Muqaddasi alternately called his hometown Bayt al-Maqdis and al-Quds. According to the testimony of the Persian pilgrim Nasir-i Khusraw, who visited Jerusalem in 1047, al-Quds was the name usually given to the city by its inhabitants. As for the Temple itself, it was henceforth called the Noble Sanctuary (al-Haram al-Sharif), on the model of those in Mecca and Medina. Thus the notions of the Holy City (al-Quds) and the Holy Land (al-Ard al-muqaddasa), sometimes employed coextensively, were shared by all of Jerusalem's inhabitants in the eleventh century, whatever their religion.[42]

JERUSALEM AROUND THE YEAR 1000: A NATIVE'S VIEW

Except for the recovered Temple, which had finally given its name to the city and which pilgrims and visitors described over and over again, few things in Jerusalem were out of the ordinary for such a small provincial city. However, medieval authors generally scant on the details of what made up their daily lives. It requires all the affection of a native, such as the geographer al-Muqaddasi, for a reader to taste even the slightest bit of the flavor of life in Jerusalem around the year 1000:

> The houses are of stone, and the building is nowhere finer or more solid. In no place will you meet with a people more chaste, and nowhere is living so agreeable, or the markets so clean. The mosque is of the largest, and not anywhere are Holy Places more numerous. Its grapes are excellent, and its quinces are unequalled. In Jerusalem are men of the highest learning and skill; the hearts of the wise are ever drawn towards it; and never for a day are its streets empty of strangers. . . . There is water in Jerusalem in plenty. Thus, it is a common saying, that "There is no place in Jerusalem but where you may get water and hear the call to prayer." Indeed, few are the houses that have not one or more cisterns. Within the city are three large tanks. . . . The baths are constructed in the vicinity of these tanks, and to them lead water channels from the streets. . . . There are few quarters of the city that have not public cisterns.[43]

Jerusalem thus had everything that made life sweet for an inhabitant of the Islamic world around the year 1000: well-built houses, water in abundance, markets and public baths readily available, fellow citizens from every corner of the earth, and some local specialities in which to take pride. But there is no place that does not have its faults:

> Thus, it is reported as found written in the Torah, that "Jerusalem is a golden basin filled with scorpions." Then you will not find baths more filthy than those of the Holy City; nor in any place are the charges so heavy. Learned men are few, and the Christians numerous; they are churlish in their man-

ners. In the Public Square and in the hostelries taxes are heavy on all that is sold. . . . The Christians and the Jews are predominant; and the mosque is void of either congregation or assembly of learned men.[44]

As numerous as the clichés are in al-Muqaddasi's writing (the dirtiness of the baths, the weight of taxation, the boorishness of Christians), there is little reason to refute the picture he paints of his city's communities. Muslims were still a minority in Jerusalem—as, for that matter, they were in most locales in Palestine and Syria around the year 1000, except in the largest cities, where Islam's intellectual and mystical life was concentrated. The Holy (al-Quds) was still predominantly Christian. The only important difference from the Byzantine era, apart from Islam's dominant position, was the presence of strong Jewish communities, both Rabbinic and Karaite.

In this regard, the testimony of the Andalusian traditionist Abu Bakr ibn al-'Arabi, who stayed in Jerusalem between 1092 and 1095 and returned in December 1098, shows that the situation had hardly changed on the eve of the Crusaders' arrival. Besides the presence of Muslim pilgrims from around the Islamic world and that of "uncountable groups of Jewish and Christian scholars," Ibn al-'Arabi noted with a hint of spite that "the land belongs to [Christians] and they cultivate its estates, frequent its monasteries and attend its churches."[45] However, Jerusalem had hardly been untouched over the course of the eleventh century.

JERUSALEM IN THE ELEVENTH CENTURY: TRIALS AND TRIBULATIONS RETURN

There is often a wish to recall in the study of history only the great scourges that marked their times. By this standard, Jerusalem's eleventh century was a period of tribulations ideal for capital-*h* History. The first of these scourges is generally presented as the folly of one man, the Fatimid caliph al-Hakim (r. 996–1021), who ordered the destruction of the Church of the Holy Sepulchre on September 28, 1009. This event had such an impact, from Jerusalem to the West, that the caliph's motivations and the destruction's actual extent were the subjects of rampant speculation. Machination of the Jews for some: this was the theory advanced by the Burgundian monk Rodulfus Glaber. Wrath of the caliph against the Christian fakery during the miracle of the sacred fire's descent on Holy Saturday: this was the explanation advanced by most Arabic chroniclers, both Muslim and Christian.[46]

The order given by the caliph in Cairo, however, has only the appearance of an impulsive decision. It was part of a series of measures that also victimized Egypt's inhabitants, Muslims as well as Christians and Jews: churches and synagogues were destroyed; various prohibitions were introduced, such as the ban on women leaving their homes; and finally the pilgrimage to Mecca was suspended. Al-Hakim, reviving Isma'ili Shi'ism's original spirit, was preparing for the End Times, imminent in this four hundredth year (which began on August 25, 1009) after the Hegira, and the consequent abolition of all religions. In Jerusalem, this search for unanimity required the destruction of the only monument capable of competing with the devotion to the recovered Temple.

If the Holy Sepulchre was indeed plundered and partially destroyed, the edifice's most solid parts were left in place. These ruins were the object first of reconstruction by the city's Christians in 1012 and then of more extensive work, which was finished only around 1048 and made possible by the accommodating diplomacy of the emperor in Constantinople. That same year, Christians from Amalfi in Italy were authorized to build a church (Saint Mary of the Latins) to the south of the Holy Sepulchre, coupled with a monastery and a hospice for Latin pilgrims, more and more of whom had been coming to Jerusalem since the beginning of the eleventh century (see map 7 in chapter 4).

A second scourge, this time natural, fell on Jerusalem in 1033. An earthquake, which struck all the communities in Palestine, destroyed Al-Aqsa Mosque and brought down part of Jerusalem's ramparts. The Fatimid caliph al-Zahir undertook the mosque's reconstruction and the restoration of the city walls. Was this an indication of demographic decline or a pragmatic choice? The course of the ramparts was reduced—on the south side, to the line of the Herodian esplanade, which then served as the city wall there. Several churches, undoubtedly ruined by the earthquake, thus found themselves *extra muros*, and the Christian chronicler Yahya al-Antaki accused the caliph of using their blocks to repair the ramparts. The Noble Sanctuary's southern doors were either fortified or walled up;

toponyms such as Gate of the Prophet and Gate of the Divine Presence later slid from the esplanade's south side to its west.[47]

As for the third scourge, which struck Jerusalem beginning in the 1070s, many contemporaries did not hesitate to attribute it to the natural order, to darken the consequences. The Seljuk Turks' conquest of Syria—Jerusalem was taken from the Fatimids in two stages, in 1071 and then 1073, before they temporarily won it back in 1098—is the subject of quite contrasting interpretations by historians. It is true that the First Crusade's Latin sources deploy all the clichés of horror, outrage, and blasphemy to justify the "liberation of Christ's tomb," which had fallen into Turkish hands, and the siege of 1099. Moreover, in their letters preserved in the Cairo Geniza, Egypt's Jews do not fail to deplore the brutal interruption of their relations with a Jerusalem under Turkish dominion nor to praise in contrast the generosity of the city's old masters, the Fatimid caliphs in Cairo.

Jerusalem certainly suffered from the Seljuk conquest's shock wave. In 1078, the repression of the uprising led by the city's Muslim notables did not spare even those who had taken refuge in Al-Aqsa Mosque. But Jerusalem's integration into the new, Iran-centered empire, while cutting its old ties to Egypt, offered other sources of prosperity. As for the city's non-Muslim communities, they were not the target of particular persecution. In 1092, with the Turks having entrusted the city's government to a Christian, the Jacobite and Coptic communities were authorized to construct a new church, dedicated to Mary Magdalene, in north Jerusalem. It was not until the approach of the First Crusade, in 1099, that the city's Christians were forced to flee persecution. As for the Jewish communities, the departure of the Yeshivat Geon Ya'aqov, Jerusalem's Rabbinic academy, which then settled in Lebanon's port of Tyre in the 1080s, has been seen as evidence of terminal decline. But at the time of the conflict between the Seljuks and the Fatimids, the choice of Tyre was the only way to maintain regular contact with Egypt and donors in the diaspora. Jews of both Rabbinic and Karaite persuasion were still numerous in Jerusalem when the Crusaders took it in 1099. The Cairo Geniza's letters record the ransom of a large number of captives by their Egyptian coreligionists. On the eve of the Franks' arrival, Jerusalem had not yet become an Islamic city.

4 Jerusalem, Capital of the Frankish Kingdom

1099–1187

The text, about ten pages long, was written in Old French, the vernacular of Frankish Jerusalem, populated by French and Flemish, Provençals and Germans, Picards and Catalans, but also Syrians, Armenians, and Greeks, who adapted to this new language come from across the sea, in the wake of the "soldiers of Christ" (*milites christi*).[1] Its exact date of composition is unknown, as is the path it traveled before being inserted, sometime in the first decades of the thirteenth century, in the *Chronicle of Ernoul and Bernard the Treasurer,* a compilation that reports the activities and difficulties of the Franks in the Middle East. A few clues suggest that the Franks had already met the defeats of 1187 and Saladin's armies. Yet in the *Estat de la cité de Jherusalem,* a guide for pilgrims that offers, in the language spoken by its twelfth-century inhabitants, the most complete description of the Frankish kingdom's capital, the city seems suspended in an eternal present, as if it had always been in Christian hands, as if it had never counted either Jews or Muslims among its residents, as if it had always had to ignore its fall.[2] Indeed, it has a perfect form:

> In the city of Jerusalem there are four Master Gates, crosswise, one over against the other, between posterns. Now I will name them to you as they follow.[3]

To the west, with Mount Zion on the right, is one of the two main entrances (the current Jaffa Gate):

> The Gate of David is towards the west. . . . This gate belongs to the Tower of David, wherefore it is called the Gate of David. Within this gate you turn to the right hand, into a street. Near the David Tower, you can go to the Mount Sion [by a postern which is there].[4]

The pilgrim has taken only a few steps inside the city, in what is now the Armenian Quarter, and already sees a church, truthful testimony of an episode of sacred history:

> In this street on the left hand, as you go towards the postern, is a church of St. James of Galicia, who was the brother of St. John the Evangelist. Here it is said St. James was beheaded, wherefore the church was built at this spot.[5]

Descending David Street toward the east, in the direction of the Temple Mount, the pilgrim encounters three covered streets to the left, which house markets and the shops of money changers—Latins on one side, Syrians on the other—whose activity extended all the way to the Holy Sepulchre's walls:

> By the Covered Street you go through the Latin Exchange to a street called the Street of the Arch of Judas, and you cross the street of the Temple. . . . This street is called the Street of the Arch of Judas, because they say Judas hanged himself there upon a stone arch.[6]

Even in the middle of the markets, surrounded by the odor of fish or of spices, in front of the stores of drapers or candlemakers, the reminders of holy history emerge at every step, caught in the snares of a half-French, half-Latin toponymy. At the end of the twelfth century, the Jerusalem of the Franks, which had just ceased to exist, and which the reader of a guide for pilgrims hoped to find again, presented two inseparable faces, associated with two simultaneous presents: that of a medium-size town of the medieval Middle East, finally prosperous after decades of precarity, and that of the Holy City, Christianity's beating heart, finally recovered after centuries of "slavery." The *Estat de la cité de Jherusalem* thus unfolds in this space the story of almost a century of history, during which the Franks sought, and were partially able, to shape the city in their image.

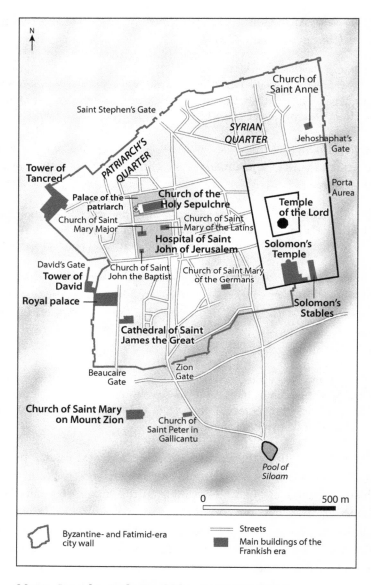

Map 7. Jerusalem in the Frankish period (1099–1244)

The labels on the map are as follows:

N

Saint Stephen's Gate

Church of
Saint Anne

SYRIAN
QUARTER

Jehoshaphat's
Gate

Tower of
Tancred

PATRIARCH'S
QUARTER

Palace of the
patriarch

Church of the
Holy Sepulchre

Temple
of the Lord

Porta
Aurea

Church of Saint
Mary Major

Church of Saint
Mary of the Latins

Hospital of Saint
John of Jerusalem

Solomon's
Temple

David's Gate

Church of Saint
John the Baptist

Church of Saint Mary
of the Germans

Tower of
David

Royal palace

Solomon's
Stables

Cathedral of Saint
James the Great

Zion
Gate

Beaucaire
Gate

Church of Saint Mary
on Mount Zion

Church of
Saint Peter in
Gallicantu

Pool of
Siloam

0   500 m

Byzantine- and Fatimid-era
city wall

Streets

Main buildings of the
Frankish era

RECOVERING JERUSALEM

How many were there to discover Jerusalem's walls in the distance, on the morning of June 7, 1099, from that height which the Crusaders would call Montjoie in memory of this return, the site of the village of Nabi Samwil, where local tradition (Jewish, Christian, and Muslim) placed and still places the tomb of the prophet Samuel? Probably just over ten thousand, including noncombatants (the wounded, servants, and women).[7] The first had left the Kingdom of France at the end of summer 1096; many had died along the way, in particular during the long crossing of the Anatolian Plateau (in what is now Turkey); others had settled, some in Edessa (now Şanlıurfa), some in Antioch (present-day Antakya), without pushing any further the fulfillment of their vow. As for those who attempted a first assault, beginning on June 13, lacking the means to conduct a formal siege and suffering a first failure against the Turkish garrison that defended the city, they probably still had in mind the words spoken by Pope Urban II—first in Clermont in November 1095 and then at each stage of the journey he had undertaken to carry his message, from Limousin to Provence—and relayed by the sermons of preachers. Of this call heard in many forms, several versions, all from after 1099, circulated in the West. The one that Robert the Monk inserted in his *History of Jerusalem* (*Historia Hierosolymitana*) was thus written in 1116, but its transmitter had been present at the Council of Clermont, where the pope, according to Robert, exhorted his listeners as follows:

> Enter upon the road to the Holy Sepulchre; wrest that land from the wicked race, and subject it to yourselves. That land which as the Scripture says "floweth with milk and honey," was given by God into the possession of the children of Israel.
>
> Jerusalem is the navel of the world; the land is fruitful above others, like another paradise of delights. This the Redeemer of the human race has made illustrious by His advent, has beautified by residence, has consecrated by suffering, has redeemed by death, has glorified by burial. This royal city, therefore, situated at the centre of the world, is now held captive by His enemies, and is in subjection to those who do not know God, to the worship of the heathens. She seeks therefore and desires to be liberated, and does not cease to implore you to come to her aid.[8]

Liberating (*liberare*) Jerusalem was thus the goal of the armed pilgrimage—what historians conventionally call the First Crusade—that the pope assigned to the Christian people, whom the church considered the "true Israel," sole legitimate heirs of the land granted by God since the New Covenant, sealed by Christ's sacrifice, had evicted the Jews from the divine heritage. Certainly, Urban II also appealed for help for the Christians who, in the east, were facing the new danger of the Seljuk Turks: be it the Byzantines, who had only ever wanted to recruit Frankish mercenaries and definitely did not want to relinquish to them what the former had regarded, since the defeats of the seventh century, as their historic rights in the provinces of the Middle East; or be it the Christian communities living in the land of Islam, whom Caliph al-Hakim's persecutions, in the early eleventh century, had recalled to the minds of their Western coreligionists and whose suffering at the hands of the Turks was outrageously exaggerated by preachers, in line with the sermon by Urban II. But more than the lot of those Christians who did not obey Rome and had distanced themselves from the "true faith" with customs and beliefs that were heretical in the eyes of the Latins,[9] it was the fate of the Holy Sepulchre, the tomb of Christ "possessed by unclean nations, [which] treated [it] with ignominy and irreverently polluted [it] with their filthiness,"[10] to use the words attributed to Urban II, that aroused the "soldiers of Christ" to enroll and led them, at the end of an almost three-year-long expedition, under the walls of Jerusalem.

Liberating the Holy City: The Crusaders' Conquest of Jerusalem

On July 15 of each year, the Latin patriarch of Jerusalem led a procession that visited the city's main holy sites and then exited through the eastern wall's Golden Gate to pay its respects at the tomb of the Crusaders who fell during the city's capture—all buried at the foot of the Herodian fortification—before skirting the ramparts and arriving at the exact spot, along the north wall, where the attackers first entered, on July 15, 1099. A wooden cross marked this new place of remembrance, where the patriarch delivered a sermon commemorating Jerusalem's *liberatio*.

The Crusaders' taking of the city was thus an event abundantly celebrated in the twelfth century, in Jerusalem itself but also in the West, where the First Crusade's chroniclers did not fail to describe this climactic moment of the armed pilgrimage of the "soldiers of Christ." Rarely having witnessed the events themselves, they employed, to make their accounts more gripping, the narrative material with which they were most familiar: the Bible.[11] The books of Isaiah, Zechariah, and Revelation are indeed the sources of sentences describing piles of corpses and rivers of blood on the Temple's esplanade splashing "as high as a horse's bridle" (Revelation 14:20). The use of biblical topoi to recount Jerusalem's capture in no way diminishes the reality of the massacre perpetrated by the Crusaders, reported by both Christian and Muslim authors, all inclined to exaggerate the numbers, either to exalt them or to denounce what they represented.

The figure of three thousand people, including women and scholars, massacred on the Haram al-Sharif—advanced by Ibn al-'Arabi, a learned Andalusian who, recently returned from Palestine, settled in Cairo in July 1099—doubtless presents a realistic order of magnitude, provided one adds the uncertain number of defenders who died during the assault and the inhabitants who were killed on their doorsteps. Certainly, Jerusalem's population—then comprising exclusively Muslims and Jews, since the Christians were expelled at the Crusaders' approach—was not entirely put to the sword. Indeed, the victors demanded that the survivors, reduced to slavery, bury their dead outside the city; furthermore, some captives saw their freedom bought by their coreligionists, as the Cairo Geniza's letters attest for the Jews. All the same, begun in the intoxication of the Crusaders' irruption through the walls and pursued all the way to the Temple's esplanade, the massacre coldly resumed the day after the city's capture—seeing, for example, three hundred people who had taken refuge on the roof of Al-Aqsa Mosque, under the protection of the Norman leader Tancred's banner, hastily and systematically decapitated, despite this defense. According to Albert of Aix—although he is the only chronicler of the First Crusade to claim this—the massacre was still in progress on July 17.

This bloody reunion with Jerusalem has several explanations, which are by no means mutually exclusive. Slaughtering the population of a city taken by force for having refused to surrender was a viable option in the medieval culture of war, although the more common preference, in the Middle East as in the West, was to capture and ransom the inhabitants. But the Franks made it almost a general rule in Syria and Palestine during the first years of the conquest that followed Jerusalem's capture, hardly letting scruples prevent them from violating even the conditions negotiated with the defenders of cities willing to submit—as in Acre in 1104.[12] This was probably a strategic choice: the desire to eliminate from these cities a Muslim population too large to accept for long the dominion of foreign Christian contingents which were formidable in combat but numerically quite small. Beginning in 1110, by contrast, more confident in the permanence of their conquests, whose prosperity they were keen to preserve, the Franks more often opted to spare the inhabitants and keep them in place, as during the capture of Sidon.

Other sentiments, however, led the "soldiers of Christ" to massacre a significant part of Jerusalem's population in July 1099: as regards the purpose of their pilgrimage, the Crusaders still had to "purify" the Holy City of the "pollution" of the pagans, to cleanse with their blood the sacred places they had usurped. In the words of Archbishop William of Tyre (d. c. 1184), the almost official historian of the Kingdom of Jerusalem, whose chancellor he had been:

> The Gentiles who were living there at the time the city was taken by force had perished by the sword, almost to a man; and if any had by chance escaped they were not permitted to remain in the city. For to allow anyone not belonging to the Christian faith to live in so venerated a place seemed like sacrilege to the chiefs in their devotion to God.[13]

The liberated Jerusalem of the Crusaders could not but be exclusively Christian, nor obey a dogma other than that of Rome. No more than the Muslims and the Jews who escaped the massacre, the native Christians who had been driven from the city shortly before could not return, at least for the time being. Two weeks later, on July 29, 1099, Pope Urban II died, unaware that the army of Christ had recovered the Holy City.

Crowning the Holy City: The Franks at the Holy Sepulchre

Many Crusaders had hoped Jerusalem's capture would hasten the coming of the kingdom of God; although it failed in that, it did give a new dimension to the Frankish conquests in the east and in itself justified the establishment of a kingdom, to which were subordinated the County of Edessa (founded in March 1098), the Principality of Antioch (conquered in June 1098), and finally the County of Tripoli (whose conquest began in 1104). But let there be no mistake: in the feudal culture of the First Crusade's barons, the king, chosen from among their ranks, occupied little more than the highest point of a hierarchy of vassals, the central link in a chain of personal loyalties that he held together—at least while the fortunes of war smiled on the Franks.

It was not the king's presence in the city that made it the capital of the Kingdom of Jerusalem, which continued to be referred to by this name long after the Franks were driven out and the king resettled in Acre. The precise location of Jerusalem's first royal residence, before Baldwin I decided, in 1104, to install his quarters in the disused Al-Aqsa Mosque (the Templum Salomonis of the Latins), is unknown (see map 7), but its extremely secondary importance is measured by the rapid deterioration of the old mosque, whose lead roof was dismantled bit by bit to be sold to the highest bidder. Not until the 1160s did the king of Jerusalem acquire a real urban palace (Curia Regis), built in the immediate proximity of the citadel (Turris David) in the reign of Amalric (1163–74): the Cambrai map of Jerusalem places it prominently among the city's most significant monuments. It was destroyed at an unknown date, but important remains have been unearthed since 1971 in the gardens of the Armenian Patriarchate.[14]

The Frankish Kingdom of Jerusalem's identity depended not on the Curia Regis but on the Holy Sepulchre. It was not only a matter of humility that Godfrey of Bouillon, chosen by his peers on July 17, 1099, refused the royal title and took, it is said, that of advocate (*advocatus*)—the title carried in the West by any layperson charged with representing, before the law or on the field of battle, a prelate or an ecclesiastical institution—of the Holy Sepulchre. On his death a year later, almost to the day, Godfrey was buried in the Holy Sepulchre complex, at the foot of Calvary and in front of the Chapel of Adam. With the exception of his immediate successor, Baldwin I, whose coronation took place in Bethlehem's Church of the Nativity, all of the kingdom's sovereigns, up to Sibylla of Jerusalem and her husband Guy of Lusignan in 1186, were crowned in the Church of the Holy Sepulchre. All up to Baldwin V, who died in 1186, were also buried there, even when their deaths occurred far from Jerusalem—like Baldwin I, who died in al-'Arish (in the Sinai) in 1118, Fulk of Anjou in Acre in 1143, and Baldwin III in Beirut in 1163.

The link between the Holy Sepulchre and the crusade was forged long before Jerusalem's conquest by the Crusaders: when, in 1009, Caliph al-Hakim had ordered the destruction of the Church of the Anastasis and the Basilica of the Martyrium. In the West, the news had led to a wave of unprecedented violence against Jews, who were accused, as in Orléans, of having intrigued with the "prince of Babylon" (the caliph of Cairo) to provoke the disaster—prefiguring the pogroms that later marked the First Crusade's itinerary. On July 15, 1099, a few hours after entering Jerusalem, the Crusaders made their first prayer of thanksgiving under the rotunda of the Anastasis, which had been raised from its ruins half a century earlier. Fifty years later, the Latin Patriarch of Jerusalem Fulk of Angoulême chose to consecrate the high altar of the new Church of the Holy Sepulchre, still under construction, on July 15, 1149, the anniversary of the city's *liberatio*.[15]

Emblematic institution of the new kingdom, the Church of the Holy Sepulchre was in fact the seat (*cathedra*) of the Latin Patriarchate of Jerusalem, which, in the conquest's wake, had replaced the Greek Orthodox Patriarchate, whose head had died just a few days before the Crusaders entered the city and whose successors continued to perform their duties in exile, in Cyprus and then in Constantinople, before Saladin returned the Holy Sepulchre to them in 1187. In the absence of the full and complete sovereignty over the Holy City dreamed of by the first two officeholders—in the image of that of the bishop of Rome over the patrimony of Saint Peter—the Latin patriarch considered himself the pastor of all the "Catholic" (i.e., faithful to the Council of Chalcedon's dogma) Christians living in the kingdom, whether Latins, Greeks, or Melchites, and regarded Jerusalem's Armenian and Jacobite metropolitans as suffragan bishops. Chosen from among the canons of the Holy Sepulchre, whose number was set at twenty in the reign of Godfrey of Bouillon (1099–1100), the patriarch had to contend with this rich and influential cathedral chapter. The first patriarchs had their quarters in the church itself, on the upper floor of the Anastasis rotunda. It was not until the entire Holy Sepulchre complex was reorganized midcentury that the patriarch was housed in a new palace (transformed into a khanqah, or Sufi convent, by Saladin in 1189 and still in place today), constructed north of the rotunda; in the meantime, the canons were installed in new houses and conventual facilities (chapter house, refectory) erected east of a new cloister on the site of the old Basilica of the Martyrium, which had not been rebuilt after 1009. An open space between the Anastasis rotunda and the cloister was set aside, however, with a view to expanding the church itself (see map 7).[16]

In a way, the Holy Sepulchre's great reconstruction was the crowing achievement of the Franks' dominion over Jerusalem. Even before 1106 or 1107—according to the testimony of the hegumen Daniel of Kiev—changes were made to the decoration of the tomb cave under the Anastasis rotunda: the tomb's walls were covered with marble facing, and a ciborium crowned by a life-size silver statue of Christ was put on top of the cave. A few years later, around 1114, another pilgrim (the anonymous author of *De situ urbis Ierusalem*) reported the construction of a large church in "the place where St. Helena found the holy cross." The Chapel of Saint Helena, accessed by a staircase that descends under the cloister and partly built on the foundations of an ancient cistern, was probably the Franks' first construction in the Holy Sepulchre; the masons reused capitals taken from Al-Aqsa Mosque's abandoned rooms in its vault.[17]

By contrast, it is not known when the much more ambitious construction of the Holy Sepulchre's new church, erected between the Anastasis rotunda and the cloister occupying the site of the old Basilica of the Martyrium, began. In the style of a large pilgrimage church, such as the Romanesque architecture raised along the routes to Santiago de Compostela (in Tours, Limoges, or Conques), but without the space for a nave—already occupied on the west side by the rotunda—the new church consisted of a vast north-south transept and a choir doubled, on the east, by an ambulatory serving three chapels. The Anastasis rotunda's apse was demolished, to allow axial circulation between the tomb cave and the new church's choir. A second cupola, smaller than the one that topped the rotunda, was built above the choir, and the roof was extended to include in a single structure, for the first time, all of the holy sites associated with Christ's Passion: the Calvary Chapel above Golgotha, the Chapel of the Finding of the Cross (Chapel of Saint Helena) below the cloister, and the tomb cave under the rotunda. As for access to the complex, which in the eleventh century was already gained via the court to the south, it was too complicated to modify. The Holy Sepulchre was still entered from the south, now by the double door in the new transept's two-story façade. In addition, from then on, a stone stairway to the main entry's right led straight to the Calvary Chapel. Finally, a new door was opened to the northwest of the complex, in Patriarch Street, not far from the namesake's palace, providing direct access to the Anastasis rotunda. The Church of the Holy Sepulchre as it can be visited today thus owes its structure as much to the work of the Franks as to that of Constantine's architects, who in the fourth century engineered the Anastasis rotunda which was reconstructed practically identically in the first decades of the eleventh century. But its overall design owes more to the Franks, since they were the ones who integrated Golgotha, the site of the Cross's discovery, and the cave of the sepulchre into a single architectural complex.

As important as this Holy Sepulchre construction was, it nonetheless left little trace in the written documentation of the Frankish era. A sole record allows the work's progress to be approximately dated. This Latin inscription, positioned above one of the Calvary Chapel's arches, visible to the right for the pilgrims who entered by the front of the transept, commemorates Patriarch Fulk of Angoulême's consecration of four new altars— including the Calvary Chapel's altar and the new choir's high altar—on July 15, 1149, exactly fifty years after Jerusalem's capture (*captio*).[18]

Reinventing the Holy City: Jerusalem's Christian Topography in the Frankish Period

Like generations of pilgrims before them, the "soldiers of Christ" came to find, in the city's actual space, the places of holy history that sustained acquaintance with the Bible—through readings, sermons, and images— had made familiar to them since childhood. Arriving in Jerusalem, they unhesitatingly recognized the streets, doors, and sacred sites identified in the city's Christian toponymy, for the most part since the fourth century. Some buildings, by contrast, and not the least important ones, did not fit into this renowned landscape even long before it was actually traversed. On the ancient Temple Mount, where no monument should have arisen since the fulfillment of Jesus's prophecy, in 1099 there stood, in fact, besides the many Muslim oratories commemorating the passage of the prophets, two structures of prestigious architecture: the Dome of the Rock and Al-Aqsa Mosque, rebuilt some sixty years earlier by Caliph al-Zahir. No matter that the Temple had been destroyed: it rose again in the middle of the esplanade, where the Latins recognized the Templum Domini, the Lord's temple. The identification of Al-Aqsa Mosque posed more problems, which were only imperfectly resolved: the Latins mobilized the polymorphous memory of Solomon, the builder king, to see it as either the Palatium Salomonis or the Templum Salomonis, his palace or his temple, in a duplication of places imposed by the double monumental heritage of the Umayyad era (see map 7).

Solomon's palace (Al-Aqsa Mosque) served as the royal residence beginning in 1104, when Baldwin I decided to establish his quarters there. It was there, in the great hall formed by the disused mosque's three central bays, that the coronation banquets for the kings of Jerusalem were held, at the end of a ceremony that successively led them from the Holy Sepulchre (where the king was crowned) to the Templum Domini–Dome of the Rock (where he offered his crown to Christ, the true king of Jerusalem) and finally to the Palatium Salomonis. Despite its prestigious functions, the building was in bad shape, having been abandoned after it was a site of fighting in 1099: Baldwin I had no choice but to demolish parts of it.

In 1119 or 1120, his successor chose to install there the group of knights surrounding Hugues de Payens and Godfrey de Saint-Omer, who had decided to live under a monastic rule (that of the Augustinian canons) while maintaining their warrior status, giving themselves the mission of protecting pilgrims on the way to Jerusalem and taking the name "Poor Knights of Christ." These monk-knights obtained recognition of their oxymoronic vocation—this association of the profession of arms and the monastic life, which feudal culture had strictly separated until then—at the Council of Troyes in 1129. Did they decide to adopt the name commonly associated with their headquarters, the disused Al-Aqsa Mosque, or did they contribute to this toponymic shift? The fact remains that the Knights Templar—the Order of the Temple—well and truly owed their name to that Templum Salomonis whose tenure the king of Jerusalem had initially granted to the "Poor Knights of Christ."

The Templars carried out important works to adapt Al-Aqsa Mosque's architecture to their needs. The side bays' vaults were partly reconstructed (as seen today) and the space divided into cells; in the disused prayer room, the south-oriented mihrab was concealed by a wall, and an east-facing chapel was furnished; a rose window was added to illuminate this part of the building, and it still survives in the masonry of the mosque's east wall.

In the 1160s, the Templars undertook the construction of a large church, of which no vestige remains, which was doubtless completely destroyed after 1187; it probably stood in the courtyard that borders the mosque to the west. The Templum Salomonis was thenceforth accessed through the Double Gate, a Herod-era structure to the south of and below the complex, one of whose entries was walled up and the other protected by a tower. The Templars also had their own stables (Stabula Salomonis), built into the Herodian esplanade's underground structures (see map 7). By a strange irony of history, the only Latin document written on parchment ever discovered in the whole Kingdom of Jerusalem is a letter from Gérard de Ridefort, then the Order of the Knights Templar's seneschal, to the society's commander in Jerusalem, which was found in the 1920s in a wall of Al-Aqsa Mosque.[19]

For its part, the Dome of the Rock / Templum Domini acquired a central place in Frankish Jerusalem's Christian topography. It is certainly not solidly established that on July 15, 1099, after the assault, as Fulcher of Chartres alone affirms, the "soldiers of Christ" went successively to the Holy Sepulchre and then to the Templum Domini to thank the Lord for their victory. Three weeks later, however, it was definitely to the Templum Domini that they went to pray before facing the Fatimid army and winning the battle of Ascalon. Afterward, the Latins recognized the Umayyad monument as the Temple where Jesus was circumcised and presented to God as a baby and from which he later drove out the merchants, leaving in its stone an imprint of his foot, which is shown to pilgrims—an exact transposition of the Muslim veneration of the footprint left by the Prophet at the time of his heavenly ascension.

The building's Christianization translated into the erection of a monumental cross on the dome's summit; the installation of a choir and an altar on the Rock, which was covered with a marble paving stone; and the

deployment of Christian iconography and inscriptions celebrating the edifice's new destination—all while leaving visible to the faithful Caliph 'Abd
al-Malik's indecipherable inscription which explicitly denies Jesus's divinity and the dogma of the Trinity. The Templum Domini thereby became
the counterpart of the Sepulchrum Domini and was likewise entrusted to
the care of a chapter of canons obedient to the rule of Saint Augustine.
These two churches were thenceforth associated in the route of the great
urban processions, such as that of Palm Sunday; the miracle of the sacred
fire, which came to illuminate the world on Holy Saturday after darkness
had covered it at the Savior's death, was awaited at both the Holy Sepulchre
and the Temple of the Lord.[20] On some seals, finally, like that of King
Amalric of Jerusalem (r. 1163–74), the two monuments flank the Tower
of David, emblem of royal authority.

However hard it was pushed, the Dome of the Rock's identification with
the Templum Domini posed at least two problems: it ignored the Temple's
destruction, prophesied by Jesus and accomplished by Roman armies, and
left unexplained the traces of the building's earlier use by Muslims. It was
to respond to this that Achard of Arrouaise, who was the prior of the
Templum Domini's canons from 1112 to 1136, composed a long historical
poem on this subject. Recalling the three previous ages of the Jerusalem
temple, which was successively consecrated during Solomon's reign, on the
Jews' return from the Babylonian captivity, and in the time of Judas
Maccabaeus before being destroyed, Achard then described it in its current state, reconstructed by Emperor Justinian—unless this had been done
by Heraclius or maybe Saint Helena, Constantine's mother. Ultimately, it
didn't matter, because the Temple would be consecrated for the fourth
time—the first time by Christians—and would eternally celebrate the
Lord's glory. The genealogy elaborated by the Templum Domini's prior was
rather popular in pilgrimage narratives, without entirely obscuring the
Muslim memory of the Dome of the Rock. Indeed, some pilgrims reported
that the edifice had been built by a Saracen chieftain, a certain Amor—it is
easy to find in this a trace of the Muslim legend of 'Umar, which already
overlaid the remembrance of the Umayyad caliphs.[21]

Other structures on the Temple Mount were reinterpreted in connection with the memory of Christ in the Frankish period and integrated into
Jerusalem's Christian topography, which then extended beyond its ancient

landmarks. The site of the cradle of Jesus, venerated by Muslims, who associated it with the mihrab of Mary and that of Zakariyya—all three transposed to a small underground mosque at the esplanade's southeast corner since the eleventh century—was identified without difficulty by the Latins with the home of Saint Simeon, where the Virgin and Child had stayed (see map 6 in chapter 3). The "Beautiful Gate" by which Christ entered Jerusalem on Palm Sunday—since the ninth century no longer thought to be the Gate of Benjamin (currently Saint Stephen's Gate or Lions' Gate; the Latins' Jehoshaphat's Gate) but rather the Golden Gate, which opened into the Temple Mount's eastern enclosure—was also transformed into a church. Elsewhere in the city and its surroundings, other places testifying to Christ's Passion were, if not newly identified, at least fixed in Frankish times by the erection of chapels—as, in Gethsemane, on the spot of the Son's three prayers to the Father and, not far from there, of his arrest.[22]

But the Latins' main legacy in Jerusalem's Christian topography concerns the identification of the route that Christ followed after his sentencing in the Praetorium to the place of his execution on Golgotha—what Latin devotion exalted from the end of the Middle Ages under the name "Via Dolorosa." Two traditions on this subject had coexisted since the Byzantine period. One placed the Praetorium, where Christ was condemned, on Mount Zion, along with the residence of the high priests Caiaphas and Annas. The Passion's itinerary therefore skirted the ancient ramparts from south to north to the site of Calvary, according to this first tradition; in the second half of the eleventh century, the Benedictine monks of the Church of Saint Mary of the Latins, located southeast of the Holy Sepulchre, thus commemorated in their house of worship the sob of the Virgin, who fainted on seeing her son carrying his wooden cross (see map 7). The second tradition preferred to place the same topographic witnesses near the Antonia Fortress, at the Temple complex's northern edge, making the Passion route pass along the east-west street that one takes from the Mount of Olives and Gethsemane to reach Golgotha; this was already the path of the annual Passion procession in the fourth century.

It was this second itinerary, following the street which the Latins called "of Jehoshaphat," that ended up dominating Christian memory: the Via

Dolorosa, along which were scattered, according to the changing topography, the first ten "stations" (this term did not appear until the fifteenth century) of the Way of the Cross. New constructions fixed two milestones of this route in the Frankish period: the Chapel of the Repose, commemorating the place where Christ was imprisoned, erected near the Temple Mount's northern wall; and the Chapel of the Flagellation, installed in the building identified as Pilate's house. In the twelfth century, when the Dome of the Rock became the Templum Domini and the Herodian esplanade was for the very first time integrated into Jerusalem's Christian topography—in contrast with its execration in the Byzantine period—the Passion's route entered the Temple Mount complex before exiting through the "Sorrowful Gate" (perhaps Bab al-Nazir or Bab al-Ghawanima). The Kursi 'Isa, "Throne of Jesus," a dome-topped aedicula located on the esplanade not far from the north wall, may preserve its memory. After 1187 and the restoration of the Haram al-Sharif, from which Christians were again excluded, the Passion's route fell back to the Street of Jehoshaphat. It was there—probably between 1229 and 1244, when the city, minus the Haram's holy sites, was once more in Frankish hands—that the small Church of Saint Mary of the Spasm was built, in memory of the Virgin's sob, and this new localization helped to fix the Passion's itinerary in north Jerusalem a little more.[23]

REBUILDING JERUSALEM

With the Crusaders' victory over the Fatimid army at the battle of Ascalon on August 12, 1099, Jerusalem's conquest became a fait accompli. The "soldiers of Christ" had reached their goal and touched their dream; most then returned home. Of those who chose to stay in the Middle East, only a few hundred settled in Jerusalem. The capital of the Frankish kingdom, devastated by the assault in July 1099 and emptied of its inhabitants, was no more than a ghost town populated by a handful of soldiers, all men of castles and villages who had never or almost never lived in a city until then. The Holy City's repopulation was the main challenge facing its new masters: the requirement for the Frankish conquest's endurance, the foundation without which it would have been futile to rebuild Jerusalem.[24]

Quarterium Patriarchae

The earliest inhabitants of Frankish Jerusalem, far too few to occupy the entire urban space, decided to settle in the city's northwest quarter, around the Holy Sepulchre and the seat of the Latin Patriarchate, the first permanent institution established in the new kingdom's capital. Another reason may have encouraged them: the good general state of the fortifications in this part of Jerusalem, defended by both the citadel (the Latins' Turris David) and the Qasr al-Jalud (which they soon renamed Turris Tancredi, in honor of the Norman leader Tancred, who had positioned himself there during the July 1099 siege). This second tower was probably built in 1063, during the reconstruction of the city's ramparts ordered by Caliph al-Mustansir (see map 7). It was also on this occasion that a vast redistribution of the urban population would have been carried out, on a religious basis, giving the city's northwest quarter a distinctly Christian identity.

The affair is known only through a single account, given a century later by the Latin chronicler William of Tyre, himself a native of Jerusalem. According to him, the Fatimid governor had divided the cost of the rampart works among the city's inhabitants, following a very widespread practice of the Middle Ages, with the Christians responsible for one quarter. Here William doubtless meant only the communities attached to the Patriarchate of Constantinople (Greeks and Melchites), because around 1060 the Christians as a whole likely still formed the majority of Jerusalem's population. William reports, moreover, that they turned to the emperor in Constantinople, who agreed to relieve them of this burden, on the condition that

> they could obtain a promise from the lord of the land [the Fatimid caliph] that none but Christians should be permitted to dwell within the circuit of the wall which they proposed to erect by means of the imperial donation. . . . Up to that time the Saracens and Christians had dwelt together indifferently. Thenceforward, by the order of the prince, the Saracens were forced to remove to other parts of Jerusalem, leaving the quarter named to the faithful without dispute. By this change, the condition of the servants of Christ was materially improved. Because of their enforced association with the men of Belial [the Devil], quarrels had often arisen, which greatly increased their troubles. When at last they were able to dwell by themselves, without the disturbance of discord, their lives flowed more tranquilly. Any disagree-

ments which arose were referred to the church, and the controversy was settled by the decision of the [Greek] patriarch then ruling as sole mediator.[25]

This passage birthed a full-fledged historiographic myth, founded on the sole authority of William of Tyre's chronicle: the genesis, in the 1060s, of an exclusively Christian neighborhood in the Holy City, in which modern historians have wanted to see the prefiguration of Jerusalem's confessional quarters as they emerged in the second half of the nineteenth century, the proof that this characteristic of the modern city already had a long medieval past. For good measure, they have also regarded the "Judaeria" that appears in the Holy Sepulchre's twelfth-century cartulary records—the "Juiverie" (Jewry) described in *Estat de la cité de Jherusalem*—as the trace of a Jewish neighborhood that existed prior to the city's capture by the Crusaders in 1099 and the prohibition against Jews (as well as Muslims) living in the Holy City from then on.[26] Jerusalem in the eleventh century would thus have been the only city in the medieval Islamic world with Jewish and Christian ghettos—when, elsewhere in the Middle East, the jurisdictional autonomy of non-Muslim communities prevailed, but not their physical grouping in denominational neighborhoods. Certainly, the temptation is great to accept the claim of the Holy City's historical singularity.

But it is simpler to explain the attestation of the toponym *Judaeria* in the Frankish period with the earlier presence of a synagogue in the city's northeast quarter, which suggests that Jews lived in the vicinity, without this making the neighborhood—in fact, far from it—a ghetto. Above all, it is more pertinent to put William of Tyre's affirmation back in its context, an excursus within the chronicle in which he intended to demonstrate the following:

> From the time the Latins entered Jerusalem, and, indeed, for many years before, the patriarch had held as his own a fourth part of the city. How this came about, together with the origin and reason for his so holding it, may be briefly stated. After carefully investigating this matter and making repeated inquiries, we have at last arrived at the facts underlying the affair.[27]

The story of the ramparts' reconstruction, the Byzantine emperor's conditional generosity, and the formation of the Christian neighborhood had no other aim than to legitimate, in the writings of the archbishop of Tyre a century later, the Latin patriarch's lordship over Jerusalem's north-west quarter—a right inherited, according to him, from the Greek Patriarchate, whose seat the Latin patriarch then occupied:

> From that day, then, and in the manner just described, this quarter of the city had had no other judge or lord than the patriarch, and the church there-fore laid claim to that section as its own in perpetuity.[28]

In truth, the Latin patriarchs had been forced to scale back their initial ambitions since Godfrey of Bouillon had promised Dagobert of Pisa, on Easter 1100, seigneury over the whole city of Jerusalem, as well as the port of Jaffa—a commitment that Baldwin I subsequently failed to honor. The patriarch was nonetheless the lord of the Quarterium Patriarchae (see map 7), the only neighborhood in the city that was inhabited in the first years of Frankish dominion and from which he drew part of his income, thanks to attendance at the public baths (Balnea Patriarchae) and the pig market (Porcharia Patriarchalis).[29]

Syrian Christians and Latin Pilgrims: Jerusalem's New Population

Some fifteen years had elapsed since the conquest of Jerusalem, during which time, under the leadership of Baldwin I (1100–1118), the Frankish kingdom had extended over a large part of the littoral plain, from north of Ascalon to south of Tyre, advancing east all the way to the Jordan River. But the Franks' military successes and the growth of the coastal cities made Jerusalem's sparse population even more striking. To follow William of Tyre's account once more:

> At this time [in 1115], the king realized with great concern that the Holy City, beloved of God, was almost destitute of inhabitants. There were not enough people to carry on the necessary undertakings of the realm. Indeed there were scarcely enough to protect the entrances to the city and to defend the walls and towers against sudden hostile attacks. Accordingly, he gave much anxious thought to the problem, turning the question over in his own mind and talking with others concerning plans for filling it with faithful people, worshippers of the true God. . . . The people of our country were so few in number and so needy that they scarcely filled one street, while the

Syrians who had originally been citizens of the city had been so reduced through the many tribulations and trials endured in the time of hostilities that their number was as nothing. . . .

The king felt that the responsibility for relieving the desolation of the city rested upon him. Accordingly, he made careful investigations in regard to some source whence he might obtain citizens. Finally he learned that beyond the Jordan in Arabia there were many Christians living in villages under hard conditions of servitude and forced tribute. He sent for these people and promised them improved conditions. Within a short time, he had the satisfaction of receiving them with their wives and children, flocks and herds, and all their households. They were attracted thither not only by reverence for the place but also by affection for our people and the love of liberty. Many, even without being invited, cast off the harsh yoke of servitude and came that they might dwell in the city worthy of God. To these the king granted those sections of the city which seemed to need this assistance most and filled the houses with them.[30]

Driven from the city by its Muslims and Jews at the approach of the Crusaders and stripped of their belongings after the conquest, the Christians of the Middle East did not return to Jerusalem before 1101, from then on simple pilgrims passing through on the occasions of the liturgical calendar's major festivals.[31] The decision made around 1115 to call for Syrian (*Suriani*) colonists—the ethnonym then designating Syrian and Palestinian (as opposed to Greek) Christians, who were mainly Melchites but also Jacobites and Maronites[32]—to repopulate the Holy City constituted a real turning point in the history of Frankish Jerusalem. As the seigneurial landowner of three-quarters of the city—the Quarterium Patriarchae being excluded—the king was in fact in a position to offer favorable settlement conditions to these new townsfolk. They were undoubtedly exempted from certain feudal dues and other obligations—just as, in the Iberian Peninsula cities that were conquered to the detriment of Muslims in the same period, new populations were granted charters (*fueros*). They may also have been given residences that had not been reoccupied since 1099 or were vacant because of the *assise de l'an et jour*—a royal decision by virtue of which homeowners in Jerusalem who were absent from their houses were dispossessed of them in favor of their occupants after one year.[33]

Whatever the motivation of these Transjordanian villagers, their arrival, with their families and animals, did not immediately modify the broad nature of the urban space's occupation. But it laid the foundations for a lasting revitalization of the city, first noticeable in the streets of the "Juiverie," which adjoined the Patriarch's Quarter, where, according to the anonymous *Estat de la cité de Jherusalem*, "dwelt most of the Syrians of Jerusalem." The Syrians were able, moreover, to preserve their customs, settling their disputes and establishing their private agreements in a special jurisdiction, the Court of the Syrians, while the Franks for their part presented themselves, according to their status, before the High Court or the Burgess Court.[34]

With time and the kingdom's stabilization, new inhabitants from overseas were added to the original nucleus of the "soldiers of Christ" who had remained in Jerusalem or who had originated there; to the *poulains* (literally "foals," from the Latin *pullani*, the young of animals) born in the Middle East from the marriages of Franks with Syrians, Armenians, or converted Muslims; and to the Syrian colonists installed at the king's instigation. Certainly, Jerusalem never offered the same commercial opportunities as the coastal cities, particularly Acre—for this reason, it is significant that no church was established in Jerusalem by any of the Italian cities that were, however, quite active throughout the Latin East; as for the community of merchants from Marseille, it was never given a church in Jerusalem, contrary to what a false royal donation forged after the city's fall in 1244 long led scholars to believe.[35] By contrast, Jerusalem's religious prestige continued to generate an ever-increasing influx of pilgrims from the West—the facilities provided by the institution of the Frankish kingdom only amplified an older trend, the rise of collective pilgrimages in the Holy Land, of which the Crusade was but an extension.

Jerusalem's renewed prosperity in the mid-twelfth century owed much to this population, ever changing and rarely permanent, of pilgrims, around which the Frankish kingdom partly organized its institutions, to meet its specific needs by channeling new resources from the West. It was thus the primary vocation of the knights of the Order of the Temple, formed in Jerusalem around 1119 and endowed with its own rule ten years later, to protect the pilgrims on the roads that led to the Holy City, before the society became, in the West, the principal institution charged with helping to prepare the holy journey (by depositing goods or sums of money redeemable overseas and organizing the transport of pilgrims) and, in the Middle East, the principal military force charged with defending the kingdom.

In Jerusalem itself, however, a second institution played a more important role than the Order of the Temple, before reorganizing and militarizing in its image, late in the century: the Order of Knights of the Hospital of Saint John of Jerusalem. Legend has it that Charlemagne founded the first Latin hospice in the Holy City. More certainly—although the hospital's early history remains unclear—in the mid-eleventh century, merchants from Amalfi (in southern Italy) established a Benedictine monastery (Saint Mary of the Latins) near the Holy Sepulchre, on which depended both a hospital and a chapel for Latin pilgrims (Saint John the Baptist), and then a Benedictine convent charged with hosting female pilgrims in a separate house (Saint Mary Magdalene). The hospital, which predated the conquest of 1099, received important donations from the first kings of Jerusalem before its independence from the monastery of Saint Mary of the Latins was recognized in 1113 by a papal bull.

Like the Knights Templar, the Knights Hospitaler had vast landholdings in the West, organized in commanderies, and they accompanied the departure of pilgrims, for whom hospices were set up in the major embarkation ports. In the Holy City, the order occupied a much more central location than the Temple's esplanade: a complex of more than 1.5 hectares (3.7 acres) between the Holy Sepulchre and David Street (what is now the Muristan area), which in the mid-twelfth century contained three churches, including the new Church of Saint John the Baptist, a large hospital and maybe a second, women-only hospital, conventual buildings for the use of the Hospitaler brothers (who numbered four hundred around 1170, according to the testimony of the Jewish pilgrim Benjamin of Tudela), and the residence of the order's grand master (see map 7). The presence of this enclave—which enjoyed privileges of exemption from both royal and ecclesiastical authorities—in the Holy Sepulchre's immediate vicinity did not fail to arouse tensions with the Latin Patriarchate, and the conflict escalated in the middle of the century when the Hospitalers contrived to ring their bells every time Patriarch Fulk of Angoulême delivered a sermon in the Church of the Holy Sepulchre.[36]

The importance attached to the hospitable institutions in Jerusalem not only reveals the extent to which the pilgrimage economy had become central to the very existence of the Frankish kingdom but also suggests that the capital continued to be marked by the particular origins of its temporary inhabitants, who never quite merged into a single population. A hospice for Hungarian pilgrims was thus attached to the Church of Saint Stephen of Hungary. Better still, a "House of the German Hospital of Notre Dame" was created within the Order of Hospitalers, which circa 1140 had its own hospice and church, Saint Mary of the Germans—which did not prevent the German pilgrim John of Würzburg from being surprised, around 1160, that "no part of the city, not even in the smallest street, was set apart for the Germans."[37] Dreamed of by the whole Christian West, Jerusalem preserved the variegation of its new origins throughout the twelfth century.

Churches and Markets: Frankish Jerusalem's Urban Heritage

In almost a century of Frankish dominion, Jerusalem was not deeply transformed, except in the composition of its population—an ambiguous heritage that only very partially survived the city's fall in 1187. The city's space, progressively reoccupied during the twelfth century, preserved the same lines of force as in the past. The Temple Mount's unprecedented Christianization and integration into the routes of urban processions did not suffice to fill the voids that had separated the Herodian esplanade from the city proper since the Byzantine era. The Franks modified neither the course of the ramparts nor the entrance gates, even though they undertook significant refortification work after several sections of the city wall collapsed in 1177. It was probably at this time that the defenses of the Gate of the Pillar (the current Damascus Gate) were reinforced by the construction of an outer bastion and the installation of an angled entry, important remains of which were recently uncovered.[38]

On the other hand, the Frankish period saw the rebuilding of most of the Holy City's churches, entrusted to the care of religious orders introduced into Jerusalem following the conquest. Certainly, in the twelfth century the Orthodox (Greek and Melchite) clergy retained control of at least twenty-five churches in Jerusalem, such as that of Saint Sabbas, which was dependent on the venerable monastery of the same name in the desert not far from Bethlehem. Also certainly, modern historians have undoubtedly exaggerated, beyond the well-documented case of the Holy Sepulchre, the extent of the destruction ordered by Caliph al-Hakim in 1009, to better exalt the magnitude of the Frankish (re)constructions. The fact remains that more than eighty churches and chapels, of all denominations, are attested in Jerusalem between 1099 and 1244, when the Frankish presence definitively came to an end—the great majority of them in the hands of a Latin clergy.[39] Among the most endowed, the monks of the Order of Saint Benedict thus served five sanctuaries (Saint Mary of the Valley of Jehoshaphat, Saint Saviour, Saint Mary of the Latins, Saint Stephen, and the chapel of the same name built at Saint Stephen's Gate), while their female counterparts served three others (Saint Mary the Great, Saint Anne, and Saint John the Evangelist). If the foundation of these churches often dated back to the Byzantine era, most were partially or completely reconstructed in the Frankish period, leaving numerous testimonies of Romanesque architecture in Jerusalem, in situ or reused.

One of the most representative edifices of Romanesque Jerusalem is the Church of Saint Anne, in the city's northeast, whose crypt, a disused ancient cistern, has been venerated since the Byzantine era as the Virgin's birthplace in the house of her parents, Joachim and Anne (see map 7). A convent of Benedictine nuns was established on the site in the first years of the twelfth century, to house Frankish noblewomen, such as the wife whom Baldwin I repudiated in 1104. The church proper, built on a three-nave plan in the 1140s and coupled with an imposing belfry, modeled on that of the Holy Sepulchre, was extensively altered after 1856, however, when it was given to France by the Ottoman sultan in the aftermath of the Crimean War and then restored.[40]

Exiting the Church of Saint Anne and leaving the city to the east by Jehoshaphat's Gate (the current Saint Stephen's Gate), pilgrims reached another sanctuary associated with Marian devotion in the valley, entrusted to the care of a Benedictine monastery established by Godfrey of Bouillon in the months following Jerusalem's conquest: the Church of Saint Mary of the Valley of Jehoshaphat (or Kidron Valley), where the sites of the Virgin's tomb and her Assumption had been revered since Byzantine times. At the beginning of the twelfth century, all that remained of the Byzantine sanctuary was the underground church housing the tomb, an ancient rock-cut *kokh,* as in the Holy Sepulchre cave; on the surface, the upper church lay in ruins. Benefiting from royal patronage and substantial donations of properties scattered through the kingdom, the Benedictine monks undertook to reconstruct the upper church and construct their conventual buildings around it; the stairway leading to the underground church was enlarged and the church decorated with murals depicting the Dormition and the Assumption of the Virgin; and, finally, the tomb cave was surrounded by a colonnaded aedicula and topped with a ciborium. In 1161, Queen Melisende, daughter of Baldwin II, wife of Fulk of Anjou, and mother of Baldwin III, for whom she served as regent, was buried in this emblematic shrine of royal patronage—in a funerary chapel still visible today, which was set up to the side of the stairway that descends to the church of the Virgin's tomb, and where the queen's mother, the Armenian princess Morfia of Melitene (now Malatya), already lay in repose. More exposed than the churches *intra muros*, the sanctuary in the Valley of Jehoshaphat was badly damaged after the city's fall in 1187: the upper church and the conventual buildings were dismantled and used as sources of stone, undoubtedly for the construction of the new city walls; the lower church, by contrast, remained unchanged, except for the mihrab added to the cave with the Virgin's tomb, a sign of Muslims' special devotion to Maryam, the mother of the prophet ʿIsa (Jesus).[41]

If the Romanesque architectural and decorative elements of Jerusalem's churches constitute the Frankish era's most visible legacy, to this day the city harbors other vestiges that, although less spectacular and less easily identifiable, only reveal the sedimentation of this heritage all the more. In the city's heart, right above the ancient Roman *cardo* where its main markets had been held for centuries, three covered streets were built in 1152, on the instructions of the regent Melisende and on whose construction sites Muslim serfs worked. Each street provides a passage three meters (ten feet) wide under a vault six meters (twenty feet) high between shops of four square meters (forty-three square feet), some of whose façades still bear the inscription *SCA* or a *T* inside a circle, depending on whether their rents went to the convent of the Church of Saint Anne (Sancta Anna) or to the knights of the Templum Salomonis. Located between the "Street of Herbs" to the west and the "Covered Street" to the east, the main road, called Malquisinat or Vicus Coquinatorum, in the Frankish period gathered together the stalls where, according to *Estat de la cité de Jherusalem,* "they cooked food for the pilgrims, and sold it," for which openings had been made in the vault, to vent the smoke. This street is probably the origin of a block, found reused in a fourteenth-century building, inscribed with Latin and decorated with the image of five kitchen utensils (ladles, knives, and cleaver).[42]

Perhaps it is here, in the modest ornamentation of a kitchen, in the marks of masons that adorn the stonework of vaulted stores still visible along David Street, in the French names given to these lanes in the twelfth century before being forgotten—who remembers Malquisinat Street, where "bad food" was served to pilgrims?—that the most significant testimony of the almost nine decades of Frankish Jerusalem's history resides.

5 From Saladin to Süleyman

Aleppo, northern Syria, 1168. Nur al-Din, son of Zengi, whose sovereignty was recognized from Mosul in Upper Mesopotamia to Damascus in central Syria, was in the process of unifying the entire region under his authority. In Cairo, the once all-powerful Fatimid caliph even called on his men, among them a certain Salah al-Din (Saladin), to repel the threat of the Franks from Egypt. That year, the man who willingly presented himself as "the fighter in the path of God" and "the pillar of Islam and the Muslims" ordered a minbar (a pulpit for the Friday sermon) of exceptional quality from the craftsmen of Aleppo. This furnishing, which was set up in the Great Mosque of Aleppo, carries a beautiful inscription that praises Nur al-Din and prays God will "grant him conquests and allow him to make them by his own hand." The conquest that his glory lacked was that of Jerusalem, in Frankish hands since 1099. The minbar, like an ex-voto, was waiting to be put in its intended place, Al-Aqsa Mosque, the day when it returned to Islam.[1]

RECONQUERING JERUSALEM

The twelfth century was certainly propitious for all such prophecies. But it would be wrong to think that its entire aim, in the minds of Muslims as in the actions of their princes, was the reconquest of Jerusalem. The city's capture by the Crusaders, of only secondary military importance, had long appeared as just another episode in the war against the Rums (Byzantines). Jerusalem had changed hands so many times since 1071 and the Seljuk conquest that one expected a reversal in favor of the Fatimids in Egypt: this was the opinion expressed a few months after the Frankish conquest by a Maghrebian Jew passing through Cairo.[2] In the first half of the twelfth century, a relative indifference still surrounded the fate of Jerusalem and the Haram al-Sharif, although it was not unknown that their sacred sites had been profaned and the mosques transformed into churches by the Franks.

Conquering Spirits: Jerusalem in Twelfth-Century Muslim Discourse and Devotions

According to a tradition (hadith) that was circulating in Syria in the 1150s, the Prophet had affirmed that of all the calamities Islam would have to suffer, the gravest (besides his own death) would be Jerusalem's conquest by infidels. It is always difficult to identify the reasons why a shift in opinion, a change in mentality, emerges at a given time. But it is certain that Jerusalem's sanctity began to color the words and guide the devotions of Muslims in the middle of the twelfth century.

The conquest of Edessa—one of the Holy Land's four Crusader states, created half a century earlier—in 1144 by the armies of Zengi, the governor of Mosul and Aleppo, had paved the way. For the first time, a territory controlled by the Franks had been retaken from them by force. The call for Muslim unity in the holy war (jihad) against the infidels proved its full effectiveness and, at the same time, its political utility for the Turkish and Kurdish warlords who de facto governed Arab-speaking civilian populations. Counselors and boosters now suggested that they make Jerusalem the horizon of their reign, however circuitous the paths to success. The poet Ibn Munir, who accompanied Nur al-Din after serving his father Zengi, thus enjoined the prince of Aleppo to pursue jihad against the Franks "until you see Jesus fleeing from Jerusalem."[3]

On Nur al-Din's death in 1174, Saladin, already master of Egypt, set out to conquer his former sovereign's Syrian domain, at the expense of its legitimate heirs. This usurpation, costly in time and human lives, was done in the name of the unity necessary for the forces of Islam to recover the Holy City. As Saladin wrote in 1175 to obtain the approbation of the caliph in Baghdad, who still represented Islam's universal legitimacy and legality, "Syria's order cannot be restored with its present government, and Jerusalem has no leader capable of governing and protecting it." This argument carried to a certain extent, because the caliph recognized, beyond the possessions already acquired by Saladin, the legitimacy of the conquests he could accomplish in the future—with the exception of the principality of Aleppo, bequeathed by Nur al-Din to his son.[4]

The theme of lamenting the Holy City (al-Quds) defiled by infidels enlivened more than just official discourse. There is no good propaganda that is not nourished by the intimate convictions of those who support it. In Damascus and Baghdad at the end of the 1140s, treatises on Jerusalem's "spiritual merits" (*fada'il al-Quds*), which had fallen into oblivion half a century earlier, began to be read publicly again. Some scholars tried their hands at composing new ones, such as the famous Damascus traditionist Ibn 'Asakir (d. 1176). To devotees and mystics, the Prophet appeared in dreams to deplore Jerusalem's fall. The scandal of the Haram al-Sharif's holy sites, transformed into churches and even stables, was felt all the more strongly now that Jerusalem was no longer strictly forbidden to Muslims. The prince of Shayzar Usama ibn Munqidh (d. 1187), who went there many times as an emissary, recounted how the Templars let him pray in a little oratory converted into a church near the old Al-Aqsa Mosque. As for al-Harawi, the author of a celebrated *Guide to Places of Pilgrimage*, he described the rare elements of the Haram al-Sharif left intact by the Franks, as he was able to observe during his visit in 1173.[5]

The heightening of collective feelings by the events immediately preceding and succeeding Saladin's seizure of the city in 1187 imbued minds with the idea of Jerusalem's sanctity. A long catalogue of the Holy City's "spiritual merits" occupied the main part of the first Friday sermon delivered at Al-Aqsa Mosque since 1099, on October 9, 1187, by Aleppo's chief judge Ibn al-Zaki, who concluded by quoting a now famous hadith: "The Holy House [Jerusalem] is the first of the two *qiblas* [before the Prophet oriented prayer toward the Ka'ba], the second of the two houses [after Mecca], the third after the two sanctuaries [*haram*] [of Mecca and

Medina]." Four years later, during negotiations with the English king Richard the Lionheart, who was leading the Third Crusade, Saladin reminded his interlocutor of the main reasons for the Muslims' attachment to Jerusalem—at least if the biographer who reported this letter's contents is to be believed: "Al-Quds is to us as it is to you. It is even more important for us, for it is the site of our Prophet's Night Journey and the place where people will assemble on Judgement Day. Therefore do not imagine that we can waver in this regard." Whatever Saladin's personal sincerity on this subject, the wide dissemination of Ibn Shaddad's text, like those of other biographies dedicated to Saladin, gives these words validity as a unanimously shared collective sentiment.[6]

Conquering the City: The Siege and Capture of Jerusalem in 1187

Jerusalem's conquest by Saladin's army was without a doubt the best-prepared feat of arms of his long career as a soldier—to such an extent that he had the luxury of inviting the leading Muslim dignitaries of Egypt and Syria to witness the long-awaited victory from his camp outside the city's walls. Echoing the sanctity of its holy places, now unanimously accepted, Saladin even had the leisure to carefully choose the day when Islam would recover al-Quds. And indeed, the city's defenders surrendered on Rajab 27, 583 AH (October 2, 1187)—when Muslims were commemorating the Prophet's celestial Ascension (Mi'raj), as they do on that date every year.

Since becoming Mosul's master in 1186, Saladin had definitively imposed himself as Syria's strong man. The offensive against the Kingdom of Jerusalem began in spring 1187, using as a pretext the pillage of a caravan traveling from Cairo to Damascus by the men of Reynald of Châtillon, the lord of Kerak. The army that Saladin assembled in a few weeks, reinforced by contingents from Egypt—probably thirty thousand men in all, including twelve thousand cavalry—was strong enough to risk the decision of a battle, a rare event in medieval warfare. Besieging Tiberias at the end of June 1187 and thereby controlling the region's main sources of water, Saladin forced the Frankish army gathered by Guy de Lusignan (perhaps twenty thousand men, including twelve hundred knights) to come and meet him. Surrounded at the Horns of Hattin, a hill that dominates the plain around Tiberias, without access to water, the Franks sustained repeated assaults from Saladin's army, which captured the red tent of Jerusalem's king on the evening of July 4.[7]

The battle of Hattin was a decisive step on the road to Jerusalem: indeed, Saladin later raised a Dome of Victory (Qubbat al-Nasr) on the site to celebrate its memory. The Frankish army was decimated and its major barons taken prisoner, leaving the Kingdom of Jerusalem's main cities without any real defense. Worse, the enemy seized the piece of the True Cross that was miraculously discovered during the conquest of 1099 and had accompanied the Franks to the battlefield of Hattin. The relic was derisively carried in procession on the end of a spear through the streets of Damascus before Saladin offered it to the caliph in Baghdad, five centuries after the Constantinian True Cross had made the journey to what is now Iraq, to the Sassanid palace in Ctesiphon. Acre, the Kingdom of Jerusalem's great port and economic capital, surrendered less than a week after the defeat at Hattin. In July and August, all the coastal cities, from Gaza and Ascalon to Sidon and Beirut, excepting Tyre, were taken in turn, leaving Jerusalem with no hope of aid. After renouncing his siege of Tyre, Saladin laid siege to Jerusalem on September 20, 1187, first along its western wall and then, five days later, having taken stock of the city's defenses, along its north and northeast walls, where the Crusaders had successfully penetrated in 1099.

Did Saladin want to take the city by force, as one of his biographers claims, to make the Christians suffer what they had done to the Muslims eight decades earlier? Did Balian of Ibelin, Jerusalem's acting commander, threaten to kill the thousands of Muslims held captive in the city and to destroy its holy places in return? Did the attackers manage to open a critical breach in the ramparts? Did the besieged lack provisions in a town that had become overpopulated owing to the influx of refugees since the summer's defeats? In any event, the adversaries agreed on the terms of surrender barely two weeks after the siege began. Jerusalem's inhabitants all had to buy their freedom, at the rate of ten gold dinars per man, five per woman, and two per child—considerable sums of money—with a payment term of forty days, failing which they would be sold as slaves. Greek Christians, Syrians, and Armenians were allowed to stay in the city, according to the provisions of the so-called pact of 'Umar; the Franks were forced into exile but permitted to take their goods, except weapons and horses. The ransoms were paid in the greatest disorder, and some managed to evade them, even though the city's doors had been shut. Others, unable to pay, were redeemed by Balian of Ibelin and even by Saladin himself, mindful of his reputation as a magnanimous sovereign. But healthy men were reduced to slavery by the thousands: there is still evidence of them a few years later on sites of fortification work in Jerusalem and Cairo. Because the city was not taken by force, Islamic law did not authorize the three-day legal looting. Churches, however, were desecrated and pillaged—with the notable exception of the Holy Sepulchre, whose treasures the Latin patriarch was permitted to take with him. Responsibility for the city's principal Christian shrine was given back to the Greek patriarch at the same time. After eighty-eight years of Frankish dominion, Jerusalem thus rejoined the Abode of Islam.[8]

Restoring the Noble Sanctuary to Islam

During the first sermon delivered at Al-Aqsa Mosque after Jerusalem was taken, a week later, the preacher did not fail to praise God for having helped his faithful in "cleansing His Holy House from the filth of polytheism and its pollutions." This vocabulary of impurity, characteristic of the religious sensibilities and controversies of the Middle Ages, is not surprising.[9] In Jerusalem, didn't Muslims nickname the Church of the Holy Sepulchre or Church of the Resurrection (in Arabic, Kanisat al-Qiyama) the Church of the Rubbish Heap (Kanisat al-Qumama) in a play on words already attested in the tenth century?

In the reconquest's aftermath, they therefore endeavored to cleanse the Noble Sanctuary's monuments of the "filth" that the Christians had left there. Al-Aqsa Mosque, which had served as the Templars' residence, was scrubbed and purified with rose water and incense. The partition they had installed to reorient the prayer room from south to east was dismantled. The southern mihrab, which had been concealed and was said to have been used as a latrine by the Templars, was restored and decorated with new glass mosaics. Saladin also ordered that the minbar prepared for this occasion by Nur al-Din two decades earlier be brought from Aleppo, thus fulfilling his illustrious predecessor's vow. This famous pulpit adorned

Al-Aqsa Mosque's prayer hall until the fire of 1969; today its fragments are in the Haram al-Sharif Islamic Museum. As for the Dome of the Rock, which the Franks had made into a church, it was stripped of its Christian ornamentation—the cross that capped the dome, the statues and paintings that decorated the interior—and the Rock, once the marble platform that covered it had been removed, was now carefully washed with rose water. Finally, the Augustine canons' conventual buildings, to the esplanade's north, were destroyed, as was the small cemetery nearby. Probably at the same time, the Chapel of the Ascension, built by the Franks on the Mount of Olives on an axis with the Dome of the Rock, was transformed into a mosque.[10]

If the Noble Sanctuary's main monuments recovered their original functions as early as autumn 1187, the restoration of its sacred topography, which presupposed the rediscovery of memories of the places effaced by the Frankish conquest, was a much longer project. In 1200–1201, for example, Jerusalem's governor al-Zanjili constructed a small building on the Dome of the Rock's terrace, also topped with a cupola and reusing elements of Frankish architecture; the foundation inscription refers to it as "the Dome of the Prophet, which historians speak of in their books."[11]

In the same period, the restoration of names for the esplanade's gates led to the displacement of certain toponyms: "Gate of the Prophet," formerly identified with the southern wall, was now connected to one of the access points in the western wall. The sanctuary's most monumental entrance, also on the west side, formed by a double door that opened on to the main road descending from Bab al-Khalil (Hebron Gate, the current Jaffa Gate), was probably reconstructed at the very end of the twelfth century, as the numerous Frankish capitals and columns reemployed in its masonry suggest. The southern access of this double door, previously Bab Dawud (David's Gate), was now called Bab al-Silsila (Chain Gate); as for the northern access, it has been referred to since as Bab al-Sakina (Gate of the Divine Presence), a name that one of the gates in the esplanade's south wall carried before the Frankish era (see map 6 in chapter 3).[12] The authority of the "historians" (ahl al-ta'rikh) must not have been very sure, or at any rate the traditions that they reported "in their books" were too confused for the places to be recognized every time.

Defending the Holy City: A Short History of
Jerusalem's Ramparts (1187–1247)

The Franks had reinforced the city's defenses in 1178. It is unlikely that they suffered much from the brief siege of 1187. Saladin waited until the end of 1191, and the winter halt of military operations in the Third Crusade, to undertake important refortification work in Jerusalem for the purposes of withstanding a siege. In accordance with well-established custom, the burdens of financing, mobilizing labor, and procuring building materials were shared among the great officers of his empire, each of whom was in charge of part of the wall and the construction of a tower. The ramparts' work sites must have mirrored the image of an army in the field.

Saladin entrusted the section between Bab al-'Amud (Gate of the Pillar, the current Damascus Gate) and Bab al-Rahma (Gate of Mercy, the ancient Porta Aurea)—in other words, the city's north and northeast walls—to his son al-Afdal Ali. This was where the assailants had entered in 1099 as in 1187 and is probably where the main reinforcement work was concentrated. But Saladin also set about extending the course of the ramparts south of the city, to include Mount Zion: the Church of Zion was henceforth *intra muros*, as a German pilgrim who passed through Jerusalem two decades later noted, and sections of the Ayyubid wall were unearthed on Mount Zion at the end of the nineteenth century. In addition to the wall, Saladin took care to reinforce the trench, which was dug deeper into the rock. Frankish captives were used for the most arduous work.[13]

The most important fortification works took place, however, after Saladin's death in 1193, in the reign of his nephew al-Mu'azzam 'Isa (1198–1227), to whom the Ayyubid family had entrusted the principality of Damascus, on which Jerusalem depended. During two building campaigns, commemorated by several inscriptions, the city's western walls were almost entirely reconstructed in 1202–3 and then its southern walls in 1212–14, reinforced by massive towers then necessitated by the new siege weapons. The remains of a gate defended by one of these towers were uncovered at the beginning of the 1970s: its location, to the east of the current Bab Dawud (David's Gate; also called Zion Gate) shows that although the Ottoman enclosure partially corresponded to the course of the Ayyubid one in its southern section, their gates did not coincide. On the other hand, the Ayyubid entrance discovered on Mount Zion's thresh-old corresponded to the ancient gate of the Nea, attested at the end of the Byzantine period (see map 5 in chapter 2).[14]

A fundamental discontinuity can thus be identified in the history of Jerusalem's ramparts. However, the rupture occurred during the reign of the same man who contributed so much to their reconstruction. In 1218, when the Fifth Crusade's troops surrounded the port city of Damietta in the Nile delta, the sultan of Damascus al-Mu'azzam 'Isa went to the aid of his brother and suzerain al-Kamil Muhammad, the sultan of Egypt; Jerusalem, stripped of most of its defenders, was at serious risk of falling back into Frankish hands. Moreover, in March 1219, as a preventive measure to keep the Franks from permanently retrenching themselves in the city should they succeed in retaking it, al-Mu'azzam gave the order to dismantle Jerusalem's fortifications—with the exception of the citadel near the Hebron Gate. The precaution was extended to other strongholds in the region, such as the fortress on Mount Tabor built just eight years earlier. Three decades after its reconquest by Saladin, his descendants rec-onciled themselves to the prospect of losing the Holy City. The chroniclers report scenes of despair: women and girls gathered on the Haram, rend-ing their clothes and hair. In fact, many of Jerusalem's Muslim inhabitants then took the road to exile, toward Kerak, Damascus, or even Egypt.

The history of Jerusalem's ramparts throughout the following decades is that of a slow but irremediable defortification of the city. In 1227, the sultan of Egypt al-Kamil proposed an alliance with Emperor Frederick II, who was preparing to go on crusade, in exchange for the return of Saladin's conquests; dreading this possibility, his brother al-Mu'azzam ordered the completion of the walls' dismantling, begun eight years earlier. In 1229, the Treaty of Jaffa, negotiated between al-Kamil and Frederick II, estab-lished a truce of ten years in return for recognition of the emperor's sover-eignty over Jerusalem (excepting the Haram's holy sites). But it also for-bade the Franks from refortifying the city during the armistice. In 1239, the works that they undertook in haste once the truce expired could not prevent al-Nasir Dawud, the Ayyubid sultan of Kerak, from conquering Jerusalem after a brief siege during which the city's last stronghold was destroyed: the old citadel that protected Jerusalem's western flank, near the Hebron Gate (the current Jaffa Gate). It was a city entirely devoid of defenses that had to face, in 1244, a consequence of the distant Mongol wars: the Khwarezm-Shah's disbanded Turkic troops, summoned by the sultan of Egypt al-Salih Ayyub, ravaged it, massacring part of the population and pillaging the churches, as had happened in the worst hours of the Persian siege of 614. Three years later, in 1247, visiting the Holy City, over which he had gained dominion after precipitating its ruin, Sultan al-Salih gave the order to measure the circumference of the old ramparts and raise the funds necessary for their reconstruction. But the decision was left a dead letter.

Making Jerusalem an Islamic City: The People

Since the Arab conquest of the seventh century, Jerusalem had never ceased to be a primarily Christian city. Its inhabitants were mostly Christians, albeit of diverse confessions. Churches and monasteries were the most influential institutions in their daily lives—at a time when the Haram al-Sharif was a distinct entity, still physically separated from the city itself. The conquest of 1187, whose victory was evidence sanctioning Jerusalem's particular sacredness in Islam, imposed on the city's new masters a program much more complex to implement: turning Jerusalem into an Islamic city.

The expulsion of the Jews and Muslims in 1099 and of the Latin Christians in 1187 posed the immediate problem of populating the city. Saladin had dealt with the most pressing issue by installing Bedouin tribes in Jerusalem and its environs to better control access to it.[15] The urgent need for settlement was nevertheless felt even in the new collections devoted to the "spiritual merits of al-Quds," which now showcased hadiths encouraging residence in the Holy City. Thus, according to a tradition attributed to the Prophet, "he who dwells in Jerusalem is considered a fighter in the path of God." Because of the material sacrifices that this decision entailed, settling there was a meritorious act, comparable to jihad itself. According to another hadith, "He who persists for one year in Jerusalem, despite the inconveniences and adversities, will be provided with daily bread and favored with paradise by God."[16] The urban environment's deterioration following the siege of 1187, the high prices of basic foodstuffs, the difficulty of establishing a business in a city long cut off from the Syrian hinterland by the Frankish domination, and the risk of seeing the Franks return in force were probably all good deterrents for potential settlers. But after the Third Crusade's failure in 1192 and despite Saladin's death the next year, the empire's stabilization at the century's end under the leadership of his brother al-Adil Abu Bakr opened up a new period of prosperity in the city's history.

Another consequence of Jerusalem's return to the Abode of Islam was the reestablishment of a perennial source of people: the arrival of Muslim pilgrims in the Holy City, where they often donned both the sacred state and the clothing symbolizing it (both called ihram) before setting off for Mecca and Medina with the Syrian pilgrimage caravan. Yet this first visit to Jerusalem often augured a long-term residence there, for study or commerce, after the return from Arabia's holy cities. Numerous pilgrims from the Maghreb thus chose to settle in Jerusalem after 1187, where they gathered in a neighborhood bordering the Noble Sanctuary's southwest corner, near an esplanade access point thereafter known as Bab al-Maghariba (Mughrabi Gate; see map 6 in chapter 3). In the mid-1190s, Saladin's son al-Afdal Ali constructed the Maghariba Mosque for them, on the Haram, as well as a madrasa that taught Malikite law (the dominant legal school in the Maghreb), this time in the city, in the heart of their district. The Afdaliyya Madrasa was destroyed along with the rest of the Mughrabi Quarter in the days following the war in June 1967. It stood in the center of what is now the open plaza before the Kotel (Wailing Wall).[17]

Moving into the Holy City was also encouraged by the hadith according to which "dying in Jerusalem is almost like dying in heaven." Mirroring the pilgrims who settled permanently in Mecca to serenely await death in the vicinity of the blessed sanctuary, devout Muslims were invited to approach paradise by residing in Jerusalem. Even if one didn't die there, it was desirable to be interred in that city, in anticipation of the Day of Resurrection, when all of humanity would be assembled there. Several of Saladin's officers who perished on different battlefields after 1187 were thus buried at the foot of the Holy City's walls.

Although Islamic law prohibits all inhumation *intra muros* as a rule, this did not prevent powerful people, such as Saladin's nephew al-Amjad Hasan, from founding madrasas in the city that were coupled with a mausoleum to receive their remains, preferably as close to the Noble Sanctuary as possible. Some devotees, like Shaykh Darbas al-Kurdi, even managed to be buried in the esplanade's surrounding wall. However, Jerusalem's Muslim cemeteries were established *extra muros:* al-Sahira, to the north, just beyond the gate of the same name (the current Herod's Gate); Mamilla, to the west, at the exit of the Hebron Gate; and Mercy, outside the gate of the same name (Bab al-Rahma), by the Noble Sanctuary's eastern wall, facing the Mount of Olives. Their development in the thirteenth century testifies to Muslims' devotion to the Holy City, gateway to paradise, and even more surely to the growing Islamization of Jerusalem's population.[18]

The process of Islamization should not obscure, however, another break that occurred in 1187 with the end of Frankish dominion: the return of the Jews, reauthorized to go on pilgrimage to Jerusalem and to make it their home. In autumn 1192, while Saladin was demolishing Ascalon's fortifications in accordance with the treaty that put an end to the Third Crusade, part of its Jewish community left to live in Jerusalem. The conquest of 1187 not only birthed a Jewish legend about Saladin, whose victories over the "uncircumcised" (Christians) foretold the advent of a Jewish king in Jerusalem—if one is to believe, for example, an apocryphal letter attributed to Maimonides (1138–1204), the great Andalusian Jewish philosopher and doctor who settled in Egypt, addressed to his coreligionists in Fez a few months before the Holy City's capture. The end of Frankish dominion also encouraged a movement of Jewish immigration, of which the Gerona scholar Nachmanides, who emigrated from his native Catalonia to Jerusalem and died in Acre around 1270, became the herald in the thirteenth century.[19] The resettlement of Jews in Jerusalem is paradoxically the most eloquent testimony of the Holy City's return to the Abode of Islam.

Making Jerusalem an Islamic City: The Institutions

Saladin, who was a great builder in other cities of his empire, did not judge it useful to enrich Jerusalem's architectural heritage. However, he left several institutions in his name in the Holy City, all established in preexisting structures which were converted to a new use.

In 1189, a small building that the Franks had erected on the Haram's south wall, against Al-Aqsa Mosque, was transformed into a *zawiya* for the accommodation of poor pilgrims during their visit to the Noble Sanctuary. In October of the same year, the former palace of the Latin Patriarchate, to the Holy Sepulchre's north, was granted to a Sufi community and turned into a khanqah (Khanqah al-Salahiyya, "of Salah al-Din," Saladin's Arabic name), a convent where these mystics performed their spiritual exercises and lived in seclusion (see map 6 in chapter 3). Three years later, the old Church of Saint Anne, built by the Franks in the first half of the twelfth century, was transformed into a madrasa (Salahiyya Madrasa) that taught Shafi'i law, the Islamic legal school to which Saladin adhered, as attested by the foundation inscription in the portal bay, dated Rajab 13, 588 AH (July 25, 1192), which is still in place today. In October of that year, Saladin ordered the conversion of the old Church of Saint Mary Major into a *bimaristan* (Bimaristan al-Salahi), both a hospital and a medical teaching facility. He thereby consecrated a remarkable continuity in the functions of this district neighboring the Holy Sepulchre, which had welcomed the first hospices established for the use of Latin pilgrims before 1099 (like that of the Amalfitani) and still housed the Hospital of Saint John of Jerusalem, whose knightly order was authorized after 1187 to keep ten of its members on site to care for the sick. Entirely transformed at the beginning of the twentieth century by the construction of modern markets, the quarter still preserves the memory of its medieval functions in its name: the Muristan. The only building that Saladin commanded be constructed—and not simply converted—in Jerusalem was finished after his death in 1193 and doesn't carry his name: an oratory (*masjid*) facing the Holy Sepulchre's main entry, which is on the site of "the blessed staircase," where tradition has it that Caliph 'Umar made the first Muslim prayer in Jerusalem, and which is named for the city's legendary conqueror (see map 6 in chapter 3).[20]

In the space of four years, Saladin thus set up a remarkably coherent program in Jerusalem. From a topographic point of view, his foundations tightly framed the city's highest place of Christian devotion: the Church of the Holy Sepulchre now found itself between the Salahiyya Khanqah and 'Umar's oratory. From an institutional point of view, they covered the whole spectrum of pious works for the greater glory of Islam with which Sunni rulers now sought to associate their names: the care of the poor (the *zawiya* and the hospital), the training of men of law and religion (the madrasa), the mystical exaltation of God (the khanqah). In accordance with Shafi'i law, Saladin built no new Friday mosque in the city (Jerusalem already had one, Al-Aqsa, which was incomparable in all respects) but instead a simple oratory, the Masjid 'Umar, intended as a reminder that the conquest of 1187 was a reconquest, five centuries after the caliph's legendary entry into the Holy City.

Such an institutional program had precedents: similar schemes had been implemented in Aleppo and Damascus by Nur al-Din, and already by Saladin himself in Cairo. The durability of the new foundations also rested on a well-established institution: the waqf, a perpetual pious endowment. Founding a waqf is a legal procedure engaged in on an individual basis by a devout donor who wishes to work in the community's interest. It consists of "immobilizing" (the literal meaning of *waqf*) land assets, real estate, and even movable goods for the benefit of pious work. These assets, the proprietary rights to which the founder renounces, are irreversibly transferred into the pious endowment's holdings: their inalienability should guarantee the waqf's perpetuity until the Day of Resurrection.

Waqf properties are divided into two categories: those whose usufruct constitutes the devout offering to the community (e.g., a mosque, the water in a fountain, the books in a library) and those whose revenues (e.g., the profit from a piece of land, the rent from a store, the entrance fee for a hammam) finance the pious foundation's operation (e.g., maintenance of buildings, payment of salaries). If it is backed by judiciously chosen real estate and land assets, a waqf can last, if not to the Day of Resurrection, at least several generations after its founder's death. Those that Saladin established in Jerusalem between 1189 and 1192 were still active more than three centuries later, when the Ottoman authorities undertook a census in 1525–26, ten years after Syria's conquest, of all the waqf holdings in their new province.[21]

In the years following the end of Jerusalem's Frankish rule, Saladin took advantage of the wealth of the Latin institutions that had been expropriated by the right of conquest, personally buying from the public treasury (*bayt al-mal*) real estate and land that had been seized in 1187, to endow it to his different pious foundations. For example, the Salahiyya Madrasa, located within the walls of the old Church of Saint Anne, derived part of its revenues from stores that had once belonged to Saint Anne's temporals (in the Suq al-'Attarin, "Perfumers' market") and from a rural settlement known as Sand Hanna (the old *casale* Santa Anna) but also from lands that had been owned by the Abbey of Saint Mary of the Valley of Jehoshaphat, some in Jismaniyya (Gethsemane) and others in 'Ayn Silwan (Siloam).

The most lucrative assets were, however, public baths: the one near the Gate of the Tribes (Hammam Bab al-Asbat), at the Haram's northeast entrance, was the main source of revenue for the Salahiyya Madrasa's waqf in the sixteenth century. Indeed, Saladin had taken care to give his urban foundations control over the hydraulic infrastructure indispensable to their operation. The Salahiyya Khanqah, installed in the former palace of the patriarch, counted among its waqf holdings two large open-air cisterns, the Mamilla Pool and the Patriarch's Pool, along with the pipes that connected them and supplied the Patriarch's Bath, a hammam adjacent to the hospital of the Knights of Saint John of Jerusalem.[22]

The origin of the Jerusalem Islamic Waqf, today still one of the largest institutional holders of the Holy City's land and real estate patrimony, thus dates back to the immediate aftermath of the conquest of 1187. But let us go further: it plunges, in fact, through the intermediary of the pious foundations that Saladin established to better make Jerusalem an Islamic city, into the property-based fortunes of the great Christian institutions in the time of Frankish dominion.

What to Do with Jerusalem? The Holy City in Ayyubid Politics

Saladin had made Jerusalem's conquest in 1187 and its return to the Abode of Islam a personal project: until his death in 1193, he was the only one to establish pious foundations there. Until the mid-thirteenth century, his descendants, the Ayyubids, did not fail to recollect, in the inscriptions that adorned their monuments in Egypt and Syria, their ancestor's claim to fame: "He who saved the Holy House from the hands of the infidels." However, they were embarrassed by the fate in store for the city that Saladin had conquered through such hard fighting.

Like so many other Islamic kingdoms born of conquest, the Ayyubid sultanate was shared among its founder's family members, even during his lifetime. After his death and for as long as the Ayyubids managed to maintain themselves in Syria and Egypt, the main political issue was the more or less straightforward ability of one of the princes to impose himself on his relatives as the family's true head. In the first half of the thirteenth century, when new Crusader expeditions targeted Egypt, the sultanate's richest province and the key to the Holy Land, the Ayyubid family's chief resided in Cairo. In this new configuration, Jerusalem, which most often fell under the jurisdiction of the sultan of Damascus, quickly lost importance.

In 1198, Saladin's brother al-Adil Abu Bakr, who was trying to assert his authority over his nephews, entrusted the principality of Damascus to his son al-Mu'azzam 'Isa. Did the latter harbor a special devotion to the Holy City, predestined by his name, that of the prophet Jesus ('Isa) in the Qur'an, which was rarely used in Muslim princely families? Or did he more simply see Jerusalem as an emblematic place to anchor his own fame, he who remained in his father's shadow? The fact remains that al-Mu'azzam 'Isa was involved in an ambitious project to reconstruct the city's ramparts, which finished only in 1214. Not only that, but in 1204 he decided to establish his primary residence in Jerusalem, which thus became the provincial capital for the first time since the Arab conquest of the seventh century—excepting the three years that separated the city's capture by the Seljuk chief Atsiz in 1073 and his entry into Damascus in 1076, as well as the interlude of the Frankish kingdom.

In Jerusalem, al-Mu'azzam 'Isa developed a particularly successful institutional and architectural program. In the Haram's heart in 1207, on the Dome of the Rock's terrace, which he enlarged, he constructed a madrasa to teach Arabic grammar; the Nahwiyya Madrasa's twenty-five students would also study Hanafi law in the Mu'azzamiyya Madrasa, which he founded in 1209 outside the Noble Sanctuary, on the north side (see map 6 in chapter 3). It was this same north side that he embellished, inside the esplanade complex this time, by adorning it with a new, ten-bay portico. Finally, in 1217–18, the year when his second madrasa was completed, he rebuilt Al-Aqsa Mosque's entrance porch, as it still appears today.[23]

Jerusalem thus almost became, with al-Mu'azzam 'Isa, Palestine's real capital. This was without taking into account the return of the Crusader menace, which made the Holy City a significant bargaining chip for Egypt's security. Al-Kamil Muhammad, who reigned in Cairo (1218–38), had already contemplated retroceding Saladin's conquests in exchange for the evacuation of Damietta, which the Crusaders had seized in 1218; his victory in the Nile delta three years later spared him from doing so. The idea resurfaced in 1227, when al-Kamil was negotiating with Emperor Frederick II on the eve of a new crusade. In 1229, the Treaty of Jaffa, concluded between the two sovereigns, ratified a division of Jerusalem to which the adversaries reconciled themselves all the more easily since it corresponded on the ground to a very clear spatial dichotomy: the city returned to the Franks, while the Haram remained in the Abode of Islam. Despite the emperor's friendly interest in Islam—it is said that he regretted not having heard the dawn call to prayer, which was suspended in deference to him during his short stay in Jerusalem—the accord resulted in exile for a good number of the city's inhabitants, Muslims as well as Jews. Vehement protests, notably in Damascus, forced al-Kamil to justify himself: thus he asserted that he had "conceded to the Franks only ruined churches and houses."[24]

Jerusalem's demographic decline (begun in 1187 and aggravated in 1229) and the dismantling of its defenses (in 1219 and then in 1227) overshadowed in people's minds the sanctity of the city that, just a few decades earlier, had mobilized so many forces to protect it from "infidels." Certainly, when the truce provided for in the Treaty of Jaffa reached its term, at the end of 1239, the sultan of Kerak al-Nasir Dawud forced the Franks to surrender Jerusalem again. But it took only the resumption of rivalries in the Ayyubid family—between al-Nasir Dawud and the new sultan of Egypt, al-Salih Ayyub, despite the solemn accord that they reached under the Dome of the Rock—for the Holy City to be exchanged once more. In 1240, al-Nasir ceded Jerusalem in return for military aid from the Franks against his cousin. The Dome of the Rock itself was handed over to the Christians, who are said to have brought in wine (probably to celebrate Mass). In 1244, al-Salih Ayyub recovered sovereignty over the city, which was not just depopulated but also devastated by the unrestrained Khwarezmian troops whom he had summoned from the east against the members of his own family. Indeed, in his will the sultan of Egypt advised his son not to hesitate to cede Jerusalem to the Franks if by chance they succeeded in capturing Damietta again.[25]

It is known that in 1249, the crusade led by the French king Louis IX (the future Saint Louis) did manage to take Damietta before being repulsed by al-Salih's Mamluk regiment, his royal guard composed of slave soldiers, who then seized the throne. Two years later, to ward off this new threat, the Ayyubid sultan of Aleppo al-Nasir Yusuf, the ruler of Jerusalem, offered to cede the Holy City to Louis IX, who had remained in Acre, in exchange for military support against the Mamluks in Cairo. That the king of France refused the proposal in no way changes the substance of the matter: the Ayyubids, descendants of Jerusalem's "savior," never stopped, even sixty years later, cheaply selling off their inheritance.

THE TURKS' LONG REIGN

Once again, a battle would decide Jerusalem's fate. But the one that took place on September 3, 1260, at the Spring of Goliath ('Ayn Jalut) in Galilee ushered in the longest period of stability in the Holy City's millennia-old history. The victory of the Mamluks (the Ayyubid sultan's Turkic slave soldiers, who had usurped the throne in 1250) over the Mongol hordes of Hülegü (Genghis Khan's grandson) saved Syria and Egypt—and probably Islam as a whole—from devastation just two years after Baghdad's capture and the caliphate's destruction.[26] The Mamluks' entry into Jerusalem in 1261 (the city's eighth change of hands since the Treaty of Jaffa in 1229) inaugurated almost seven centuries of Turkic rule over the Holy City. Indeed, contrary to a persistent myth maintained by the Ottomans after their victory over the Mamluks in 1516–17, few things ever distinguished the two Turkic dynasties in the daily lives of their Palestinian subjects, except the imperial capital's relocation from the banks of the Nile to those of the Bosporus, from Cairo to Istanbul.

One proof of this continuity is that the Mamluk and then the Ottoman sovereigns were eager to enrich and decorate the Noble Sanctuary without ever again disrupting the layout of its sites inherited from the Ayyubid conquest. The great fourteenth-century Mamluk sultan al-Nasir Muhammad (r. 1310–41), who visited Jerusalem in person, restored the cupola of the Dome of the Rock, raised the colonnades that border it to the north, and built both the large portico that marks the esplanade's western boundary and the minaret of the Chain Gate (Bab al-Silsila). His sixteenth-century counterpart, the Ottoman sultan Süleyman the Magnificent (r. 1520–66), without ever going to the Holy City, in 1537 had the mosaics that had adorned the Dome of the Rock's exterior walls since Umayyad times replaced with Iranian-style cuerda seca polychrome tiles (see map 8 in chapter 6).[27]

The Mamluk and Ottoman sultans also made it their duty, and an honor, to ensure the water supply and the maintenance of the massive hydraulic infrastructure which was the only way to quench "the thirst of Jerusalem." In 1399, Sultan Barquq restored the large reservoir outside the city's walls near the Hebron Gate (the current Jaffa Gate), which was thenceforth known as the Sultan's Pool (Birkat al-Sultan). In 1482, Sultan Qaytbay built a monumental *sabīl* on the Haram, both cistern and public fountain, topped with a cupola like the Dome of the Rock and like most of the Noble Sanctuary's aediculae. Finally, in 1536–37, in line with his Mamluk predecessors, Süleyman the Magnificent restored both the Sultan's Pool near Jerusalem's wall and the aqueducts and basins that collected water from the springs between Hebron and Bethlehem, and built six small *sabīls* in different parts of the city, where they can still be admired today (see map 8 in chapter 6).[28]

The political stability that characterized the Turks' long reign in Jerusalem, as elsewhere in the Middle East, should not hide, however, the profound transformations that affected the city's urban space. It gave birth, between the fourteenth and sixteenth centuries, to what is today called the Old City.

BIRTH OF THE OLD CITY

A clear division of space today contrasts the *intra muros* Old City and the modern neighborhoods that have developed outside Jerusalem's walls since 1850. The powerful urban enclosure erected by order of Süleyman the Magnificent between 1537 and 1541 both delimits and identifies the Old City. It would be a mistake, however, to see the latter as more or less the image, minus the walls, of what Jerusalem was like at the end of the Middle Ages. Süleyman's walls powerfully fixed a teeming urban topography, the result of more than two centuries of development and construction in the time of the Mamluks.

Jerusalem beyond Its Walls

Of the walls that al-Mu'azzam 'Isa built at the beginning of the thirteenth century and then dismantled between 1219 and 1227, numerous vestiges remain. There were, on the one hand, accumulations of rubble that were never cleared away, like those visible even today in the Old City's south-west corner, which in places gave it the appearance of a ruined town raised by a number of pilgrims and other foreign travelers, and, on the other hand, entire sections of the old structure, still partially upright, against which the inhabitants erected new buildings as Jerusalem was repopulated, to the point of making them disappear into the body of the city. The gates had also escaped destruction, which allowed the Holy City to be closed at night, with the aligned constructions between entrances forming makeshift ramparts.

In 1283, the German Dominican Burchard of Mount Zion counted eight gates in Jerusalem. In 1496, in his *Ta'rīkh al-Quds wa l-Khalīl* (*History of Jerusalem and Hebron*)—the first book that ever endeavored to encompass not only the Holy City's "spiritual merits" but also its history from the time of the prophets to that of its author, a description of its monuments, and biographies of its notables—Mujir al-Din al-'Ulaymi, a Jerusalem native, for his part enumerated twelve gates in the city, two of which had been walled up. Should one conclude that new gates had been installed in the interval or more simply that some had escaped the German pilgrim's notice? It is known, incidentally, that between 1260 and 1340, all of the gates on the Haram's west side (that of the city) were reconstructed and at least two new entrances (Bab al-Hadid, Bab al-Mathara) built. The increase in gates on the Haram's west side—and probably also along the line of the city's ancient walls—is one of many signs of Jerusalem's urban development and the densification of its built area, especially in the first half of the fourteenth century.[29]

The habit of identifying places as *intra* or *extra muros* also survived the dismantled enclosure, a usage to which clerks and notaries conformed long after the wall's physical disappearance. However, the legal actions concluded in Jerusalem even before the erection of Süleyman's wall (1537–41), such as a sale or the endowment of a waqf, mention numerous buildings located "outside the city." They thus confirm the testimony of al-'Ulaymi, the Jerusalem historian, who here and there reports the existence of new neighborhoods (*hara*) beyond the walls, such as Harat al-Jawalida to the northwest or Harat al-Maghariba (the Mughrabi Quarter) to the south. The *extra muros* construction in 1263 of the Khan al-Zahir (caravansary of Sultan al-Zahir Baybars), to the city's northwest, is perhaps explained by the density of buildings *intra muros* and the need for easy access to the khan's warehouses; it nonetheless attests to Jerusalem's budding outside its ancient walls from the first years of Mamluk dominion. The khan was destroyed in 1530 by decision of the new Ottoman authorities, who feared that this edifice might threaten the security of the nearby Citadel, and its blocks reused in the construction of the Lions' Gate in the city's northeast—which takes its name from the "lions passant" carved in the stone, the personal emblem of Baybars (literally "Lord panther"), which can still be admired on the gate's external face.[30]

Monuments in the City

The antiquity of Jerusalem's churches and the Haram's mosques often makes people forget that the city itself owes a significant proportion of its monuments and its configuration to a more recent period, the fourteenth and fifteenth centuries, and to the generosity of a military aristocracy foreign to the country, the Mamluks. The prosperity of the Mamluk era— at least until the great plague of the mid-fourteenth century, and then again, after the troubles of the 1400s, throughout the fifteenth century— translated into a large number of projects in most of the cities of Egypt and Syria; those in Jerusalem were intended to provide the city with new pious institutions and a monumental setting worthy of its reputation of sanctity. The Mamluk regime's particular organization, in which the great emirs (senior army officers) were often as rich and powerful as the sultan himself, encouraged a veritable competition in the building of facilities and the multiplication of pious foundations. Jerusalem was thus favored by the Mamluk sultans (six of whom visited the Holy City from Cairo) and the governors of Damascus (who long had authority over the officers stationed in Jerusalem) but also by numerous emirs, put on extended leave, who chose the Holy City as a place of temporary or permanent exile. In the 1460s, for example, Emir Qansuh al-Yahyawi, a deposed former governor of Damascus, lived there, where he built a funerary complex (*turba*) in the cemetery near the Haram's eastern wall; two decades later, having recovered his office, he stayed in his mausoleum during a visit to Jerusalem (see map 6 in chapter 3).[31]

Between the middle of the thirteenth and the beginning of the sixteenth century, no fewer than eighty-six pious institutions were established in Jerusalem—the most prestigious by the sultans, their emirs, and their great civil servants, as well as by some foreign rulers. Whatever the term by which it was designated (madrasa, khanqah, *zawiya*, etc.), each one bore the name of its founder, who often planned to be buried there. To honor his memory and contribute to the salvation of his soul, students, Sufis, or sometimes both at once were pensioned within the foundation's walls, provided they pursue their studies or perform their spiritual exercises while dedicating their prayers to their benefactor. If these characteristics did not distinguish Jerusalem's pious foundations from those of Cairo or Damascus, the Holy City was unique in its significant number of hospices (ribat) intended to accommodate pilgrims who were passing through, devotees who wished to end their days there, and particularly older, widowed, and divorced women. The Tankiziyya Madrasa, founded in 1328–29 by Emir Tankiz, the all-powerful governor of Damascus, not only hosted hadith classes but also boarded fifteen Sufis, who lodged in cells constructed on the roof. The institution also included, opposite the main building, a hospice for women (see map 6 in chapter 3). Moreover, the founder reserved lodging priority in the khanqah and the ribat for his own freed slaves, both men and women.[32]

The number of pious institutions founded in the Holy City in the fourteenth and fifteenth centuries was disproportionate to its altogether modest dimensions. The construction of imposing edifices to house them adorned Jerusalem with a new crown of monuments. Furthermore, the distribution of these building sites in the urban environment significantly changed the spatial relationship between the Haram and the city. The Second Temple's destruction in 70 CE had banished its powerful foundation—the Herodian esplanade—from Jerusalem proper. Neither the presumed construction of the Temple of Jupiter Capitolinus in the second century nor the building of the Dome of the Rock at the end of the seventh had reintegrated the ancient Temple Mount into the urban space. The Herodian walls had thus remained visible for centuries under the esplanade's four sides, contributing to the sacredness of the boundaries and thresholds that defined the Haram's space.

In the Mamluk era, in contrast, no fewer than ten monuments were erected just outside the Noble Sanctuary's northern limit (from the Karimiyya to the Jawiliyya Madrasa, from east to west) and another ten just outside its western limit (from the Manjakiyya to the Tankiziyya Madrasa, from north to south; see map 6 in chapter 3). Moreover, the new foundations were concentrated on the routes leading to the Haram's western entrances: the streets of the Inspector's Gate (Bab al-Nazir), the Iron Gate (Bab al-Hadid), the Cotton Merchants' Market (Suq al-Qattanin), and the Chain Gate (Bab al-Silsila)—the last of which led straight along the road from the Hebron Gate (the current Jaffa Gate) to the Noble Sanctuary's main access point at the end of the Middle Ages and grouped no fewer than nine of the new foundations (from the Tankiziyya to the Tashtimuriyya Madrasa, from east to west).

These monuments, however, were only the most visible part of more important real estate transactions, which associated, within the framework of a waqf, investment assets and the pious institutions whose operations they financed. The facing madrasa and hospice for women founded in 1328–29 by Emir Tankiz, at the Chain Gate's entrance, thus formed the charitable side of a waqf whose assets were centered less than a hundred meters (328 feet) away, at a Haram entry farther north. The latter has been known since the fourteenth century as the Cotton Merchants' Gate— on the Haram side, it opens with a monumental porch approximately in line with the Dome of the Rock; on the city side, it serves a vast covered market almost a hundred meters long and down a flight of stairs. The whole complex is the work of Emir Tankiz, who also built a caravansary (khan), a covered market (qaysariyya), and two public baths (hammams) behind the markets' shops (see map 6 in chapter 3). The baths catered to the faithful who wished to visit the Haram in a state of ritual purity. But we also know that they were the safest of all the investment assets, with the most-regular revenue. All in all, in less than a decade Emir Tankiz had not only fully equipped an entire neighborhood and ensured the long-term funding of its foundation but also entirely reconfigured one of the Haram's entrances. An inscription repeated on the brass strips adorning the monumental gate's doors has commemorated since 1336 the achievements of Emir Tankiz.[33]

The rapid urbanization of the Noble Sanctuary's immediate surroundings, essentially completed in the mid-fourteenth century, thus redefined the spatial relationship between the city and the Haram. The deliberate raising of the street level to facilitate access to the esplanade and the founders' desire that their monuments overlook the panorama of holy sites had the effect of filling the void that had more or less separated, for more than a millennium, the city and the Temple Mount. The venerable Herodian walls now served as the foundations of Mamluk monuments and mostly ceased to be visible from north and west of the esplanade.

Crowning Jerusalem: The Construction of Süleyman's Wall

Jerusalem's expansion beyond its dismantled enclosure and the proliferation of monuments housing pious institutions around the Haram gave substance to "the Old City" as early as the fourteenth century. But it was really the reconstruction of the surrounding wall, between 1537 and 1541, that gave it its final shape. In the absence of systematic archaeological excavations, it is difficult to establish the extent to which the new wall deviated from the courses of the Byzantine, Fatimid, Frankish, and Ayyubid fortifications. Thanks to test pits on each side of David's Gate (the current Zion Gate), we know that the Ottoman architects aligned the southern section with the early thirteenth-century enclosure—but didn't, however, put their towers and gates in exactly the same spots. Elsewhere, particularly in Jerusalem's northwest, the neighborhoods that had developed outside the line of the old dismantled wall were integrated by the new one's route (see map 8 in chapter 6).

The Ottoman enclosure's construction was not only the culmination of a long reurbanization phase over the three centuries that followed Saladin's conquest of Jerusalem: it literally crowned the monumental program with which Sultan Süleyman the Magnificent, then at the height of his power—three years after victoriously entering the Islamic Empire's ancient capital of Baghdad—wanted to associate his name with the Holy City. The start of this work—whose first, heavily symbolic act was the reconstruction in 1537 of Jerusalem's main gate, Bab al-ʿAmud (Gate of the Pillar; the current Damascus Gate)—was exactly contemporaneous with that undertaken to improve the city's water supply and give new luster to the Dome of the Rock's exterior decoration. Incidentally, the Ottoman officer who supervised the wall's construction, Muhammad Çelebi al-Naqqash (the Sculptor), was already present in Jerusalem in 1536, as a tax collector for the sultan.[34]

No urgency presided over such a colossal project, which was initiated twenty years after the Ottomans conquered the city from the Mamluks in December 1516. Neither regularly occurring unrest caused by the Bedouins of Jabal al-Quds nor the more than distant threat of European piracy in itself justified the elevation of a wall a dozen meters high and more than three kilometers (two miles) long, studded with thirty-four towers and pierced with seven monumental gates. Süleyman sought neither to defend nor to restore Jerusalem but to join the august line of builders who had distinguished themselves there from earliest antiquity, starting with the first of them, whom jinns themselves had helped to construct the First Temple in mythical times, that king whom the Qur'an makes a prophet and whose name the sultan himself bore: Solomon. Collective memory, so valued by Maurice Halbwachs, was not mistaken in soon attributing to the prophet-king the hydraulic infrastructure renovated by the sultan: the aqueduct and the pools of Solomon/Süleyman.

The wall was completed in only four years, as the inscriptions commemorating the successive constructions of doors attest: begun in 1537 in the city's north (Gate of the Pillar and Gate of al-Sahira), it was simultaneously extended to the eastern (Lions' Gate) and western (Hebron Gate) sections and finished in 1541 with the southern section (David's Gate and Mughrabi Gate). The new fortifications passed by the foot of Mount Zion without including it within their circuit, unlike the old Ayyubid walls—further proof that Jerusalem's defense was not the primary concern of its designers. The tradition which says that the sultan executed his two architects for this reason and that their remains have rested near the Hebron Gate ever since is an Ottoman legend for which the history of the Istanbul projects of Mehmed II (r. 1451–81) already offered a precedent.[35]

The efficiency of the builders—a construction manager from Aleppo paired with two architects, one from Istanbul and the other a Jerusalem

native—can certainly be explained by the partial reuse of the Ayyubid fortifications' foundations and of blocks from the walls dismantled in the
thirteenth century. They also used stone taken from other buildings, such
as the cells of the Franciscan monastery on Mount Zion, destroyed by
order of the sultan. But it is more the rapid funding of the operations that
commands admiration. The tax collector Muhammad Çelebi al-Naqqash,
named "superintendent of the wall" at the end of 1536, employed part of
the taxes paid by the districts (sanjaks) of Palestine for this purpose: those
of Jerusalem, Gaza, Ramla, and, for much greater amounts, Nablus, the
most prosperous sanjak in the whole province. The sultan's treasury contributed directly as well: significant sums were sent from Damascus in
three heavily guarded convoys of gold coins in 1537.[36]

Repopulating Jerusalem? The Holy City's Inhabitants in the Sixteenth Century

The new Ottoman order materialized not only in Sultan Süleyman's monumental projects. In Jerusalem as in every other new province of the
empire, the authorities undertook to identify the waqf assets that that had
escaped all taxation until then, as well as the heads of families whose
households were subject to taxes. The Ottoman state's stability and exceptional longevity helped to preserve the archives of these inventory operations to the present day. They thus deliver the first photograph of
Jerusalem's population, three and a half centuries after Saladin's conquest
of the city.[37]

The first census, carried out in 1525–26, counted 934 family heads in
Jerusalem, or around 4,500 inhabitants—assuming an average of five
people per household. In 1553–54, the number of family heads was
2,724, in addition to 179 students and 20 tax-exempt persons, or nearly
14,000 inhabitants. Had Jerusalem's population tripled in thirty years?
Such growth is highly unlikely. To read the effect of the Ottoman order's
establishment in these disparate numbers would be to misunderstand the
challenges of constructing Süleyman's wall and to retrospectively over-
state the demographic consequences of the insecurity that had reached
the region at the beginning of the sixteenth century. Certainly, since
the Black Death of 1348, the Holy City had been regularly struck by the

epidemic's return (in 1429, 1437, 1468, and 1476–77). But it is known that after the disaster's first few months the urban population underwent a rapid recomposition, driven by the rural exodus.

The Mamluk government's bad historical reputation, fostered by the Ottomans, cannot alone support the hypothesis of a city abandoned at the beginning of the sixteenth century, with only four thousand inhabitants. It is much more likely that the first Ottoman census was incomplete or its records incompletely saved. If Jerusalem's fourteen thousand or so inhabitants in 1553–54 register a probable demographic renewal, they also give a fairly accurate idea of the Holy City's population in the fourteenth century's finest hours: the town was of average importance but differed from its neighbors in the weight of its non-Muslim communities.

Non-Muslims—"protected people" (dhimmi) according to the provisions of the so-called pact of 'Umar—were in fact counted separately, which is not surprising in the context of censuses for tax purposes, since they had to pay a head tax to which Muslims were not subject. In 1553–54, of 2,724 family heads registered in Jerusalem, 413 were Christian (of different denominations) and 324 Jewish, representing communities of around 2,000 and 1,600 individuals, respectively, 15% and 12% of the total population. Jewish taxpayers, however, considered themselves unjustly overcounted and contested the census before the qadi's court. Indeed, temporary residents had been tallied as part of Jerusalem's Jewish community, even though they were already paying taxes in their city of origin. A new census carried out in 1572 brought the number of heads of Jewish families down to 115—that is to say, a permanent community of 500 or 600 persons, 4.5% of Jerusalem's total population. Despite the settlement of many Jews in the Islamic Middle East at the beginning of the sixteenth century, notably after their expulsion from the Catholic Kingdoms of Castille and Aragon in 1492 and then from the Kingdom of Portugal in 1496, the community established in Jerusalem thus remained relatively modest. In the sixteenth century, the one housed in the city of Ṣafad in Galilee was larger and more influential.[38]

Nonetheless, the correction of the census of 1553–54 reveals both that non-Muslims could defend their rights before the qadi's Islamic tribunal and that a large number of their coreligionists temporarily resided in

Jerusalem. The regular influx of pilgrims and the coexistence of communities were thus two major issues in the Holy City's government.

GOVERNING THE HOLY CITY

The Ottomans' entrance into Jerusalem on December 29, 1516, four months after Sultan Selim's victory over the Mamluks at the battle of Marj Dābiq in northern Syria and one month before the capture of Cairo, was accomplished without a blow. Selim, taking time for a detour on his way to Egypt, visited the Holy City in person and was given the keys to the Dome of the Rock and Al-Aqsa Mosque—thereby signifying that he was taking on the role of the Noble Sanctuary's protector, which the Mamluk sultans had performed for two and a half centuries. Continuity prevailed in the distant government of the Holy City.

Jerusalem as a Provincial City

Whether subject to Cairo's "Noble Gates" in the time of the Mamluks or to Istanbul's "Sublime Porte" in the time of the Ottomans, Jerusalem occupied the lower rung of provincial administration. In the fourteenth century, its governor (wali) was appointed by the viceroy (na'ib) of Gaza, who was himself under the authority of the viceroy of Damascus. From 1375, however, he too held the rank of viceroy and was appointed directly by the sultan or the sultan's officer in Damascus. Belonging to the Mamluk, Turkic, or Circassian military aristocracy, Jerusalem's governor was consequently a stranger to the city; the brevity of his mandate (an average of seventeen months in the fifteenth century) prevented him from confusing the duties of his office with his personal interest for very long. Furthermore, his authority over the city was severely limited by a strict division of responsibilities. The citadel's garrison was in fact placed under the command of another officer. More important, the administration of the Noble Sanctuary and its numerous waqfs was in principle entrusted to a high-ranking civil servant, sometimes appointed by the sultan himself, who jointly performed his duties over the shrines of Jerusalem and Hebron: the administrator of the two sanctuaries (nazir al-haramayn) was headquartered in the Tankiziyya Madrasa, at the Haram's entrance. The dangers of combining the functions of governor and administrator of the Noble Sanctuary did not escape the authorities in Cairo: at the beginning of the fifteenth century, Sultan Faraj formally forbade it by decree. This did not, however, prevent his successors from tolerating it. At century's end, the position had long been held by a civil administrator, a certain Nasir al-Din al-Nashashibi—whose surname did not leave, from then until the twentieth century, the first rank of Jerusalem's great families of notables.[39]

The Ottomans' arrival hardly changed this division of roles. The head of Jerusalem's district (sanjak), which thenceforth included Hebron, was a Turkish officer appointed to a renewable one-year term and placed under the authority of the governor of the province (*eyalet*) of Damascus. The garrison of Janissaries (an elite regiment composed of slave soldiers like the Mamluks) installed in the citadel was put under the command of its *duzdar,* who took his orders only from the Sublime Porte. However, judicial and religious affairs were no longer entrusted, as in the Mamluk period, to four chief judges (representing Sunni Islam's four legal schools) from among Jerusalem's notables but rather to a single magistrate, usually an Istanbul native, who was appointed for one year. Court sessions were now held within the walls of the Tankiziyya Madrasa, at the entry to the Haram. In contrast, Jerusalem's great families, which had built their fame and fortune through the hereditary exercise of prestigious civic charges and the management of the Holy City's main pious foundations since the end of the fourteenth century, retained control of the offices of mufti (the principal authority in religious matters) and administrator (nazir) of the Haram in the Ottoman era.

This was the case for the Banu Ghanim, so deeply rooted in Jerusalem's social landscape that one of the city's neighborhoods (Harat al-Ghawanima) has been known by their name since at least the late fourteenth century, as are the Haram gate that borders it and the minaret that towers over it. Their forebear, Ghanim ibn Ali, had been named to head the Salahiyya Khanqah by Saladin himself, who founded this Sufi convent in the former palace of the Latin Patriarchate. Two centuries later, one of Ghanim ibn Ali's descendants, Sharaf al-Din ʿIsa ibn Ghanim, was Jerusalem's chief Shafiʿi judge. It is to his dishonest management of the waqfs placed under his jurisdiction that we owe the preservation of almost nine hundred legal acts, most dating from the years 1391–94, that were probably assembled on the occasion of an investigation into accusations of corruption against him and which were rediscovered by chance in the Haram al-Sharif Islamic Museum in 1978; historians have not finished exploiting this mine of information on daily life in late fourteenth-century Jerusalem.[40] Despite Sharaf al-Din's woes, the Banu Ghanim family retained its hereditary prebend. In 1435, however, it had to share the Salahiyya Khanqah office and its revenues with another notable Shafi'i family, the Banu Jama'a. In the sixteenth century, this time under the Ottoman government, the latter were regularly appointed to the very prestigious position of mufti of Jerusalem.[41]

Jerusalem and Its Communities: Coexistence
and Conflicts over Land

The presence of strong Christian and Jewish communities, reinforced each year by the influx of pilgrims during religious holidays, had been an integral part of Jerusalem's landscape since the conquest of 1187. Thus the most prestigious of their places of worship were among the monuments that contributed to the city's fame. In his *History of Jerusalem and Hebron*, completed in 1496, al-'Ulaymi lists about twenty churches, which he dates to the Byzantine era, and describes four in detail: the Church of the Cross (Kanisat al-Musallabiyya), which belonged to the Georgians and had been given to them after being briefly transformed into a mosque at the beginning of the fourteenth century; the Church of Saint James (Kanisat Mar Ya'qub), which was part of the Armenian monastery (see map 7 in chapter 4); the Church of Zion (Kanisat Sahyun), which belonged to the "Franks," meaning the Franciscans of the Custody of the Holy Land, which was established in Jerusalem by virtue of a privilege accorded by the sultan and regularly renewed since around 1335; and the Church of the Resurrection (Kanisat al-Qiyama), which Muslims derisively called the Church of the Rubbish Heap (Kanisat al-Qumama) and which al-'Ulaymi describes as "an imposing edifice of extremely robust construction and fine work, visited each year on numerous occasions [by pilgrims] from the territory of the Byzantines, that of the Franks, and that of the Armenians, as well as from Egypt, Syria, and other countries." In contrast, al-'Ulaymi describes only a single synagogue (Kanisat al-Yahud) in the whole city, incidentally mentioned as a means of locating a nearby mosque in the section of the book devoted to Jerusalem's minarets.[42] Thus Jewish and Muslim city dwellers, neighbors and partners in commercial as well as real estate transactions, coexisted in the same quarter.[43] However, the density of urban buildings and the entanglement of usage rights and restrictions did not fail to provoke disputes between neighbors, which could rapidly degenerate into religious conflicts, even riots.

The so-called pact of ʿUmar, in fact, while protecting non-Muslims' property, religious liberty, and use of their places of worship, forbade, in addition to overly visible manifestations of their faith, the construction of new churches or synagogues. In the eyes of a legal practitioner like the historian al-ʿUlaymi, Jerusalem's *kanisat* could only be Byzantine, because they had to predate the founding moment of the seventh-century conquest. Likewise, judicial authorities had to inspect all restoration work on churches and synagogues, to prohibit the extension or any modification of the use of the premises. The Franciscan monastery in Jerusalem thus preserves in its archives the clearances following restoration work that were granted in 1446 and 1447 by the sultan himself, the governor, and the chief Hanafi judge and which confirm the ownership and residence rights on Mount Zion of the Friars Minor. In 1447, the governor and the chief Shafiʿi judge similarly authorized the sisters of a convent outside the city to renovate their cells.

If Christians and Jews were protected by the law, the extensive judicialization of social relations, the competition among the courts of different legal schools, and the possibility of introducing a legal opinion (fatwa) to contest a ruling and have the case retried all encouraged repeated reconsideration of the rights of the "protected." In the fifteenth century, in a social context tenser than it had been in the past, Jerusalem did not lack militants of the Muslim faith who were quite determined to exploit every recourse of the law, and even to rely on mob violence, to drive them out.

In 1458, an earthquake collapsed the dome of a church in the vicinity of the Holy Sepulchre. As the restoration work, authorized by the governor and the chief Hanafi judge, was coming to an end, a Hanbali judge—who said he was uncomfortable with the prayers of the faithful in that church—obtained an order from the sultan in Cairo that an inquiry be made. A complaint was filed by the shaykh of a Sufi brotherhood—in the court of the very judge who had initiated the affair. The verdict was rendered to the detriment of the Christians, and a mob soon demolished the dome.

In November 1473, heavy rain caused the collapse of a house in the Jewish quarter (Harat al-Yahud) that belonged to the waqf of the synagogue next door—dhimmis could indeed establish waqfs before the qadi on the same basis as Muslims. The damage had an unexpected consequence: it enlarged the access to the main entrance of a mosque in the synagogue's immediate vicinity. The neighborhood's Muslims thus occupied the ruined plot, which they claimed as a waqf of the mosque. The legal titles presented by the Jews shifted the dispute to the question of the age of the synagogue itself. First, deeming the building recent, the judicial authorities forbade its use as a place of worship. Then, against the demands of the sultan, who had tried to make them reverse their decision, they even rendered a legal opinion (fatwa) in favor of the edifice's outright destruction, which was very quickly implemented. Finally, however, the Muslim dignitaries responsible for this murky affair were arrested, sent to Cairo, and punished in the sultan's presence, and the synagogue was exactly reconstructed in 1475, on the sultan's express order.[44]

The Ottoman conquest of 1516 changed nothing in the legal conditions that governed the coexistence of Jerusalem's different communities. On the other hand, the *status quo ante* was called into question simply because the interlocutors had changed and the new regime did not retain the old one's memory. The Franciscans' uninterrupted presence since 1335 in their monastery on Mount Zion—which was only suspended briefly in the fifteenth century, in reprisal for Frankish acts of piracy in the Mediterranean—was soon threatened by the installation of a Sufi brotherhood on the supposed site of David's tomb on Mount Zion, which was also venerated and disputed by the Jews. Disturbed first in 1536, the Franciscans saw some of their cells destroyed to furnish stones for the construction of Süleyman's wall before being purely and simply dispossessed of their monastery, which was transformed into a waqf by order of the sultan in 1549. They were finally expelled from Mount Zion in 1551 but authorized to settle in the Monastery of the Column (Dayr al-ʿAmud, the current Convent of Saint Saviour) after proving that it had belonged to them before the Ottoman conquest of 1516 and had been usurped at their expense by the Georgian community.[45]

Another memory quest would prove detrimental to those same Georgians. Already in 1537, they had to defend themselves against charges of annexing a mosque to the Monastery of the Cross (Dayr al-Musallaba), which they possessed outside Jerusalem, and of using a wall to conceal the evidence of this usurpation. A new investigation, conducted in 1571 on the sultan's orders, uncovered stone blocks bearing Muslim religious inscriptions in the monastery's walls. On the strength of this discovery, the Monastery of the Cross was taken from the Georgians and transformed into a mosque. It had been forgotten that almost three centuries earlier the monastery had been improperly converted into a mosque—for the first time—before being returned to its monks in 1305 following the intervention of the Byzantine emperor and the king of Georgia. It was the vestiges of the building's first conversion, in Mamluk times, that justified its ultimate reconversion in Ottoman times.[46] The Monastery of the Cross was soon given back to the Georgians, however, but they were overwhelmed by debts and ceded it to the Greeks in 1685.

. . . . .

The half century that followed the Ottomans' entry into Jerusalem had thus seen adjustments in the respective positions of the different Christian communities that fought over the city's sacred sites, thanks to the change in imperial dominion and the authorities' amnesia. But Jerusalem's new masters quickly resumed the custom best suited to ruling the Holy City: that of an Islamic order of people, places, and things whose legendary founder was Caliph ʿUmar and whose first master builder, three and a half centuries before Süleyman the Magnificent, was Saladin.

6 The Peace of the Ottomans

SIXTEENTH TO NINETEENTH CENTURIES

If the major projects that Süleyman the Magnificent began in the 1530s are certainly part of the glorious and memorable episodes in the history of the Holy City, the rest of Ottoman Jerusalem's story has not enjoyed the same preferential treatment. After reaching its territorial apogee in the seventeenth century, the empire spent the following two hundred years in what is generally portrayed as the long and inexorable decline of an exhausted power, rebaptized "the sick man of Europe" by Western observers.

Ottoman Jerusalem suffers from this historiographic tradition, which is as unjust as it is tenacious: between the construction of Süleyman's walls (1537–41) and the entry of the British general Allenby (1917), the Holy City practically disappears from the history books, and when it is briefly mentioned, this period is presented as a prolonged fall. According to conventional wisdom, Jerusalem was forsaken by an Ottoman power whose back was against the wall, and its image soon merged, in Western representations, into that of an immense field of ruins.[1] The famous lithographs by David Roberts, which circulated widely throughout Europe beginning in the 1840s, are perfect illustrations of this Western gaze imbued with nostalgia, ignorance, and melancholy: fallen columns, vegetation-covered ruins, and sand, everywhere, hiding the ancient monuments. . . .

Everything contributes to the portrait of a frozen, immobile, almost forgotten city.

To tell, despite everything, the story of Ottoman-era Jerusalem (see map 8), it is thus necessary to turn back the clock against the tide of this declinist view. Let us stress first of all that if there was "neglect of Jerusalem," it was especially in the perception of Europeans themselves, who largely abandoned the practice of pilgrimage to the Holy Land in the early modern period in favor of an "interior crusade" against Protestantism as part of the vast movement of the Counter-Reformation.[2] Between the end of the Crusades in the thirteenth century and the rise of the great collective pilgrimages at the end of the nineteenth, an enduring gap opened between Europe and Jerusalem, and this distance largely explains Westerners' vision of a city that was almost moribund in the modern age. The orientalist Constantin-François de Volney thus stressed, on returning from a voyage undertaken in 1784, that "we with difficulty recognize *Jerusalem.*"[3] A few years later, in 1806, Chateaubriand emphasized the virtual disappearance of Catholic pilgrimage to Jerusalem: "During the last century the fathers of St. Saviour [the headquarters of the Franciscan Custody of the Holy Land] have not seen, perhaps, two hundred Catholic travellers, including the religious of their orders, and the missionaries in the Levant. That the Latin pilgrims have never been numerous, may be proved from a thousand circumstances. . . . Very often the number of pilgrims did not amount to twelve, since it was found necessary to take some of the religious to make up that number at the ceremony of foot-washing on Maundy Thursday. In fact, in 1589, . . . Villamont found only six European pilgrims at Jerusalem."[4] This long neglect of terrestrial Jerusalem by Europe, which was the essential driving force of the new "race for holy sites" that began at the end of the nineteenth century, allows us to put in perspective the Western historiography on the Holy City in the Ottoman era: during the early modern period, it was not the Ottoman Empire that forgot Jerusalem—it was Europe.

A second argument contradicts the declinist view: it passes over in silence the profound changes that the Holy City underwent beginning in the 1840s, when the Ottoman Empire undertook a renovation of its administrative structures by embarking on a phase of intense reforms (*tanzimat*).[5] Jerusalem benefited from these modernization efforts,

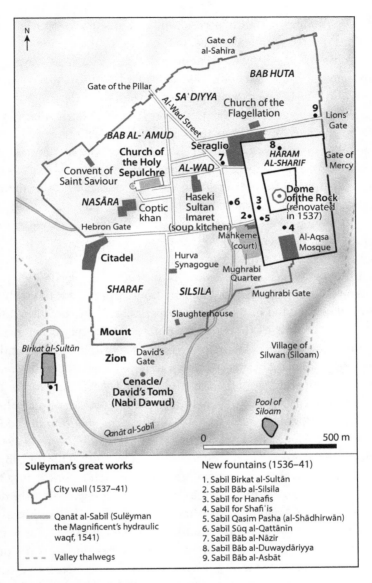

N

Gate of
al-Sahira

BAB HUTA

Gate of the Pillar

SA'DIYYA

Al-Wad Street

Church of the
Flagellation

9
Lions'
Gate

BAB AL-'AMUD

Seraglio

Church of
the Holy
Sepulchre

AL-WAD

7

8
*HARAM
AL-SHARIF*

Gate of
Mercy

Convent of
Saint Saviour

NASĀRA

Coptic
khan

Haseki
Sultan
Imaret
(soup kitchen)

•6

3

2•

Dome
of the Rock
(renovated
in 1537)

•5

Hebron Gate

Mahkeme
(court)

•4

Al-Aqsa
Mosque

Citadel

Hurva
Synagogue

Mughrabi
Quarter

SHARAF

SILSILA

Mughrabi Gate

Slaughterhouse

Mount

Village of
Silwan (Siloam)

Birkat al-Sultān

Zion

David's
Gate

•1

Cenacle/
David's Tomb
(Nabi Dawud)

*Pool of
Siloam*

Qanāt al-Sabīl

0   500 m

Sulëyman's great works	New fountains (1536–41)
City wall (1537–41)	1. Sabīl Birkat al-Sultān 2. Sabīl Bāb al-Silsila 3. Sabīl for Hanafis 4. Sabīl for Shafi'is
Qanāt al-Sabīl (Sulëyman the Magnificent's hydraulic waqf, 1541)	5. Sabīl Qasim Pasha (al-Shādhirwān) 6. Sabīl Sūq al-Qattānīn 7. Sabīl Bāb al-Nāzir 8. Sabīl Bāb al-Duwaydāriyya
- - - Valley thalwegs	9. Sabīl Bāb al-Asbāt

Map 8. Ottoman Jerusalem (sixteenth to nineteenth centuries)

notably by establishing an intercommunity municipal institution at the start of the 1860s, well before most of the empire's major cities.[6] Against this background, the Holy City's population grew at a steady pace, from fifteen thousand inhabitants in 1850 to around seventy thousand on the eve of World War I. A new town appeared beyond the walls constructed by Süleyman, constituting a major rupture in Jerusalem's urban history (see map 9 in chapter 7): thenceforth, a distinction would have to be made between the city *intra muros,* in which most of the holy sites and religious institutions were concentrated, and the city *extra muros,* which was more secularized and open to the outside world.[7] This radical transformation of the urban environment, whose effects are still being felt today, happened in the Ottoman period's last sixty years—and this alone is enough to call into question the frozen chronology that still too often prevails in the historiography concerning this historical sequence.

A third element must be taken into account to avoid describing Jerusalem's Ottoman history as a long motionless sequence: the Holy City, at first fully integrated into Ottoman imperial ideology, as Süleyman the Magnificent's great works show, in the nineteenth century became one of the focal points of the nationalist movements of the Zionists and the Arabs—Palestinians. This process of an imperial city's double *nationalization* was long and complex: first it played out, beginning in the mid-nineteenth century, in cultural rhetoric and representations, and then it translated into fact by leading to the effective *capitalization* of the Holy City, which became an autonomous regional capital in 1872 and Mandatory Palestine's administrative capital after 1922. This transformation represented a considerable political turning point: for the first time since the biblical period, the Holy City was no longer regarded as the decorative jewel of a Christian or Muslim imperial crown but rather as the political capital of two aspiring nations, Israel and Palestine.[8] The current discussions of "Jerusalem as a capital for two states" are thus the direct result of the changes that took place at the end of the nineteenth century: as we can see, whether in terms of urban topography ("real Jerusalem") or of religious or political representations ("ideal Jerusalem"), it is simply impossible to understand the Holy City of today without reference to its long Ottoman history.

A HOLY, IMPERIAL, AND PROVINCIAL CITY (SIXTEENTH TO EIGHTEENTH CENTURIES)

The Western vision of a sleeping Holy City in the Ottoman period can be explained by the decline in exogenous sources (European pilgrims were few in the modern era) and by historians' overly parsimonious use of endogenous administrative sources but also more globally by a myopia characteristic of the historiography of Jerusalem, which essentially focuses on episodes of trouble, of war, of conquest—that is, on the shattering ruptures that do indeed punctuate its millennia-old history—to the extent that the periods of stability are automatically neglected. However, there was a staggering breaking point in the Ottoman era: it was indeed the "Status Quo" that prevailed, to use the term for the typically Ottoman politico-juridical notion that governed the balance among communities and was stabilized little by little by firmans (sultan's decrees) issued in 1767 and 1852. To enrich the history of Ottoman Jerusalem before Napoleon's expedition of 1799, it is therefore necessary to focus on direct testimony and endogenous administrative sources.[9] They reveal a Holy City characterized by a certain number of fiscal privileges, by a surprising hybridization of religious references, and especially by the very particular attention paid to it by the Ottoman administration.

Holy City, Free City?

Jerusalem theoretically occupied the Ottoman provincial administration's lower level, because its governor had the title of *sanjak bey* and until 1872 was under the authority of the provincial governor of Damascus.[10] However, it enjoyed a special status because it was officially recognized as a "Holy City" (*Kudüs* in Ottoman Turkish), just like Mecca, Medina, or Hebron. Far from merely symbolic, this recognition gave the inhabitants a certain number of privileges, particularly in matters of taxation and conscription. An imperial decree (firman) signed by the sultan on Rebiyulahir 27, 976 AH (September 19, 1568), and addressed to Jerusalem's judge (qadi) provides proof of these privileges of exemption. The sultan begins by recalling that an extraordinary levy of fifteen hundred archers was ordered in the province of Damascus the previous spring, to meet the needs of the military campaign then being conducted in Yemen. Concerning Jerusalem, it was planned that every twenty households would finance the conscripting, arming, and monthly pay of an archer, but "the inhabitants of Jerusalem and Hebron produced a noble firman to the effect that no extraordinary levies should be collected from them" and argued that this privilege had lasted "from olden times." In response, the sultan commands that the judge "shall not allow anybody to collect anything from [the people of] Jerusalem and Hebron."[11] Jerusalem, Islam's third holy city, and Hebron, the city that houses the tombs of the four Patriarchs (Adam, Abraham, Isaac, and Jacob), thus benefited from a privilege of tax exemption that was officially recognized by the imperial authority and whose memory local notables carefully maintained.

As in the medieval period, many pilgrims en route to Mecca made a stop in Jerusalem to pray together, and this particular situation conferred on the Holy City an essential strategic function in the eyes of the Ottoman authorities, who were responsible before God for the safety of pilgrimage. Pillaging by Bedouin tribes is the danger most frequently mentioned in the imperial archives, which made the Jerusalem garrison of paramount importance. On August 7, 1567, the sultan thus transmitted to Jerusalem's governor the complaint of a certain Fatima: "When I went with my son on a pilgrimage to Jerusalem, rebellious Bedouins suddenly attacked [us] on our return journey, plundered my luggage, and took my son prisoner. They demand a price [as ransom]. This is iniquitous." The rest of the letter addressed to the governor shows that the security of pilgrims was the subject of considerable attention on the imperial power's part: "This is the first time that Bedouins have taken anyone prisoner. This affair has now occurred in your days and you are fully answerable in this matter. To liberate the son of the above-mentioned [woman] is necessarily your responsibility. . . . If [such] a complaint is made again, you will be blamed."[12]

It would be erroneous, however, to imagine the inhabitants of Ottoman Jerusalem hiding behind Süleyman's high walls to escape the Bedouin tribes' cruelty. In reality, the archives reveal that cases of exchange and even cooperation between Bedouins and townspeople were far more frequent than might at first be imagined, as this letter, addressed to Jerusalem's judge and governor on March 31, 1593, illustrates:

Certain inhabitants of Hebron co-operate with the Banī ʿAṭa and Banī ʿAṭīya, who are in a state of permanent rebellion. They receive and sell goods that those Bedouins take from Mecca pilgrims, at times buying them cheaply and at others accepting them for safe-keeping. The year before they also served the Bedouins as guides into the Hebron mountains, with the result that four or five villages were sacked.

The culprits are to be captured and punished.[13]

Here again we see that Jerusalem's holy sites gave the city a special status in the eyes of the Ottoman authorities—far removed, in any case, from its modest administrative status as a district (sanjak) capital. Palestine, located exactly at the Ottoman Empire's geographic center, between the Anatolian Plateau, the Arabian Desert, and North Africa, and along the strategic Damascus-Cairo route, was an essential part of the empire's territorial cohesion. Jerusalem, located in the center of the Palestinian ridge, along the road that connects Nablus, Bethlehem, and Hebron from north to south, was a decisive link in the system.

City of All Pilgrimages

The question of free access to sacred places for pilgrims of the three monotheisms is a sensitive subject in the Holy City's historiography, for all periods, because the issue is both historical and political. What can be said and what precisely known about the Ottoman era? We do know that the imperial authorities in principle allowed pilgrims of all religions access to their respective shrines, with a toll for Jews and Christians, but forbade ostentatious religious demonstrations and the construction of new sanctuaries. The travel narrative of David Reubeni, a mystical adventurer in the early sixteenth century, goes further, however, suggesting that some Jewish pilgrims could de facto enter the Haram, the ancient Temple Mount, to pray: "I journeyed from Hebron on the 24th Adar and came to Jerusalem, and there were robbers on the way. . . . Behold, the Turkish judge had come from Hebron with many servants. The robbers saw him and all of them fled, and I journeyed with him to Jerusalem. I entered it on the 25th Adar, 283 ([April 24,] 1523), and that day I entered the house of the Holy of Holies, and when I came to the sanctuary all the Ishmaelite guardians came to bow before me and to kiss my feet." Here we find the omnipresent theme of travelers' insecurity but also the strange mention of an authorized visit inside the Dome of the Rock, which Reubeni calls "the Holy of Holies," and even "to the cavern which is under the *Eben Shethiah* [Foundation Stone]" (see map 6 in chapter 3).[14]

Of course, it cannot be excluded that David Reubeni sought to enhance his prestige by thus staging himself in prayer in "the Temple court," but the rest of his account gives credence to his testimony, so precise is it: he recounts being dislodged that evening by other, less accommodating guards, then managing to mingle the next day with the crowd of Muslims who arrived to pray, and finally, at a cost of ten ducats, arranging to "[stay] in the sanctuary and [fast] in the Holy of Holies five weeks," to which he adds that he "ate no bread and drank no water except from Sabbath eve to close of Sabbath." Afterward he went to Mount Zion, reporting that Muslims there showed him "the grave of King David," and when he left Jerusalem, "a number of Ishmaelites came on horseback to accompany me five miles [eight kilometers]."[15] This narrative, from the very beginning of the reign of Süleyman the Magnificent (1520–66) and a few years before the launch of his giant wall construction (1537–41), testifies to the complexity and also to the probable diversity of the customs governing the access of Jewish and Christian pilgrims to Jerusalem's emblematic holy sites. It shows above all that contingent variables (the traveler's personality, social skills, and financial means; the sitting governor's character) played a role equal to if not greater than those of the official regulations and strict religious identities of visiting pilgrims.

Other accounts bear witness to the vexations that pilgrims sometimes endured to access their sanctuaries. François-Charles du Rozel, a French noble from Orne, on pilgrimage in Jerusalem in September 1644, quite precisely described the procedure for entering the Holy City: "We went into that place by the Gate of Rama, also called the Shepherd's Gate [the present Damascus Gate], which is the one for pilgrims, who are not allowed to enter by any other, whatever might have happened to you, otherwise they put you in prison and make you pay a heavy fine. . . . And although the gate was open, our entrance was not lawful until we had first informed the monastery to announce it to the Bacha [governor] and the Qadi [judge], who sent a janissary via the aforesaid monastery to take us to the gate, where they made us wait a good hour and a half, during which time we had to suffer an abundance of insults and opprobrium from Turks and Moors, even several blows with sticks and stones, which the above-mentioned janissary made stop."[16] Concerning the Haram, Du Rozel was less fortunate (or less bold) than David Reubeni: "One of the most beautiful things in the world is the Temple, built in the same place as that of Solomon, it is said, by Saint Helena [sic], and in the same form, where it is not permitted for Christians to enter, although the doors are always open, nor even its enclosure. But I saw it almost as well as if I had been inside, from the house of a Turk that is against and looks onto it." For Du Rozel, the Dome of the Rock is indeed "the Temple," and it is to "Saint Helena," Constantine's mother, that we owe the construction of this architectural marvel. In passing, let us remember the description that Du Rozel gives of the city itself, which sharply refutes the traditional view of a town abandoned in the Ottoman period: "It is still quite large, more than three *mils* [4.5 kilometers, or 2.8 miles] around, well enclosed by good walls, most refurbished, with seven iron gates. The houses are built in the Turkish style; the city retains quite beautiful ones, and many old ones can still be found there. The streets are large for the country and the city well populated."[17]

To enter the Holy Sepulchre, Du Rozel had to disburse twenty-four piastres, "for distribution to those who have the keys, who are the bacha, the qadi, and the santum [guardian] of the aforesaid Holy Sepulchre, whose house and mosque are adjacent to it. These three keys are different, and none can do anything without the others; this is why they must take the time to send their people there together."[18] The description is precise enough to be authentic, and it indeed testifies to the complexity of admittance to holy sites: the sanctuaries were theoretically accessible, but entrance to them was tightly controlled. To add nuance to this description, let us quote another passage of Du Rozel's account: while traveling along the Via Dolorosa, he stopped at what he calls the house of Saint Matthew, "which the Turks use as their hotel Dieu, and all the poor, both Turks and Christians, are welcome there and can go daily to fetch soup and bread."[19] As we can see, the real contacts between the different religions were much richer than a Manichaean vision would suggest: Christian pilgrims who were wealthy had to pay to access the Holy Sepulchre, but the poorest among them were willingly housed and fed by a pious Muslim institution.

Hybrid Sanctuaries

The lack of confessional assignment for some of Jerusalem's holy places is a subject rarely mentioned, since most historians prefer to stick to the catalogue of clearly labeled sanctuaries as if the impermeability of religious memories were a fundamental part of Jerusalem's heritage landscape. However, it seems clear that the hybridization of sanctuaries was particularly prevalent in the Ottoman period and in any case before the nineteenth century—that is, before the popularization of Western pilgrimages and new competition among monotheisms contributed to a logic of religious polarization that was epitomized by the "race for holy sites."[20] The long duration and stability of Jerusalem's Ottoman administration were doubtless the main factors in this slow process of hybridization; Islam, the third and final monotheist revelation, was then the dominant religion in the Holy City, and it is not surprising that its believers appropriated, little by little, previous religious traditions—both Jewish and Christian—as well as the shrines attached to them.

Let us walk again with François-Charles du Rozel (1644), this time on the slopes of the Mount of Olives, to take the phenomenon's full measure. On a visit to the Tomb of the Virgin (see map 5 in chapter 2), he noticed "in the rock a large hole like a small cave, where the Turks say 'that Our Lord hid when the Jews were looking for him to crucify him, and that when they had gone away he came out and flew to heaven through a small window in the form of a cellar vent at the end of the aforesaid wing; that since that time no one has seen him, and that the Jews, not finding him, took one of his disciples who resembled him, believing that it was him, and crucified that man.'"[21] This shows the Qur'an's disbelief in the face of the theological scandal represented by the account of the Crucifixion (Qur'an 4:157): if Jesus really was a prophet (and he is, without any possible doubt, in the Qur'anic text), then he could not have suffered the indignity of death by crucifixion.[22]

Du Rozel's following testimony is even more explicit: "All the Turks and Moors believe he was a great prophet, even as great as Muhammad. They say that the law he had made was a bit too harsh and that God sent them their prophet Muhammad to mitigate it. Nonetheless, they strongly revere him, just like the Virgin and all the apostles, whom they consider great saints. So they seized all the Holy Sites where Our Lord performed so many miracles, most of which they turned into mosques."[23] Du Rozel reports the stories peddled by his guides, attesting to the appropriation of evangelical texts by Jerusalem's Muslim inhabitants. He interprets the transformation of certain churches into mosques not as a sign of an intrinsic gulf between Islam and Christianity but, on the contrary, as proof of the closeness between the two traditions and of the sincere veneration of the prophet Jesus/'Isa by Jerusalem's Muslims.

A few days later, while visiting the "Fountain of the Virgin" in the Kidron Valley and noting that "the Turks made a mosque there," he expressed the same idea: "This testifies to their devotion to it." There is no reason to doubt the testimony of Du Rozel, who, incidentally, expresses no sympathy for those he calls "Turks and Moors." The signs of sanctuary hybridization are too numerous in his text to be considered insignificant: stopping at the Garden of Gethsemane (the location of Jesus's arrest), he reports that the place's Muslim proprietor had refused to sell it to his neighbor, "which bears witness to the reverence they [Muslims] have for Our Lord."[24]

Finally reaching the summit of the Mount of Olives, he visited the little mosque that commemorates Christ's Ascension, "where the mark of one of his feet imprinted on a stone can still be seen. He left the prints of both there, but the Turks took the other, which was more distinct, to Solomon's Temple. There is a little round church on this site, which the Turks have made into a mosque; they venerate it highly and allow Christians to come."[25] The Mosque of the Ascension, which still exists today, is one of the most remarkable material witnesses of the old mixing of religious traditions in Jerusalem—but pilgrims hardly ever visit it now, as if such "uncertain holy sites" had become inconvenient for travelers in search of well-established identity boundary posts and well-sealed religious borders.[26]

De Jure Separation, De Facto Hybridization

In the nineteenth century, these local traditions, which attest to an undeniable hybridization of religious references in the Ottoman period, were denigrated, mocked, and discredited little by little by the Western pilgrims who were then flocking to the Holy City. In his commentaries on Du Rozel's travels, which he published in 1864, the scholar Émile Bonneserre de Saint-Denis never ceases to ironize this "nonsense" and these "superstitions"; he who never set foot in the Holy Land fashions the image of holy sites cleansed as if purified, cleared of all traces of an ancient confessional crossbreeding: "Du Rozel is not the only one who has, in Palestine, lent a too-attentive ear to the absurd tales so willingly spouted there by heavy and ignorant ciceroni," he wrote, contributing with so many others to the polarization of the Holy City's religious memories through a strict faith-based assignment of its sanctuaries.[27]

Had François-Charles du Rozel, then, let himself be fooled by the flim-flam of his guides, by what Bonneserre de Saint-Denis calls "Mohammedan greed" and "the historical trickery of the Saracen gentlemen"?[28] Were these hybrid traditions just superficial legends, intended only to encourage the support of passing visitors? The Ottoman administrative archives prove the opposite: they ceaselessly denounce mixed religious practices and recall the rules of separation that theoretically governed relations between communities, which indicates that the opportunities for contact and exchange were in fact probably frequent. In July 1613, an imperial decree specifically mentioned the Mosque of the Ascension, described as "the domed building which is [the shrine of] the sacred foot[print] of the Lord Jesus, God's blessing be upon him, and its courtyard outside it at the village of [At-]ṭūr, situated on the east side of Jerusalem," and makes clear that the restoration of its walls and the mending of its paving "are the privilege of the Armenian Christians living and domiciled in Jerusalem."[29] Further on, the decree reports that "some Muslims, solely in order to gain money and to annoy and tyrannize over the said infidels, have come with the intention of living there," and asks Jerusalem's judge to enforce the Armenians' rights. This decree, written just thirty years after Du Rozel's journey, demonstrates that use and access rights and confessional assignments were not definitively fixed for Jerusalem's sanctuaries, which were the subjects of claims, negotiations, and sometimes de facto sharing between different communities. The Status Quo, contrary to popular belief, thus governed the sharing of not just the most emblematic sacred sites, such as the Holy Sepulchre: this legal concept also protected the rights of communities in sanctuaries of lesser importance.

Fifty years later, in August 1565, another imperial decree revealed that many Christian sanctuaries were frequented as such by Muslim faithful who went there to pray, especially women: this was the case for the Tomb of the Virgin Mary in particular, which regularly welcomed "[Muslim] women and infidel women and infidels (Christian women and men) [who] come and assemble," but also for the Haram, whose "door-keepers . . . do not guard the gates [properly]" and where "some ladies come to the Aqṣā Mosque . . . on the pretext of pilgrimage and worship [but in fact] merely for [enjoying] the spectacle." The contacts between communities were therefore not a strictly religious issue, as attested by a decree of July 1565 which recalls that "it is strictly forbidden to bring wine to Jerusalem" and that "the non-Muslim inhabitants are to be warned against advertising and selling wine to any Muslim"—evidence that such exchanges must have been commonplace. In the same vein, a decree from December 1565 denounces the establishment of five bars in Jerusalem, meeting points for "*levendāt*" (rascals) and other disreputable characters, whose pernicious conduct was "keeping the Muslims from pious devotion and divine worship." Once again, these imperial firmans must be read for what they are: if the sultan's functionaries took the trouble all the way from Istanbul to regularly reaffirm these rules and prohibitions, that is proof that these everyday practices did indeed exist.[30]

In September 1578, another decree targeted mixed clothing practices:

> The Samaritans [equated with the Jews by the Ottoman authorities] and Christians in the province of Damascus dress like Muslims. They buy pieces of fine muslin (*dülbend*), get them dyed yellow, and wind them round their heads as turbans, thereby causing annoyance to the Muslims.
> Henceforth this is to be strictly forbidden.[31]

In short, dress, food, and religious practices testify much more—and quite logically—to the imbrication of religious traditions in the daily lives of Jerusalem's inhabitants than to strict separations between the communities. By comparing narrative and administrative sources and trying to understand the daily reality of Ottoman Jerusalem's city life without artificially slapping our current categories on it, we can thus lift part of the veil on the Holy City's *lived* history, its history at ground level.

EUROPE AND EGYPT AT JERUSALEM'S GATES

In spring 1799, General Napoleon Bonaparte, coming from Egypt, seized Gaza and Jaffa before being defeated before the walls of Acre and finally returning to Europe without having approached the Holy City. In December 1831, Khedive Muhammad 'Ali's army seized Jerusalem, which it occupied until 1840, initiating a number of administrative reforms in the process. In 1839, taking advantage of the new room for maneuver offered by this Egyptian interlude, the United Kingdom installed the first European consulate in the Holy City, soon followed by Prussia (1842), Sardinia and France (1843), Austria (1849), and then Russia (1857). Neglected by Europe since the failure of the Crusades, Jerusalem was once more the center of attention. Western travelers crowded around holy sites, which were proliferating like never before. In the first half of the nineteenth century, Jerusalem's history thus resonated with those of nearby Egypt and distant Europe, which contributed to the gradual emergence of its status as the capital of a new territory both imaginary and political: this was the "Holy Land" of Europeans, which became the "Palestine" of Zionists and Arab nationalists in the century's second half.

Napoleon, Liberator of Jerusalem?

In its edition of May 22, 1799, *Le Moniteur universel* disclosed breaking news to its French readers: "Politics, Turkey, Constantinople—28 Germinal, year VII [April 17, 1799]: Bonaparte has published a proclamation in which he invites all the Jews of Asia and Africa to come line up under his banners to reestablish the ancient Jerusalem. He has already armed a great number of them, and their battalions are threatening Aleppo."[32] One year after leaving Toulon and ten months after his resounding victory at the Battle of the Pyramids, General Bonaparte was thus trying to rely on Jewish "battalions" to fight the Ottoman troops in Palestine and liberate Jerusalem.[33] The same paper repeated the news with even more assurance in its edition of June 27, 1799: "On Bonaparte's probable conquest of the Ottoman Empire. Let us await the confirmation of this happy news. If it is premature, we like to think that it will come true one day. It was not only to return their Jerusalem to the Jews that Bonaparte conquered Syria."[34]

In his monumental "biography" of Jerusalem, Simon Sebag Montefiore even quotes a proclamation that Napoleon is said to have written with his own hand on 1 Floréal, year VII (April 20, 1799), while garrisoned in Ramla, some forty kilometers (twenty-five miles) from the Holy City: "Bonaparte, Commander in Chief of the Armies of the French Republic in Africa and Asia, to the rightful heirs of Palestine—the unique nation of Jews who have been deprived of the land of your fathers by thousands of years of lust for conquest and tyranny. Arise then with gladness, ye exiled, and take unto yourselves Israel's patrimony."[35] There are many and very different versions of this surprising document—and for good reason: the historian Henry Laurens, after meticulously combing through the materials in French archives, already demonstrated more than thirty years ago that the original document does not exist and the text is a fake, fabricated by the disciples of Jacob Frank, a messianic leader who was somewhat popular in central Europe at the end of the eighteenth century; found in 1940 in a version translated into German, it has since enjoyed undeniable popularity.[36]

Yet if it is now proved that Napoleon never planned to support any Jewish national revival in Palestine, the idea was apparently plausible enough for *Le Moniteur universel* to disseminate the news twice. This rumor's success illustrates the change in the West's view of the Holy City at the turn of the eighteenth into the nineteenth century: the impact of the Egyptian expedition put the Middle East, the "Holy Land," and more specifically Jerusalem back at the center of European imaginations. Of course, in the short term this had no effect on the concrete history of the Holy City and its inhabitants. But in the longer term this shift was important: for the first time since the end of the Crusades, Jerusalem was again at the heart of Western preoccupations and projections. As Europe began a long secularization process in the nineteenth century, sacred places regained the function they had lost in the modern era: keepers of biblical memories, they had to bear witness to a bygone age. The enormous manufacture of holy sites that started then would accentuate the polarization of communities and delineate the physiognomy of present-day Jerusalem.

Chateaubriand in Jerusalem: A Founding Voyage

The journey that François-René de Chateaubriand started in 1806 and his account of it, published in 1811 under the title *Itinéraire de Paris à Jérusalem* (Itinerary from Paris to Jerusalem), constituted the founding moment of a tradition with a bright future. He portrayed the Holy City as a closed, macabre, and sepulchral place, an exact illustration of the Passion narrative. Four years after releasing *The Genius of Christianity*, François-René de Chateaubriand stayed in Jerusalem for just a week, from October 5 to 12, 1806. It is while describing Jerusalem's domestic architecture that he brutally reveals his point of view: "The houses of Jerusalem are heavy square masses, very low, without chimneys or windows . . . , and look like prisons or sepulchres."[37] Chateaubriand further elaborates this quite astonishing vision of a literally *dead* city, comprising not houses for the living but "prisons" and "sepulchres" for the deceased, as his description continues: "On beholding these stone buildings, encompassed by a stony country, you are ready to inquire if they are not the confused monuments of a cemetery in the midst of a desert." The New Testament filter through which Chateaubriand regarded the city here discloses itself: it was not an inhabited city that he went to visit but rather the fantasized materialization of the story of Christ's Passion, polarized at its two extremities by the motifs of prison (place of the flagellation) and tomb (place of the burial and resurrection).

When he describes the city's interior, this morbid vision's influence extends to the way he regards the residents themselves, pitiful puppets of a terrifying theater: "Enter the city, but nothing will you there find to make amends for the dulness of its exterior. . . . A few paltry shops expose nothing but wretchedness to view, and even these are frequently shut, from apprehension of the passage of a cadi. Not a creature is to be seen in the streets, not a creature at the gates." Passing by a butcher's stall, where he witnesses a quite ordinary scene, Chateaubriand reveals the pervasiveness of the religious representations that he mobilizes to comprehend what he sees: "Aside, in a corner, the Arab butcher is slaughtering some animal suspended by the legs from a wall in ruins: from his haggard and ferocious look, and his bloody hands, you would rather suppose that he had been cutting the throat of a fellow creature than killing a lamb." The folklorization process at work in the pilgrim's cultural representations clearly appears here: rather than a professional butcher simply doing his job, Chateaubriand describes a "textual scene," imaginary but foundational for the three monotheisms, that of the sacrifice of Isaac/Ishmael, who was saved in extremis by the immolation of the lamb (Gn 22). Nothing in this scene, however, should have made Chateaubriand's narrative go off the rails. . . . Nothing except the essential: his imagination and his interpretations—in other words, everything at his disposal for understanding the city he surveyed.

Moreover, Jerusalem in its globality appeared to him like a condemned entity: "The only noise heard from time to time in this deicide city is the galloping of the steed of the desert: it is the janissary who brings the head of the Bedouin, or returns from plundering the unhappy Fellah." This truly extravagant vision should be interpreted in the general context of Christian pilgrimage's psychic economy, which makes Jerusalem the setting and, in a way, the guilty principle of Christ's death. The morbid view of the Holy City, reduced to a collection of prisons and tombs in which every mundane scene becomes macabre, stems without a doubt from this global system of representations. After Chateaubriand's founding account, which all pilgrims thenceforth carried in their luggage, this vision imposed itself as a topos of Jerusalem travel literature.

Imperial City, Consular City

Anyone traveling in Jerusalem today cannot help but be struck by the huge number of vehicles with white license plates with the abbreviation "CC," for "consular corps." World city, global city, meeting point of all powers, the Holy City indeed became, in the nineteenth century, a "consular" city—that is, a conglomeration in which, in addition to diverse local communities, an incalculable number of international emissaries, mediators, and diplomats lived together. This particular physiognomy dates back to the 1830s to 1850s, when the first consulates established a foothold in Jerusalem. The Western powers' interference is attributable to the renewed interest generated by the Middle East since Napoleon's expedition but especially by fallout from the occupation of Palestine by the army of Muhammad ʿAli, Egypt's viceroy, who was in revolt against the Ottoman government: between 1831 and 1840, the Holy City was in fact ruled from Cairo, with the active support of France, which hoped to see the anti-Ottoman insurrection that Napoleon had dreamed of three decades earlier finally come to fruition.[38] To counter French aims, the United Kingdom backed the Ottoman government in its battle to contain its restless Egyptian vassal, but also took advantage of this opportunity to establish a first consulate in Jerusalem. Indeed, Muhammad ʿAli was a fervent reformer, open to European influences, and he considerably reevaluated the rights of non-Muslim residents in the cities that he governed.

The project to establish a British consular post in Jerusalem initially came up against the city's exceptional character, as Patrick Campbell, the British consul in Alexandria, emphasized in a letter addressed to his superiors on September 19, 1838: "Jerusalem being one of the Holy Cities, he [Muhammad ʿAli] could not take upon himself to sanction such an appointment there, unless he (the Pacha) should have a Firman to that effect from the Sultan. . . . It is true that there is not a Consular Agent of any other Power in Jerusalem." A few weeks later, the negotiations were successful and the future consul William Young's area of operation had to be specified: "As Mr. Young is appointed Vice Consul for all Palestine, I have directed him to take under his charge and Jurisdiction the Several Parts in Palestine where there are British Consular Agents, and I have made a communication to that effect to Her Majesty's Consuls at Damascus and Beyrout." This apparently innocuous administrative decision was in fact crucially important in Jerusalem's history: for the first time since the fall of the Latin Crusader states, the European powers were placing the Holy City at the center of a clearly identified territory, "Palestine." The process by which Jerusalem gradually acquired the status of *capital*—which led to its administrative reevaluation by the Ottoman government in 1872 (from that date, the district of Jerusalem was directly connected to Istanbul) and then resulted in its "political nationalization" by Zionist and Arab nationalist leaders at the beginning of the next century—finds its origin here. The British consul's installation had another future-deciding consequence: the very first framework letter sent to the new consul by the British government explicitly highlights his role among Palestine's Jewish populations, stating, "Mr Young's duties in Palestine will not be merely commercial, but I should suppose that one great and perhaps the chief object of his duties will be the protection of the Jewish Nation in general."[39] Here is the first concrete manifestation of Protestant millenarian support for the establishment of a Jewish homeland in Palestine.

The British consul's installation was not slow to provoke a response from other European powers: Prussia opened its own consulate in 1842, and then it was the turn of France, which put the comte de Lantivy in place in summer 1843. On that occasion, the French tricolor was raised at the consular officer's house and a riot broke out against what was considered provocative interference.[40] This affair sheds light on the figure of Jerusalem's *nakib el-eshraf*, representative of the major aristocratic families and defender of the interests of the city's notables: Abdallah al-Alami, who then occupied the position and whom France's consul named "the Leader of Jerusalem's Greats," denounced the actions of Governor Rashid Pasha and provided the names of the rioters in a letter to Istanbul.[41] In the end, he secured the incriminated governor's dismissal: "The *nakib el-eshraf*'s journey from Jaffa to Jerusalem was a triumphal march; he entered, accompanied by the Cadi of Jaffa and Ramla and a large procession of effendis [notables]. . . . The diploma confirming his titles, rank, and post in Jerusalem, which I transmitted to him, brought him great joy. . . . The [new] Pasha promised me that he himself would give the *nakib* a robe of honor."[42] This piece of consular correspondence is a measure of the *nakib el-eshraf*'s eminent role in representing local notables and defending the Holy City's interests, even against high-ranking Ottoman officials.

In a report addressed to Paris, the French consul described the authority, not only moral but also properly political, that Jerusalem's *nakib el-eshraf* enjoyed: "The *nakib* also has indirect jurisdiction over the guilds of merchants and tradesmen. This is how: the heads of all these guilds are poor nobles with no livelihood other than their work or trade. A large number of simple craftsmen and merchants are also in the 'sharif,' or noble, class. It follows that no ruling can be enforced against these individuals without notice first being given to the *nakib*, who generally endeavors to reconcile disagreements even before they go before the judge."[43] A representative figure of a particular urban consciousness, the *nakib* thus served both to mediate and to resolve conflict, thanks to the control he exercised over the guilds of merchants and craftsmen. As we can see, in certain circumstances his authority allowed him to evade the governor's theoretically eminent authority.

In any event, the installation of the first European consulates provoked a rearrangement of the powers inside the Holy City. In the mid-nineteenth century, Jerusalem became both an imperial and a consular city, housing a more open society in which each could take advantage of the room for maneuver presented by the appearance of these opposing forces.[44] On March 1, 1848, on the occasion of the new governor's arrival, the French consul straightforwardly asserted the role that the European consulates intended to play from then on: "The pasha openly declares that he intends to deal with the Holy Land's affairs without consular intervention. . . . Is this pasha in his second childhood?"[45]

JERUSALEM AT THE END OF THE NINETEENTH CENTURY: UNDER THE HOLY SITES, THE CITY

The Ottoman period's final decades are little known, although they were a pivotal moment in Jerusalem's history: between 1850 and 1914, the city underwent dramatic changes. At the institutional level, the reforms initiated in the 1830s by the Egyptian occupiers were extended within the framework of the Ottomans' administrative reforms (*tanzimat*) and then continued from the 1860s onward through a "municipalization" of urban powers: at century's end, Jerusalem's city council, a mixed and intercommunal institution, established itself as the unavoidable pivot of city politics by progressively enlarging its range of authority. This administrative modernity went hand in hand with the spectacular modernization of the urban environment thanks to the organization of numerous municipal facilities, which contributed to the blossoming of a new urbanite identity, more secularized and better shared by the city's different communities.[46] At the demographic level, the Holy City experienced a meteoric rise beginning in the 1860s: it counted fifteen thousand inhabitants in 1850 and seventy thousand in 1914—in fifty years, the population multiplied fivefold and a new city emerged outside the walls, profoundly modifying Jerusalem's physiognomy (see map 9 in chapter 7). At the time of the

Young Turk Revolution in summer 1908, the Ottoman constitution's restoration was loudly fêted by the Holy City's residents, who marched side by side and expressed themselves in every language to celebrate the strengthening of civil liberties. In these few decades, Jerusalem enjoyed a rich and singular moment in its history, during which a real city community seems to have emerged, even if the increasing power of nationalisms beginning in the 1920s would soon overcome this "age of possibilities."[47]

The Municipalization of Urban Powers

To clear away the hackneyed notion of a Holy City ruined and immobile at the end of the Ottoman era, fragmented among religious communities in perpetual conflict, it is necessary to go back to local sources and turn toward the history of lay institutions of urban management, which, in Jerusalem as elsewhere, made the city and its residents. Indeed, Jerusalem was one of the first Ottoman Empire cities to establish a mixed council, in 1863 or 1867—in any case, well before an imperial law of 1877 required it.[48] It was at the end of an endogenous process spurred on by local notables that the Holy City formed an interfaith municipal council at an early stage, belying the image of a "battlefield city," just an unstable aggregate of competing holy places.

This municipal institution's history has long been passed over in silence, as it accords poorly with traditional clichés. Its importance has been reevaluated only in the past ten years or so, thanks in particular to the discovery of records of municipal proceedings (preserved for the period 1892–1917 with just a few gaps), which are now the subject of exhaustive transcription and translation work.[49] This never-before-seen source provides access to the daily administrative practice of this organization that was able to resolve conflicts between the city's different communities until the mid-1930s. Of course, the municipalization of urban powers was not without its difficulties: over the nineteenth century, the city councillors had to assert, little by little, their legitimacy against the Ottoman governor and the European consuls, who at first jealously defended their prerogatives.

In this regard, the 1830s were decisive. While Palestine was occupied by Egyptian troops, many sources report, a *majlis alshura* (literally "council assembly") was put in place by the new authorities, with representatives of all the religious communities, great families, and guild heads, under the personal leadership of the *nakib el-eshraf*.[50] The opening of the first European consulates, beginning in 1839, doubtless accelerated the municipalization process, which the local notables envisaged as a means of fighting against attempts at interference by the consular powers. In 1853, the British consul James Finn asserted that the council of notables had been meeting regularly in Jerusalem "for at least four years."

In the 1860s, the signs of a municipal action multiplied in the archives: in 1866, the Convent of the Sisters of Zion on the Via Dolorosa received a construction permit (*mazbata*) from the municipality for expansion work;[51] the archives of the same convent yield, from two years later, in 1868, a "construction permit from the municipality authorizing the construction of an orphanage, subject to alignment with the public road, with a copy of the boundary report."[52] It is clear that an authentic municipal institution (*belediye*) had already been in place for some time, capable of affecting the built environment thanks to proven monitoring tools. In 1875, the famous British Jewish philanthropist Moses Montefiore, who could hardly be suspected of an indulgent attitude toward local institutions, enthused over the progress made by the municipality during one of his frequent visits to Jerusalem: "All houses must now be built . . . according to a plan approved of by the Government. . . . It being part of [the mayor's] duty to see the law in question carried out in the proper sense of the word, he finds it sometimes difficult to convince the builders of the utility and importance thereof."[53]

The Ottoman law of 1877 on provincial city councils (*vilayet belediye kanunu*) reinforced the Jerusalem municipality's autonomy vis-à-vis foreign powers, for example by specifying that a municipal councillor "should not be employed and consequently protected by a foreign power or lay claim to a foreign nationality" (Article 19).[54] Already in 1868, the British consul had complained that foreign residents were obliged to pay the municipal taxes without being able to sit on the council. Besides the electoral code, the law of 1877 clarifies the extent of municipal jurisdiction (in particular the supervision of building construction, the road network, and public transportation; the monitoring of drinking water, sewers, and public health; the maintenance of public order; and firefighting). Here again we see that Jerusalem was ahead of the empire's other cities, because its council had a good number of these responsibilities before the law of 1877. In January 1873, for instance, the mayor, Yusuf Diya al-Khalidi, wrote (in French) to the German consul as "municipal president," whose duty was "to protect the population of his city from all harmful things," to demand that Jewish butchers of German nationality stop slaughtering "thin and anemic" steers in Jerusalem's abattoirs.[55] Three years earlier, during the particularly dry summer of 1870, the same al-Khalidi had succeeded in reaffirming municipal ownership of an underground spring at the end of a power struggle against the French consul.[56]

It should be added that the municipalization of urban powers, from the 1830s to the law of 1877, was accompanied by a geographic extension of the municipality's jurisdiction, thus helping to reinforce the Holy City's stature as the capital of the gestating Palestinian territory. Beginning in 1872, the district (sanjak) of Jerusalem was no longer a dependency of the province of Damascus but was directly connected to Istanbul. Jerusalem's area of influence expanded: its city council controlled, for example, the budget of the Bethlehem municipality from the latter's foundation in 1894, was also responsible for granting building permits "in the neighboring villages" starting in the 1880s, and played a decisive role in the construction and renovation of regional roads toward Jaffa, Hebron, Jericho, and Nablus.[57]

Municipal Taxation: Under the Communities, the Social Classes?

Beyond the institutional and geographic bounds of its operations, did Jerusalem's municipality have the financial resources to match its ambitions? The sources clearly indicate municipal revenue growth during the period from 1860 to 1914, with a city budget of around one thousand Turkish liras at the end of the 1860s, three thousand at the end of the 1870s, eight thousand in the 1890s, and up to about twelve or even fourteen thousand just before World War I.[58] The increase in municipal budgets was directly linked to the city's economic development, since the municipality's revenues came from three types of levies (rüsumu): first, taxes on merchandise licenses and tolls on the Jaffa-Jerusalem road and railway; second, various taxes relating to the slaughter and sale of livestock; and third, taxes on construction permits and capital gains on land. These three major income streams were joined by diverse levies of less significance, such as taxes on cars and carts, on street lighting and cleaning, and on garbage disposal. Some of this revenue was directly allocated to specific expenditures: the toll on the Jaffa-Jerusalem road, for example, financed the construction and then the operation of the new municipal hospital, inaugurated in 1891 to offer free medical care to all the city's inhabitants (whether Muslims, Jews, or Christians), as well as the expenses of the municipal pharmacy, established the following year (see map 9 in chapter 7). In 1887, the French consul noted that the annual revenue generated by this toll had risen to twenty-five hundred Turkish liras, or sixteen times what it had been when the road opened in 1869.[59]

Beginning in the 1880s, the municipality sought to consolidate its financial base by renting stores that it had constructed outside the city walls, near the Jaffa Gate. This increased fiscal autonomy allowed it to undertake more beautification and modernization projects (see map 9 in chapter 7): paving the city's main arteries in 1885; creating a municipal park (al-Muntazah al-Baladi) in 1892; inaugurating the new railway station, also in 1892; building a new town hall in 1895; inaugurating a monumental public fountain, by the Jaffa Gate, in 1900; financing and opening Jerusalem's first theater in 1904; modernizing the street lighting, with the installation of "Lux" lamps in the area of the municipal park, in 1906; inaugurating a monumental clock twenty-five meters (eighty-two feet) high at the Jaffa Gate in 1907; and inviting bids on a tramway project in 1910—a project that was interrupted by the war and finally saw the light of day, in a very different form . . . only in 2011.

Local taxation is thus a good window onto municipal actions and the city's dynamism at the turn of the nineteenth into the twentieth century. But its interest to the historian goes much further, because it was also the laboratory of an urban consciousness and a public opinion that emerged then. In fall 1909, for example, Jerusalem's inhabitants struggled to find a new revenue source capable of financing the modernization of the drinking-water distribution network, which was sorely lacking because of the city's rapid population growth. The Palestine Chamber of Commerce, Industry, and Agriculture, whose members were the most influential local notables of all the city's communities, fully engaged in the debate and suggested funding the work with "the leather concession for butchered animals, which serious experts say produces more than 120,000 francs [5,000 Turkish liras] per year."[60] The tax on pelts, a direct legacy of the market police's premunicipal powers, appears to have been the preliminary base of municipal budgetary autonomy for the large Ottoman cities, which the petition's signatories indeed confirmed by evoking "the precedents established in Beirut and Damascus."

Beyond the fiscal and technical debate, the specifically political argument put forward by this affair's lead actors must be considered: "This indirect tax will in no way strain the budgets of the poorest, as meat is still for the rich in Jerusalem. . . . No country was ever seen to double the price of water to reduce that of meat by 5 percent." The rich and the poor—in other words, the meat eaters and the water drinkers . . . search though we might, in this debate there is no place for religious identities or intercommunal conflicts. This example, among others, enables the observation of a largely ignored feature of Ottoman Jerusalem's history: under the religious and community categories definitively affixed by outside observers, other categories and other conflicts are perceptible if one takes the trouble to read local sources. The conduct of municipal business and the discussions that arose among residents about taxation and spending priorities thus lift the veil on a Holy City that is also a city and on its Muslim, Jewish, and Christian inhabitants, who were also city dwellers.

Demographic Growth and Increase of Urban Diversity

Jerusalem's Old City—in Ottoman times and today—is generally presented as a juxtaposition of four homogenous neighborhoods with impermeable boundaries: the "Muslim" Quarter in the northeast, the "Christian" Quarter in the northwest, the "Armenian" Quarter in the southwest, and the "Jewish" Quarter in the southeast. This rough quadripartition testifies to a number of historical misinterpretations. First, it prevents perception of the internal differences that ran through each of these supposed "communities," erasing the complex history of a settlement composed of successive migrations, to which toponyms still in use among the local population refer. More seriously, this rough-hewn cartography, which focuses exclusively on the city *intra muros*, stops us from seeing late nineteenth-century Jerusalem's most important urban phenomenon: namely, its expansion beyond the walls. The causes of the new *extra muros* town's rise were mundanely demographic: Jerusalem counted ten thousand inhabitants around 1800, about fifteen thousand around 1850, twenty thousand in 1870, forty-five thousand in 1890, and more than seventy thousand in 1914. The population, which thus increased sevenfold in a century, quickly found itself cramped inside an enclosure measuring barely one square kilometer (0.4 square miles).

Beginning in the 1880s, when Jewish immigration to Palestine and Jerusalem swelled, this change accelerated: in 1880, the population *extra muros* comprised only two thousand of the city's thirty thousand inhabitants (6 percent); in 1897, at the moment when the economic crisis temporarily interrupted real estate speculation, it was twenty-five of fifty-five thousand (almost 50 percent). The impact of this process must be carefully assessed: the Holy City, entirely concentrated between narrow walls, all of whose residents had lived for long centuries in close proximity to its holy sites and places of traditional power, literally cut itself in half to allow the emergence, in less than twenty years, of an entirely new city, characterized in some neighborhoods by an even greater denominational diversity than was found in the city *intra muros* (the 1905 census shows, for example, that the population in the Talbiyeh and Baka neighborhoods, near the railway station, was 32 percent Jewish, 47 percent Christian, and 21 percent Muslim; see map 9 in chapter 7).

Far from the legacy of an ancient tradition, the Old City's simplistic division into four impermeable community-based segments rests on a late cartographic invention. Before 1837, no cartographer of Jerusalem assigned the slightest ethnic or religious characterization to any part of the Old City; its segmentation into four solid-color blocks first appeared only in 1853, on a German map, after which tourist maps for pilgrims systematically adopted the model, which persists today.[61] Local administrative sources, for their part, largely contradict this Western view and refer to the great diversity of the different neighborhoods, including in the Old City. Figures from the 1905 census thus reveal that in the al-Wad area, which is immediately northwest of the Haram and an integral part of the so-called Muslim Quarter, there were more Jewish (388) than Muslim (383) family heads. In the Bab al-Silsila neighborhood, in the heart of the "Jewish" Quarter, 548 family heads were Muslim, against 711 Jewish (see map 8). Final example: in the Sa'diyya area, east of the Damascus Gate and thus in the middle of the so-called Muslim Quarter, 124 family heads were Christian, while 161 were Muslim.[62]

Clearly, working with endogenous administrative sources reveals that there was no ethnoreligious homogeneity within the four supposed quarters of Jerusalem. If we sum up such deviations from the "norm" based on the 1905 census, we find that 29 percent of the Muslim families in Jerusalem lived in the so-called Jewish Quarter, while 32 percent of Jewish families and 24 percent of Christian families lived in the "Muslim" Quarter. . . . The numbers speak for themselves: at the beginning of the twentieth century, Jerusalem's four famous community-based quarters did not correspond to the city's demographic reality.

Identity Projections: City Dwellers or Citizens?

How can we know if Jerusalem's inhabitants shared a common urban identity at the end of the nineteenth and beginning of the twentieth century or if they were already projecting themselves into the citizenships of nations yet to be constructed? The question is essential, going to the heart of past and present developments in the Holy City, but it is difficult to answer. If we place ourselves at the end of the nineteenth century, we must first of all avoid anachronistically focusing on national or religious associations alone and recall the Ottoman imperial background's importance in structuring the identities of the Holy City's inhabitants. Indeed, the Ottoman Empire gathered together majority-Muslim and majority-Christian provinces but also cities quite strongly marked by Jewish culture, such as Salonika (now Thessaloníki), which in 1900 counted 90,000 Jews in a total population of 130,000. At the empire's head, the sultan had the title of caliph (the commander of the Muslim faithful) but also derived his legitimacy from a certain universalism, the foundation of all supranational imperial ideology.

Far from losing ground, this imperial ideological matrix was reactivated at the end of the nineteenth century when the Young Turks—heirs of the Young Ottomans, whose movement had been active since the 1850s—burst onto the Ottoman political scene. Inspired by the French

Revolution's universalism and by the Masonic lodges that had multiplied throughout the empire's major cities, the Young Ottomans and then the Young Turks brought together the various minorities and proposed a regeneration of the supranational imperial ideology to overcome emerging religious and national rivalries: deeply involved in carrying out administrative reforms (*tanzimat*), the Young Turks thus traced the contours of a possible new *Pax Ottomanica* which could preserve the empire's territorial integrity by canalizing national aspirations.[63] As is well known, the acceleration of centrifugal nationalist demands, the imperial government's Turkist and nationalist turn after 1912, the alliance with Germany in 1913, and then the empire's dismemberment at the end of World War I ultimately defeated this project of "Ottoman revival." But its failure should not obscure Ottomanism's appeal in the 1870s to 1910s, particularly in the most cosmopolitan cities, such as Alexandria, Beirut, Salonika . . . and Jerusalem.[64]

It is all the more difficult to grasp the identity postures of Jerusalem's inhabitants at the end of the nineteenth century because individual trajectories reveal many surprises. The celebrated scholar Eliezer Ben-Yehuda, a native of what was then the Russian Empire's Lithuania governorate who emigrated to Palestine in 1881 as a resolute Zionist, thus described the identity unease that he felt on his arrival there by evoking the Arab residents: "I sensed that they felt themselves to be citizens of the land of my forefathers, and I, despite being a descendant of those forefathers, was coming to it as a stranger, a citizen of a foreign country, a member of a foreign nation. . . . Here is the reality, the actuality! These are citizens of the land, they dwell in it, they lead their lives in it, and we—we are scattered in the Diaspora throughout every country in the world." When he went to Jerusalem for the first time, his distress only worsened: "I entered, by way of Jaffa Gate, this holy city, this city of David, King of Israel, desolate, destroyed, and utterly humiliated, and no special feeling was aroused in my heart. . . . Almost in complete apathy, as if I were walking along any street in any city in the world, I passed all the way from Jaffa Gate to the site of the Temple."[65] To fully appreciate this astonishing narrative's significance, it must be understood that in 1881 Ben-Yehuda was already convinced of the Zionist project's relevance, of the necessity for a Jewish national revival in Palestine as protection against European anti-Semitism;

he was a great biblical expert and at the origin of Hebrew's restoration as a
national language. . . . A priori, his attachment to Jerusalem should therefore have been immediate. The unease that Ben-Yehuda expressed is perhaps explained by the discovery of a city that was doubtless more modern
and secularized than he had imagined from afar.

Another document helps to identify the uncertain contours of the
"Jerusalem urbanity" that seems to have emerged at the end of the nineteenth century: the letter that Jerusalem's former mayor Yusuf Diya al-
Khalidi sent on March 1, 1899, to the founder of the modern Zionist
movement, Theodor Herzl, via the chief rabbi of France Zadoc Kahn.
Declaring that he was acting "for the tranquillity of the Jews," against
whom he feared a possible "popular movement," al-Khalidi asked Herzl to
reorient his national project toward other territories and concluded his
missive (written in French) with "In the name of God, leave Palestine
alone."[66] This letter was penned less than two years after political Zionism's
founding congress, held in Basel in August 1897. Historians agree that it
is one of the first examples of the anti-Zionist reaction in Palestine, but
they fail to point out that this attitude emanated from one of the Jerusalem
municipality's eminent figures, since Yusuf Diya al-Khalidi was the city's
mayor between 1870 and 1876 before being elected as its deputy in the
first Ottoman legislative elections, also in 1876. Let us quote the passage
of his letter that refers to a "Jerusalem urbanity" joining interreligious syn-
cretism, defense of the "common good," and sincere loyalty to the Ottoman
Empire: "I was mayor of Jerusalem for ten years, and afterward this city's
deputy in the imperial parliament, which I still am; I am now working for
the good of this city, to bring it clean water. I am thus in a position to speak
to you with full knowledge of the facts. We consider ourselves, we Arabs
and Turks, guardians of the sites equally sacred to the three religions—
Judaism, Christianity, and Islam. Well, how can the leaders of Zionism
imagine that they might wrest these sacred sites from the two other religions, which account for the vast majority?" Yusuf Diya al-Khalidi's position thus highlights the singularity of Jerusalem's urban identity, which he
considered to be historically based on surmounting religious categories.

This type of identity positioning, far from the prerogative of the city's
Muslim elites, was shared by some of the Jewish community's most
eminent members. Albert Antébi, the director of the Alliance israélite

universelle (AIU; Universal Israelite alliance) in Jerusalem, to whom the French diplomatic corps granted the unofficial title "consul of the Jews," thus addressed Narcisse Leven, the president of the AIU in Paris, on January 8, 1900: "You know I'm not a Zionist. Situated in Jerusalem for more than three years . . . , I can measure the extent of the evil done to Judaism by this noxious campaign. It has set the Ottoman authorities against us, made the Muslim population distrustful of any progress of ours. . . . I esteem Jerusalem for its historic past, but I don't believe in its future for our nation."[67] This last sentence rings oddly today, since it is clear that Antébi's predictions have turned out to be wrong. Yet this is exactly what makes the forgotten testimonies of Ben-Yehuda, al-Khalidi, and Antébi valuable: they are reminders that history is never written in advance and that at the end of the Ottoman period the city of Jerusalem was the crucible of an urban identity undoubtedly less compartimentalized than has been believed until now.

The Revolution of 1908 in Jerusalem: Fraternité?

Comparing sources thus reveals that Jerusalem's nineteenth-century history cannot be written exclusively from a teleological perspective: if one aligns one's gaze with that of the inhabitants themselves, one cannot consider this period the simple prehistory of the regional and international drama that played out over the next century. To understand the particular historical dynamics at play in the Holy City in the nineteenth century, the story of the celebration of the Young Turk Revolution is a good vantage point, even if this event is generally absent from great historical panoramas of Jerusalem.

At the beginning of August 1908, three weeks after the promulgation of the constitution by the Young Turks, Jerusalem was jubilant. This liberal constitution, first promulgated in 1876 but suspended several months later, allowed national minorities to envisage the empire's genuine democratization within a renovated federal framework. Although Governor 'Ali Ekrem Bey had planned to publicly proclaim the new constitution on Saturday, August 8, all the sources report that huge, spontaneous demonstrations of tens of thousands of people began gathering the day before:

They shout, they sing; the band tries to make itself heard, but the musicians, separated by the crowd, cannot come together and are unable to finish a single bar. . . . The soldiers form a solid honor guard but they are overwhelmed, and the crowd crushes in along the path they form from the gate to the official gallery, as in the surrounding areas. . . . The demonstrations also continue, to the despair of the peaceful bourgeois, who no longer sleep at night. Turks, Greeks, Jews, Latins, and Armenians meet in different neighborhoods and then roam the streets, singing and firing guns. They make many speeches, they call one another "brother," they embrace, they swear allegiance to the Young Turks' motto, "Liberty, equality, justice, fraternity." [68]

This explosion of collective joy lasted several weeks, accompanied by strikes and petitions of all kinds, and uncorked the creation of multiple political newspapers, such as the Hebrew *Ha-Ḥerut* (Liberty) and the Arabic *Falestin* (Palestine).

What struck witnesses the most was the simultaneous presence in the streets of all the components of urban society:

All the races rub elbows, all the religions fraternize there. The Jews, with magnificent yellow or purple velvet coats and fur hats, surround their banner, which has the Tables of the Law embroidered in gold on a blue ground. . . . The Armenian seminarians are no less enthusiastic: they sing at the top of their lungs and carry small red flags. The Greeks surround about a dozen Hellenic flags. . . . The black turbans of the Copts are also spotted. . . . The imams circulate in the middle of the crowd, and the dervishes are recognized by their big yellow felt hats, which strangely call to mind overturned flower vases. Everyone wears the red-and-white cockade, the constitutional cockade. [69]

The great local Hebrew newspaper *Ha-Ḥavatzelet* (The lily) very straightforwardly interpreted the exaltation that had seized Jerusalem's population: "All those who are under the Ottoman government's protection, without any distinction of religion or nationality, will be called Ottomans." [70] Many Jerusalem inhabitants thus sincerely partook in Ottomanist ideology as a potential bulwark against nationalist competitions at the beginning of the twentieth century.

Speeches, incessant and polyglot, were the other element that struck observers. Sir John Gray Hill, a lawyer from Liverpool who had owned a large estate on Mount Scopus since the end of the 1880s, thus wrote for the London *Times* that "speeches are made daily in public places and in the streets, which are nightly crowded and illuminated."[71] The official authorities spoke, but so did ordinary city dwellers who tried to make the Young Turks' motto their own: "A young Jews shouts to us in French: 'Hey! We have it—freedom! Long live the Constitution!' 'Will it last?' 'Oh! yes, it will last, why don't you want it to last?' . . . On the Armenian group's exit, a young seminarian climbs onto the rim of a cistern and, from this improvised pulpit, harangues the crowd. He praises the sultan. . . . The Greek group comes next, still surrounding its white-and-blue flags. They all shout, '*Zito eleftheria!* Long live liberty!' with extraordinary ardor."[72] The public speeches, the spread of debates and ideas, testified to the emergence of an educated middle class capable of expressing itself, reading, and communicating in several languages.

That revolutionary time was also an opportunity to make economic and social demands beyond ethnic or religious differences. The Jerusalem-Jaffa route's coach drivers thus went on strike for pay raises; a movement also crystallized that demanded the end of census suffrage and a transition to universal male suffrage in municipal elections. Some speakers denounced the administration's taxation excesses, with a tone that clearly borrowed from the vocabulary of the class struggle:

> The speaker is railing against the government, its pillages and injustices, when, spying a group of effendis, he shouts, "And you too, you must repent your injustices! You have pressured the people by again demanding the taxes that have been paid, by taking three or four times the tithe. You have starved the poor while you have plenty. Change your ways, repent, and repair the past if you don't want the people's justice to take revenge and punish you!" And the speaker sits, tired, but one of the effendis rises and, offering him a glass of lemonade, says: "What you say doesn't offend us, because it's the truth. Rest, then continue!"[73]

This surprising scene says a lot about the atmosphere and the freedom of speech then prevailing in the Holy City, both of which its inhabitants seized hold of. There is no doubt about it: in Jerusalem, in August 1908, the revolution did indeed take place.

Beyond the rhetoric of fraternization, most witnesses observed that the slogan "Liberty, equality, justice" ("Hurriyya, musawah, 'adala" in Arabic) was concretized by the free access of all the inhabitants to all the city's holy sites. However, a detailed analysis of the processions and the reactions to them in each of the communities reveals that behind this facade of unanimity, conflicts were reappearing, but not in the expected ways:

> Rumor has it that from now on one can freely circulate everywhere, even in the Mosque of 'Umar, which one could formerly enter only if escorted by a Turkish kavass or soldier. . . . The Jewish group, banner ahead, goes directly to the Mosque of 'Umar, toward that corner of land which, for eleven centuries, from Solomon to Jerusalem's destruction by Titus, was the unique theater of the people of God's religious life. For fifteen hundred years, entry was forbidden to the children of Israel; today the imams enthusiastically welcome them, embrace them, serve them refreshments: all are brothers, all are Ottomans! Let's hope it lasts![74]

This scene well illustrates the fraternal mood during those revolutionary days; it supports the theory of a real appropriation of Ottomanist ideology by Jerusalem's inhabitants. To appreciate the significance of this symbolic image, one must remember the bullying that David Reubeni suffered in 1523 and imagine the group of visiting Jews carrying at its head a banner with "the Tables of the Law embroidered in gold on a blue ground" and being welcomed "enthusiastically" by the Muslim authorities who guarded the Esplanade of the Mosques. This simple anecdote gives an idea of how singular Jerusalem's history was in the first decade of the 1900s and how difficult it is to represent today but also how necessary it is to preserve a record of it.

In the Holy City, the Revolution of 1908 was not, however, synonymous with systematic fellowship among all the inhabitants. Despite the collective jubilation, fault lines appeared or reappeared within the urban community, but the conflicts were not structured on the binary, current today, that opposes Jews against Arab Palestinians. For proof, let us read the rest of the correspondent's account in the Catholic magazine *Jerusalem*, which suddenly takes a deliberately anti-Semitic turn:

> Liberty! This word has not yet been precisely defined, and each person understands it in their own way. The Jews interpreted it in a sense that almost became tragic. It is known that entrance to the Holy Sepulchre is forbidden to them. What would they do there anyway? Does this place not

remind them of their crime? . . . The Jews, however, thought otherwise. To assert their liberty, they resolved to come in a crowd to the Holy Sepulchre's parvis. . . . But we were warned. Greeks, Armenians, Latins—all were ready and waiting for them. They argued, they jostled one another, the Jews threatened, the Christians held steady, and, before this resolute attitude, the Jews understood that they would not be the strongest and retreated to their ghetto, swearing to return. They did not return and did well not to.[75]

The description of this pathetic scene recollects a truth that, however distressing it may be today, is no less incontestable: at the beginning of the twentieth century, Christian anti-Judaism was the real main breeding ground for anti-Semitism, including in Jerusalem.

7 The Impossible Capital?

JERUSALEM IN THE TWENTIETH CENTURY

After four centuries (1516–1917) of Ottoman presence marked by a certain continuity, Jerusalem entered the twentieth century in a phase of great instability resulting from ruptures and plans for partition. The image that emerges is one of a city engaged in a war, or rather a succession of wars that each redirected the Holy City's destiny: World War I, by bringing about the fall of the Ottoman Empire, which had allied with Germany, placed Jerusalem under British mandate; starting in the 1930s, the competition between Zionist Jews and Arab nationalists resulted in a situation of guerrilla insurrection, including in Jerusalem; the first Arab-Israeli conflict, of 1948–49, led to its partition between Jordan, which controlled the eastern half and the Old City, and the new State of Israel, which controlled the western half and the new part of town; the Six-Day War of 1967 ended with Israel's annexation of the whole agglomeration and marked the beginning of its East Jerusalem settlement policy (see map 10); the First Intifada (1987–93) and then the "al-Aqsa" (Second) Intifada (2000–2004) showed that the reunification of the Holy City unilaterally decreed by the Israeli parliament (Knesset) in 1980 had not narrowed the gap between West and East Jerusalem, which are still characterized by profound disparities. In less than a century, Jerusalem became a capital claimed by two peoples, the pivotal element of the Israeli-Palestinian conflict, and this is how most observers regard the city today.

However, the history of twentieth-century Jerusalem cannot be reduced to that of a battlefield, the mere theater of a war that extended well beyond it. If we wish to grasp its materiality, we must not cling to the staggering geopolitical ruptures that have occurred recently but rather bear in mind a certain amount of long-term topographical and demographic data. Over the course of the twentieth century, for instance, the Holy City's population grew from around seventy thousand before World War I to today's eight hundred thousand. Despite the vagaries of history, the overall demographic balance between Jerusalem's Jewish and Arab inhabitants has not undergone any real upheaval: the Holy City housed about forty thousand Jews (63 percent) and about thirty thousand Arabs (Muslims and Christians) in 1914; today it counts five hundred thousand Jews (63 percent) and three hundred thousand Arabs within the limits of the current Israeli municipality. Geographically, the city's expansion was evident: in the early 1880s, almost all of Jerusalem's population was squeezed tight between the Old City's ramparts, in an area of barely one square kilometer (about 0.4 square miles); on the eve of World War I, the new part of town extended over a little less than ten square kilometers (less than 4 square miles; see map 9); and today the municipal boundaries of "Greater Jerusalem" surround two hundred square kilometers (77 square miles). If the dividing wall that Israeli authorities began constructing in 2002 had not isolated Jerusalem from its Palestinian neighbors, the Holy City would have formed a conurbation with the agglomerations of Ramallah to the north and Bethlehem to the south, within a metropolitan area of around four hundred square kilometers (154 square miles) if the settlement blocks to the north (Givat Ze'ev), south (Gush Etzion), and east (Ma'ale Adumim) were included (see map 10).

The maps and the numbers speak for themselves: Jerusalem's demographic and geographic expansion in the twentieth century went beyond strictly urban logic and illustrates the double process of "capitalization" that took just one century to transform a universal Holy City into a bicephalous political capital claimed by two states—one that already existed, Israel, and the other still to come, Palestine. In fact, Jerusalem's millennia-old history teaches us that this tension between universal and

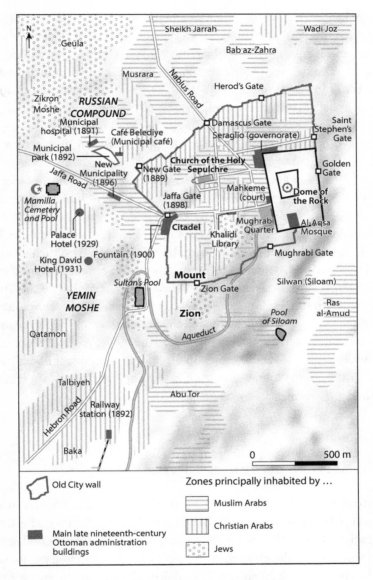

Map 9. Jerusalem "outside the walls" (1850–1948)

Map labels:

N

Sheikh Jarrah
Wadi Joz
Geula
Bab az-Zahra
Musrara
Herod's Gate
Nablus Road
Zikron Moshe
RUSSIAN COMPOUND
Municipal hospital (1891)
Café Belediye (Municipal café)
Damascus Gate
Saint Stephen's Gate
Seraglio (governorate)
Municipal park (1892)
New Municipality (1896)
New Gate (1889)
Church of the Holy Sepulchre
Golden Gate
Jaffa Road
Jaffa Gate (1898)
Mahkeme (court)
Dome of the Rock
Mamilla Cemetery and Pool
Citadel
Khalidi Library
Mughrabi Quarter
Al-Aqsa Mosque
Palace Hotel (1929)
Fountain (1900)
Mughrabi Gate
King David Hotel (1931)
Mount
Sultan's Pool
Zion Gate
Silwan (Siloam)
Ras al-Amud
YEMIN MOSHE
Zion
Pool of Siloam
Qatamon
Aqueduct
Talbiyeh
Abu Tor
Hebron Road
Railway station (1892)
Baka
0   500 m

Legend:

Old City wall

Main late nineteenth-century Ottoman administration buildings

Zones principally inhabited by …

Muslim Arabs

Christian Arabs

Jews

state polarities, between religious and political perspectives, far from being a twentieth-century novelty, is constitutive of the city's very identity. What is specific to the twentieth century is instead the change of political scene from an imperial to a national or even binational model: with the fall of the Ottoman Empire (1917) and then the British mandatary experiment's failure (1948), Jerusalem ceased to be just an ornamental jewel in a supranational (Egyptian, Roman, Byzantine, Persian, Umayyad, Fatimid, Mamluk, Ottoman, British) imperial crown and became the heart of dual nation-building projects. This new sequence of events in Jerusalem's age-old history resonates with the biblical narrative, in which the city appears as the capital of the Kingdom of Israel, which was founded about three thousand years ago by David and his son Solomon, but this chronological short circuit should not make us forget a fundamental historical reality: the contemporary "national" perspective, turned upside down by the rise of nationalisms in the nineteenth century, had nothing to do with the one that was current in the various "kingdoms" of the Middle East some three thousand years ago. It is precisely the supranational imperial framework's suspension and the national perspective's reconfiguration that have put Jerusalem's contemporary fate at stake. Contrary to appearances and to widespread opinion, this fate is unknown, if one admits that history is never written in advance—and that of Jerusalem less than any other.

JERUSALEM UNDER BRITISH MANDATE: THE CLASH OF COMMUNITARIANISMS

If Jerusalem's twentieth-century history is that of the passage from a supranational to a national or binational framework, then the British occupation (1917–48) appears as a tortuous and complex period of transition from one to the other. Legally, the mandate entrusted by the fledgling League of Nations to the United Kingdom in 1923 was a hybrid model, symptomatic of the passage from "the age of empires" to "the age of nations": on the one hand, Palestine was de facto integrated into the British imperial crown and the Colonial Office managed this small piece of land from London, but, on the other hand, the league explicitly requested that the mandatary authority allow the principle of the right of peoples to self-determination to bloom and flourish—which, it was not hard to imagine, would prove particularly difficult in the Palestinian context. Article 22 of the Covenant of the League of Nations thus stipulates that the territories placed under mandate "are inhabited by peoples not yet able to stand by themselves under the strenuous conditions of the modern world," that "the well-being and development of such peoples form a sacred trust of civilisation," and that "the best method of giving practical effect to this principle is that the tutelage of such peoples should be entrusted to advanced nations who by reason of their resources, their experience or their geographical position can best undertake this responsibility."[1] The mandate's original legal and political contradiction is obvious: this regime of colonial occupation was intended to be temporary and theoretically should have allowed the full development of the national aspirations of the people who were colonized—or, to use the official terminology, placed under "tutelage."

Article 22 goes on to specify that "the character of the mandate must differ according to the stage of the development of the people, the geographical situation of the territory, its economic conditions, and other similar circumstances." Regarding the Ottoman Empire's former territories, the decision was made to include the Middle East in the so-called Class A mandates because of the region's political, economic, and social maturity: "Certain communities formerly belonging to the Turkish Empire have reached a stage of development where their existence as independent nations can be provisionally recognised subject to the rendering of administrative advice and assistance by a Mandatory until such time as they are able to stand alone." Starting in the 1920s, therefore, Palestine fell under a complex and intrinsically contradictory politico-legal regime. In this new context, the competition between the Zionist project and Palestinian nationalism further accentuated the mandate's legal contradiction. In Jerusalem in particular, this new framework encouraged religious communitarianism, which the occupying power saw for a while as a way to maintain control of the situation, according to the principle of divide and conquer. In hindsight, the clash of communitarianisms in Jerusalem throughout the 1920s and 1930s thus seems like a symptom of the delicate transition from a supranational imperial framework to a binational one.

World War I, a Historic Ordeal for Jerusalem

Unlike World War II, which Jerusalem passed through almost without mishap and with a strangely peaceful atmosphere (see below), World War I was a particularly painful time for the Holy City, as attested by the decline in its population, which fell from seventy thousand in 1914 to only forty-five thousand in 1917. A critical juncture between the Ottoman imperial and British mandatary periods, the three years from November 1914 to December 1917 are nonetheless little known and poorly documented.[2] The closure of the consulates of the Triple Entente (France, the United Kingdom, and Russia), which are essential sources of information for historians of the Holy City, may partly explain this abrupt "vacuum" in Jerusalem's history. Let us try, however, to reconstruct the sequence of events.

The Ottoman Empire did not immediately make public the alliance it had sealed with Germany in August 1914, but it officially annulled the so-called regime of capitulations, which guaranteed a number of privileges to foreign subjects in Jerusalem, on October 1, 1914. The Turkist-nationalist wing had taken over the Young Turks' revolutionary movement in January 1913 and then imposed its will on the Ottoman government—the defeats suffered by the Ottoman army during the Balkan Wars in 1912 had discredited the liberal-federalist wing and started the imperial government on a headlong rush toward authoritarianism. Between November 2 and 5, 1914, Russia, France, and the United Kingdom declared war on the Ottoman Empire, and the consuls of these three powers had to hastily vacate the Holy City. William Hough, the British vice-consul, thus reported that he "burnt . . . the [consulate's] Confidential archives" before being detained for fifteen days with his French and Russian counterparts. "Shortly before I left," he added, "an official proclamation from the Commandant at Damascus was circulated at Jerusalem, stating that all enemy subjects would be kept for the time being as hostages against the bombardement [*sic*] of open ports and that anybody trying to leave without permission would be shot without pity."[3] Reading this testimony leaves no room for doubt: in fall 1914, for the first time since the end of the Middle Ages, the Holy City was at war.

Jerusalem's Armenians and Jews were the two communities hit the hardest by the new geopolitical situation. The abolition of the regime of capitulations and the departure of the French, British, and Russian consuls left without any protection Jews who had recently immigrated. The Ottoman law on the conscription of non-Muslims, enacted in 1909 and reinforced in 1914, left only two options to Jerusalem's Jewish residents: exile or enlistment in the Ottoman army. Many chose the first, and most of them took refuge in Alexandria in Egypt (under British rule since the 1880s). It is estimated that twenty-five thousand Jews left Palestine during the war; the French government took in a few hundred in Corsica.[4] Others, such as Albert Antébi (the former director of the Alliance israélite universelle school in Jerusalem), opted for loyalty to the Ottoman Empire: he enrolled in the Ottoman army, was sent to the Caucasus front in 1917, and died in Istanbul, of typhus, on March 18, 1919, shortly after the end of the war.[5] His tragic fate is a symbol of the historic rupture that the Ottoman Empire's fall represented in Jerusalem: Albert Antébi the "Levantine," born in Damascus, both Jewish and Arab, Ottoman citizen, French in his education and universalist convictions, found himself in an awkward position when the war broke out and the principle of nationalities irresistibly imposed itself.

For their part, Jerusalem's Armenians suffered the repercussions of the Ottoman power's extermination policy, pursued from 1915 onward. At the end of November 1917, several hundred were explicitly threatened with mass expulsion, which was only narrowly averted by the approach of British troops. Some Arab nationalists (Christians and Muslims) were also victims of Turkish governmental repression, which contributed to the "Ottoman black legend" in Arab historiography for several decades.[6]

Perched on the Palestinian mountaintop, Jerusalem did not represent a large military stake for the Ottoman army, allied with Germany, nor for the British army commanded by Allenby. However, Djemal Pasha, the supreme commander of the Ottoman Fourth Army, established his headquarters in the Holy City, precisely in the Augusta Victoria Hospital, on the summit of the Mount of Olives. For the British, military operations in the Middle East in 1917 aimed above all to protect the Suez Canal, a vital element of their maritime empire; in a difficult situation on the European fronts, they also sought to prod Germany's Ottoman ally in order to force the hand of destiny and hasten their own victory. At the end of October the front line was breached; the British seized Beersheba in the Negev desert and then, in mid-November, Gaza and Jaffa. At the beginning of December, Jerusalem's encirclement was complete, despite fairly hard fighting to the city's northwest, especially around Nabi Samwil's hill.

On the evening of Saturday, December 8, the Ottoman governor Izzet Pasha left the city by car on the Jericho Road, and the last Ottoman garrisons did the same later that night. The next morning, the mayor himself, Hussein al-Husseini, organized the city's surrender: first he procured a white flag from the hospital in the American Colony Hotel (in the Sheikh Jarrah neighborhood) and then went in search of British officers to hand over the letter of capitulation that the governor had signed the night before (see map 9). On his way, he met Menache Elyashar, the young son of one of the city's Jewish families, and a Swedish photographer, who both decided to accompany him. The improvised delegation—which, as history later remembered, was composed of a Muslim, a Jew, and a Christian—came across Sergeant Frederick Hurcomb and another British soldier, who were looking for supplies for their superiors. An impromptu photograph, preserved in the American Colony archives, has immortalized this improbable surrender: Mayor Hussein al-Husseini, leaning on a cane, a cigarette in his hand, stands proudly in the center of the group; beside him are Menache Elyashar, the two British soldiers, and a few curious people; behind them an exultant man bears the white flag; all are dazzled by the morning sun and look at the photographer, for posterity.[7]

The moment was indeed historic: it marked the end of four centuries of Ottoman presence in the Holy City. The historian Tom Segev underlined the mythic dimension that subsequently attached to the story of Jerusalem's takeover by the British:

Jerusalem being Jerusalem, the conquest was decked in the trappings of myth. The Jews saw it as a Hanukkah miracle; on the evening of the conquest they lit the holiday's first candle. Avraham Yitzhak Hacohen Kook, the Yishuv's leading rabbi, who was then in London, later composed a special prayer of thanks. Across the city people quoted a prophecy the Arabs used to tell to glorify the Ottoman Empire: the Turks would leave Palestine only when a prophet of God brought the water of the Nile to Palestine. The British had laid pipes that supplied their army with water in the desert, and so Allenby was called *Allah an-nabi*, a prophet of God.[8]

In fact, Jerusalem was taken during the Jewish holiday of Hanukkah, one Sunday not long before Christmas. . . . That was all it took to forge the legend of General Allenby, whose name, the local press pointed out, could be spelled *al-Nebi* in Arabic—that is, literally "the Prophet."

How to Enter Jerusalem?

Allenby's formal entry into Jerusalem, on December 11, 1917, was meticulously prepared and negotiated; it can be analyzed as a result of the balance of power then being decided between France and the United Kingdom in the future of the Middle East, but also as a reflection of the contradictions of British foreign policy.

To understand the uncertainty in which the actors of this historic moment were immersed, it is necessary to bear in mind a few previous episodes. In spring 1916, the agreement negotiated by the Englishman Mark Sykes and the Frenchman François Georges-Picot planned to entrust the administration of the northern Middle East (today's Lebanon and Syria) to France and the southern part (the current Iraq, Kuwait, and Saudi Arabia) to the United Kingdom, and to put Palestine, including Jerusalem and its holy places, under an international management regime.[9] This first project to internationalize Palestine and Jerusalem undoubtedly responded, in the minds of the French and British negotiators, to an implicit intuition: in Palestine, the concentration and entanglement of holy sites and religious communities made difficult, if not impossible, a strict application of the Wilsonian principle of the right of peoples to self-determination. In any case, one can say that this first project of Jerusalem's internationalization was chronologically situated at the point of contact between the close of the Ottoman imperial era and the rise of Jewish and Arab nationalisms in Palestine: the idea of internationalizing the Holy City was suitably envisaged as a response to the challenge posed by the end of the Ottoman supranational framework.

The second element in the background of Allenby's entry into Jerusalem was the famous Balfour Declaration, issued on November 2, 1917, just before the Holy City's conquest. In this open letter addressed to the Zionist leader Lord Rothschild, the British foreign secretary Lord Balfour declares that "His Majesty's Government view with favour the establishment in Palestine of a national home for the Jewish people, and will use their best endeavours to facilitate the achievement of this object."[10] Lord Balfour then offsets this commitment by including non-Jewish populations in the envisaged scenario: "Nothing shall be done which may prejudice the civil and religious rights of existing non-Jewish communities in Palestine." In this balancing act we find the seed of the future British mandate policy's inextricable contradiction. At any rate, when Allenby was poised to enter the Holy City, the constraints of the moment doubled the stakes: it was a question of, on the one hand, accommodating—measuredly—French diplomacy (following the Sykes-Picot Agreement) and, on the other hand, not ruffling the feathers of Arab nationalists (after the Balfour Declaration).

It was this double constraint that determined the form of the ceremonial entry on December 11. To avoid giving the impression of behaving like an heir to the Crusaders, Allenby conspicuously got out of his car outside the Jaffa Gate and passed through the Holy City's wall on foot (see map 9). This demonstration of informality also helped to differentiate him from the German emperor Wilhelm II, who, in 1898, persuaded the Ottoman authorities to demolish a section of the wall so he could enter Jerusalem in his imperial carriage. Moreover, to respect the terms of the Sykes-Picot Agreement, Allenby organized a procession with a strict parity of British and French representatives: he marched at the head, flanked closely by Georges-Picot, who had just been named the French high commissioner for Palestine; behind them appeared the British general Bols and the French colonel Piépape; and then came the French Louis Massignon and Colonel Lawrence, who was not yet called Lawrence of Arabia but was there to remind the British government of the promises it had made to the Arab nationalists. On the face of it, parity was thus respected, not only between France and the United Kingdom but also between Jewish and Arabic national aspirations.

However, with regard to the Holy City's future status, Allenby did all he could to ward off the prospect of an internationalization that he considered too favorable to French interests. Even if, as a matter of form, he had his statutory declaration read in English, French, Arabic, Hebrew, Greek, Russian, and Italian, the proclamation's substance was unambiguous.

Allenby refused to hand over the city's management to an international civil power and affirmed (without setting an expiration date) the new British occupier's military prerogatives:

> To the Inhabitants of Jerusalem the Blessed and the People Dwelling in Its Vicinity:
> The defeat inflicted upon the Turks by the troops under my command has resulted in the occupation of your city by my forces. I, therefore, here now proclaim it to be under martial law, under which form of administration it will remain so long as military considerations make necessary.

He added that he would scrupulously respect the *status quo ante* regarding the administration of holy places: "I make it known to you that every sacred building, monument, holy spot, shrine, traditional site, endowment, pious bequest, or customary place of prayer of whatsoever form of the three religions will be maintained and protected according to the existing customs and beliefs of those to whose faith they are sacred."[11]

On closer inspection, all the elements of the coming drama were already in place on that morning of December 11, 1917: the United Kingdom dismissed the prospect of an internationalization of Palestine and Jerusalem, made promises to both Jewish and Arab nationalists, and imagined itself able to separate religious questions from political issues. It was precisely this pile of insurmountable contradictions that led, thirty years later, to Jerusalem's split into two distinct entities.

Jerusalem on the Road to Communitarianization

In April 1920, during the Muslim pilgrimage to Nabi Musa (the tomb of Moses, near Jericho), the processions degenerated into violent clashes between Jews and Arabs in Jerusalem. With the British police proving incapable of maintaining order, the Russian Zionist Ze'ev Jabotinsky organized Jewish self-defense groups to protect his coreligionists. In two days, the death toll was six on each side and several hundred were injured.[12] How could the urban community formed by Jerusalem's inhabitants in the first decade of the 1900s fall into such violent confrontations just two decades later? Only the new institutional and political context can explain this abrupt communal polarization. Beginning in 1913, as we have seen, the failure of the supranational Ottomanist model contributed to the exacerbation of tensions, but it was really the political blindness of the new British authorities that definitively undermined the civic community's internal equilibrium: by privileging religious institutions to the detriment of secular administrative bodies, the new occupiers set off an uncontrollable downward spiral.

One symbolic act illustrates this fundamental error: barely arrived in Jerusalem, the British decided to destroy the clock tower, twenty-five meters (eighty-two feet) high, that overlooked the Jaffa Gate, which gave all city dwellers a secularized time detached from any religious reference and which had been erected in 1907 thanks to a subscription launched by the municipality (see map 9). By pulling down this interfaith urban monument, the bearer of a shared modernity, to enhance the city's "authentic biblical and medieval character," the new authorities conveyed their distorted view of a Holy City essentially frozen in the past and governed exclusively by religious concerns. As is always mentioned, among the first measures implemented by Jerusalem's British governor Ronald Storrs was the military order of April 1918 that subjected "demolish[ing], erect[ing], alter[ing], or repair[ing] the structure of any building in the City of Jerusalem" to the express agreement of the new authorities and to the obligation to use "Jerusalem stone" for future edifices, meant to give an appearance of unity to the Holy City's eclectic architecture.[13] But it is often forgotten that the British emblematically marked their arrival with the deliberate destruction of the first interfaith monument constructed in Jerusalem, at the end of the Ottoman period.

This architectural and symbolic measure corresponded to a more directly political and much more serious decision: in spring 1920, after the Nabi Musa unrest, the governor dismissed Mayor Musa Kazem al-Husseini, accused of having encouraged the rioters, and replaced him with Raghib Bey Nashashibi, a member of an influential Arab family, rivals of the Husseinis, who was known for his benevolence toward the Zionist project. The city council was no longer the emblem of the community but thus became the plaything of British diplomatic temporizing. Already in March 1918, on the death of Hussein al-Husseini, the British authorities had appointed two Muslims, two Christians, and two Jews to the city council, unilaterally modifying its composition, as if the municipality's sectarianization could extinguish the risk of conflict. This same obsession with religious categories appeared again in the municipal reform of 1926, which organized future city elections on the basis of denominational districts. The municipal institution's communitarianization, thus encouraged and even instituted, was not long in producing predictable results: after the elections in 1934, the municipal board was torn between Jewish and Arab (Muslim and Christian) councillors. Mayor Hussein Fakhri al-Khalidi was exiled to the Seychelles in 1937 and replaced first by his Jewish deputy mayor, Daniel Auster, and then by his brother Mustapha al-Khalidi, who remained in office until his death in 1944, but from 1934 the municipality was de facto split into two distinct entities. The territorial partition of 1948 had therefore existed, in terms of municipal management, since the mid-1930s.

The Artas water conflict, which in 1925 pitted the municipality of Jerusalem against the crop farmers of the village of Artas (eleven kilometers [seven miles] south of Jerusalem, between Bethlehem and Hebron), reveals the communitarianization of the city's management (see map 10). In May 1925, after a particularly dry winter, the mandatary authorities decided to divert some of Artas's water to Jerusalem; on June 9, the Arab Executive Committee sent a strong protest to High Commissioner Herbert Samuel explicitly denouncing a "Zionist" maneuver to benefit Jerusalem's Jewish population at the expense of the Arab villagers in Artas. The case, first heard by the Supreme Court of Palestine, was referred in 1926 to the Privy Council in London, the highest British judicial body. In their complaint, the Arab nationalists questioned what they saw as the "biased" policy of the Jerusalem Water Supply (managed by a Hungarian Jew, Andrew Koch); condemned Jewish immigration, which in 1925 reached a historic peak in Palestine (thirty-five thousand immigrants); and asserted that the vast real estate projects undertaken in Jerusalem (the Hebrew University, for example, which happened to be inaugurated in 1925) were dangerously exacerbating an already quite serious water crisis. Beyond the arguments advanced, this affair reveals the deterioration of the debates within the municipal authority: beginning in the mid-1920s, questions were apparently no longer addressed according to technical or urban-planning criteria but as part of a thenceforth explicit competition between Zionists and Arab nationalists.

The fragile calm that prevailed in Jerusalem during the 1920s thus masked a process of communitarian polarization already well under way. Having become the administrative capital of a Palestinian territory in the making, the Holy City found itself the privileged stage of verbal and physical clashes between Zionists and Arab nationalists. Beginning in autumn 1918, the project launched by Chaim Weizmann to buy the Wailing Wall (Kotel) and part of the adjacent "Mughrabi Quarter" had provoked Arab residents' anger (see map 9). However, although Jerusalem became the Arab Executive Committee's seat in 1920, Arab nationalism's various branches did not unanimously recognize its status as Palestine's political capital: in January 1919, when the congress of Muslim-Christian associations met in the Holy City, the motion to integrate Jerusalem into a Pan-Arab "Greater Syria" under the authority of Damascus passed by a large majority. There are echoes here of a decades-long debate that divided Palestine's Arab nationalists, some favoring the Pan-Arab option, others supporting an autonomous Palestine with Jerusalem as its capital.

The arrival in June 1920 of the new Palestinian civil administration's first high commissioner, Herbert Samuel, a Jew and a fervent Zionist, fueled Arab concerns without, however, reassuring Zionist leaders, who themselves worried about the measures immediately taken to counterbalance his appointment's disastrous effect on the Arabs. That is why the new high commissioner decided, against all expectations, to name the young Hadj Amin al-Husseini to the recently created position of grand mufti of Palestine, after quashing the prison sentence to which he'd been condemned for having participated in the bloody Nabi Musa riots in April 1920. The energetic Hadj Amin al-Husseini, known for his strongly anti-Zionist positions, took the lead in the Palestinian uprising of the 1930s and was noted for his closeness to Hitler during World War II. Here we see the impasse in which the mandatary authorities were gradually mired: muddled alternation between harassment and gestures of appeasement, intimidation and the first steps toward reconciliation, targeting both parties, and without any political regulatory body being set up, because the project to elect a "universal" legislative assembly (bringing together all of Palestine's communities) was rejected by the Arab Executive Committee, which feared that supporting it would endorse the mandatary framework and especially the Balfour Declaration of 1917.

Urban Expansion and Territorial Polarization

Beyond the intensification of political fractures, the history of Jerusalem's mandatary period is marked by a process of territorial polarization that accompanied the Holy City's demographic expansion. Nonetheless, the raw demographic data show that the overall balance was maintained: the city had 70,000 inhabitants in 1914 (44,000, or 63 percent, Jewish), 45,000 in 1918 (25,000, or 56 percent, Jewish), and 90,000 in 1931 (50,000, or 56 percent, Jewish and 40,000 or 44 percent, Arab). Within the Arab population, parity was reached in 1931, when 20,000 Christians and 20,000 Muslims were tallied.[14] In 1944, coming out of World War II, Jerusalem counted 150,000 residents, of whom 90,000 (60 percent) were Jews and 60,000 (40 percent) were Arabs. Although the quantitative demographic facts are generally advanced to explain the deterioration of the situation on the ground, it is thus clear that they are not what threatened the internal equilibrium of Jerusalem's society. In reality, it was the qualitative disintegration and disarticulation of the urban fabric that readied the Holy City for its split into two distinct entities, one Jewish, the other Arab.

Indeed, in terms of city planning, the mandatary authorities failed to give any real consistency to the municipal territory, whose borders obeyed political constraints more than urbanist considerations: from seventeen square kilometers (seven square miles) in 1921, the municipal territory increased to forty-four square kilometers (seventeen square miles) at the end of the mandate, but the Zionist organizations pushed to limit its extension, for fear that integrating the neighboring Arab villages would challenge Jerusalem's Jewish majority. The Jerusalem Town Planning Commission, established in 1921 as a result of the Town Planning Ordinance, had to deal with the numerous real estate projects meant exclusively for Jewish residents, financed by the Palestine Zionist Executive, and succeeded in tracing only a few elementary guiding lines, such as King George Street, which in 1924 was the first circular thoroughfare west of the Old City.

The separation of the urban utility network into two discrete systems was one of the symptoms of the city council's inability to make development coherent: the water supply grid was dense to the west, starting from the new reservoir built on Romema's hill in 1919, but largely absent from

Jerusalem's east (Old City, Sheikh Jarrah, Wadi Joz, At-Tur, and Mount of Olives), which continued to be furnished by traditional channels and water drawn from Wadi Kelt, farther to the east (see map 9). Public transport was also split into two in the 1920s: there were now a Jewish company and an Arab company, each privileging service to the most polarized neighborhoods. A gap emerged and then widened bit by bit between the city's east and west, although the communitarian polarization of housing didn't accelerate until the mid-1930s. In the end, the Old City was the only area where the mandatary authority was able to make its mark, according to the principles of an explicitly backward-looking restoration notably defended by C. R. Ashbee, at the head of the omnipresent Pro-Jerusalem Society: "Our aim is . . . to discover and preserve all that remains of the past and to undo so far as we can the evil that has been done."[15] With the aim of showcasing the walls, everything was done to separate the Old City from the rest of the agglomeration by means of a green belt that must have formed a jewel box for the ornament of the sanctuary-filled city. If the project made sense from a heritage viewpoint, it also increased the fracturing of the urban landscape, which became a collection of mismatched and poorly connected isolates.

In the context of this fairly disjointed urban territory, political clashes gradually transformed into physical clashes. After the Nabi Musa riots in 1920, the most serious incident happened in August 1929, following a dispute over the rights of passage and use in the area facing the Wailing Wall (Kotel). In November 1928, the president of the Supreme Muslim Council, Grand Mufti Hadj Amin al-Husseini, created an association for the protection of the holy sites, to which the ultranationalist Jews around Ze'ev Jabotinsky responded with demonstrations near the wall. Riots broke out among the Arab population, spreading through the Old City, into the *extra muros* residential neighborhoods, and even to Jaffa, Hebron, and Safed. A few days later, there were some 30 dead in Jerusalem (of almost 250 in the whole of Palestine, 133 Jews and 116 Arabs). In October 1933, anti-British demonstrations by Arabs in Jerusalem resulted in the deaths of eleven protesters. At the same time, the outburst of anti-Semitism in Europe intensified the migratory pressure in Palestine, which reached a maximum between 1933 and 1936 (160,000 arrivals in three years). In Jerusalem, Hadj Amin al-Husseini's rise accompanied the radicalization, the sectarianization, and the militarization of the Palestinian nationalist movement, which turned into an armed insurrection in spring 1936. Jerusalem's municipal institution did not resist political pressure for long: Mayor Hussein Fakhri al-Khalidi, who was clearly committed to the nationalist movement, was arrested and exiled in 1937 by the British authorities. . . . That was the end of Jerusalem's mixed municipality, the last instrument of a possible coexistence.

Jerusalem from 1939 to 1945: A Strange Calm

In contrast to the periods that preceded (1936–39) and followed (1946–49), the years of the Second World War were marked by a surprising calm in Jerusalem.[16] While the advance of Rommel's German troops to El Alamein, Egypt, in November 1942 may have occasionally worried the inhabitants, the Holy City was spared the direct ravages of the war. As a matter of fact, in their strategic plan, the British made the Palestinian mandate and its capital a linchpin in protecting the Suez Canal's east side. But the lull's decisive factor was undoubtedly the publication of a UK government white paper in May 1939: after the Arab uprising, the British partially satisfied the insurgents' demands, with a strict limitation on Jewish immigration (seventy-five thousand entries maximum over five years) and the prospect of creating a single, independent Palestinian state in the next ten years. With Arabs then clearly having achieved preponderance in Palestine (around one million, versus about half a million Jews in 1939), the specter of partition receded, and there gleamed the guarantee of imminent independence in the form of a majority-Arab state with Jerusalem as its capital. A British soldier garrisoned in Jerusalem could thus write to his family, in December 1939: "The country is very quiet and peaceful, probably more so than in the last two thousand years [sic]. Jews and Arabs are beginning to work together and it looks as if Palestine is in for a prosperous time in the coming years."[17]

At the same time, Jerusalem's residents closely followed events in Europe. Hala Sakakini thus recounts in her memoir that she was fifteen when she heard the British declaration of war against Germany over the radio: "When the announcement came to an end, all of us sat in complete silence, stunned by the terrible news." Later, she underlines that family conversations constantly revolved around the conflict: "We speculated on the future—what the world would be like after the War."[18] Amos Oz, born in Jerusalem in May 1939, also remembered the global war's invasion of domestic space: "Throughout the years of the World War there hung on the wall in the passage a large map of the theaters of war in Europe, with pins and different-colored flags. Every day or two Father moved them in accordance with the news on the wireless."[19] A war "so near, so far," then. Jerusalem's inhabitants were surely aware that their fates and that of the Holy City were being decided elsewhere, in Europe and the Pacific—in any case, far from Palestine. As it happened, intercommunal violence decreased immediately after the declaration of war: according to the French consulate's numbers, eighty-seven people were killed in Palestine in August 1939, compared to only fifteen in October.[20] The political tensions were anything but settled, but they seemed frozen, as if hanging on the global conflict's uncertain outcome, which everyone believed would be crucial to the region's future. After his clandestine flight in October 1937, the distant wanderings (Beirut, Baghdad, Tehran, Istanbul, Rome, Berlin, Sarajevo, Zagreb, etc.) of the "mufti beyond the walls" Hadj Amin al-Husseini were perhaps the best symbol of violence's temporary remoteness from Palestine and Jerusalem: between 1939 and 1945, the Holy City indeed experienced a strange peacefulness.

One question rarely addressed by historiography, however, deserves some time: beyond the available information on the major geostrategic developments in progress, what could Jerusalem's residents have known about the Holocaust? How was the destruction of Europe's Jews, a pivotal event in Jewish history and memory, experienced, or rather perceived, by the Holy City's ninety thousand Jews? The question is important for the urban history of Jerusalem itself, because after the war the city became a privileged site of Jewish memory of the Shoah: the Yad Vashem memorial was established there in 1953 and opened to the public in 1957.

It is clear that from autumn 1939 to autumn 1942, accurate perception of the facts was still attenuated by distance, even if some Zionist cadres with strong connections to Europe were already expressing their apprehension, such as Arthur Ruppin, who wrote in his journal on November 5, 1939: "Hitler wants to concentrate Polish and other Jews (from Vienna, Prague) in the region of Lublin. A Jewish state or a Jewish ghetto by the grace of Hitler!"[21] In the local papers, the subject became omnipresent in autumn 1942 (nine months after the Wannsee Conference), as the French consul in Jerusalem directly testified on December 4, 1942: "For several weeks the Hebrew press has not stopped publishing information on the Nazis' extermination of the Jews. . . . This week the Jewish community declared three days of national mourning across the whole country. On Sunday a 'conclave of rabbis' met in the Old City's large synagogue, from which the audience went to the Weeping Wall to pray en masse and commemorate the dead. The whole city is draped with black flags. . . . The Arab press refrained from expressing sympathy for the victims of the Nazi atrocities, with the exception of the *Falestin*."[22] A few days earlier, during the general assembly of the Va'ad Le'umi (Jewish National Council), Yitzhak Ben-Zvi had drawn a strong link between the Shoah's victims and Jerusalem's Jews: "We are gathered in Jerusalem, our Holy City, our eternal city. . . . A terrible calamity has befallen the whole of European Judaism, a situation with no equal in our history. We are gathered to express the distress of the people living in Zion in the face of our nation's destruction." Thus, Jerusalem's Jewish residents did not ignore the Holocaust: days of mourning followed one another, as did calls for donations, so much concrete evidence of a "shared horror."[23]

JERUSALEM FROM 1948 TO TODAY: PLANS FOR COHABITATION, PARTITION, AND ANNEXATION

Jerusalem's history in the second half of the twentieth century is particularly difficult to deal with. This is the case for any "history of the present," in which it is hard to distinguish historical realities from contemporary issues, but especially so for Jerusalem, which has become an inescapable symbolic and political issue for Israel, Palestine, and the whole world. However, this difficulty should not stop us from taking a step back and considering this period as a cohesive cycle in the Holy City's millennia-old history.

Two fundamental facts structured this period and gave it a unique profile: for the first time since the biblical era, the Holy City was no longer governed within an imperial or supranational framework but became the

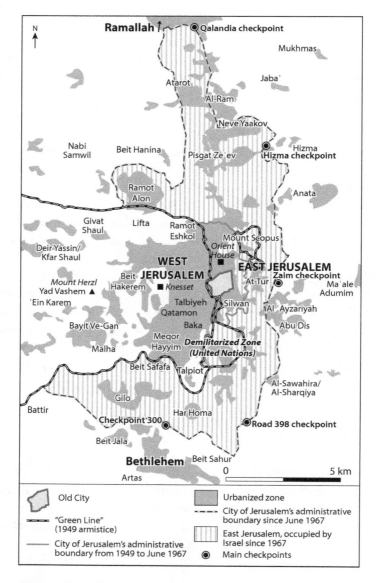

Map 10. *From division to annexation (since 1948)*

pivot of two concurrent nation-building projects; also for the first time, it was divided into two distinct urban entities, West Jerusalem and East Jerusalem. This partition, today still visible in the civic fabric and operative at the level of international law, was militarily concretized during the first Arab-Israeli War, in 1948, but it had been germinating since the mid-1930s in municipal institutions and the representation of residents, as we have seen. Israel's conquest of the city's east side in the Six-Day War in June 1967 did not bridge the gap that still separates the two Jerusalems. Today, most of West Jerusalem's inhabitants are hesitant to go "east."

To grasp the specificity and coherence of this new sequence of Jerusalem's history, these two phenomena must be considered together. The tensions running through Jerusalem today, in terms of both its cityness (cohesion of the urban fabric) and its city life (cohesion of urban society), are undoubtedly due to the intrinsic difficulty of integrating a city with a universal vocation into two projects to construct specific nations. But, as often happens in history, the problem might partly contain its own solution: Jerusalem, universal and binational Holy City, capital of two states, must today reinvent itself to remain itself.

1948: Partition

The "1948 moment," a brief and brutal episode in Jerusalem's history, at first glance resembles a simple military event: the fortunes of war seem to have decided the Holy City's fate in just two months of spring and summer 1948. After the departure of the last British mandatary soldiers and the declaration of Israel's independence by David Ben-Gurion in Tel Aviv on May 14, 1948, fighting immediately began in Jerusalem's outskirts between the new Israeli army (the Haganah) and the Transjordanian Arab Legion. The front line stabilized on July 17 and hardly budged until the signing of the cease-fire by Moshe Dayan, the Israeli troop commander in Jerusalem, and Abdullah al-Tal, the Arab Legion's representative, on the following November 30.

From summer 1948 to summer 1967, nineteen years, Jerusalem remained split into two distinct entities, separated by a line of demarcation, barbed wire, and military posts (see map 10). However, contrary to appearances, the territorial partition of 1948 is attributable less to the immediate military history than to the city's social and political history in the preceding period. Indeed, from the viewpoint of both Zionist officials and Jordanians, the city's territorial division seemed the most likely and the most desirable scenario, even before the outbreak of hostilities. Each side considered this a "lesser evil" to prevent the enemy from seizing the entire urban area, and they both agreed on refusing interference from the UN. The international community's approach, in all versions of the plans for a shared Palestine published from 1937 to 1947, had been to try to ward off the very specter of partition by imagining the creation of a *corpus separatum* for the Holy City and its environs. The Jewish and Arab nationalists were not mistaken in opposing this project, considering that it aimed above all to preserve Western hegemony over the sacred sites.[24]

From the perspective of Jerusalem's inhabitants themselves, the partition had already begun, following the bloody riots from 1928 to 1939, which had considerably reinforced the communitarian polarization of the city's different neighborhoods, and increased after the organized attacks that began in 1946. Finally, with regard to the municipality, an institution that regulated conflict and represented a certain urban identity, partition went back to the elections of 1934, when the Jewish and Arab councillors stopped meeting regularly. In the end, the battle for Jerusalem served only for plotting the details of the line of demarcation: the gap between the city's west and east had been formed well before. In terms of representation and political temporality, we can say that Jerusalem's residents then ceased to be *city dwellers* in a town that was lived in the present and became above all *citizens* of two future nations.

On both sides of the new border, the inhabitants of mixed districts were the war's first victims. To the west, Baka, Talbiyeh, Qatamon, Musrara, and part of the Abu Tor hill, notably, were emptied of their Arab populations.[25] To the east, the Jewish residents of the Sheikh Jarrah neighborhood had to flee in haste. Farther north, Atarot and Neve Yaakov, located between Jerusalem and Ramallah, were evacuated in the face of the Transjordanian troops' advance (see map 10). The battle of 1948 accelerated and finalized the process of segregation that had been observable on the ground since the 1930s. The Old City, which had passed entirely under Jordanian control, lost its whole Jewish populace; the synagogues and talmudic schools (yeshivot) were looted and set on fire; and the Jewish cemetery on the Mount of Olives was partially destroyed.

Direct testimony is rare for this dramatic episode, which was similar, at Jerusalem's scale, to a civil war. With regard to the Old City, Constantine Mavrides's account is irreplaceable: at the age of fifty-eight, he was an interpreter at the Greek General Consulate in Jerusalem; from the beginning of combat in May 1948, he took refuge at the Greek Orthodox Patriarchate, where he kept a diary. Mavrides depicts "crowds with plenty of enthusiasm" and "indescribable scenes . . . manifested in front of the Gethsemane Gate [Saint Stephen's Gate]," facing the Mount of Olives, on the evening of Wednesday, May 19, when the Arab Legion entered the Holy City to keep it from falling into Israeli hands. He reports the destruction of the Hurva Synagogue on Thursday, May 27, and then, the next day, the fall of the entire Jewish Quarter: "The *Haganah* soldiers were taken as prisoners of war to Zarqa in Transjordan, but the women and children were handed over to the Red Cross. . . . Many corpses were found unburied and almost in a state of decomposition, and the Arabs had to burn them on May 28 and 29 after the capture of the Jewish Quarter." Finally, he precisely relates the scenes of pillage on Saturday, May 29, taking care to emphasize that Jerusalem's inhabitants were not involved, as if to extenuate the violence of the events he had witnessed: "What was left was still plundered, swarms of Arab children and women came into the quarter, most of them from the surrounding villages, and tore out window shutters, half-burned doors, railings, etc., and took them away either to sell them in the Arab market or out of the city to their villages."[26]

As regards the new city, one can quote the account of the writer Khalil Sakakini's daughter Hala, then a young resident of the Qatamon district, whose memoir describes the consequences of the Semiramis Hotel's bombing by the Haganah (then a Jewish self-defense group) in January 1948, which killed twenty-four: "All day long you could see people carrying their belongings and moving from their houses to safer ones in Katamon or to another quarter altogether. They reminded us of pictures we used to see of European refugees during the war. People were simply panic-stricken. The rumour spread that leaflets had been dropped by the Jews saying that they would make out of Katamon one heap of rubble.

Whenever we saw people moving away we tried to encourage them to stay."[27] This direct testimony confirms the early desire of the future Israeli army's leaders to see as many Arab inhabitants as possible leave the neighborhoods west of the city, even before hostilities officially commenced. This theory is confirmed by a Haganah Intelligence Service report from January 5, 1948, the day after the Haganah bombed the Semiramis Hotel: "Many families are leaving [Qatamon]. . . . The explosion of the houses in the area had instilled fear in all the people of Qatamon. They argue that the Jews are well-organised economically and the Arabs cannot withstand such organization."[28] Reading these lines, one understands the uncertainty that the inhabitants of Jerusalem's mixed districts must have felt in the first months of 1948, when, before the actual war, the threat of unpredictable attacks nonetheless hovered.

Jerusalem's partition in 1948 was an ambivalent historical event, quite difficult to decipher: its direct causes were military, but its distant origins were political and its long-term consequences profound for urban planning. It seemed like a violent break but in reality was deeply anchored both upstream and downstream of its immediate chronology. The ceasefire line drawn in November 1948 indeed left a scar on Jerusalem's very heart, at the exact junction of the Old City and the new, of millennia-old sanctuaries and modern neighborhoods. In so doing, it eliminated the dynamic interface that had been formed since the end of the nineteenth century by the contact of these two urban polarities, especially around the Jaffa Gate. Between Israeli strongholds and Jordanian positions, the city's no-man's-land is several dozen meters wide, and in places several hundred, in particular to the north of the Old City, in the Musrara district; to the west, facing the Jaffa Gate; and to the south, on the slopes of Mount Zion. In total, the so-called neutral zone covers three square kilometers (one square mile), which is enormous for Jerusalem, whose city *intra muros* measures barely one square kilometer (0.4 square miles). In 1962 (the same year that the Berlin Wall was completed), after multiple fatal incidents, the two sides decided to materialize the demarcation line with a series of barriers and concrete blockhouses.[29] In the mid-1980s, twenty years after Israel's conquest of East Jerusalem, this gash carved right through the middle of the urban fabric was still quite visible, even to an unwitting stroller. Today the northern tramway and, in the west, the

Mamilla Mall have begun to attenuate the stigmata of the 1948 war, but as soon as political tension seizes hold of the city again, mobile Israeli police cordons almost naturally resume their places, on the sites of the old block-houses from 1948–67. It's as if the city preserved the memory of this heart-breaking historical episode in its very fabric.

Jordanian Jerusalem, 1948–1967: Back to the Provinces

King Abdullah's Transjordan had an ambiguous relationship with Jerusalem, to say the least. Of course the nascent kingdom took legitimate pride in possessing Islam's third holy city, even if the Hashemite dynasty had long reigned in Mecca, whose prestige remains unequaled for Muslims. Moreover, it was the conquest of "Cisjordan" and Jerusalem that allowed the national horizon of the ephemeral "Transjordan" to expand, giving birth to Jordan, which was officially proclaimed in January 1949. As its name thereafter explicitly indicated, the Hashemite Kingdom of Jordan's center of gravity was located along the Jordan Valley, and it found its balance in two large cities that faced each other across fifty kilometers (thirty-one miles), Jerusalem to the west and Amman to the east. Starting on December 1, 1948, Abdullah took care to gather a few hundred Palestinian notables in Jericho (that is, exactly halfway between Jerusalem and Amman) to have himself declared the "king of Palestine": therefore, the war of spring and summer 1948 was not a side event in Jordan's history but, on the contrary, a baptism by fire, a founding moment both symbolically and territorially.[30] However, Abdullah's strategy aimed not to make Jerusalem the bridgehead of a specifically "Palestinian" nationalism but, quite the reverse, to place the Holy City under the banner of "Arab unity," which the new Kingdom of Jordan would prefigure.

To a certain extent and as far as Jerusalem's Jordanian part is concerned, the period from 1949 to 1967 represents the final sequence in the Holy City's long supranational history: East Jerusalem again became—in the proper sense of the term and for almost two decades—a "provincial" city, marginalized and no longer a capital. In the Hashemite sovereign's crown it was a prestigious but peripheral jewel. Other elements fed the Hashemite monarchy's distrust of Jerusalem: the new kingdom had to deal with a population that was two-thirds Palestinian, of whom a third were refugees, which could entail the risk of sedition or even partition if the city were to be considered a genuine political capital.

Jerusalem was thus strictly confined to its status of Holy City: the municipality had its first elections only in 1951, and the Jordanian authorities quickly dismissed the new mayor, 'Aref el-'Aref, because of his strong nationalist convictions.[31] In a historical irony, it was Raghib Bey Nashashibi, the city's mayor from 1920 to 1934, who received the purely honorific title of "superintendent of the Haram al-Sharif and custodian of the Holy Places." Nashashibi's nephew, present at the investiture ceremony on January 5, 1951, described the scene: "We both knew in our hearts that a leader of the Arabs of Palestine, a former mayor of Jerusalem, had, at the end of a distinguished career, been reduced to a local personality, a player on the periphery—a Jordanian administrator in a dusty corner of Jerusalem."[32] A few months later, on Friday, July 20, 1951, when emerging from the Friday prayer at Al-Aqsa Mosque, King Abdullah was assassinated by a young Palestinian-nationalist militant who was close to the former mufti Hadj Amin al-Husseini. This consummated the divorce between Jerusalem and the Jordanian kingdom, which was thereafter wary of the potentially explosive nature of the Holy City's political base.

Once again, political history dictated Jerusalem's urban physiognomy. On the Jordanian side, it was understood that everything was done to contain the city's growth within strict limits: the Jordanian municipality covered barely six square kilometers (two square miles), of which only three were developed. Within city limits, construction was prohibited in many areas, particularly on the slopes of Mount Scopus, northeast of the Old City. Meron Benvenisti, Jerusalem's deputy mayor from 1971 to 1978, responsible in particular for the former Jordanian districts, testified in his own way to this strange paradox: "It was because they had become wastelands that the Israelis had no difficulty in confiscating them after the Six-Day War and establishing new Jewish neighborhoods there."[33] The same Meron Benvenisti indicated that just after the war in 1967, the Jordanian municipality's budget represented an expenditure of around one hundred dollars (at 1992 rates) per inhabitant, compared to about five hundred in the city's Israeli half. Such a fiscal disparity, primarily explained by the general poverty that prevailed in the Jordanian kingdom, could only widen the gap between the city's east and west.

Topographic constraints also added to the difficulties of the city's eastern part, especially with regard to water distribution: from the inauguration of the Ras al-Ain aqueduct in January 1936, most of the potable water consumed by Jerusalem's inhabitants came from the west (Ras al-Ain is on the coastal plain, near Tel Aviv) and was stored in the immense Romema reservoir at the city's northwestern end.[34] The 1949 Green Line thus cut off the Jordanian neighborhoods from the water distribution network that the municipality had put in place thirteen years earlier. To address this, the Jordanian authorities tried to reactivate the old hydraulic lines that had supplied the eastern districts before the 1930s.

Thanks to the personal archive of Yussuf al-Budeiri, the Jordanian municipality's chief engineer, we can fully appreciate the operation's difficulty: the new Ain Farah pumping station, located about ten kilometers (six miles) northeast of the city, was not inaugurated until July 13, 1958, ten years after the partition. Two months later, on September 12, a reservoir built to store water from Ain Farah, Ain Fawar, and Wadi Kelt was inaugurated in the city's northern neighborhood of French Hill. These emergency measures were clearly insufficient, as a report was written in 1960 on the feasibility of installing a desalination plant in Ain Fashkha, on the shore of the Dead Sea near the archaeological site of Qumran.[35] The water question illustrates a more general fact: after 1949, Jordanian Jerusalem was isolated from its western hinterland and the rich coastal plain and found itself turning exclusively to the east—that is, toward the desert and the Jordan Valley, which are much less dynamic. Beyond political factors, this topographic reality was a fundamental reason for East Jerusalem's disengagement from West Jerusalem between 1949 and 1967.

Israeli Jerusalem, 1948–1967: The Holy City Capitalized

West Jerusalem's situation after 1949 appeared to be the reverse of East Jerusalem's: far from neglected by political authorities, the city was, on the contrary, the object of every care and benefited from important investments; it was proclaimed the capital of the new State of Israel in January 1950, and the Knesset (the Israeli parliament) moved there from Tel Aviv that year, as did most ministries; to accommodate new immigrants, housing construction sites multiplied and the municipal territory's boundaries were extended westward until it reached thirty-eight square kilometers (twenty-four square miles). West Jerusalem's population thus rose from 90,000 to 190,000 between 1949 and 1967.[36] However, urban planning west of the Green Line helped in its own way to widen the gap with the city's eastern part: the areas near the line of demarcation, dangerous and isolated, were abandoned to social dropouts and stray dogs. The Mamilla neighborhood, the beating heart of city life before 1948, was deserted. In addition to the official no-man's-land that separated the Israeli and Jordanian sides, a buffer zone of several hundred meters further enlarged the chasm between the two Jerusalems. In contrast, the hills west of the residential districts were thenceforth the new Israeli Jerusalem's hub. The "Government Quarter" (also called the Ben-Gurion neighborhood) sprang up in the 1950s, around the Eastern Orthodox Monastery of the Cross, about two kilometers (one mile) west of the Old City's walls. The Israel Museum, which houses the renowned Dead Sea Scrolls, discovered in Qumran beginning in 1947, was inaugurated there in 1965, followed by the new seat of the Knesset in 1966.

Other institutions, previously located in the city's east, were forced to move, thus bolstering the westward shift of its center of gravity. For instance, the prestigious Hebrew University of Jerusalem, built on Mount Scopus (north of the Mount of Olives) in 1925, found itself isolated in the middle of Jordanian territory after the 1948 war (see map 10). In 1950, the university was obliged to hold its silver jubilee celebration in its temporary premises, at the Franciscan Terra Sancta College, crowned then as now by an immense statue of the Virgin Mary. . . . Norman Bentwich, who was then in charge of international relations for the university, wrote that it had incongruously fêted this anniversary "as a Displaced Person."[37] Beginning in 1953, students and professors made their way to the new campus under construction in the Givat Ram neighborhood, across from the new Israel Museum and the new government complex.

The Hadassah Hospital, also established on Mount Scopus before 1948, moved west to the former Arab village of 'Ein Karem in 1961. Likewise, one of the outlying western hills was chosen in 1949 to house the remains of Theodor Herzl, the founder of political Zionism, who had died in Austria forty-five years earlier. In 1953, the same hill was slated for the construction of the Yad Vashem Holocaust memorial, which opened to the public in 1957: both functionally and symbolically, a new urban center was being put in place several kilometers west of the Old City's walls. From this point of view, the immense Yad Vashem complex— which includes archives, memorials, museums, and a cemetery in which some of Israel's eminent historical figures are buried (such as the former prime minister Yitzhak Rabin, who was assassinated in 1995)—constituted a symbolic center that was an alternative to the religious sanctuaries in the Old City, newly inaccessible to Jerusalem's Jews. There was one notable exception, however: after fierce fighting in summer 1948, Mount Zion, immediately south of the walls, was integrated into Israeli territory. King David's Tomb, which had been Jerusalem's Franciscan headquarters in the Middle Ages before transforming into a Muslim holy site in the sixteenth century (under the name Nabi Dawud), thus found itself in a frontier zone and became a sacred place visited regularly by passing Jewish tourists. From 1948 to 1967, as if by a trick of history, the Mount Zion that had given its name to the project of Jewish national rebirth happened to be the Holy City's only heritage feature that could be part of the new State of Israel.

All in all, between 1948 and 1967, everything contributed to widening the gap that separated the two Jerusalems. Economically, Israeli Jerusalem looked toward Tel Aviv, fifty kilometers (thirty-one miles) to the west and with four hundred thousand inhabitants in 1960, while Jordanian Jerusalem looked toward Amman, fifty kilometers to the east, where a large part of the old Arab urban bourgeoisie converged, anxious to provide their children with good future prospects. Politically, Israeli Jerusalem was at the heart of a nation-building process, while Jordanian Jerusalem was deliberately kept in a marginal position. Demographically, Israeli Jerusalem attracted many immigrants and counted 190,000 residents in 1967, compared to 70,000 in Jordanian Jerusalem at the same time. On the religious and ethnic front, the old mixed neighborhoods that had existed on both sides of the demarcation line disappeared. Finally, topographically and symbolically, Israeli Jerusalem was focused on the coastal plains, the Mediterranean, and Europe, whereas Jordanian Jerusalem was oriented toward the desert, the Jordan Valley, and the Arab world. The Holy City's urban fabric, weakened by the intercommunal clashes of the 1930s and torn apart by the line of demarcation in 1948, thus disintegrated even more profoundly. On the eve of the Six-Day War, two fragments of the city coexisted, albeit at a distance, but the urban landscape's cohesion had completely vanished.

1967: Annexation

Nineteen years after the territorial partition of 1948, the new Arab-Israeli War in June 1967 allowed Israel to annex Jerusalem's eastern part, thanks to its military occupation of the whole West Bank. That month, the Jordanian municipality was abolished and the Holy City proclaimed "reunified." Seemingly, then, 1967 ended the sequence of events that began in 1948: Jerusalem, divided for a time by the fortunes of war, was newly unified as a result of a new conflict. This idea of a short "parenthesis" that closed in 1967, although accurately descriptive of the geopolitical situation, does not take into account the lived reality on the ground: just as it did not appear with the war in 1948, the gap between the city's east and west did not disappear with the war in 1967, as anyone can still observe today (see map 10).

Indeed, this gap is not a simple military cease-fire line that may appear or disappear with armed conflict; it is, as we have seen, a much deeper tear in Jerusalem's *cityness* and even *urbanity*—that is, the ability of the Holy City's inhabitants to interact, live together, and build a common destiny. As often happens, making 1967 a date of rupture which erases that of 1948 confuses Jerusalem's urban history with the Middle East's geopolitical history and, by focusing solely on diplomatic or military aspects of the region's history, only pretends to tell the city's story. This towering perspective reduces the Holy City to a mere theater of operations.

In studying the time line of events in June 1967, one is struck first and foremost by the extreme rapidity of the succession of causes and effects which led Israeli authorities to decide on an annexation that they hadn't anticipated just a few weeks earlier. The first stage, which was military, responded to an international chronology: following Egyptian troop movements in the Sinai beginning on May 15 and the Egyptian navy's closure of the Straits of Tiran (between the Gulf of Aqaba and the Red Sea) on May 21, a national unity government was formed in Israel on the evening of Saturday, June 3. On the morning of Monday, June 5, a preemptive strike by the Israeli Air Force destroyed almost all of the Egyptian Air Force on the ground, and Israel ground troops entered the Sinai. At morning's end, Jordan's King Hussein, bound to Egypt by a mutual defense treaty signed with Gamal Abdel Nasser on May 30, ordered his artillery to open fire on Israeli positions, including in Jerusalem. In the afternoon, the Israeli Air Force, freed from the Egyptian front, destroyed the Royal Jordanian Air Force on the ground. In Jerusalem itself, Jordanian infantry passed into no-man's-land and seized the Hill of Evil Counsel, which is south of the Old City and housed the city's UN headquarters.

On the evening of June 5, there was still no consensus on the Holy City in the Israeli cabinet: some ministers, such as Menachem Begin, advocated an immediate conquest, but Prime Minister Levi Eshkol feared an international response and wanted to delay any decision. On the morning of Tuesday, June 6, without waiting for an explicit political order, Generals Moshe Dayan and Yitzhak Rabin successfully undertook a movement around the Old City, making a link with the Mount Scopus enclave to the north. At the end of the day in New York (in other words, around one in the morning in Jerusalem), the UN Security Council unanimously passed a resolution calling for an immediate cease-fire; faced with the threat of a refrozen front line, the paratroopers commanded by Uzi Narkiss entered Jerusalem *intra muros* through the Lions' Gate in the early hours of Wednesday, June 7, and quickly reached the Kotel (the Wailing Wall), followed a few hours later by Moshe Dayan, Yitzhak Rabin, and several ministers and members of parliament. It should be noted that, unlike in 1948, there was no combat in the Old City itself, as the Jordanian soldiers had withdrawn en masse during the night. In less than forty-eight hours, Jerusalem's fate had turned again.

After the phase of military conquest, the second annexation stage involved the appropriation of a religiously and culturally important space. The idea was to give the Wailing Wall an esplanade designed to host large public ceremonies. As Alain Dieckhoff writes, it is striking that the very first "territorial gesture" which the Holy City's new occupier decided to make focused on this "place of hierophany" (manifestation of the sacred), explicitly underlining the exclusively religious link that united the Jewish people in Jerusalem.[38] On Sunday, June 11, only four days after the city's conquest, the Mughrabi Quarter, which faced the wall, was evacuated in a few hours and the houses of its inhabitants razed by bulldozers (see map 9). On Wednesday, June 14, 250,000 Israelis went to the Wailing Wall Plaza to celebrate Shavuot, thus inaugurating a tradition that made this new open space the young Israeli nation's symbolic heart. The rabbinical authorities of course participated in this symbolic reappropriation and even increased the pressure on the political authorities: when the city was taken on June 7, Israeli's chief military rabbi, Shlomo Goren, suggested dynamiting the Haram al-Sharif's mosques, and a few days later Israeli's chief rabbi clearly alluded to the prospect of restoring "service in the Temple" at some point.[39] Israeli political leaders rejected these two proposals, but from then on Jerusalem remained solidly attached to the project of Jewish national rebirth: the Holy City, long on the margins of the Zionist ideological framework, constituted one of the new religious Zionism's main symbolic centers beginning in 1967, on par with, in particular, the Tomb of the Patriarchs in Hebron.

The annexation's third stage was of a legal nature. However, contrary to popular belief, the Israeli political authorities did not immediately proceed to the actual annexation of East Jerusalem but instead advanced extremely cautiously: On June 27, the Knesset adopted a deliberately technical text that officially aimed only to ensure the continuity of public services on both sides of the old demarcation line. On June 28, the Arab municipality was dissolved and its archives confiscated. On July 4, the UN General Assembly passed a resolution declaring Jerusalem's annexation "invalid."[40] On July 10, Abba Eban, the Israeli minister for foreign affairs, declared to the UN that the term *annexation* was improper because the measures taken by Israel were purely technical. Here we find one of the constitutive traits of the Israeli Jerusalem strategy, which consisted of bringing about a certain number of faits accomplis before making them openly official. As it happens, it wasn't until July 30, 1980, thirteen years after the military occupation began, that the Knesset shouldered an explicitly political vote on Jerusalem, adopting a Basic Law that makes the "complete and united" Holy City the capital of Israel.[41]

The matter of the municipal area's new boundaries was particularly delicate: there was no question of adding to the Israeli municipality's territory (thirty-eight square kilometers, or fifteen square miles, before the war) only the Jordanian municipality's territory (six square kilometers, or two square miles), but at the same time it was necessary to avoid integrating too many Arabs into the new city. Meron Benvenisti, who was in charge of East Jerusalem's urban planning in the early 1970s, recounts that debates were intense throughout June 1967 between those who advocated annexing a large band of two hundred square kilometers (seventy-seven square miles) that would have cut the West Bank in half and those who worried about "too many Arab residents in the annexed area," which would have made Arabs the majority in the new municipality.[42] It should be noted in passing that this discussion frames Israel's current Jerusalem strategy, notably with respect to the creation of a settlement corridor between West Jerusalem and Jordan, via Ma'ale Adumim, effectively splitting the West Bank in two. The plan chosen by the government on June 26, 1967, was a compromise solution which expanded the municipal territory to seventy-one square kilometers (twenty-seven square miles) in total, confiscating some land adjacent to nearby Arab towns (El Bireh, Ramallah, Bethlehem), whose residential areas were not included (see map 10). It should be pointed out that these new municipal borders were still the subject of discussion over the following decades, since it was only on November 27, 2000, that an amendment was added to the Basic Law of 1980 definitively fixing the municipal territory within the limits decided at the end of June 1967. This outline, which Benvenisti stresses was "drawn in haste and without serious consideration or attention to urban exigencies, and on the basis of short-sighted historical and political presumptions," is one of the keys to the urban issues facing the Holy City today.[43]

The Failure of Reunification, 1967–1980

East Jerusalem's annexation, which Israel unilaterally decreed in 1967 but took legal and political responsibility for only in 1980, did not lead to the actual reunification of the Holy City's two parts. Whatever the chosen criterion of analysis, everything indicates that the policy of integrating the two Jerusalems failed, even if it was begun with fervor by the Labour mayor Teddy Kollek. Whether at the level of international law, municipal institutions, or the inhabitants themselves, the trend was even the opposite: illusions still perceptible in the first months of the occupation were rapidly succeeded by growing mutual distrust. Far from forming a coherent urban whole, the two Jerusalems seem to have gradually drifted apart instead.

First, on the level of international law, the condemnation of East Jerusalem's Israeli occupation grew clearer and stronger over the years. The specific case of Jerusalem is not explicitly mentioned in the well-known Resolution 242 enacted by the UN Security Council on November 22, 1967, which simply demands a comprehensive "withdrawal of Israeli armed forces from territories occupied in the recent conflict." Passed six months later, on May 21, 1968, Resolution 252 is much more precise: in it, the Security Council "*deplores* the failure of Israel to comply with the [previous] General Assembly resolutions" and emphasizes that "all legislative and administrative measures taken by Israel, including expropriation of land and properties thereon, which tend to change the legal status of Jerusalem are invalid and cannot change that status." At the time, Israel still enjoyed relative leniency from the United States, which abstained from the vote, along with Canada. That was no longer the case a year later, on July 3, 1969, during the vote on Resolution 267, dedicated exclusively to Jerusalem. During the preliminary debate, the US ambassador Charles W. Yost sharply criticized Israel's Holy City policy and pronounced, one by one, all the key words that have sealed international legal condemnation to this day: "the expropriation or confiscation of land," "the demolition or confiscation of buildings," and "the application of Israeli law to occupied portions of the city." The ambassador reminded his audience that according to the Geneva Convention, occupying powers must abstain from any modification of temporarily occupied territories. The final text of the resolution, this time unanimously approved by the Security Council's fifteen members, was definitive, reaffirming that "acquisition of territory by military conquest is inadmissible" and censuring "in the strongest terms all measures taken to change the status of the City of Jerusalem." Two years after the military conquest, the annexation unilaterally decided on by Israel was officially condemned by the international community.

On a local scale and perhaps more important, the situation on the ground worsened in the months following the war of June 1967. In fact, the speed of the lightning conquest in the face of a helpless and unmotivated Jordanian army seems to have masked the existence of a Palestinian popular resistance, which gradually gained organization and structure. It is too often forgotten that the founding congress of the Palestinian Liberation Organization (PLO) was convened in Jerusalem itself, in May and June 1964, and this despite the Hashemite monarchy's great mistrust of the Palestinian cause. Three years later, Palestinian nationalists saw the Israeli occupation of Jerusalem as an intolerable assault. After the Mughrabi Quarter's destruction on June 11, 1967, the dynamiting of the house of Fatah's military leader in Jerusalem (Kamal Nammari) on March 8, 1968, provoked the indignation of the local Arab press. On August 18, 1968, grenades were thrown at Israeli buses, injuring ten people. On November 2, 1968, the anniversary of the Balfour Declaration of 1917, the merchants of East Jerusalem held a general strike. On November 22, a car bomb exploded in the popular Mahane Yehudah, then an outdoor market, killing twelve. Already in October 1967, a bomb was discovered under a seat at the Zion Cinema on busy Ben Yehudah Street, but it produced no casualties.[44] The situation deteriorated further when an Australian Christian fundamentalist started a serious fire in Al-Aqsa Mosque on Thursday, August 21, 1969, calling for the construction of the Third Temple. It is plain to see: all the elements of today's political conflict over Jerusalem were put in place during the two years that followed the Israeli military conquest.

Besides international reactions and the local mobilization of Palestinian nationalists, the condition of municipal institutions is probably the best indicator of Israeli disillusionment and reunification's overall failure. Teddy Kollek, West Jerusalem's Labour mayor from 1965 onward, at first tried to include some members of the dissolved Jordanian municipality in his staff—for example, Yussuf al-Budeiri, the chief engineer of the former municipality, who served as the new municipal team's deputy engineer until 1972. However, the policy of integrating the two groups very quickly hit its limits and most of the former civil servants of the Jordanian municipality found themselves unemployed. Even reunification's most ardent partisans had to face the facts: Gideon Weigert, a journalist for the *Jerusalem Post*, thus wrote in his 1973 book *Israel's Presence in East Jerusalem* that "the hope, co-operation and enthusiasm vanished, to be replaced by a mood of despair and bitterness."[45] If the failure was obvious at the level of the municipal team's internal composition, it was even more manifest in the participation of Jerusalem's Palestinians in local elections: in the municipal poll of October 1969, no Arab stood as a candidate, and the Holy City's Palestinian inhabitants overwhelmingly followed an instruction to boycott the vote. The British historian Martin Gilbert, who visited Jerusalem for the first time in 1971, in the company of the left-wing Israeli writer Amos Elon, testified frankly to his disappointment, despite his positive appraisal of Mayor Teddy Kollek's policies: "Kollek . . . did his utmost to draw the Arabs into his plans and his improvement. But the divide was always there. The breaking-down of the physical barriers in 1967 had not removed it."[46]

The failure of the urban master plan is another concrete sign of reunification's failure: although the annexation of the city's eastern part could have made it possible to finally put in place a comprehensive program for the entire agglomeration, political difficulties constantly delayed the project. In 1967, when the war broke out, the last town plan for construction in West Jerusalem dated to 1959 and a new version was indeed being prepared.[47] The scheme proposed for discussion in 1968 incorporated the recent annexation and highlighted the necessity "to establish an urban structure for a unified city," but the Palestinian urban planners boycotted the commissions of inquiry that were set up, and in June 1973 the project was finally rejected. In 1981, a shorter, less ambitious program was advanced, explicitly aiming to seam together the city's two halves as a prerequisite for all future planning.[48] The discussions bogged down, and the 1981 plan still hadn't been approved in 1987 when the First Intifada erupted, further delaying the possibility of a real forward-looking urban analysis. If the start of the Oslo process (1993) allowed people to hope for a time when there would be a negotiated solution for Jerusalem, the Second Intifada (2000–2004) again dispelled the prospect of a shared urban planning vision in the Holy City: the "Master Plan 2000," proposed in 2004, to this day has not been approved by the municipal authorities.

Jerusalem since 1980: The Conquest Relaunched

At the end of the 1970s, the new Israeli strategy in Jerusalem stemmed from an admission of failure: the Holy City's unilateral "reunification" was not followed by the effects expected on the ground. Indeed, the decade only confirmed the initial trends observed after the war in 1967. On the international level, the Arab armies' surprise attack on Yom Kippur in 1973 increased the Israeli authorities' distrustfulness. On the local level, violence continued, widening the gap between Arab and Jewish neighborhoods: Fourteen dead on July 4, 1975, in a bombing at the end of Ben Yehudah Street claimed by the PLO; two dead on June 29, 1978, in the Mahane Yehudah marketplace. On April 11, 1982, a Jew born in the United States, a reservist in the Israeli army, Alan Goodman, opened fire on the Haram al-Sharif, killing a Muslim worshiper. On the governmental level, for the first time since the country's founding in 1948, the 1977 Israeli legislative elections brought the right to power, under Menachem Begin (Likud), opening the way to colonization projects in the occupied West Bank and East Jerusalem.

It is in the context of this violence and political radicalization that the Knesset's July 30, 1980, enactment of the "Jerusalem, Capital of Israel" Basic Law must be understood: faced with the failure of reunification, the Israeli right plunged headlong and unilaterally forward, believing that Jerusalem's true reconquest remained to be accomplished. International observers were not deceived, however, and their reactions indicate the magnitude of the change effected by Israel vis-à-vis the Holy City: on August 3, 1980, the *New York Times* denounced a "capital folly" and a "gratuitous and provocative new law"; the dozen countries that had installed embassies in Jerusalem after 1967 moved them to Tel Aviv; and after Prime Minister Begin announced his intention to set up his office in the city's eastern half, the unanimous outcry compelled him to renounce the idea in the end.

The Israeli reconquest strategy went beyond the legislative domain, unfolding on the ground: the Jerusalem agglomeration's current physiognomy is largely a result of choices made since 1977 (see map 10). Beyond the municipal border, at a distance of ten to fifteen kilometers (six to nine miles) from the city center, a new belt of colonies was created (notably Efrat to the south, Ma'ale Adumim to the east, and Beit El to the north) to form what Alain Dieckhoff has called a "peripheral ring" intended to protect the capital and limit its area of expansion. Subsequently, starting in the mid-1980s, settlements were founded between these external projections and the city center (Psagot, Anatot, Har Gilo . . .), forming "an ultimate safety belt for the Holy City and also a potential propagation front that could fill the still empty gap before the peripheral ring in order to create a real conurbation."[49]

In the absence of a rapid reunification of the city's different neighborhoods, this desire to "girdle" Jerusalem has been the guiding principle of Israeli policy since the early 1980s, regardless of which party is in power. The strategy relies on a certain number of legal zoning tools designed to make available the peripheral territories chosen to house new settlements. The Jabal Abu Ghneim hill, between Jerusalem and Bethlehem, was thus declared a "protected green zone" in 1969 before being transformed into a "residential zone" in 1996, allowing the construction of the vast colony of Har Homa (literally "Wall mountain"), which has almost fifteen thousand inhabitants today (see map 10).[50] However, this strategy, which consists of moving the colonization front beyond city limits, may have enabled an indisputable seizure of the peri-urban territory, but it has not enabled Israel to tilt the demographic balance in its own favor in Jerusalem's municipal territory. The figures speak for themselves: the Jewish population represented 74 percent and Arabs 26 percent of Jerusalem's inhabitants in 1967. The ratio was 64 percent to 36 percent in 2006 and 61 to 39 in 2016—and this despite the high fertility rate of the city's Jewish residents.[51] Since 1967, Jerusalem's Jewish population has multiplied by 2.5, while the Arab population has quadrupled. This is the paradox: by focusing on the peripheral settlements, the Israeli strategy is thus threatened by a powerful Palestinian demographic resilience in the agglomeration's very center. This structural fact, rarely mentioned by observers, is one of the keys to Jerusalem's political future.

In December 1987, the First Intifada broke out, coupling the Palestinian demographic resilience with a popular uprising that definitively sapped Israeli hopes for an imminent reunification of the Holy City. Until 1993, the attacks were accompanied by riots, nighttime violence, demonstrations, the closure of Arab shops, and strikes, which the Israeli army was unable to contain. In November 1988, at the PLO's Palestinian National Council meeting in Algiers, Yasser Arafat proclaimed the independence of the State of Palestine, with Jerusalem as its capital, while endorsing the UN's Resolution 242, which was tantamount to implicitly recognizing

Israel. In the years that followed, the clashes were particularly deadly in the Holy City. Five Israeli Jews were killed in Jerusalem by Palestinians in 1989; on October 8, 1990, twenty Palestinians were killed by the Israeli army on the Esplanade of the Mosques. On June 2, 1989, in the London *Jewish Chronicle*, Eric Silver frankly noted that "Jerusalem is still a divided city."[52]

The Palestinian uprising finally marked the failure of the optimistic and moderate political approach incarnated since 1967 by the Labour mayor Teddy Kollek. In 1987 he acknowledged that "coexistence is dead," and according to his deputy Meron Benvenisti, "he was the first to admit publicly: 'We really have done nothing for the Arabs.'"[53] During the local elections in 1993, the contradictions of Kollek's municipal policy and the increasing demographic power of the ultra-Orthodox Jews contributed to the victory of Ehud Olmert (Likud), Jerusalem's mayor until the city elections of 2003, which saw the ultra-Orthodox Uri Lupolianski win before the right regained the direction of civic affairs in 2008 with Nir Barkat's triumph at the polls. Once again, the municipality offered a good vantage point on the historical developments at work in the Holy City.

·   ·   ·   ·   ·

Jerusalem's several-thousand-year history did not stop at the threshold of the twenty-first century. Quite the contrary: it is now at a surprising junction. It was proclaimed the eternal and indivisible capital of Israel in 1980, but statistically it is the least Jewish of the country's three major metropolises (compared to Tel Aviv and Haifa), due to both the strong Palestinian demographic resilience and the significantly negative migration balance of the city's Jews, who today are only 64 percent of its total population, versus 74 percent in 1967. Geopolitically, Jerusalem's unilateral "capitalization" is still not recognized by the international community, and the city is also claimed as the capital of the State of Palestine, whose United Nations status was changed to "non-member observer state" in November 2012. Within the population itself, divisions are widening between secular Jewish residents and ultra-Orthodox communities, which today represent almost a third of the Jewish populace and have a strong impact on the conduct of municipal affairs. Jerusalem is thus more than ever a paradoxical—even an "impossible"—capital, torn apart by its triple standing as universal, national, and binational capital. As a sign of this historical uncertainty, the Holy City was deliberately excluded from the negotiations, begun in 1993, between the Israelis and the Palestinians: no one knows how to include "the Jerusalem question" in a two-state solution and comprehensive settlement of the conflict.

To illustrate the paradoxical moment that Jerusalem is currently traversing, let us return one last time to the concrete spaces and living conditions of its inhabitants: today, although the eastern part constitutes 37 percent of the city's territory, only 13 percent of the municipal budget is devoted to it, compared with 87 percent for West Jerusalem, which contributes to the gap between the two Jerusalems that widens more with each year. According to the urban researcher Jonathan Rokem, this means that the Holy City "is developing into two distinct growth poles, with the crossover parts and old border areas remaining mainly as division points between the two sides of the city." Let us be even more precise, to underline what separates the city's Palestinian and Jewish inhabitants today. According to municipal statistics for Jerusalem, 37 percent of Palestinians live in homes with more than six people, compared to 8 percent of Israelis. The average housing density of Palestinian lodgings (0.7 rooms per person) is almost three times higher than that of Israeli lodgings (1.9 rooms per person).[54] As one might imagine, this overpopulation generates a multitude of other problems, relating to comfort, privacy, safety, and hygiene. The desire of Israeli authorities to constrict Jerusalem's Palestinian population growth thus has very concrete urban planning consequences. In other words, geopolitical issues today have generated and maintained a serious urban crisis in the Holy City's eastern half.

Given this situation, there are only two possibilities: a top-down approach, which is to say an attempt at a global political solution as a precondition for the modification of the local city planning rules; or, on the contrary, a bottom-up approach, meaning an immediate reorientation of the urban planning rules as the first step of the conflict's final resolution. The second approach, today advocated with some success by the Israeli association Ir Amim ("City of peoples" in Hebrew) and by the Palestinian association Peace and Democracy Forum, will perhaps pave the way to a shared future for the city's current eight hundred thousand inhabitants, five hundred thousand Israelis and three hundred thousand Palestinians. At once a universal holy city, binational metropolis, and capital of two states, Jerusalem will have to invent a singular political model in the years to come in order to face the yet unwritten pages of its history.

Conclusion

THE MEMORY OF THE DEAD, THE HISTORY OF THE LIVING

> The chronicles of Jerusalem are a gigantic quarry from
> which each side has mined stones for the construction of its
> myths—and for throwing at each other.
>
> Meron Benvenisti, *City of Stone*

At the end of this journey, how can we characterize Jerusalem's inscription in its past, if not as a shared history that is as indispensable as it is impossible, a story of the living always suffocating under the memory of the dead? Meron Benvenisti, the city's deputy mayor after the 1967 war and Israel's annexation of East Jerusalem, is one of the rare historians to have essayed a local, political, and contemporary account of Jerusalem. Almost thirty years later, the pessimistic key to interpreting his attempt, quoted in the epigraph to this conclusion, remains a vital aid for every historian of the Holy City: Jerusalem's history is a quarry of rocks intended for the construction of myths and destruction of adversaries. If the image of a historiographic intifida can seem forced, what it reveals is indisputable: because Jerusalem's sites have been shared for centuries, its history is a permanent instrument of struggle and possession.[1]

The forced or imagined unity of these places has no equivalent in speech, and histories that do not use space as their main narrative vehicle are rare. Jerusalem by turns "captive" and "delivered"? Mirroring its walls, the city's successive conquests, captures, and recaptures have imprisoned the periodization of its history: 587 BCE to 70 CE, 638 to 1187, 1917 to 1967. The topographical persistence of Jerusalem and its sanctuaries, alternately enshrined and challenged, hinders their being placed in history. The obvious polyphony of sources—from the Old Testament chronicles to those of the Crusades, from Jewish, Christian, and Muslim pilgrimage accounts to travel books about nineteenth-century grand tours—doubles the paradox: excepting the works by a few rare locals, such as the historian Flavius Josephus, the geographer al-Muqaddasi, and the chronicler Mujir al-Din al-'Ulaymi, the narratives are almost all from outsiders, fascinated by the contemplation of a topography that had become universal and thus imaginary.

But what exactly did these travelers see and retranscribe, if not that famous "legendary topography" glimpsed by Maurice Halbwachs, which they tried with all their might to make coincide with their own perceptions?[2] Jerusalem is first and foremost an imaginary, imagined, transportable, projectable, and finally fantasized city. Christianity, because it was founded on an empty tomb and on the theological injunction to abandon and forget Jerusalem, undoubtedly differs from the two other monotheist traditions in its ability to "duplicate" the Holy City, and with it a significant share of biblical toponyms. From Constantinople to Ethiopia's Lalibela, from Rome to Paris, the New Jerusalems are legion, to the point that each parish has celebrated and delineated, ad infinitum, on its own patch of land and at every Easter, the imaginary map of the Stations of the Cross, from the Garden of Olives to Golgotha. As for the destroyed Temple, it became the architectural model for "houses of God"—that is, churches.

This duplication goes as far as the very real removal of material fragments from the city. Without even mentioning the numerous relics from tombs, the most significant extraction was without doubt the one effected in 1225, after the Fifth Crusade's failure, by fifty galleys from Pisa: to supply the soil for the Italian city-state's new *campo santo* (cemetery), they transported from the other side of the Mediterranean mounds of earth taken from beneath the Holy City. This massive puncture in Jerusalem's terrain is echoed by the thousands of bags of earth from the Mount of Olives deposited on myriad Jewish tombs around the global to this day. In this first sense, Jerusalem is indeed an open-air quarry, which founds its own avatars *extra muros;* it is thus in a strict sense a "global city," through its capacity for universal diffusion and duplication—to the extent that visiting the actual city and its monuments, which sometimes appear quite modest in comparison with their multiple transpositions, gives the traveler a strange feeling of displacement.

Even when brought to these places by religious belief, contemporary visitors, like their predecessors, generally experience a form of disappointment, born of the obvious disparity between their mental map and what they observe. At the point of contact between the celestial and the terrestrial, the sightseer is perturbed by a strange sense of disproportion between the universality of the toponyms and the meager reality of their physical survival. This book has tried, in its own way, to account for this gap in perception, which can be detected in many testimonies. But is it really about "survivals"—or, rather, permanent reconstructions? For it must be admitted that Jerusalem, despite its status of collective good inherited by and disputed within monotheistic humanity, is an eminently anti-heritage place. This remark is not innocent and forms the first conclusive idea to emerge from this history: if nothing is physically authentic anymore, all discourse must be.

A full history of Jerusalem must thus deal with the incessant back-and-forth between the real and legendary cities, which has produced an indisputable plasticity of sites, according to beliefs and their successive translations. From the "City" to the "Tower" of David, the Dome of the Rock to the Mosque of 'Umar, the Via Dolorosa to Christ's sepulchre—not to mention the walls, pools, and aqueducts of Solomon/Süleyman—the pages of this book have shown how much intentional reconstructions can prevail over the history of the real things on which they are based (see maps 6, 7, and 8 in chapters 3, 4, and 6, respectively). The sanctuaries' cyclical reparation is thus a mark of an obsession with actualizing the sacred, to the point that the work sites are always inscribed within the same "restorative" chronology: in the mid-sixteenth century, the early nineteenth century, and then the 1960s and 1970s, the massive reconstruction phases of the Church of the Holy Sepulchre and the Dome of the Rock were concurrent. Jerusalem's face has never stopped being renewed.

Most historical overviews are thus condemned to situate their remarks, without fully coming to terms with this, as if in suspension between the city as it is represented and as it is experienced: to take only one example, such narratives constantly superimpose the Valley of Jehoshaphat, the valley of the Last Judgment, charged with eschatological significance in the three monotheisms, over the modest valley formed by the intermittent Kidron stream (see maps 1 and 2, in the introduction and chapter 1, respectively). And the very name of the principal shrine—Mount Moriah, Temple Mount, Templum Domini, Haram al-Sharif—at every step commits the historian to writing a universal story with definitive pretensions, when it should instead be simply urban and humbly local (see map 3 in chapter 1 and maps 4 and 5 in chapter 2).

TELLING THE LOCAL STORY OF A GLOBAL CITY

How to write the history of a city trapped in its symbolic "global" function? It is clear that a local and social history of Jerusalem is, by that measure, almost impossible. The preceding pages have nonetheless tried to stick to this unlikely scale of the story. In this regard, it seems that two factors, closely linked for a very long time, emerge from all the analyses: the city's political alienation and its structural demographic deficit.

The presumed capital of the kings of Israel in biblical times, Jerusalem has nonetheless tended to be marginalized by historically attested political powers. With the exception of local princes such as Herod; Emperor Hadrian, who gave it his name for a time; Caliph ʿAbd al-Malik, who erected the only monument of its kind with the Dome of the Rock; and the Frankish feudal barons who assumed the title of king of Jerusalem to rule what was in fact a mere county, potentates with universal claims indirectly took over the city but strangely avoided it. To the great regret of historians, Alexander the Great, Constantine, Saint Louis IX, Süleyman, and Napoleon never visited Jerusalem, even though they stayed in the surrounding area. In the fifth century, the repudiated Empress Eudocia made it her place of exile and residence; in the eighth century, one of Saladin's nephews, a second-rank prince who bore the Arab name of the prophet Jesus (al-Muʿazzam ʿIsa), linked his political fate to the city's, all the way to defeat. Then, in 1229, Emperor Frederick II, *stupor mundi* (wonder of the world) and an Antichrist figure for the papacy, who dreamed about his power as much as he exercised it, spent a night there to organize his self-coronation as the kingdom's ruler before his double excommunication doomed his career as a universal emperor. Although Baybars stayed briefly as a pilgrim, Tamerlane overtly despised the city and its notables. And until Paul VI's trip in 1964, no pope had ever gone to Jerusalem. Certainly, from Heraclius to the Armenian king Hetum II and from Saladin to Moshe Dayan by way of Selim I and Allenby, Jerusalem has known a fine procession of conquerors, but until the mid-twentieth century none of them transformed the city into the administrative headquarters of a new power.

This apparent anomaly has been transposed, however, into political fictions with very real historical effects: for example, the legendary tale of Jerusalem's conquest by Caliph 'Umar and the writing of the pact that bears his name, elaborated by the Muslim tradition more than a century after his death, integrate the Holy City and its Christian population into the Islamic imperial order; as for "the pilgrimage of Charlemagne," literally invented in the eleventh century, it was one of the grounds that justified the launching of the First Crusade, preached in 1095.

The political extraterritoriality of this impossible capital is linked to a second common thread that runs through this book's chapters: Jerusalem has never really been able to stabilize its population; the city of the dead has always prevailed over the city of the living there, as if the necropolis had always hindered the development of the metropolis. The city's demographic growth dates only to the twentieth century—that is to say, precisely to its political *recapitalization* (see maps 9 and 10 in chapter 7); until then, Jerusalem's indigenous demographic base was always fragile. It is easy to presume as many exoduses as more or less voluntary exiles from 70 to 1187. The demographic projections are indeed instructive: the trading post of the sacred that the nineteenth century reinvented, thanks to Ottoman benevolence, struggled to reach the hypothetical figures of the brief Herodian capital (between forty thousand and eighty thousand inhabitants).

This stagnation of the urban population undoubtedly masks a migration problem that each new conqueror tried to overcome. After the Franks, Saladin installed new residents, notably from the Maghreb, thus echoing other migratory waves, in which it is difficult to differentiate between mystical journey, temporary retirement, and permanent settlement, but whose mark remained on the city's toponymy at the beginning of the twentieth century (e.g., Harat al-Saltin, "Quarter of the inhabitants of Salt," a town in Jordan; Harat al-Mashraqa, "Quarter of the Easterners"; Harat al-Maghariba, "Mughrabi Quarter"; Bab al-Sarb, "Gate of the Serbs").

The city's social stratification is a matter of debate: patrician genealogies existed, of course, particularly around the guardianship of the holy places, but new ones replaced them at a steady pace. The time of the Turks, from the fourteenth to the nineteenth century, was certainly a moment of low water and fairly strong stabilization, with Jerusalem's oldest notable families dating back to the Mamluk era, although the local dignitaries of the nineteenth century, who would try their hand at the municipal venture after the 1860s, could not invoke a true genealogical antiquity. As for the city's paupers, they blend in with pilgrims of all persuasions—not those who passed through and could afford the luxury of coming back, for they were not poor, but rather those who went to Jerusalem to die, destitute and finally facing the foundation myth that justified the pilgrimage: the expectation of the Last Judgment and the End Times.

Writing a local, social, and urban history of Jerusalem remains an almost inaccessible objective, whose first difficulty lies in the nature of the sources, all more or less deceitful and turned against one another. They have yet to be discovered—that is to say, in the literal sense, to be laid bare. The city's "archives"—produced, amassed, and sorted by institutions, social groups, religious communities—are dispersed throughout the world, from Istanbul to Moscow, Rome to Yerevan, Nantes to London, Athens to Addis Ababa, Amman to Abu Dis. . . .

In Jerusalem itself, as might be expected, owing to misrepresentations of communities, political exploitation, and identity differentiation, there is no repository that could act as a settling tank or buffer space; the city's memory thus remains fractured, smashed, in tatters. The rediscovery, twenty-five years ago, in the Israeli municipal archives of some fifteen registers recording the minutes of the mixed city council's meetings at the end of the Ottoman period has, however, given rise to another way of considering the city's history. In the wake of this discovery, the Open Jerusalem program, funded by the European Research Council, has been a catalyst of invigorating experiments that lay the foundations for a local, social, and urban history of the Holy City.[3]

FROM MYTH TO TOPOGRAPHY: A UNIVERSAL NECROPOLIS?

This book has offered a collective stroll through this "quarry" of sources, incomplete remnants from which grafted-on myths can become fragments of history, closely associating, in joyous disorder, stories that copy one another, truncated or otherwise transformed quotations, visible and hidden monuments, and data reconstructed by recent archaeology. Confined to the rare observation windows that the permanence of dwelling and sacred spaces have afforded it—notably excluding the Esplanade of the Mosques / Temple Mount, which has been virtually untouched by any modern excavation operation—archaeology alone has not enabled the resolution of the contradiction that would allow an escape from the obsessive rut of a *besieged* history. Put in the service of current planning policies and urban conquests, ancient and medieval remains are trapped in their relationships to preexisting textual traditions, from the Bible to the Muslim tradition and Crusader chronicles. This is so much the case that since the end of the nineteenth century, Western-style biblical archaeology has provoked another undeclared war, of ruins and relics, whose principal objective remains the conquest of new holy places.

Here is just one example of many: when, in 1863, the Frenchman Félix de Saulcy discovered a cavity at the foot of a giant staircase nine meters (thirty feet) high north of the city's walls, he hoped to have found nothing less than King Solomon's tomb, whose location no tradition had ever fixed. . . . Then as now, archaeological sites, like so many whiffs of the sacred, offered the starting point for a perpetual war of sepulchres: because Saulcy discovered bones in this tomb, the Hebrew-language newspaper *Ha-Magid* was disturbed by this "profanation"; it was even imagined that the remains of Rabbi Akiva (second century CE), one of the leading founders of Rabbinic Judaism after the Temple's destruction, could be found there. That was why a Frenchwoman of Jewish origin, Bertha Bertrand, acquired the parcel, to make it an element of the Jewish people's heritage. One of her heirs, Henri Pereire, nonetheless donated it to France in 1886, and since then a blue, white, and red flag has flown on the site, whose gate announces, without irony, "French Republic / Tomb of the Kings." Recent excavations there, however, have identified the family vault of Queen

Helena of Adiabene, who reigned over a territory in what is now northern Iraq before converting to Judaism at the beginning of the first century CE and traveling from so far away to Jerusalem, where she died.

A little to the south of this site, beyond the École biblique et archéologique française and toward the Damascus Gate, is the "Garden Tomb": in the midst of ancient quarries, antique tombs by the dozen. . . . One of them, which Anglican scholars found, empty, in 1867, has since become a supposed location of Christ's burial, an increasingly successful alternative Holy Sepulchre (see map 3 in chapter 1). Opportunely, the old crumbling limestone cliff that borders this vast enclosure is pierced by two closely spaced holes that appear, with a bit of imagination, to be part of the face of a human skull, justifying the attribution of the name Golgotha— "Skull" in Aramaic—to a site that is certainly outside the city walls.

While fueling mythography, these archaeological operations, long carried out "with Bible in hand," will undoubtedly offer, with time, the means to go beyond it. Following the work of Neil Asher Silberman and Israel Finkelstein, a rich recent summary gives a glimpse of the promise of a progressive invalidation of the strict "biblical" reading of Jerusalem's archaeological space, and thus a circumvention of the mythical narrative, for the attempt to write a real urban history of the city, including its earliest periods.[4]

That being said, it is impossible to reduce Jerusalem entirely to its *local history:* its mythical dimension, its function as a *global memorial,* cannot be evaded. Recognized by all the monotheistic traditions as the place of both their origin and the end of the world, Jerusalem seems unable to belong to itself; indeed, it is in this second sense that Jerusalem is a global city. The rock that gives its name to the Dome is thus assimilated to the stone on which the Creator founded the world—a historian's analysis must deal with this symbolic detail. But how? How to historically account for the foundations of the sacredness of this modest city perched eight hundred meters (0.5 miles) above the shores of the Mediterranean and some twelve hundred meters (0.75 miles) above those of the Dead Sea?

The question posed by any global history of Jerusalem is precisely situated in the silence of an apparently eternal confrontation between contemporary tombs, mythical necropolises, and the universal mausoleum of the unburied Holocaust dead: it demands a voyage in time that starts with prebiblical horizons but is also a tour of the city's space, a journey that takes off from the first archaeological traces present under the houses and streets—tombs, rightly—and interrogates the very origins of the sacredness conferred by the vast monotheistic world on the city of Jerusalem. This is a sacredness that ceaselessly explores and contradicts the never-broken links between the presence of the dead, the development of the city, and the production of the sacred itself.

The situation, the site, and especially the intimate topography of Jerusalem itself have closely depended, over the very long term, on the dialogue, the friction, the overlapping, and even the confusion between the space of the dead and the city of the living, whether "indigenous" urbanites or pilgrims on a one-way trip, keeping in mind that the latter went and still go to Jerusalem certainly to pray, sometimes to live, but above all to die while awaiting the End Times promised by the apocalyptic traditions of the three monotheisms. Jerusalem's eschatological function as both local urban space and global sacred esplanade must thus be grasped differently in order to finally understand why this city is the theater for a singular score in which the symphony of origins constantly mixes with the cacophony of the End of Days, genesis always combined with apocalypse, and all of this reactivated by the stagecraft of the global media with each new battle, each new attack, each new confrontation where the stone-throwing teenager is *both* a young Palestinian fighting against the Israeli occupier *and* a new incarnation—with the positions reversed—of David versus Goliath.

Should the image of "tomb of history" thus be added to that of "quarry of the past"? Can the city's resistance to its historical takeovers find some kind of rational explanation here? The superimposed quarries of history, memory, and myth are in fact meaningless without the omnipresence of the dead, even as a large number of the stone quarries in the outskirts have periodically been converted into cemeteries or sanctuaries, as in the disturbing case of the Nabi Samwil site, which overlooks the city from the northwest (see map 10 in chapter 7). In the heart of a stone quarry, which recent archaeology shows was in operation up to the Herodian era, stands the prophet Samuel's cenotaph, now the double base of a mosque (in the former nave) and a synagogue (in the crypt) after having been, in the time of the Crusades, the seat of a church, whose choir and transept can still be visited today.

An exceptional promontory from which one can see the Holy City for the first time when coming from the sea, this hill that the Crusaders baptized Mount of Joy (Mons Gaudi) now offers a singular view: below the tomb of the prophet who anointed the first two kings of Judah, Saul and David, stretch the dual peaks of contemporary Israel's remembrance—the memorial hill of Yad Vashem and Mount Herzl, the symbolic sepulchre for the victims of the Holocaust adjoining the commemorative site for the "Visionary of the State," whose body was moved there from a Vienna cemetery in 1949.

It is thus impossible to tell the story of Jerusalem and its imaginaries without considering the vast collective cemetery that it has represented for centuries for millions of believers around the world. Moreover, this is partially what the power of its places and the necessity of the journey are based on, because the omnipresence of tombs strung like beads around the city and its walls cannot fail to strike the traveler, like Chateaubriand in 1806. If one tried to map the phenomenon, one would realize that tombs appear almost everywhere, as if they were Jerusalem's true bedrock. Indeed, this deceptively invisible population is not confined to the immense and still active cemeteries on the Mount of Olives (Jews and Christians) and along the wall at the foot of the Esplanade of the Mosques (Muslims). Smaller ones nestle together according to community and national affiliations, as on Mount Zion, whose slopes notably house Protestant and German necropolises—where Oskar Schindler, for instance, reposes today. His tomb can be visited a few steps from the Chamber of the Holocaust, the first memorial to the Shoah dead, established in 1948 as a giant collective cenotaph, which illustrates, with plaques donated by members of the diaspora's disappeared communities, the diffracted motif of an impossible burial.

Vast operations of urban reconquest are in the process of covering still other graves, such as those of Ma'min Allah (Mamilla), the Muslim cemetery in West Jerusalem's heart, over part of which a pleasure garden already extends and on which is rising, by a sad twist of fate, the future Museum of Tolerance Jerusalem, constructed by the Simon Wiesenthal

Center (see map 9 in chapter 7). As for the Mount of Olives, it reached saturation long ago and is now reserved for famous, wealthy, or foreign dead. If the Arab suburb of Silwan resists, albeit with difficulty, this cemetery's extension, a counterattack by archaeological and funerary spaces on urban spaces, most of the dead to come will await the End Times a little farther afield, in the new, peripheral modern multistory cemeteries.

At the mercy of territorial struggles and political hopes, the memory of the dead and the history of the living thus devour each other. Will Jerusalem's ever-increasing dead agree to make room for the living, to let them write a new chapter of a shared history?

Chronology

19th century BCE	Jerusalem's name (as *Rushalimum*) appears on an Egyptian figurine.
18th century BCE	Remains of a walled fortress dating to this period; first phase of construction of the well called Warren's Shaft.
1550–1200 BCE	Decline of most sites in the Canaan highlands.
14th century BCE	Presence of tombs on the west slope of the Mount of Olives.
	The king or governor Abdi-Heba (or Abdi-Hepa) rules Jerusalem (named Urushalim); he is subject to the Egyptian pharaoh's authority.
	Akkadian clay tablet from this period found on the Ophel is the oldest written document discovered in Jerusalem.
12th or 11th century BCE	Stepped Stone Structure, identified by E. Mazar as supporting the foundations of the "Palace of David," built on the Ophel.
12th–11th centuries BCE	"Jebusite" period.
10th century BCE	Supposed period of the reigns of David and Solomon, per biblical chronology.
	Construction of a sanctuary and a palatial complex on the future Temple Mount.

8th century BCE	Unprecedented urban development; construction of walls and the so-called Hezekiah's Tunnel.
722 BCE	Capture of Samaria, the Kingdom of Israel's capital, by the Assyrian king Shalmaneser V.
701 BCE	Assyrian siege of Jerusalem (during Hezekiah's reign).
586 BCE	Babylonian siege and destruction of the Temple.
539/538 BCE	The Persian king Cyrus II authorizes the return of exiles to Jerusalem and the reconstruction of the Temple.
521 BCE	Supposed date of the beginning of the Temple's reconstruction, attributed to Zerubbabel.
302 BCE	Capture of Jerusalem by Ptolemy I Soter, bringing it under Lagid (Ptolemaic) dominion.
198 BCE	Capture of the city by Antiochus III—Jerusalem comes under Seleucid control.
196 BCE	Death of the high priest Simon II, the initiator of important works in the Temple.
174/173 BCE	Supposed date of the founding of the Seleucid city of Antiochia in Jerusalem.
167 BCE	Desecration of the sanctuary by Antiochus IV and uprising of the priest Mattathias (according to 1 Maccabees).
164 BCE	Purification of the sanctuary by Judas Maccabaeus.
141 BCE	Simon Maccabaeus takes control of the Akra fortress; relative independence of Judaea.
135–104 BCE	High priesthood of John Hyrcanus.
134–133 BCE	City besieged by Antiochus VII.
129/128 BCE	Death of Antiochus VII; independence of the Kingdom of Judah.
Late 2nd–early 1st century BCE	Erection of a fortress (Baris) northwest of the Temple Mount and of a palace in the Upper City's north.
103–76 BCE	Reign of Alexander Jannaeus, apogee of the "Hasmonean" period.
63 BCE	Capture of the city by Pompey, who penetrates the Temple.
54 BCE	Crassus takes part of the Temple's treasure.
37 BCE	City comes under the control of Herod the Great.

37–4 BCE	Reign of Herod the Great; construction of a palace and numerous public buildings, reconstruction of the Baris (the future Antonia Fortress), and enlargement of the Temple and the esplanade.
6 CE	Judaea comes under Rome's direct control.
26–36	Pontius Pilate serves as prefect of Judaea.
Early 30s	Preaching and execution of Yehoshua Ben Yosef ("Jesus of Nazareth" in the Gospels).
40–41	Emperor Caligula plans to put a statue of himself in the Temple.
41–42	Construction of the third city wall by Agrippa I, grandson of Herod the Great.
Circa 50	Conjectural date of the "Council of Jerusalem." Beginning of Paul's preaching.
Circa 56	Queen Helena of Adiabene solemnly buried in Jerusalem on the site now known as the Tombs of the Kings.
70	Conquest of the city and destruction of the Temple by Titus. Installation of the Legio X Fretensis.
Circa 75–79	Flavius Josephus writes *The Jewish War*.
Circa 130	Foundation by Hadrian of a Roman colony, Aelia Capitolina, on the site of Jerusalem.
132–35	Bar Kokhba Jewish revolt.
201	Emperor Septimius Severus visits Aelia Capitolina, where he perhaps meets Yehudah ha-Nasi (Judah the Prince), to whom the Mishnah's compilation is attributed.
230	Origen is ordained as a priest in Aelia Capitolina. He nonetheless establishes his Christian theological school in Caesarea (231).
Circa 240	The Legio X Fretensis garrison leaves Aelia Capitolina, probably in connection with the Roman Empire's military crises.
258–73	Aelia Capitolina in the orbit of the ephemeral independent "kingdom" of Palmyra (Odaenathus and Zenobia).
312	Emperor Constantine converts to Christianity.
323–24	Eusebius of Caesarea composes his *Ecclesiastical History*.

325	Council of Nicaea.
325–27	Stay in Jerusalem of Helena, Constantine's mother. Invention of the legend of the rediscovered Cross and supposed foundation of the Church of the Holy Sepulchre.
333	Journey of the Bordeaux Pilgrim (author of the oldest known Christian pilgrimage account).
335	*September 13:* Official dedication of the new Basilica of the Holy Sepulchre, per the Liturgy of Jerusalem.
Circa 360	Composition of the Jerusalem Talmud.
361–63	Emperor Julian the Apostate plans to rebuild Jerusalem's Jewish Temple.
380	The Edict of Thessalonica proclaims that all the Roman Empire's peoples must accept the Christian faith.
381–84	Egeria's pilgrimage.
386	Pilgrimage of Paula, accompanied by Jerome, who had moved to Bethlehem to translate the Bible into Latin.
417	Stay in Jerusalem of Melania the Younger, who founds many monasteries.
420	Death of Jerome, whose remains are buried in Jerusalem.
422–58	Episcopate of Juvenal, bishop of Aelia.
437–38	Peter the Iberian's pilgrimage.
437–60	Exile of Empress Eudocia (wife of Theodosius II) in Jerusalem.
438	Construction of the Church of Saint Stephen on Eudocia's impetus.
451	Council of Chalcedon.
452	Aelia obtains the title of patriarchate under the name of Jerusalem.
Early 6th century	Theodosius writes his pilgrimage guide.
After 530	Jerusalem benefits from investments by Emperor Justinian (r. 527–65).
543	Dedication of the Nea Ekklesia (New Church of Saint Mary).
560–70	Journey of the Piacenza Pilgrim.

Late sixth century	The Madaba Mosaic Map (from present-day Jordan) illustrates part of the city.
614	Capture of the city by the Persians, who, however, prefer Caesarea as the provincial capital.
	Alleged exile of the "True Cross" to Ctesiphon.
628	Retaking of Jerusalem by Emperor Heraclius.
630	Return of the "True Cross" relic; forced baptisms and expulsion of the Jewish population.
635–38	City under the control of Caliph 'Umar's troops; "True Cross" transferred to Constantinople (c. 636).
	Probable installation of a first Muslim sanctuary in Jerusalem, on the present site of the Citadel (Tower of David).
640–60	Probable construction of the city's first Muslim place of worship, at Al-Aqsa Mosque's current location.
661	Mu'awiya proclaims himself caliph in Jerusalem.
Circa 680	Pilgrimage of Bishop Arculf from Gaul.
685	'Abd al-Malik is proclaimed caliph in Jerusalem and rebuilds the city's mosque, on Al-Aqsa Mosque's current site.
688–92	'Abd al-Malik has the Dome of the Rock built, under the direction of Raja ibn Haywa.
713–14	Earthquakes collapse 'Abd al-Malik's mosque, which his son and successor al-Walid restores.
758	Reconstruction of the esplanade mosque following the Abbasid revolution. Caliph al-Mansur personally supervises the work on-site.
770	Caliph al-Mansur's second stay in Jerusalem.
780	Caliph al-Mahdi stays in Jerusalem.
831	Last great intervention in Jerusalem of the Abbasid caliphs: al-Ma'mun has a bronze door installed in the esplanade mosque.
Circa 960	Inhumation of Egyptian Ikhshidid princes at the Haram al-Sharif's northwest corner.
Circa 990	Description of Jerusalem by al-Muqaddasi, a native of the city.

1009	The Fatimid caliph al-Hakim orders the dismantling of the Church of the Holy Sepulchre.
1012	First reconstruction of the Holy Sepulchre by the city's Christians.
1019	Al-Wasiti composes *The Spiritual Merits of the Holy House [Jerusalem]*, a text contemporaneous with Ibn al-Murajja's *The Spiritual Merits of the Holy House [Jerusalem] and Hebron and the Spiritual Merits of Syria.*
After 1021	The Fatimid authorities grant the Jews a sanctuary (the Cave, *ha-Me'ara*) in one of the gates of the Haram's western wall.
1033	An earthquake destroys numerous buildings and the city's ramparts; it is seen as a harbinger of the End Times.
1034	The Fatimid caliph al-Zahir launches the restoration of Al-Aqsa Mosque.
1039	The Georgian king Bagrat IV finances the construction of the Monastery of the Cross.
1047	Pilgrimage of the Persian Nasir-i Khusraw.
	Al-Quds becomes the usual way to refer to the city.
1048	Completion of the Holy Sepulchre's reconstruction, financed by the Byzantine emperor.
	Christians from Amalfi found the Church of Saint Mary of the Latins, to the south of the sanctuary, and an associated hospice for pilgrims.
Circa 1050	Dedication to the parchment codex with the Hebrew Bible's transcription (called the Aleppo Codex) written for Jerusalem's Karaite Jewish community.
1063	Reconstruction of the city's ramparts ordered by the Fatimid caliph al-Mustansir.
1073–76	Al-Quds comes under the control of Atsiz's Seljuk Turks (Sunnites), who make it their capital for three years.
1078	Repression of the Muslim urban elites by the Seljuk authorities.
Circa 1080	The Yeshivat Geon Ya'aqov quits Jerusalem and settles in the port of Tyre.
1090	Stay of the great mystic al-Ghazali.

1092	The Seljuk Turks entrust Jerusalem's government to a Christian; the city's Jacobite and Coptic communities are authorized to construct a sanctuary dedicated to Mary Magdalene on the north side.
1092–95	Stay of the Andalusian traditionist Abu Bakr ibn al-'Arabi.
1095	Council of Clermont, including Pope Urban II's call to crusade.
1098	Brief reconquest of the city by the Egyptian Fatimids.
1099	*July 15:* Capture of Jerusalem and massacre of its civilian population by the Crusaders.
	July 17: Godfrey of Bouillon refuses Jerusalem's royal title; later (Easter 1100), as the Holy Sepulchre's "advocate," he promises Patriarch Dagobert of Pisa seigneury over the whole city.
1100	Death of Godfrey of Bouillon, who is buried just outside the Chapel of Adam in the Holy Sepulchre complex.
	Coronation of Baldwin I on December 25.
1101	Resumption of pilgrimages to Jerusalem by Middle Eastern Christians.
1104	Baldwin I establishes his royal residence in Al-Aqsa Mosque, later conventionally called "Solomon's palace."
	Installation of an abbey in the Dome of the Rock, referred to as Templum Domini.
1113	Pope Paschal II recognizes the Hospital of Saint John of Jerusalem's independence from the Church of Saint Mary of the Latins.
1114	Construction of the Chapel of Saint Helena in the north part of the Anastasis, which shortly precedes the Romanesque remodeling of the Holy Sepulchre.
1115	Repopulation of Jerusalem through an appeal for voluntary immigration by Middle Eastern Christians.
1116	Robert the Monk, an eyewitness of the Council of Clermont, writes his *History of Jerusalem*.
1118	Death of Baldwin I, the first king of Jerusalem. He is buried in the Chapel of Adam in the Church of the Holy Sepulchre, which becomes the necropolis for Jerusalem's kings, the last of whom will be interred there in 1186.

1119 or 1120	King Baldwin II supports the foundation of the order of the "Poor Fellow-Soldiers of Christ" (future Order of the Temple, or Knights Templar), which installs itself in "Solomon's palace" (Al-Aqsa Mosque).
1129	Recognition of the Order of "Solomon's Temple" at the Council of Troyes.
1130	Construction of a double church dedicated to the Assumption on the presumed site of Mary's tomb in the Valley of Jehoshaphat.
1140	Foundation of the Church of Saint Mary of the Germans and the Church of Saint Anne.
1149	*July 15:* Consecration of the Church of the Holy Sepulchre's new high altar by the Latin Patriarch of Jerusalem Fulk of Angoulême.
1152	The regent Queen Melisende has three covered streets built in the heart of the city.
	Construction of the Chapel of the Ascension atop the Mount of Olives.
Circa 1160	The "Templars" build a large church in the courtyard to the west of Al-Aqsa Mosque.
	Pilgrimage of John of Würzburg.
1161	Queen Melisende is buried in the Church of Saint Mary of the Valley of Jehoshaphat.
Circa 1163	King Amalric of Jerusalem establishes his court and his palace near the "Citadel of David."
1166–71	Holy Land visit of the Jewish pilgrim Benjamin of Tudela.
1170	Construction of a Crusader chapel near Gethsemane.
1173	The Muslim pilgrim al-Harawi visits Jerusalem.
1178	Restoration and reinforcement of the city's walls by the Franks.
1186	Death of Baldwin IV, the Leper King. His sister Sibylla and her husband Guy de Lusignan are crowned the following year.
1187	*July 4:* Defeat of the Frankish army at Hattin.
	October 2: Saladin seizes Jerusalem.

1189	Granted to a Sufi community, the palace of the Latin Patriarchate becomes the Khanqah al-Salahiyya. Saladin converts the Church of Saint Anne into a madrasa that teaches Shafi'i law.
1191	Saladin reinforces the city walls to face the Third Crusade.
1192	Part of Ascalon's Jewish community settles in Jerusalem.
	The Church of Saint Mary Major is converted into a *bimaristan* (hospital and medical teaching facility).
1193	Saladin orders the erection of a mosque of "the blessed staircase," on the southern edge of the Church of the Holy Sepulchre and under the patronage of Caliph 'Umar.
Circa 1195	Construction of the Maghariba Mosque and a Malikite madrasa under the impetus of Saladin's son al-Afdal Ali, and growth of the so-called Mughrabi Quarter.
1201	The Dome of the Prophet built on the Haram al-Sharif.
1204	Al-Mu'azzam 'Isa (the last part is "Jesus" in Arabic), Saladin's nephew and the governor of the principality of Damascus, makes Jerusalem his capital. He works on renovating the city walls until 1214.
1207	Construction of a madrasa to teach Arabic grammar in the Haram al-Sharif and embellishment of the esplanade with a portico on its north side.
1219	Demolition of part of the city walls on the order of the Ayyubid sultan al-Mu'azzam 'Isa, under the threat of the Fifth Crusade.
1227	With Sultan al-Mu'azzam's death, the city loses its status as capital.
1229	Treaty of Jaffa, in which Sultan al-Kamil concedes sovereignty over the city of Jerusalem, with the exception of the Haram al-Sharif, to Emperor Frederick II for ten years.
1229–44	Construction of the Church of Saint Mary of the Spasm, on Jehoshaphat Street, marking the Via Dolorosa's relocation to within the city.
1239	Reconquest of the city by the sultan of Kerak al-Nasir Dawud and dismantling of the Citadel of David's main fortifications.

1240–44	Sultan al-Nasir gives Jerusalem back to the Franks in exchange for military aid against his cousin al-Salih, the sultan in Cairo.
1244	City looted by the Khwarezm-Shah's Turkic troops.
1247	Al-Salih, the last Ayyubid sultan of Egypt, visits the city and plans to rebuild its ramparts.
1251	From Acre, the French king Louis IX refuses the offer of al-Quds/Jerusalem in exchange for military support of the sultan of Aleppo al-Nasir Yusuf against the Cairo-based Mamluks.
1260	Mamluk victory against Hülegü's Mongol hordes at the Spring of Goliath in Galilee.
1261	Jerusalem comes under Mamluk control.
1263	Construction *extra muros* of the Khan al-Zahir, in honor of Sultan Baybars, on pilgrimage to Jerusalem, to the city's northwest, to facilitate its provisioning.
1267	Rabbi Moses Ben Nachman (Nachmanides or Ramban) builds a synagogue on Mount Zion.
1291	Fall of Saint John of Acre. The Franks leave the Holy Land.
1299	Without damaging the city and with the aid of a Mongol army, the Christian king of Armenia Hetum II occupies Jerusalem.
1310/11	Beginning of the reconstruction of the mosque in the "Tower of David" (Mihrab Dawud) and construction of its present minaret by Sultan al-Nasir Muhammad.
1317	Pilgrimage of Sultan al-Nasir Muhammad.
1328/29	Emir Tankiz, the Mamluk governor of Damascus, builds a madrasa and lodging for fifteen Sufis at the entrance to the Chain Gate. Madrasas cover the area around the Haram al-Sharif.
1333–35	After a brief interruption, the Holy Sepulchre is reopened to Christian worship by Sultan al-Nasir Muhammad, at the urging of the king of Naples Robert of Anjou.
1335/36	The Franciscans acquire the so-called Cenacle on Mount Zion.

1336	Completion of a vast urban complex (warehouse, market hall, public baths) near "Cotton Merchants' Gate," financed by Emir Tankiz.
1342	A bull issued by Pope Clement VI names the Franciscan Order the guardian (custodian) of the Holy Land.
1375	The city's governor briefly holds the rank of viceroy, appointed directly by the Mamluk sultan in Cairo.
1391–94	Investigation into the Banu Ghanim family's fraudulent management of the Holy City's waqfs.
1393	Pilgrimage of Henry Bolingbroke, the future king of England Henry IV.
1399	Sultan Barquq restores the large reservoir near the Hebron Gate (now the Jaffa Gate), thereafter known as the Sultan's Pool.
1400	The notables of the city plan to hand it over to Tamerlane, who had just conquered Damascus.
1405	Anti-tax revolt and exile of the Mamluk governor.
1429	Plague epidemic.
1432	Bertrandon de La Broquière's pilgrimage and mission (in view of a possible Crusade) on behalf of the duke of Burgundy.
1440	Tax imposed on Jewish communities by the Mamluk government.
1446	The Mamluk sultan confirms the Franciscans' right to their Mount Zion properties.
1475	Reconstruction of Ramban's synagogue on the order of the Mamluk sultan Qaytbay, then on pilgrimage.
1476–77	New plague epidemic.
1480	Emir Qansuh al-Yahyawi builds a funerary complex east of the Haram al-Sharif.
1482	Erection of a monumental *sabīl* by Sultan Qaytbay on the Haram al-Sharif.
1483	Second pilgrimage of the Dominican Felix Fabri, who deplores the Holy Sepulchre's state.
1496	Mujir al-Din al-'Ulaymi composes his *History of Jerusalem and Hebron,* which lists about twenty churches.

1516	*December 29:* Al-Quds/Jerusalem passes under Ottoman dominion under the name Kudüs i-Sherif; Sultan Selim comes in person to take possession of the keys to the city.
1523	Pilgrimages of the Jewish mystic David Reubeni.
	September: The Spanish monk Ignatius of Loyola spends three weeks on pilgrimage in Jerusalem before being asked to leave the Holy City by the Franciscans.
1525–26	Ottoman census of the population and all waqf holdings in Kudüs/Jerusalem.
1537	Süleyman has the Dome of the Rock's mosaics replaced with cuerda seca polychrome tiles.
1537–41	Reconstruction of the city wall by Süleyman the Magnificent, construction of new fountains (*sabīls*), and restoration of the so-called Solomon's Pools in the Artas Valley, ten kilometers (six miles) south of Jerusalem.
1549	The Franciscans' seat on Mount Zion is transformed into a Muslim waqf dedicated to the memory of King David (Nabi Dawud).
1551	Acquisition of the *intra muros* Convent of Saint Saviour by the Franciscans.
1552	Construction of the Haseki Sultan Imaret charitable complex, including a soup kitchen for the city's poor, under the patronage of Sultan Süleyman's wife Roxelana (the *haseki sultan*).
1553–54	The second Ottoman census of Jerusalem counts 2,724 family heads (including 413 Christians and 324 Jews), meaning probably some 14,000 inhabitants total.
1555	Emperor Charles V obtains permission to restore the Holy Sepulchre. Control of the church is alternately entrusted to the Franciscans and the Orthodox clergy.
1565	Firman denouncing the opening of drinking establishments for Christian pilgrims in Jerusalem.
1568	Firman partially exempting the city from tax levies.
1572	A new Jerusalem population census counts 115 "Jewish" family heads, about 600 total "Jewish" people.
1578	Firman requiring that pilgrims wear distinctive clothing according to their religion.

1589	Pilgrimage of Villamont, who encounters only six "Frankish" pilgrims in Jerusalem.
1604	The king of France Henri IV obtains an agreement from Sultan Ahmed I on the protection of Catholic pilgrims and access to the Holy Sepulchre.
1611	Pilgrimage to Jerusalem by George Sandys, son of the Anglican archbishop of York.
1613	Firman confirming that the maintenance of the Chapel of the Ascension, within the mosque of the same name on top of the Mount of Olives, is the responsibility of the city's Armenian community.
1615	Attempt by two Jesuit brothers to establish a mission of the Society of Jesus in Jerusalem. They are driven out by the Franciscans.
1621–39	Muhammad ibn Farrukh, a local clan chief and the governor of Kudüs/Jerusalem and Nablus, is the commander of the pilgrimage to Mecca.
1623	The installation of a French consul in Jerusalem fails.
1644	Pilgrimage of François-Charles du Rozel to Jerusalem.
1650	The Turkish traveler Evliya Çelebi visits the city, as described in his famous *Seyâhatnâme*.
1658	The Monastery and Church of Saint James become the full and entire property of the Armenian Church in accordance with a sultanic firman.
1660	Sabbatai Zevi, a self-proclaimed messiah, preaches the Last Judgment in Jerusalem.
1670	Publication of the Medinese al-Khiyari's travelogue.
1686	The appointment of an official Ottoman administrator, Ahmed Pasha Tarazi, as the governor of Kudüs/Jerusalem and the commander of the pilgrimage to Mecca marks the decline of the local dynasties' control over the city.
1693	Visit to Jerusalem of ʿAbd al-Ghani al-Nabulusi, as described in an account of his travels.
1707	Revolt of the city against the Ottoman governor, led by the *nakib el-eshraf* Muhammad al-Husaini, who is later executed in Istanbul.

1719	Restoration of the Holy Sepulchre's dome, whose former mosaic is sold off in pieces as pilgrimage relics.
1721	Restoration of the Dome of the Rock, ordered by Sultan Ahmed III.
1757	A riot chases the Franciscans from the Holy Sepulchre.
1767	A sultanic firman entrusts the Holy Sepulchre's custodianship to the Orthodox clergy—the origin of the Status Quo.
After 1776	Under the "reign" of Ahmad Pasha al-Jazzar (the Butcher) over the province of Sidon, Jerusalem remains neutral and loyal to the Ottoman power.
1784	Constantin-François de Volney's trip to Jerusalem.
1791	The Moroccan al-Zayyani visits Jerusalem and writes an account of his journey.
1799	Napoleon present in Jaffa during the Egyptian expedition.
1806	Journey of François-René de Chateaubriand.
1808	Fire in the Holy Sepulchre, causing the dome's collapse.
1816	Restoration of the Dome of the Rock, Al-Aqsa Mosque, and Nabi Dawud.
1831	Kudüs/Jerusalem comes under the control of the khedive of Egypt Muhammad ʿAli.
1836	Reconstruction of the Hurva Synagogue authorized.
1837	An earthquake destroys many buildings.
1839	The United Kingdom establishes a consulate in Jerusalem.
	Beginning of the Ottoman Empire's *tanzimat* reforms.
1840	Reestablishment of direct Ottoman rule over Jerusalem.
1841	Construction of Jerusalem's Etz Chaim Yeshiva.
1842	Prussia sets up a consulate in the city.
1843	Installation in Jerusalem of a first French consul and a consul from the Kingdom of Piedmont-Sardinia.
1849	The emperor of Austria establishes a consulate and an imperial post office in the city.
1850	Ottoman tax sources count some fifteen thousand inhabitants in Kudüs/Jerusalem.

1852	A sultanic firman confirms the one from 1767 granting the holy places' guardianship to the Orthodox clergy. This arrangement has been known since then as the Status Quo.
1853	The Old City's division into four quarters appears for the first time, depicted on a German map.
1855	First houses built outside the city walls (Mishkenot Sha'anim neighborhood), by Moses Montefiore.
1856	In return for aiding the Ottoman sultan during the Crimean War, France is given ownership of the Church of Saint Anne.
1857	The Ottoman sultan recognizes the Russian Ecclesiastical Mission in Jerusalem.
1858	Alphonse de Ratisbonne builds the Convent of Ecce Homo to house the Sisters of Sion.
1860–80	Construction of the Russian Compound, covering almost seven hectares (seventeen acres). Its hospice is the biggest Christian establishment in Jerusalem (one-thousand-person capacity).
1865	Foundation of the Palestine Exploration Fund in London, in response to Charles Wilson's Ordinance Survey of Jerusalem (1864–65).
1866	Enlargement of the Convent of the Sisters of Zion, north of the Haram al-Sharif.
1867	Mixed city council set up in Kudüs/Jerusalem.
1870–76	Mayor Yusuf Diya al-Khalidi's term of office.
1872	Kudüs/Jerusalem becomes an autonomous regional capital, placed directly under the Ottoman sultan's supervision.
1873	Establishment of the German Colony in the Qatamon neighborhood.
1876	First Ottoman Constitution and legislative elections; Yusuf Diya al-Khalidi is the city of Jerusalem's first deputy.
1877	Ottoman law on provincial municipal councils, confirming the prohibition on foreign powers' intervention in the city's affairs.
	The Society of the Missionaries of Africa ("White Fathers") moves into the Saint Anne monastery.

1877 *(cont.)*	Foundation of the Deutsche Verein zur Erforschung Palästinas (German Society for the Exploration of Palestine), which has published the journal *Zeitschrift des Deutschen Palästina-Vereins* since 1878.
1878	The Congress of Berlin declares the Status Quo of 1852 inviolable.
1881	Eliezer Ben-Yehuda emigrates to Palestine and soon settles in Jerusalem.
	Foundation of the American Colony in Jerusalem.
1882	First Aliyah, mostly from Western Jewish communities. Formation of the "New Yishuv."
1883	General Charles Gordon identifies the "Garden Tomb"—the purported location of the true tomb of Christ—north of the city's ramparts.
1885	The main roads of Kudüs/Jerusalem are paved.
1888	Inauguration of the French pilgrimage complex Notre Dame de France (now Notre Dame of Jerusalem), outside the city walls.
1889	Construction of the New Gate (Bab al-Jedid), north of the Convent of Saint Saviour, at France's request and facing Notre Dame de France.
1890	Father Marie-Joseph Lagrange founds the École pratique d'études bibliques (Practical school of biblical studies), which will become the École biblique et archéologique française de Jérusalem (French biblical and archaeological school of Jerusalem) in 1920.
1891	Opening of the municipal hospital, which offers free medical care to all the city's inhabitants.
1892	Inauguration of the Jerusalem terminus of the Jerusalem-Jaffa railway line; creation of a municipal park.
	Nathan Birnbaum, a cofounder of the Vienna-based Jewish student association Kadimah, coins the term *Zionism*.
1895	Construction of Jerusalem's new city hall outside its walls, near the Jaffa Gate.
1896	Albert Antébi becomes the director of the Alliance israélite universelle (Universal Israelite alliance) in Jerusalem.

1897	First Zionist Congress, in Basel, Switzerland, at which Theodor Herzl founds the Zionist Organization (since 1960 the World Zionist Organization).
1898	Journey to Jerusalem of the German emperor Wilhelm II and opening of the wall south of the Jaffa Gate in his honor.
1899	Letter from Yusuf Diya al-Khalidi, the former mayor of Kudüs/Jerusalem, asking Theodor Herzl to "leave Palestine alone."
1900	Completion of the Notre Dame de France complex by the Augustinian Fathers of the Assumption.
1901	Creation of the Jewish National Fund, for the purchase of land in Palestine.
	Eliezer Ben-Yehuda begins his *Dictionary of Ancient and Modern Hebrew* (first volume published in 1910), the root of modern Hebrew.
1904	Opening of Jerusalem's first theater.
1904–14	Second Aliyah (forty thousand immigrants), primarily from the Russian Empire.
1905	The Zionist Congress in Basel officially approves the establishment of a Jewish national homeland in Palestine.
1907	The Jerusalem municipality inaugurates a monumental clock tower at the Jaffa Gate.
1908	Young Turk Revolution, including the restoration of the 1876 constitution.
1909	Ottoman law on conscription forces city residents to go into exile or to enlist.
1910	Bids are invited for the construction of a tramway, the installation of electrical lighting, and the establishment of a telephone network in Jerusalem.
1914	The consulates of the Triple Entente's European powers are expelled from Jerusalem.
1915–17	Islamic university on the grounds of the Church of Saint Anne.
1916	Secret treaty between France and the United Kingdom to divide up the Ottoman Empire's territories, known as the Sykes-Picot Agreement.

1917	*November 2:* Letter from the UK foreign secretary Lord Balfour to Lord Rothschild, a representative of the Zionist movement in Great Britain, with what is now known as the Balfour Declaration.
	December 9: The former mayor of Kudüs/Jerusalem Hussein al-Husseini gives General Allenby the keys to the city.
1918	The British governor Ronald Storrs issues a military order prohibiting the demolition or construction of any building in Jerusalem—yet nonetheless has the Jaffa Gate clock tower razed.
	Chaim Weizmann offers to buy the Kotel (Wailing Wall) and its immediate surroundings in the Mughrabi Quarter.
1919	Palestine Arab Congress in Jerusalem, organized by Muslim-Christian Associations, declares the desire to integrate the city into a reunified "Greater Syria."
	Construction of the new Romema reservoir in the city's northwest.
1919–22	Third Aliyah, mostly of Jews from Galicia (east central Europe) and Russia (thirty-five thousand people).
1920	Jerusalem becomes the seat of the Arab Executive Committee.
	Riots between Jews and Arabs during the Nabi Musa Muslim pilgrimage.
	Ze'ev Jabotinsky organizes Jewish self-defense groups into the Haganah.
1921	A commission starts work on a town planning act for the city.
1923	The United Kingdom receives a mandate to govern Palestine from the League of Nations.
1924	Opening of King George Street on the city's west side, outside the wall.
1924–28	Fourth Aliyah (sixty thousand people).
1925	Protests by the villagers of Artas after their water is diverted for Jerusalem's benefit.
	Inauguration of the Hebrew University, on Mount Scopus.

1926	A municipal reform organizes city elections on a denominational basis.
1927	*July 11:* Last major earthquake in Jerusalem.
1928	Palestine's Grand Mufti Hadj Amin al-Husseini creates a Muslim association for the protection of Jerusalem's holy places.
1929	Deadly riots over Jewish pilgrims' right of passage to the Kotel (Wailing Wall).
1931	Population census counts ninety thousand inhabitants in Jerusalem, fifty thousand Jews and forty thousand Arabs (Christians and Muslims).
	Creation of the Istiqlal (Independence) Party in Jerusalem, bringing together Syrians, Lebanese, Palestinians, and Moroccan representatives.
	Splintering of the Haganah and creation of the Irgun Tsva'i Leumi (National military organization).
1933	Anti-British demonstrations by Arabs leave eleven dead in Jerusalem.
1933–39	Fifth Aliyah (about a quarter of a million people, including those fleeing Nazism).
1934	Municipal elections are held. For the first time, Jerusalem's city council is clearly divided between representatives of the Jewish community and representatives of the Arab communities (Muslim and Christian).
1936	Inauguration of the water supply from Ras al-Ain, on the western coastal plain.
	Near-continuous armed insurrection in Palestine, including Jerusalem, encouraged by Grand Mufti al-Husseini.
1937	Exile to the Seychelles of Mayor Hussein al-Khalidi, who is replaced by his deputy, Daniel Auster.
1939	White paper on Britain's Palestine policy, notably limiting Jewish immigration there to seventy-five thousand people for five years.
1942	*December:* An assembly of rabbis meets in Jerusalem to declare three days of mourning for the extermination of Europe's Jews, reports of which had gradually arrived.

1944	Death of Jerusalem's mayor Mustapha al-Khalidi.
1946	Bombing of the King David Hotel, site of British administrative headquarters, by the Irgun (almost a hundred dead).
1947	First discoveries of biblical-era manuscripts and scrolls in Qumran, near the Dead Sea.
	The UN partition plan for Palestine (Resolution 181) provides for Jerusalem's establishment as a *corpus separatum*.
1948	*April 9:* The Irgun massacres 120 civilians in Deir Yassin, a village near Jerusalem.
	May 14: David Ben-Gurion declares the State of Israel's independence.
	May 27: The Arab Legion destroys the Hurva Synagogue.
	November 30: Cease-fire line, the future Green Line, set between Moshe Dayan's troops and Abdullah al-Tal's Arab Legion.
	December 1: Transjordan's King Abdullah is proclaimed the "king of Palestine" in Jericho.
1948–51	In the "Great Aliyah," 750,000 Jews from Arab countries and from Europe emigrate to Israel/Palestine.
1949	Transfer of Theodor Herzl's body from Vienna to Jerusalem. Mount Herzl becomes Israel's national military memorial.
1950	The Knesset adopts the Law of Return.
1951	Assassination of King Abdullah on his way out from the Friday prayer at Al-Aqsa Mosque.
1957	The Yad Vashem memorial, on a hill neighboring Mount Herzl, opens to the public.
1958	Inauguration of the Ain Farah pumping station to supply potable water to East Jerusalem, which had been cut off from West Jerusalem's distribution network.
1959	Israeli urban plan for Jerusalem's development to the west.
1962	A series of barriers and bunkers concretizes the demarcation line between Israel and Jordan.
1964	Jerusalem hosts the founding congress of the Palestinian Liberation Organization.

1965	Teddy Kollek becomes Jerusalem's mayor, a post he will hold for twenty-eight years thanks to five reelections.
1965–66	Inauguration of the new "Government Quarter" and installation of the Knesset there, near the Israel Museum.
1967	*June 11:* At the end of the Six-Day War, the State of Israel takes control of Jerusalem's Old City. The Israeli army's chief rabbi, Shlomo Goren, suggests dynamiting the Haram al-Sharif's mosques.
	June 14: A quarter of a million Israeli pilgrims gather to celebrate Shavuot at the foot of the Kotel (Wailing Wall), whose surroundings had been completely razed over the course of forty-eight hours (destruction of the Mughrabi Quarter).
	July 4: The UN declares Israel's unilateral actions in Jerusalem "invalid."
1968	*August 18:* Ten people injured in a bus attack in Jerusalem.
	November 2: General strike by East Jerusalem merchants on the fifty-first anniversary of the Balfour Declaration.
	November 22: First car bomb in the Mahane Yehuda market.
1969	Arson of Al-Aqsa Mosque by an Australian Christian fundamentalist.
	Adoption of UN Resolution 267, condemning the State of Israel's occupation of East Jerusalem.
1971	Meron Benvenisti becomes Jerusalem's deputy mayor, responsible for the city's former Jordanian neighborhoods.
1972	Yussuf al-Budeiri, the former Jordanian municipality's chief engineer, definitively quits "reunified" Jerusalem's city council.
1973	Yom Kippur War.
1975	Bomb attack claimed by the Palestinian Liberation Organization (fourteen dead).
1977	Israeli legislative elections bring the right to power for the first time, under Menachem Begin (Likud).
	The Egyptian president Anwar al-Sadat visits Jerusalem.

1980	The reunification of Jerusalem is declared by an Israeli law affirming its status as the country's "complete and united" capital.
1982	Terror attack by Alan Goodman, an American Jewish extremist, on the Haram al-Sharif.
1987–93	First Intifada.
1988	In Algiers, Yasser Arafat accepts UN Resolution 242 (implicit recognition of the State of Israel) and declares Palestine's independence.
1990	"Temple Mount" or "Al-Aqsa" massacre (twenty Palestinians killed by the Israeli army).
1993	Ehud Olmert (Likud) becomes Jerusalem's mayor.
	Oslo I Accord signed by Yitzhak Rabin and Yasser Arafat.
1994	Creation of the Palestinian Authority.
1995	*September 4:* Commemoration of Jerusalem's third millennium (on Elul 9, 5755, in the Hebrew calendar), presided over by Yitzhak Rabin.
	November 4: Assassination of the Israeli prime minister Yitzhak Rabin by the extremist Yigal Amir following the Oslo II Accord, regarding the extension of zones of Palestinian autonomy.
1996	Launch of the construction of the Har Homa settlement (fifteen thousand residents in 2016), between Jerusalem and Bethlehem.
1998	Adoption of the "Greater Jerusalem" plan proposed by Benjamin Netanyahu.
2000	An amendment to the Basic Law of 1980 fixes Jerusalem's municipal limits around the territories conquered since 1967.
2000–2004	Second ("al-Aqsa") Intifada.
2001	Ariel Sharon (Likud) becomes Israel's prime minister.
2002	Beginning of construction on a dividing wall between Jerusalem and its Palestinian suburbs.
2003	Election of the ultra-Orthodox Uri Lupolianski as the Jerusalem municipality's head.

	The Geneva Initiative proposes shared sovereignty over Jerusalem, which would be the capital of both Israel and Palestine.
2004	Publication of the "Master Plan 2000" for the city's development, which is still awaiting approval.
	Death of Yasser Arafat. Mahmoud Abbas is elected president of the Palestinian Authority two months later.
2008	Nir Barkat, a former Likud member, is elected mayor of Jerusalem.
2009	The European Union calls attention to the fact that Jerusalem should be the capital of two sovereign states, Israel and Palestine.
2011	Inauguration of Jerusalem's new tramway.
2012	Palestine's UN status is changed from "observer entity" to "non-member observer state."

Notes

1. It is also not a coincidence that the only two authors to have attempted a form of chronological synthesis aren't professional historians, even less Jerusalem specialists, but popular writers and essayists personally excited by the subject. Simon Sebag Montefiore, a novelist and biographer who specializes in czarist Russia, in 2011 offered a thick "biography" of Jerusalem, an impressive and impassioned volume, whose title has the merit of honesty: it is not a "history" of the city but indeed a "biography," constructed as a narrative sequence of anecdotes and personal stories. The city's inhabitants are clearly visible, but the city, in its materiality, disappears behind the gallery of portraits (Simon Sebag Montefiore, *Jerusalem: The Biography* [New York: Alfred A. Knopf, 2011]). Fifteen years earlier, in 1996, the writer Karen Armstrong, a specialist in myths and religions, offered a long-term history of Jerusalem focusing almost exclusively on the mystical and religious issues, which the work's subtitle emphasizes (*A History of Jerusalem: One City, Three Faiths* [London: HarperCollins, 1996]). We can add to these two books that of the archaeologist Eric H. Cline, who in 2004 published a military history of "Jerusalem besieged," a chronicle of blockades of the city from its origins to the present day (*Jerusalem Besieged: From Ancient Canaan to Modern Israel* [Ann Arbor: University of Michigan Press, 2004]).

CHAPTER 1. THE BIRTH OF A HOLY CITY

1. Flavius Josephus, *The Jewish War* 5.140.

2. Katharina Galor and Hanswulf Bloedhorn, *The Archaeology of Jerusalem: From the Origins to the Ottomans* (New Haven: Yale University Press, 2013), ch. 2, "Natural and Built City Limits."

3. For the history of archaeological research at Jerusalem since the nineteenth century, see Katharina Galor and Gideon Avni, eds., *Unearthing Jerusalem: 150 Years of Archaeological Research in the Holy City* (Winona Lake, IN: Eisenbrauns, 2011), pt. 1, "The History of Research."

4. See especially Israel Finkelstein and Amihai Mazar, *The Quest for the Historical Israel: Debating Archaeology and the History of Early Israel*, ed. Brian B. Schmidt (Leiden: Brill; Atlanta: Society of Biblical Literature, 2007).

5. Israel Finkelstein, "The Great Transformation: The 'Conquest' of the Highlands Frontiers and the Rise of the Territorial States," in *The Archaeology of Society in the Holy Land*, ed. Thomas E. Levy (London: Leicester University Press, 1995), 349–65; Finkelstein and Neil Asher Silberman, *The Bible Unearthed: Archaeology's New Vision of Ancient Israel and the Origin of Its Sacred Texts* (New York: Free Press, 2001), 113–18.

6. Ronny Reich, *Excavating the City of David: Where Jerusalem's History Began* (Jerusalem: Israel Exploration Society, Biblical Archaeology Society, 2011), 286–87.

7. All Bible quotes are from the New Revised Standard Edition.

8. Amarna letters EA 287: 25, 46, 61, 63; EA 290: 15.

9. Eilat Mazar, Wayne Horowitz, Takayoshi Oshima, and Yuval Goren, "A Cuneiform Tablet from the Ophel in Jerusalem," *Israel Exploration Journal* 60, no. 1 (2010): 4–21.

10. Eilat Mazar, Yuval Goren, Wayne Horowitz, and Takayoshi Oshima, "Jerusalem 2: A Fragment of a Cuneiform Tablet from the Ophel Excavations," *Israel Exploration Journal* 64, no. 2 (2014): 129–39.

11. Moshe Weinfeld, "Jerusalem: A Political and Spiritual Capital," in *Capital Cities: Urban Planning and Spiritual Dimensions*, ed. J. Goodnick Westenholz (Jerusalem: Bible Lands Museum, 1998), 15–40.

12. Eilat Mazar, "Did I Find King David's Palace?," *Biblical Archaeology Review* 32, no. 1 (2006): 16–27, 70; Eilat Mazar, *The Palace of King David: Excavations at the Summit of the City of David; Preliminary Report of Seasons 2005-2007* (Jerusalem: Shoham Academic Research and Publication, 2009).

13. Amihai Mazar, "Archaeology and the Biblical Narrative: The Case of the United Monarchy," in *One God, One Cult, One Nation: Archaeological and Biblical Perspectives*, ed. R. G. Kratz and H. Spieckermann (Berlin: De Gruyter, 2010), 29–58.

14. A suggestion also made by Avraham Faust, "Did Eilat Mazar Find David's Palace?," *Biblical Archaeology Review* 38, no. 5 (2012): 47–52.

15. Reich, *Excavating the City of David*, 307.

16. Israel Finkelstein, "A Great United Monarchy? Archaeological and Historical Perspectives," in Kratz and Spieckermann, *One God, One Cult*, 3–28.

17. Yosef Garfinkel, Katharina Streit, Saar Ganor, and Michael G. Hasel, "State Formation in Judah: Biblical Tradition, Modern Historical Theories, and Radiometric Dates at Khirbet Qeiyafa," *Radiocarbon* 54, nos. 3–4 (2012): 359–69.

18. Reich, *Excavating the City of David*, 306–14.

19. Trans. K. C. Hanson, "Sennacherib Prism: Column 3," www.kchanson.com/ANCDOCS/meso/sennprism3.html, adapted from Daniel David Luckenbill, *The Annals of Sennacherib*, Oriental Institute Publications 2 (Chicago: University of Chicago, 1924).

20. Nadav Na'aman, "When and How Did Jerusalem Become a Great City? The Rise of Jerusalem as Judah's Premier City in the Eighth–Seventh Centuries B.C.E.," *Bulletin of the American Schools of Oriental Research* 347 (2007): 21–56.

21. Joe Uziel, Esther Eshel, and Nahshon Szanton, "A Late Iron Age Inscribed Sherd from the City of David," *Israel Exploration Journal* 65, no. 2 (2015): 167–78.

22. Yigal Shiloh, "Jérusalem ancienne: Une ville cananéenne et une capitale israélite," in *Archéologie, art et histoire de la Palestine*, ed. E.-M. Laperrousaz (Paris: Cerf, 1988), 119–32.

23. Ronny Reich, "A Fiscal Bulla from the City of David, Jerusalem," *Israel Exploration Journal* 62, no. 2 (2012): 200–205.

24. Joseph Blenkinsopp, "Temple and Society in Achaemenid Judah," in *Second Temple Studies*, vol. 1, *Persian Period*, ed. Philip R. Davies (Sheffield: JSOT Press, 1991), 22–53.

25. Reich, *Excavating the City of David*, 319–21; Israel Finkelstein, "Jerusalem in the Persian (and Early Hellenistic) Period and the Wall of Nehemiah," *Journal for the Study of the Old Testament* 32 (2008): 501–20. See also Oded Lipschits, "Between Archaeology and Text: A Reevaluation of the Development Process of Jerusalem in the Persian Period," in *Congress Volume Helsinki 2010*, ed. M. Nissinen (Leiden: Brill, 2012), 145–65.

26. See in this regard the testimony of Flavius Josephus, *Jewish Antiquities* 13.62ff.

27. Josephus, *Jewish Antiquities* 11.325–40.

28. Diodorus Siculus, *Historical Library* 40.3, trans. Andrew Smith, "Diodorus Siculus, Book 40," *Attalus*, www.attalus.org/translate/diodorus40.html.

29. Sirach 50:1–4. The "sea" in question is the large bronze basin placed in the Temple's vestibule, according to 1 Kings 7:23–26.

30. Josephus, *Jewish Antiquities* 12.138–45.

31. Elias Bickerman, "La Charte séleucide de Jérusalem," *Revue des études juives* 100 (1935): 4–35; Elias Bickerman, "Une proclamation séleucide relative au temple de Jérusalem," *Syria* 25, no. 1 (1946): 67–85.

32. Josephus, *Jewish Antiquities* 12.145–46. All translations of this text are by Ralph Marcus, from the Loeb Classical Library edition (Cambridge, MA: Harvard University Press, 1998; first published 1934).

33. John Ma, "Relire les *Institutions des Séleucides* de Bikerman," in *Rome, a City and Its Empire in Perspective: The Impact of the Roman World through Fergus Millar's Research*, ed. S. Benoist (Leiden: Brill, 2012), 59–84.

34. Dan Bahat, *The Illustrated Atlas of Jerusalem* (Jerusalem: Carta, 1996).

35. Elias Bickerman, *Der Gott der Makkabäer: Untersuchungen über Sinn und Ursprung der Makkabäischen Erhebung* (Berlin: Schocken, 1937), trans. Horst Moehring as "The God of the Maccabees" (1978), repr. in *Studies in Jewish and Christian History*, ed. Amram Tropper, vol. 2 (Leiden: Brill, 2007), 1025–149.

36. Claude Orrieux and Édouard Will, *Ioudaïsmos-Hellènismos: Essai sur le judaïsme judéen à l'époque hellénistique* (Nancy: Presses Universitaires de Nancy, 1986), 113.

37. According to Josephus (*Jewish Antiquities* 13.215), who diverges from 1 Maccabees on this point, Simon razed the Akra to the ground. Recent archaeological digs seem to indicate that the Akra was indeed destroyed, but probably not before the beginning of the first century BCE (Ayala Zilberstein, "New Evidence from Jerusalem" [speech, 9th Nangeroni Meeting on the Middle Maccabees, Milan, June 13, 2018]).

38. Lee I. Levine, *Jerusalem: Portrait of the City in the Second Temple Period (538 B.C.E.-70 C.E.)* (Philadelphia: Jewish Publication Society of America, 2002), 91–92.

39. Josephus, *Jewish Antiquities* 12.136.

40. *Letter of Aristeas*, §89, trans. Moses Hadas, *Aristeas to Philocrates (Letter of Aristeas)* (Eugene, OR: Wipf and Stock, 2007; first published 1951 by Harper Brothers [New York]), 135. The passage about Jerusalem is in §§83–111; for the equilibrium between city and *chōra*, see §§105–7.

41. *Letter of Aristeas*, §106, trans. Hadas, *Aristeas to Philocrates*, 143.

42. Josephus, *Jewish Antiquities* 13.236–48.

43. According to Josephus, *Jewish War* 1.99–103; *Jewish Antiquities* 13.389–92.

44. Pliny the Elder, *Natural History* 5.14.70. All translations of this text are by H. Rackham, Loeb Classical Library edition (London: Heinemann; Cambridge, MA: Harvard University Press, 1952).

45. Ehud Netzer, *The Architecture of Herod, the Great Builder* (Tübingen: Mohr Siebeck, 2006).

46. Babylonian Talmud, *Baba Bathra* 4b, trans. Michael L. Rodkinson, *New Edition of the Babylonian Talmud*, vol. 5 (Boston: Talmud Society, 1918), 6.

47. Josephus, *Jewish War* 5.222–23, trans. H. St. J. Thackeray, Loeb Classical Library edition (London: William Heinemann; Cambridge, MA: Harvard University Press, 1961).

48. Josephus, *Jewish Antiquities* 15.425.

49. Reich, *Excavating the City of David*, 329–30. On the demography and impact of pilgrimages, see also Levine, *Jerusalem*, 340–43.

50. Trans. Jonathan J. Price in *Corpus Inscriptionum Iudaeae/Palaestinae*, vol. 1, *Jerusalem*, pt. 1, *1–704*, ed. Hannah M. Cotton, Leah Di Segni, Werner Eck, Benjamin Isaac, Alla Kushnir-Stein, Haggai Misgav, Jonathan Price, Israel Roll, and Ada Yardeni (Berlin: De Gruyter, 2010), 43.

51. Josephus, *Jewish War* 5.227.

52. Levine, *Jerusalem*, xiv.

53. Josephus, *Jewish War* 2.176–77.

54. Josephus, *Jewish War* 2.223–27.

55. Thirty-six hundred dead, according to Josephus, *Jewish War* 2.293–308.

56. Josephus, *Jewish War* 6.201–13.

57. Josephus, *Jewish War* 5.160.

58. Josephus, *Jewish War* 6.272–76.

59. Another reason frequently invoked to explain the revolt's outbreak is Hadrian's prohibition of circumcision, but this theory is based on a dubious source, the *Historia Augusta*.

60. Nicole Belayche, *"Dimenticare . . . Gerusalemme:* Les Paganismes à Aelia Capitolina du IIᵉ au IVᵉ siècle de notre ère," *Revue des études juives* 158, nos. 3–4 (1999): 308–9; Nicole Belayche, *Iudaea-Palaestina: The Pagan Cults in Roman Palestine (Second to Fourth Century)* (Tübingen: Mohr Siebeck, 2001), 169–70.

61. Bordeaux Pilgrim, *Itinerary from Bordeaux to Jerusalem: 'The Bordeaux Pilgrim' (333 A.D.)*, trans. Aubrey Stewart (London: Palestine Pilgrims' Text Society, 1887), 22; original cited by Nicole Belayche, "Du mont du Temple au Golgotha: Le Capitole de la colonie d'*Aelia Capitolina*," *Revue de l'histoire des religions* 214, no. 4 (1997): 400.

62. Eusebius of Caesarea, *Demonstration of the Gospel* 8.3; Cyril of Jerusalem, *Catechetical Lectures* 16.18.

63. Shimon Gibson and David M. Jacobson, *Below the Temple Mount in Jerusalem: A Source Book on the Cisterns, Subterranean Chambers and Conduits of the Haram al Sharif*, BAR International Series 637 (Oxford: Tempus Reparatum, 1996), xxiv.

64. Cassius Dio, *Roman History* 69.12.

65. On the highly debated issue of the location of the temple of Jupiter Capitolinus, see Belayche, "Du mont du Temple," which supports a construction near Golgotha. Hillel Newman favors a site on the Temple esplanade, based on a reexamination of Byzantine evidence: see "The Temple Mount of Jerusalem and the Capitolium of Aelia Capitolina," in *Knowledge and Wisdom: Archaeological and*

Historical Essays in Honour of Leah Di Segni, ed. Giovanni C. Bottini, L. Daniel Chrupcała, and Joseph Patrich (Milan: Terra Santa, 2014), 35–42.

66. Caroline Arnould, *Les Arcs romains de Jérusalem: Architecture, décor et urbanisme* (Fribourg: Éditions universitaires de Fribourg; Göttingen: Vandenhoeck und Ruprecht, 1997), 281.

67. Nir Hasson, "Archaeologists Bringing Jerusalem's Ancient Roman City Back to Life," *Haaretz,* February 21, 2012.

68. Jean-Christophe Attias and Esther Benbassa, *Israël, la terre et le sacré* (Paris: Flammarion, 2001).

CHAPTER 2. ROMAN PANTHEON, CHRISTIAN RELIQUARY, AND JEWISH TRADITIONS

1. Charles Baudelaire, "The Swan," *Les Fleurs du mal,* trans. Richard Howard (Boston: David R. Godine, 2003), 90.

2. Cassius Dio, *Roman History* 69.12.2–3, 69.14.2, trans. Earnest Cary, vol. 8, Loeb Classical Library (Cambridge, MA: Harvard University Press, 1925), 451.

3. See the fine article by Belayche, *"Dimenticare . . . Gerusalemme."*

4. Josephus, *Jewish War* 7.218, trans. Thackeray, 567, quoted in Martin Goodman, *Rome and Jerusalem* (New York: Vintage, 2008), 433.

5. Eusebius of Caesarea, *Ecclesiastical History* 4.5.2, 4.5.4, trans. Kirsopp Lake, vol. 1, Loeb Classical Library (Cambridge, MA: Harvard University Press, 1961), 309, 311.

6. *Chronicon Paschale* 224.3 (year 119), quoted in Hugues Vincent and Félix-Marie Abel, *Jérusalem: Recherches de topographie, d'archéologie et d'histoire,* vol. 2, *Jérusalem nouvelle* (Paris: Joseph Gabalda, 1914), 15.

7. For a discussion of these historical aporias, see Belayche, "Du mont du Temple."

8. Yvon Thébert, "À propos du 'triomphe du christianisme,'" *Dialogues d'histoire ancienne* 14 (1988): 324.

9. Thébert, "'Triomphe du christianisme,'" 325.

10. Eusebius of Caesarea, *Life of Constantine* 3.29–32, 3.26, 3.29, trans. Ernest Cushing Richardson in *Eusebius: Church History, Life of Constantine, and Oration in Praise of Constantine the Great,* vol. 1 of *A Select Library of the Nicene and Post-Nicene Fathers of the Christian Church: Second Series,* ed. Philip Schaff and Henry Wace (New York: Christian Literature, 1890), 528–29, 527, 528.

11. Eusebius, *Life of Constantine* 3.30, trans. Richardson, *Eusebius,* 528.

12. Socrates of Constantinople, *Ecclesiastical History* 1.17, trans. A. C. Zenos, in *Nicene and Post-Nicene Fathers, Second Series,* vol. 2, *Socrates, Sozomenus: Church Histories,* ed. Philip Schaff and Henry Wace (Buffalo, NY: Christian Literature, 1890), 21.

13. Eusebius, *Life of Constantine* 3.31, 3.32, trans. Richardson, *Eusebius,* 528, 529.

14. Eusebius, *Life of Constantine* 3.37–38, trans. Richardson, *Eusebius,* 530.

15. Michael Tarchnišvili, *Le Grand Lectionnaire de l'Église de Jérusalem (Vᵉ-VIIIᵉ siècle),* vol. 1 (Corpus Scriptorum Christianorum Orientalium 188, Scriptores iberici, vol. 9, text; 189, Scriptores iberici, vol. 10, translation) and vol. 2 (Corpus Scriptorum Christianorum Orientalium 204, Scriptores iberici, vol. 13, text; 205, Scriptores iberici, vol. 14, translation) (Leuven: Peeters, 1959–60).

16. Egeria, *Itinerarium* 48.1, 48.2, trans. M. L. McClure and C. L. Feltoe, *The Pilgrimage of Etheria* (London: Society for Promoting Christian Knowledge, 1919), 95.

17. Egeria, *Itinerarium* 49.1–3, trans. McClure and Feltoe, *Pilgrimage of Etheria,* 95–96.

18. Arculf, quoted in Adomnán, *De Locis Sanctis* 1.1, trans. James Rose McPherson, *The Pilgrimage of Arculfus in the Holy Land (about the Year A.D. 670)* (London: Palestine Pilgrims' Text Society, 1895), 3–4.

19. "Post talem Hierusolimitanam baptizationem," reads the original text (Adomnán, *De Locis Sanctis* 1.1, trans. McPherson, *Pilgrimage of Arculfus,* 4).

20. Ammianus Marcellinus, *History* 23.1.2–3, trans. John C. Rolfe, vol. 2, Loeb Classical Library (Cambridge, MA: Harvard University Press, 2000), 311.

21. Maurice Halbwachs, *La Topographie légendaire des évangiles en Terre sainte* (1941; repr., Paris: Presses universitaires de France, 2008), 14.

22. Bordeaux Pilgrim, *Itinerarium Burdigalense* 590, trans. Aubrey Stewart, *Itinerary from Bordeaux to Jerusalem: 'The Bordeaux Pilgrim' (333 A.D.)* (London: Palestine Pilgrims' Text Society, 1887), 21.

23. Bordeaux Pilgrim, *Itinerarium Burdigalense* 591, trans. Stewart, *Itinerary from Bordeaux to Jerusalem,* 21. For a recent consideration, see Yoram Tsafrir, "70–638: The Temple-less Mountain," in *Where Heaven and Earth Meet: Jerusalem's Sacred Esplanade,* ed. Oleg Grabar and Benjamin Z. Kedar (Jerusalem: Yad Ben-Zvi Press; Austin: University of Texas Press, 2009), 72–99.

24. Bordeaux Pilgrim, *Itinerarium Burdigalense* 591, trans. Stewart, *Itinerary from Bordeaux to Jerusalem,* 21–22.

25. Halbwachs, *Topographie légendaire,* 24.

26. Bordeaux Pilgrim, *Itinerarium Burdigalense* 592, trans. Stewart, *Itinerary from Bordeaux to Jerusalem,* 23.

27. Halbwachs, *Topographie légendaire,* 48.

28. Egeria, *Itinerarium,* in Pierre Maraval, *Récits des premiers pèlerins chrétiens au Proche-Orient* (Paris: Cerf, 2002), 59.

29. Egeria, *Itinerarium* 27.1, trans. McClure and Feltoe, *Pilgrimage of Etheria,* 57.

30. Jerome, letter to Eustochium (404), 12.1, trans. Joan Ferrante, Epistolae: Medieval Women's Letters (website), Columbia Center for New Media Teaching and Learning, https://epistolae.ctl.columbia.edu/letter/445.html.

31. John Rufus, *Life of Peter the Iberian* 38, trans. Cornelia B. Horn and Robert R. Phenix Jr. in *John Rufus: The "Lives" of Peter the Iberian, Theodosius of Jerusalem, and the Monk Romanus*, ed. Horn and Phenix (Atlanta: Society of Biblical Literature, 2008), 51.

32. John Rufus, *Life of Peter the Iberian* 134, trans. Horn and Phenix, *John Rufus*, 197.

33. See Dominique Trimbur, *Une école française à Jérusalem: De l'École pratique d'études bibliques des Dominicains à l'École biblique et archéologique française de Jérusalem* (Paris: Cerf, 2002).

34. Eucherius, *The Epitome of S. Eucherius about Certain Holy Places* 1, trans. Aubrey Stewart in *The Epitome of S. Eucherius about Certain Holy Places (circ. A.D. 440), and The Breviary or Short Description of Jerusalem (circ. A.D. 530)* (London: Palestine Pilgrims' Text Society, 1890), 7–8.

35. Eucherius, *Epitome* 2, 3, trans. Stewart, *Epitome*, 8.

36. Theodosius, *On the Topography of the Holy Land* 1–39, trans. J. H. Bernard, *Theodosius (A.D. 530)* (London: Palestine Pilgrims' Text Society, 1893), 7–10.

37. Theodosius, *Topography* 46, trans. Bernard, *Theodosius*, 11.

38. Theodosius, *Topography* 40–41, trans. Bernard, *Theodosius*, 10 (italics in the original).

39. *Breviary or Short Description of Jerusalem*, trans. Aubrey Stewart in *The Epitome of S. Eucherius about Certain Holy Places (circ. A.D. 440), and The Breviary or Short Description of Jerusalem (circ. A.D. 530)* (London: Palestine Pilgrims' Text Society, 1890), 14–15.

40. Halbwachs, *Topographie légendaire*, 145.

41. Piacenza Pilgrim, *Itinerarium* 16, trans. Aubrey Stewart in *Of the Holy Places Visited by Antoninus Martyr (circ. 530 A.D.)* (London: Palestine Pilgrims' Text Society, 1887), 13–14.

42. Piacenza Pilgrim, *Itinerarium* 25, trans. Stewart, *Of the Holy Places*, 21.

43. Piacenza Pilgrim, *Itinerarium* 19, trans. Stewart, *Of the Holy Places*, 16.

44. Vincent Lemire, *La Soif de Jérusalem: Essai d'hydrohistoire (1840–1948)* (Paris: Publications de la Sorbonne, 2010), ch. 1.

45. Piacenza Pilgrim, *Itinerarium* 18, trans. Stewart, *Of the Holy Places*, 15.

46. Piacenza Pilgrim, *Itinerarium* 22, trans. Stewart, *Of the Holy Places*, 18–19.

47. Halbwachs, *Topographie légendaire*, 7 (italics added).

48. Piacenza Pilgrim, *Itinerarium* 23, trans. Stewart, *Of the Holy Places*, 19.

CHAPTER 3. IN THE EMPIRE OF THE CALIPHS

1. Max van Berchem, *Matériaux pour un corpus inscriptionum arabicarum*, pt. 2, *Syrie du Sud*, vol. 1, *Jérusalem "ville,"* Mémoires publiés par les membres de l'Institut français d'archéologie orientale 43 (Paris: E. Leroux, 1922), 17–30.

2. Cyril Mango, "The Temple Mount, AD 614–638," in *Bayt al-Maqdis*, Oxford Studies in Islamic Art 9, pt. 1, *Abd al-Malik's Jerusalem*, ed. Julian Raby and Jeremy Johns (Oxford: Oxford University Press, 1992), 4–5.

3. Tsafrir, "70–638," 72–99.

4. Mango, "Temple Mount," 8–15.

5. Alfred-Louis de Prémare, *Les Fondations de l'islam: Entre écriture et histoire* (Paris: Seuil, 2002), 138–48.

6. Heribert Busse, "'Omar's Image as the Conqueror of Jerusalem," *Jerusalem Studies in Arabic and Islam* 8 (1986): 149–68; Prémare, *Fondations de l'islam*, 155–59.

7. Prémare, *Fondations de l'islam*, 153–55, 409–11.

8. Bernard Flusin, "L'Esplanade du Temple à l'arrivée des Arabes d'après deux récits byzantins," in Raby and Johns, *Abd al-Malik's Jerusalem*, 17–31; Arculf, quoted in Adomnán, *De Locis Sanctis* 1.14, trans. McPherson, *Pilgrimage of Arculfus*, 4.

9. Amikam Elad, *Medieval Jerusalem and Islamic Worship: Holy Places, Ceremonies, Pilgrimage* (Leiden: Brill, 1995), 23–24.

10. Sebeos, *History* 43, trans. R. W. Thomson, in *The Armenian History Attributed to Sebeos*, pt. 1, *Translation and Notes* (Liverpool: Liverpool University Press, 1999), 103.

11. Eilat Mazar and Orit Peleg, "'The House of the Menorot' in the Temple Mount Excavations: The Earliest Synagogue Discovered in Jerusalem" [in Hebrew; includes an abstract in English], *Cathedra* 94 (1999): 55–74.

12. H. I. Bell, "Translation of the Greek Aphrodito Papyri in the British Museum," *Der Islam* 2 (1911): 269–83, 372–84.

13. Oleg Grabar, "The Umayyad Dome of the Rock in Jerusalem," *Ars Orientalis* 3 (1959): 33–62; Nasser Rabbat, "The Meaning of the Umayyad Dome of the Rock," *Muqarnas* 6 (1989): 12–21.

14. Christel Kessler, "'Abd al-Malik's Inscription in the Dome of the Rock: A Reconsideration," *Journal of the Royal Asiatic Society* 102 (1970): 2–14.

15. Pierre Lory, "Abraham," in *Dictionnaire du Coran*, ed. Mohammad Ali Amir-Moezzi (Paris: Robert Laffont, 2007), 9–14.

16. S. D. Goitein and O. Grabar, "Al-Ḳuds," in *Encyclopaedia of Islam*, 2nd ed., ed. P. Bearman, T. Bianquis, C. E. Bosworth, E. van Donzel, and W. P. Heinrichs (Leiden: Brill, 2006–), http://dx.doi.org/10.1163/1573-3912_islam_COM_0535.

17. Al-Muqaddasi, *Aḥsanu-t-taqāsīm fī maʿrifati-l-aqālīm*, trans. G. S. A. Ranking and R. F. Azoo (Calcutta: Asiatic Society of Bengal, 1897), 262.

18. Prémare, *Fondations de l'islam*, 297–301.

19. All Qur'anic quotations are from *The Qur'an*, trans. M. A. S. Abdel Haleem (Oxford: Oxford University Press, 2004).

20. Mathieu Tillier, "'Abd al-Malik, Muḥammad et le Jugement dernier: Le Dôme du Rocher comme expression d'une orthodoxie islamique," in *Les Vivants et les morts dans les sociétés médiévales*, ed. Société des historiens médiévistes de l'Enseignement supérieur public (Paris: Éditions de la Sorbonne, 2018), 341–65.

21. Elad, *Medieval Jerusalem*, 51.

22. Bell, "Greek Aphrodito Papyri."

23. Elad, *Medieval Jerusalem*, 33–39.

24. Max van Berchem, *Matériaux pour un corpus inscriptionum arabicarum*, pt. 2, *Syrie du* Sud, vol. 2, *Jérusalem "ḥaram*," Mémoires publiés par les membres de l'Institut français d'archéologie orientale 44 (Cairo: Imprimerie de l'Institute français d'archéologie orientale du Caire, 1927), 235–39, 379.

25. Al-Muqaddasi, *Aḥsanu-t-taqāsīm fī ma'rifati-l-aqālīm*, trans. Ranking and Azoo, 276.

26. K. A. C. Creswell, *A Short Account of Early Muslim Architecture* (Harmondsworth: Penguin, 1958), revised and supplemented by James W. Allan (Cairo: American University in Cairo Press, 1989), 73–82. Page references are to the 1989 edition.

27. Emmanuel Sivan, "The Beginnings of the 'Faḍā'il al-Quds' Literature," *Der Islam* 48 (1971): 100–110.

28. Elad, *Medieval Jerusalem*, 16–22.

29. Busse, "'Omar's Image."

30. Flavius Josephus, *Jewish War* 1.417.

31. Heribert Busse, "The Tower of David / *Miḥrāb Dāwud:* Remarks on the History of a Sanctuary in Jerusalem in Christian and Islamic Times," *Jerusalem Studies in Arabic and Islam* 17 (1994): 142–65.

32. Heribert Busse, "Die 'Umar-Moschee im östlichen Atrium der Grabeskirche," *Zeitschrift des Deutschen Palästina-Vereins* 109 (1993): 73–82.

33. Prémare, *Fondations de l'islam*, 170–71, 418–20.

34. Paul Ballanfat, "Jour du Jugement," 454–57, and "Résurrection," 747–49, in Amir-Moezzi, *Dictionnaire du Coran;* Geneviève Gobillot, "Sceau des prophètes," in ibid., 795–97.

35. Heribert Busse, "Jerusalem in the Story of Muhammad's Night Journey and Ascension," *Jerusalem Studies in Arabic and Islam* 14 (1991): 1–40.

36. Elad, *Medieval Jerusalem*, 48–50, 73–76, 97–102.

37. Elad, *Medieval Jerusalem*, 78–84, 93–97.

38. Andreas Kaplony, "635/638–1099: The Mosque of Jerusalem (*Masjid Bayt al-Maqdis*)," in Grabar and Kedar, *Where Heaven and Earth Meet*, 100–131.

39. Oleg Grabar, "A New Inscription from the Haram al-Sharif in Jerusalem: A Note on the Mediaeval Topography of Jerusalem," in *Studies in Islamic Art and Architecture: In Honour of Professor K. A. C. Creswell* (Cairo: American University in Cairo Press, 1965), 72–83.

40. Elad, *Medieval Jerusalem*, 85–86; Michael H. Burgoyne, "1187–1260: The Furthest Mosque (*al-Masjid al-Aqsa*) under Ayyubid Rule," in Grabar and Kedar, *Where Heaven and Earth Meet*, 167–68.

41. Moshe Gil, "Dhimmi Donations and Foundations for Jerusalem (638–1099)," *Journal of the Economic and Social History of the Orient* 27 (1984): 170; Kaplony, "635/638–1099," 116–18, 129–30.

42. Goitein and Grabar, "Al-Ḳuds."

43. Al-Muqaddasi, *Aḥsanu-t-taqāsīm fī ma' rifati-l-aqālīm*, trans. Ranking and Azoo, 272, 274–75.

44. Al-Muqaddasi, *Aḥsanu-t-taqāsīm fī ma' rifati-l-aqālīm*, trans. Ranking and Azoo, 273, 274.

45. Shimon Gat, "The Seljuks in Jerusalem," in *Towns and Material Culture in the Medieval Middle East*, ed. Yaacov Lev, Medieval Mediterranean 39 (Leiden: Brill, 2002), 14–15.

46. Marius Canard, "La Destruction de l'Église de la Résurrection par le calife Ḥākim et l'histoire de la descente du feu sacré," *Byzantion* 35 (1965): 16–43, repr. in Canard, *Byzance et les musulmans du Proche-Orient* (London: Variorum Reprints, 1973).

47. Gat, "Seljuks in Jerusalem," 16; Grabar, "New Inscription," 78–79.

CHAPTER 4. JERUSALEM, CAPITAL OF THE
FRANKISH KINGDOM

1. Cyril Aslanov, *Le Français au Levant, jadis et naguère: À la recherche d'une langue perdue* (Paris: Champion, 2006).

2. *Chronique d'Ernoul et de Bernard le Trésorier*, ed. L. de Mas Latrie (Paris: Librairie de la Société de l'histoire de France, 1871), 189–210; *Estat de la cité de Jherusalem*, trans. C. R. Conder as *The City of Jerusalem* (London: Palestine Pilgrims' Text Society, 1896).

3. *Estat de la cité de Jherusalem* 4, trans. Conder, *City of Jerusalem*, 4–5.

4. *Estat de la cité de Jherusalem* 4, trans. Conder, *City of Jerusalem*, 5.

5. *Estat de la cité de Jherusalem* 4, trans. Conder, *City of Jerusalem*, 5.

6. *Estat de la cité de Jherusalem* 16, trans. Conder, *City of Jerusalem*, 18–19.

7. John France, *Victory in the East: A Military History of the First Crusade* (Cambridge: Cambridge University Press, 1994), 131, estimates this as the number of Frankish forces at the battle of Ascalon, in August 1099.

8. Robert the Monk, *Historia Hierosolymitana*, excerpted in *Urban and the Crusaders*, trans. Dana Carleton Munro, vol. 1, no. 2 of *Translations and Reprints from the Original Sources of European History* (Philadelphia: University of Pennsylvania, 1895), 7.

9. Camille Rouxpetel, *L'Occident au miroir de l'Orient chrétien: Cilicie, Syrie, Palestine et Égypte (XIIᵉ-XIVᵉ siècle)*, Bibliothèque des Écoles françaises d'Athènes et de Rome 369 (Rome: École française de Rome, 2015).

10. Robert the Monk, *Historia Hierosolymitana*, trans. Munro, *Urban and the Crusaders*, 6.

11. Benjamin Z. Kedar, "The Jerusalem Massacre of July 1099 in the Western Historiography of the Crusades," *Crusades* 3 (2004): 15–75.

12. Joshua Prawer, "The Settlement of the Latins in Jerusalem," *Speculum* 27 (1952): 490.

13. William of Tyre, *Historia rerum in partibus transmarinis gestarum* 11.27, trans. Emily Atwater Babcock and A. C. Krey, *A History of Deeds Done beyond the Sea*, vol. 1 (New York: Columbia University Press, 1943), 507.

14. Adrian J. Boas, *Jerusalem in the Time of the Crusades: Society, Landscape and Art in the Holy City under Frankish Rule* (London: Routledge, 2001), 79–82.

15. Denys Pringle, *The City of Jerusalem*, vol. 3 of *The Churches of the Crusader Kingdom of Jerusalem: A Corpus* (Cambridge: Cambridge University Press, 2007), 20–21.

16. Pringle, *City of Jerusalem*, 18; Boas, *Jerusalem*, 84.

17. Pringle, *City of Jerusalem*, 14–15; Boas, *Jerusalem*, 79.

18. Pringle, *City of Jerusalem*, 68.

19. Felix-Marie Abel, "Lettre d'un Templier trouvée récemment à Jérusalem," *Revue biblique* 35 (1926): 288–95; Benjamin Z. Kedar and Denys Pringle, "1099–1187: The Lord's Temple (*Templum Domini*) and Solomon's Palace (*Palatium Salomonis*)," in Grabar and Kedar, *Where Heaven and Earth Meet*, 142–47.

20. Camille Rouxpetel, "Trois récits occidentaux de la descente du feu sacré au Saint-Sépulcre (Pâques 1101): Polyphonie chrétienne et stratégies discursives," *Mélanges de l'École française de Rome—Moyen Âge* 126-1 (2014): https://doi.org/10.4000/mefrm.1932.

21. Kedar and Pringle, "1099–1187," 136–41.

22. Pringle, *City of Jerusalem*, 4, 98–102, 103–8, 310–13.

23. Halbwachs, *Topographie légendaire*, 83–88; Pringle, *City of Jerusalem*, 4, 93–96, 132–36, 319–21.

24. Prawer, "Latins in Jerusalem," 493.

25. William of Tyre, *Historia rerum* 9.18, trans. Babcock and Krey, *History of Deeds*, 407.

26. Prawer, "Latins in Jerusalem," 491–92; Boas, *Jerusalem*, 84, 88; *Estat de la cité de Jherusalem* 22, trans. Conder, *City of Jerusalem*, 25.

27. William of Tyre, *Historia rerum* 9.17, trans. Babcock and Krey, *History of Deeds*, 405.

28. William of Tyre, *Historia rerum* 9.18, trans. Babcock and Krey, *History of Deeds*, 407.

29. Boas, *Jerusalem*, 83–85.

30. William of Tyre, *Historia rerum* 11.27, trans. Babcock and Krey, *History of Deeds*, 507–8.

31. Rouxpetel, "Trois récits occidentaux."

32. Rouxpetel, *L'Occident*, 140–44.

33. Prawer, "Latins in Jerusalem," 494–95.

34. Michel Balard, *Les Latins en Orient, XIᵉ–XVᵉ siècle* (Paris: Presses universitaires de France, 2006), 84, 90; *Estat de la cité de Jherusalem* 22, trans. Conder, *City of Jerusalem*, 25.

35. Pringle, *City of Jerusalem*, 5.

36. Benjamin Z. Kedar, "A Twelfth-Century Description of the Jerusalem Hospital," in *Welfare and Warfare*, ed. Helen Nicholson, vol. 2 of *The Military Orders* (Aldershot: Ashgate, 1998), 3–26; Boas, *Jerusalem*, 27, 85–88.

37. Boas, *Jerusalem*, 89, 125–26; Pringle, *City of Jerusalem*, 228–35; John of Würzburg, *Descriptio terrae sanctae* 13, trans. Aubrey Stewart, *Description of the Holy Land by John of Würzburg (A.D. 1160–1170)* (London: Palestine Pilgrims' Text Society, 1890), 41.

38. Hillel Geva and Dan Bahat, "Architectural and Chronological Aspects of the Ancient Damascus Gate Area," *Israel Exploration Journal* 48 (1998): 223–35.

39. In what is to date the most systematic inquiry on the subject, Denys Pringle's *The City of Jerusalem* identifies and documents the history of eighty-seven churches and chapels in Jerusalem between 1099 and 1244.

40. Pringle, *City of Jerusalem*, 142–55.

41. Henri-François Delaborde, *Chartes de Terre sainte provenant de l'abbaye de N.-D. de Josaphat* (Paris: Ernest Thorin, 1880); Pringle, *City of Jerusalem*, 287–305; al-Harawī, *Kitāb al-Ishārāt ilā Maʿrifat al-ziyārāt*, trans. Josef W. Meri, *A Lonely Wayfarer's Guide to Pilgrimage* (Princeton, NJ: Darwin, 2004), 74.

42. Boas, *Jerusalem*, 142–55; *Estat de la cité de Jherusalem* 10, trans. Conder, *City of Jerusalem*, 11.

CHAPTER 5. FROM SALADIN TO SÜLEYMAN

1. Max van Berchem, *Matériaux pour un corpus inscriptionum arabicarum*, pt. 2, *Syrie du Sud*, vol. 2, *Jérusalem "ḥaram,"* Mémoires publiés par les membres de l'Institut français d'archéologie orientale 44 (Cairo: Imprimerie de l'Institute français d'archéologie orientale du Caire, 1927), 393–402; Nikita

Elisséeff, *Nur al-Din: Un grand prince musulman de Syrie au temps des croisades (511–569 H. / 1118–1174)*, vol. 2 (Damascus: Institut français de Damas, 1967), 684.

2. Shelomo D. Goitein, "Contemporary Letters on the Capture of Jerusalem by the Crusaders," *Journal of Jewish Studies* 3 (1952): 169–70.

3. Emmanuel Sivan, "Le Caractère sacré de Jerusalem dans l'Islam aux XIIe–XIIIe siècles," *Studia Islamica* 27 (1967): 149–82.

4. Sivan, "Caractère sacré de Jerusalem," 160; Anne-Marie Eddé, *Saladin*, trans. Jane Marie Todd (Cambridge, MA: Belknap Press of Harvard University Press, 2011), 90–95 (quote on 94).

5. André Miquel, *Ousâma: Un prince syrien face aux croisés* (Paris: Tallandier, 2007), 75–76; al-Harawī, *Kitāb al-Ishārāt ilā Maʿrifat al-ziyārāt*, trans. Meri, *Lonely Wayfarer's Guide*, 70, 72, 74, 76.

6. Eddé, *Saladin*, 225–26; Donald P. Little, "Jerusalem under the Ayyubids and Mamluks, 1187–1516 AD," in *Jerusalem in History: 3000 BC to the Present Day*, ed. Kamil J. Asali, 2nd ed. (London: Kegan Paul, 1997), 178–79 (includes translations, slightly modified here).

7. Benjamin Z. Kedar, "The Battle of Hattin Revisited," in *The Horns of Hattin: Proceedings of the Second Conference of the Society for the Study of the Crusades and the Latin East, Jerusalem and Haifa, 2–6 July 1987*, ed. Benjamin Z. Kedar (Jerusalem: Yad Izhak Ben-Zvi, 1992), 190–207.

8. Eddé, *Saladin*, 218–21.

9. Little, "Jerusalem under the Ayyubids and Mamluks," 177 (includes translation). But cf. Pascal Buresi, "Les Conversions d'églises et de mosquées en Espagne aux XIe–XIIIe siècles," in *Religion et société urbaine au Moyen Âge: Études offertes à Jean-Louis Biget par ses élèves*, ed. Patrick Boucheron and Jacques Chiffoleau (Paris: Publications de la Sorbonne, 2000), 333–50.

10. Burgoyne, "1187–1260," 152.

11. Berchem, *Jérusalem "ḥaram,"* 37–54.

12. Grabar, "New Inscription," 78–79; Lorenz Korn, "The Structure of Architectural Patronage in Ayyubid Jerusalem," in *Governing the Holy City: The Interaction of Social Groups in Jerusalem between the Fatimid and the Ottoman Period*, ed. Johannes Pahlitzsch and Lorenz Korn (Wiesbaden: Reichert, 2004), 81.

13. Korn, "Structure of Architectural Patronage," 78; Mohammad Ghosheh, "The Walls and Gates of Jerusalem before and after Sultan Süleymān's Rebuilding Project of 1538–40," in Pahlitzsch and Korn, *Governing the Holy City*, 118.

14. Moshe Sharon, "The Ayyubid Walls of Jerusalem: A New Inscription from the Time of al-Muʿaẓẓam ʿĪsā," in *Studies in Memory of Gaston Wiet*, ed. Miriam Rosen-Ayalon (Jerusalem: Institute of Asian and African Studies, Hebrew University of Jerusalem, 1977), 179–93.

15. Little, "Jerusalem under the Ayyubids and Mamluks," 179.

16. Sivan, "Caractère sacré de Jerusalem," 166.

17. Burgoyne, "1187–1260," 158–59.

18. Burgoyne, "1187–1260," 170; Tawfiq Da'ādli, "Mamlūk Epitaphs from Māmillā Cemetery," *Levant* 43, no. 1 (2011): 78–97.

19. Eddé, *Saladin*, 404–6, citing Joshua Prawer, *The History of the Jews in the Latin Kingdom of Jerusalem* (Oxford: Clarendon, 1988), 66–71, 85–86, 146 et seq., 154–58.

20. Johannes Pahlitzsch, "The Transformation of Latin Religious Institutions into Islamic Endowments by Saladin in Jerusalem," in Pahlitzsch and Korn, *Governing the Holy City*, 47–69; Donald S. Richards, "Saladin's Hospital in Jerusalem: Its Foundation and Some Later Archival Material," in *The Frankish Wars and Their Influence on Palestine: Selected Papers Presented at Birzeit University's International Academic Conference Held in Jerusalem, March 13–15, 1992*, ed. Khalil Athamina and Roger Heacock (Beir Zeit: Birzeit University Publications, Mediterranean Studies Unit, 1994), 70–82.

21. David S. Powers, "Revenues of Public 'Waqfs' in Sixteenth-Century Jerusalem," *Archivum Ottomanicum* 9 (1984): 166–69.

22. Pahlitzsch, "Transformation of Latin Religious Institutions."

23. Burgoyne, "1187–1260," 163–64, 168–70; Korn, "Structure of Architectural Patronage," 82–83.

24. Louis Pouzet, "De la paix armée à la négociation et à ses ambiguïtés: L'Accord de Jaffa (1229/626) entre Frédéric II et al-Malik al-Kamil," in *Chrétiens et musulmans au temps des croisades: Entre l'affrontement et la rencontre*, ed. Louis Pouzet and Louis Boisset (Beirut: Presses de l'Université Saint-Joseph, 2007), 91–116; Burgoyne, "1187–1260," 172; Little, "Jerusalem under the Ayyubids and Mamluks," 183 (includes quote).

25. Korn, "Structure of Architectural Patronage," 74–75; Little, "Jerusalem under the Ayyubids and Mamluks," 185–86; Claude Cahen and Ibrahim Chabbouh, "Le Testament d'al-Malik aṣ-Ṣāliḥ Ayyūb," in "Mélanges offerts à Henri Laoust," vol. 1, special issue, *Bulletin d'études orientales* 29 (1977): 100.

26. Julien Loiseau, *Les Mamelouks (XIIIᵉ–XVIᵉ siècle): Une expérience du pouvoir dans l'Islam médiéval* (Paris: Seuil, 2014).

27. Michael Hamilton Burgoyne, *Mamluk Jerusalem: An Architectural Study*, with additional historical research by D. S. Richards (London: World of Islam Festival Trust, 1987), 77; Gérard Degeorge and Yves Porter, *L'Art de la céramique dans l'architecture musulmane* (Paris: Flammarion, 2001), 212.

28. Lemire, *Soif de Jérusalem*, 203–10; Mujīr al-Dīn al-'Ulaymī, *Al-Uns al-jalīl bi-ta'rīkh al-Quds wa l-Khalīl*, vol. 2 (Cairo: n.p., n.d.), 92, 94; al-'Ulaymī, *Histoire de Jérusalem et d'Hébron depuis Abraham jusqu'à la fin du XVᵉ siècle de J.-C.: Fragments de la "Chronique" de Moudjîr-ed-dyn traduits sur le texte arabe*, trans. Henri Sauvaire (Paris: Ernest Leroux, 1876), 245–46, 249–50; Burgoyne, *Mamluk Jerusalem*, 606–12; Myriam Rosen-Ayalon, "On Suleiman's *Sabīls* in Jerusalem," in *The Islamic World from Classical to Modern Times: Essays in*

Honor of Bernard Lewis, ed. Clifford E. Bosworth, Charles Issawi, Roger Savory, and Abraham L. Udovitch (Princeton, NJ: Darwin, 1989), 589–607.

29. Al-ʿUlaymī, *Al-Uns al-jalīl,* 56–57; Donald P. Little, "Mujīr al-Dīn al-ʿUlaymī's Vision of Jerusalem in the Ninth/Fifteenth Century," *Journal of the American Oriental Society* 115 (1995): 237–47; Grabar, "New Inscription," 79–82; Ghosheh, "Walls and Gates of Jerusalem," 122–24.

30. Burgoyne, *Mamluk Jerusalem,* 59; Ghosheh, "Walls and Gates of Jerusalem," 124–26.

31. Loiseau, *Mamelouks,* 215–18, 225–28, 262–63.

32. Burgoyne, *Mamluk Jerusalem,* 69, 223–43; Yossef Rapoport, *Marriage, Money and Divorce in Medieval Islamic Society* (Cambridge: Cambridge University Press, 2005), 44–50.

33. Grabar, "New Inscription," 72–77; Burgoyne, *Mamluk Jerusalem,* 224–25.

34. Amnon Cohen, "The Walls of Jerusalem," in *The Islamic World from Classical to Modern Times: Essays in Honor of Bernard Lewis,* ed. Clifford E. Bosworth, Charles Issawi, Roger Savory, and Abraham L. Udovitch (Princeton, NJ: Darwin, 1989), 470–71.

35. Ghosheh, "Walls and Gates of Jerusalem," 126–28.

36. Cohen, "Walls of Jerusalem," 471–73; Amnon Cohen, "The Ottoman Approach to Christians and Christianity in Sixteenth-Century Jerusalem," *Islam and Christian-Muslim Relations* 7, no. 2 (1996): 208.

37. Amnon Cohen and Bernard Lewis, *Population and Revenue in the Towns of Palestine in the Sixteenth Century* (Princeton, NJ: Princeton University Press, 1978); S. D. Goitein and O. Grabar, "Al-Ḳuds," in Bearman et al., *Encyclopaedia of Islam,* http://dx.doi.org/10.1163/1573-3912_islam_COM_0535.

38. Kamil J. Asali, "Jerusalem under the Ottomans, 1516–1831 AD," in Asali, *Jerusalem in History,* 204; R. Amitai-Preiss, "Ṣafad," in Bearman et al., *Encyclopaedia of Islam,* http://dx.doi.org/10.1163/1573-3912_islam_SIM_6435.

39. Burgoyne, *Mamluk Jerusalem,* 60; Donald P. Little, "The Governance of Jerusalem under Qāytbāy," in *The Mamluks in Egyptian and Syrian Politics and Society,* ed. Michael Winter and Amalia Levanoni, Medieval Mediterranean 51 (Leiden: Brill, 2004), 143–62.

40. Donald P. Little, *A Catalogue of the Islamic Documents from al-Ḥaram aš-Šarīf in Jerusalem,* Beiruter Texte und Studien 29 (Beirut: Orient-Institut der Deutschen Morgenländischen Gesellschaft, 1984); Huda Lutfi, *Al-Quds al-Mamlûkiyya: A History of Mamlûk Jerusalem Based on the Ḥaram Documents* (Berlin: K. Schwarz, 1985); Christian Müller, *Der Kadi und seine Zeugen: Studie der mamlukischen Haram-Dokumente aus Jerusalem* (Wiesbaden: Harrassowitz, 2013).

41. Burgoyne, *Mamluk Jerusalem,* 62, 178; Asali, "Jerusalem under the Ottomans," 203.

42. Al-ʿUlaymī, *Al-Uns al-jalīl*, 49, 51.

43. Donald P. Little, "Haram Documents Related to the Jews of Late Fourteenth Century Jerusalem," *Journal of Semitic Studies* 30, no. 2 (1985): 227–64.

44. Al-ʿUlaymī, *Al-Uns al-jalīl*, 263–65, 300–314; Donald P. Little, "Communal Strife in Late Mamlūk Jerusalem," *Islamic Law and Society* 6, no. 1 (1999): 69–96.

45. Amnon Cohen, "The Expulsion of the Franciscans from Mount Zion," *Turcica* 18 (1986): 147–57.

46. Al-ʿUlaymī, *Al-Uns al-jalīl*, 51; Butrus Abu-Manneh, "The Georgians in Jerusalem during the Mamluk Period," *Egypt and Palestine: A Millennium of Association (868-1948)*, ed. Amnon Cohen and Gabriel Baer (Jerusalem: Ben-Zvi Institute; New York: St. Martin's, 1984), 102–12; Cohen, "Ottoman Approach to Christians," 209–10.

CHAPTER 6. THE PEACE OF THE OTTOMANS

1. Simon Sebag Montefiore, in his monumental history of Jerusalem (*Jerusalem: The Biography* [New York: Alfred A. Knopf, 2011]), thus writes of a city that "decayed" (336) and later of "a benighted ruin ruled by a shabby pasha in a tawdry seraglio" (351).

2. Christine Géraud-Gomez, *Le Crépuscule du grand voyage: Les Récits de pèlerins à Jérusalem (1458-1612)* (Paris: Honoré Champion, 2000).

3. Constantin-François de Volney, *Voyage en Syrie et en Égypte (1783-1785)* (Paris: Dienne and Volland, 1787), trans. as *Travels through Syria and Egypt, in the Years 1783, 1784, and 1785* (Dublin: White, Byrne, W. Porter, Moore, Dornin, and Wm. Jones, 1793), 439 (italics in original).

4. François-René de Chateaubriand, *Itinéraire de Paris à Jérusalem* (Paris: Le Normant, 1811), trans. F. Shoberl, *Travels in Greece, Palestine, Egypt, and Barbary, during the Years 1806 and 1807* (New York: Van Winkle and Wiley, 1814), 361.

5. Robert Mantran, *Histoire de l'Empire ottoman* (Paris: Fayard, 1989).

6. Yasemin Avci and Vincent Lemire, "De la modernité administrative à la modernisation urbaine: Une réévaluation de la municipalité ottomane de Jérusalem (1867-1917)," in *Municipalités méditerranéennes: Les Réformes urbaines ottomanes au miroir d'une histoire comparée (Moyen-Orient, Maghreb, Europe méridionale)*, ed. Nora Lafi (Berlin: K. Schwarz, 2005), 73–138.

7. Vincent Lemire, *Jerusalem 1900: The Holy City in the Age of Possibilities*, trans. Catherine Tihanyi and Lys Ann Weiss (Chicago: University of Chicago Press, 2017), originally published as *Jérusalem 1900: La Ville sainte à l'âge des possibles* (Paris: Armand Colin, 2013).

8. Henry Laurens, *La Question de Palestine* (Paris: Fayard, 1999–2015), vols. 1–2.

9. The Başbakanlık Osmanlı Arşivleri (BOA; Prime Minister's Ottoman Archives) in Istanbul, for example, preserves around 250 volumes of the "Register of Public Affairs" (*Mühimme Defteri*), which has copies of more than two hundred thousand decrees (firmans) that were addressed to imperial functionaries over three centuries (sixteenth to nineteenth) and cover all the subjects relating to provincial administration. Most often written in response to an individual or collective petition (summarized in the document's opening lines), these imperial firmans provide a close-up view of the reality of the ties between the central administration and the people in the provinces. About three hundred of these documents, touching on Palestine, were published in 1960: Uriel Heyd, *Ottoman Documents on Palestine, 1552–1615: A Study of the Firman according to the Mühimme Defteri* (Oxford: Clarendon, 1960).

10. David Kushner, ed., *Palestine in the Late Ottoman Period: Political, Social and Economic Transformation* (Jerusalem: Yad Izhak Ben-Zvi, 1986).

11. Heyd, *Ottoman Documents on Palestine*, document 23 (pp. 71–72); see also document 21 (p. 69).

12. Heyd, *Ottoman Documents on Palestine*, document 41 (pp. 87–88).

13. Heyd, *Ottoman Documents on Palestine*, document 38 (p. 85).

14. Elkan Nathan Adler, ed., *Jewish Travellers* (London: Routledge and Sons, 1930), 263.

15. Adler, *Jewish Travellers*, 263–66.

16. François-Charles du Rozel, *Voyage de Jérusalem et autres lieux saincts effectué et décrit en 1644*, ed. Émile Bonneserre de Saint-Denis (Paris: Dumoulin, 1864), 40–41.

17. Du Rozel, *Voyage de Jérusalem*, 44–45.

18. Du Rozel, *Voyage de Jérusalem*, 94–95.

19. Du Rozel, *Voyage de Jérusalem*, 73.

20. Maurice Halbwachs, *La Topographie légendaire des Évangiles en Terre sainte* (1941; repr., Paris: Presses universitaires de France, 2008).

21. Du Rozel, *Voyage de Jérusalem*, 48.

22. Marie-Thérèse Urvoy, "Jésus," in *Dictionnaire du Coran*, ed. Mohammad Ali Amir-Moezzi (Paris: Robert Laffont, 2007), 438–41.

23. Du Rozel, *Voyage de Jérusalem*, 48–49.

24. Du Rozel, *Voyage de Jérusalem*, 60, 50.

25. Du Rozel, *Voyage de Jérusalem*, 51–52.

26. Lemire, *Jerusalem 1900*.

27. Du Rozel, *Voyage de Jérusalem*, 75n1.

28. Du Rozel, *Voyage de Jérusalem*, 54n.

29. Heyd, *Ottoman Documents on Palestine*, document 122 (pp. 180–81).

30. Heyd, *Ottoman Documents on Palestine*, documents 98 (pp. 152–54), 106–7 (pp. 160–61).

31. Heyd, *Ottoman Documents on Palestine*, document 115 (p. 173).

32. A reproduction of this *Moniteur universel* was presented at the French Ministère des Affaires étrangères exhibition on the State of Israel's sixtieth anniversary (2008); it is available via the Bibliothèque nationale de France at https://www.retronews.fr/journal/gazette-nationale-ou-le-moniteur-universel/22-mai-1799/149/1524827/1.

33. Jacques Derogy and Hesi Carmel, *Bonaparte en Terre sainte* (Paris: Fayard, 1992).

34. Laurens, *La Question de Palestine*, 1:14–15.

35. Sebag Montefiore, *Jerusalem*, 331.

36. Henry Laurens, "Le Projet d'État juif attribué à Bonaparte," *Revue d'études palestiniennes* 33 (Autumn 1989): 69–83, reprinted as "Le Projet d'État juif en Palestine attribué à Bonaparte" in Laurens, *Orientales* (Paris: CNRS Éditions, 2007), 123–43.

37. All of this section's quotes are from Chateaubriand, *Itinéraire*, trans. Shoberl, *Travels*, 389–90.

38. Laurens, *La Question de Palestine*, 1:48–52.

39. Mordechai Eliav, *Britain and the Holy Land, 1838–1914: Selected Documents from the British Consulate in Jerusalem* (Jerusalem: Yad Izhak Ben-Zvi Press, 1997), 114, 121.

40. Archives of the Ministère des Affaires étrangères (MAE), Paris, Correspondance consulaire et commerciale (CCC), Jérusalem, vol. 2, 22–82, 6 août–20 novembre 1843.

41. MAE, Paris, CCC, Jérusalem, vol. 2, 33, 13 août 1843.

42. MAE, Paris, CCC, Jérusalem, vol. 2, 102, 15 janvier 1844.

43. MAE, Paris, CCC, Jérusalem, vol. 2, 199, 10 juin 1844.

44. Robert Ilbert, "De Beyrouth à Alger: La Fin d'un ordre urbain," *Vingtième siècle: Revue d'histoire* 32 (octobre–décembre 1991): 15–24.

45. MAE, Paris, CCC, Jérusalem, vol. 3, 11, 1er mars 1848.

46. Vincent Lemire, *La Soif de Jérusalem: Essai d'hydrohistoire (1840–1948)* (Paris: Publications de la Sorbonne, 2010).

47. Lemire, *Jerusalem 1900*.

48. Avci and Lemire, "De la modernité administrative."

49. Yasemin Avci, Vincent Lemire, and Falestin Naïli, "Publishing Jerusalem's Ottoman Municipal Archives (1892–1917): A Turning Point for the City's Historiography," *Jerusalem Quarterly* 60 (Autumn 2014): 110–19.

50. ʿAref el-ʿAref, "The Closing Phase of Ottoman Rule in Jerusalem," in *Studies on Palestine during the Ottoman Period*, ed. Moshe Maʿoz (Jerusalem: Magnes Press, Hebrew University, and Yad Izhak Ben-Zvi, 1975), 334–40.

51. MAE, Nantes, Jérusalem, série A, Dames de Sion, carton 98, mai 1866.

52. MAE, Nantes, Jérusalem, série A, Dames de Sion, carton 98, juillet 1868.

53. Moses Montefiore, "A Narrative of a Forty Days' Sojourn in the Holy Land," in *An Open Letter Addressed to Sir Moses Montefiore . . .*, by Meyer Auerbach and Samuel Salant, 2nd ed. (London: Wertheimer, Lea, 1877), 91–92.

54. George Young, *Corps de droit ottoman*, vol. 1 (Oxford: Clarendon, 1905), 73.

55. Israel State Archives, Jerusalem, Record Group 67, German Consulate, January 9, 1873.

56. Lemire, *La Soif de Jérusalem*, 277–90.

57. Historical Archives of the Jerusalem Municipality, Deliberations, 15 Cemaziyel-evvel 1312 (November 14, 1894).

58. Emanuel Gutmann, "The Beginning of Local Government in Jerusalem," *Public Administration in Israel and Abroad* 8 (1968): 52–61.

59. Avci and Lemire, "De la modernité administrative."

60. *Bulletin de la Chambre de commerce, d'industrie et d'agriculture de Palestine* 3 (septembre–octobre 1909).

61. Ancient Maps of Jerusalem (website), Hebrew University of Jerusalem, http://maps-of-jerusalem.huji.ac.il.

62. Adar Arnon, "The Quarters of Jerusalem in the Ottoman Period," *Middle Eastern Studies* 28, no. 1 (January 1992): 1–65.

63. Michelle Campos, *Ottomans Brothers: Muslims, Christians and Jews in Early Twentieth-Century Palestine* (Stanford, CA: Stanford University Press, 2011).

64. Ilbert, "De Beyrouth à Alger."

65. Eliezer Ben-Yehuda, *A Dream Come True*, ed. George Mandel, trans. T. Muraoka (Boulder, CO: Westview, 1993; originally published as "Ha-Halom ve-Shivro," a series of articles in the Hebrew-language magazine *Ha-Toren*, New York, 1917–18), 56–57.

66. Central Zionist Archives, Jerusalem, H.197, 1er mars 1899.

67. Archives of the Alliance israélite universelle, Israel IV/E.11, n. 2693/4.

68. "Proclamation de la Constitution turque à Jérusalem," *Jérusalem* 52 (octobre 1908): 218–22. This report is illustrated with five photographs.

69. "Proclamation de la Constitution turque."

70. *Ha-Ḥavatzelet*, August 5, 1908.

71. Sir John Gray Hill, "Jew, Christian, and Musulman in Jerusalem," *Times* (London), September 3, 1908.

72. "Proclamation de la Constitution turque."

73. "Proclamation de la Constitution turque."

74. "Proclamation de la Constitution turque."

75. "Proclamation de la Constitution turque."

CHAPTER 7. THE IMPOSSIBLE CAPITAL?

1. "Covenant of the League of Nations," Wikisource, last edited April 12, 2018, 08:27, https://en.wikisource.org/wiki/Covenant_of_the_League_of _Nations.

2. For two exceptions, see Abigail Jacobson, *From Empire to Empire: Jerusalem from Ottoman to British Rule* (Syracuse, NY: Syracuse University Press, 2011); Roberto Mazza, *Jerusalem from the Ottomans to the British* (London: Tauris, 2009).

3. Mordechai Eliav, *Britain and the Holy Land, 1838–1914: Selected Documents from the British Consulate in Jerusalem* (Jerusalem: Yad Izhak Ben-Zvi Press, 1997), 408, 409.

4. Florence Berceot, "Une escale dans la tempête: Des Juifs palestiniens en Corse (1915–1920)," *Archives Juives: Revue d'histoire des Juifs de France* 38, no. 1 (2005): 129–38 (English abstract available at https://www.cairn-int.info /article-E_AJ_381_0129--any-port-in-a-storm-palestinian-jews.htm).

5. Élisabeth Antébi, *L'Homme du Sérail* (Paris: NiL, 1996).

6. Adel Mannâ, "Jérusalem sous les Ottomans," in *Jérusalem: Le Sacré et le politique,* ed. Farouk Mardam-Bey and Élias Sanbar (Arles: Actes Sud, 2000), 191–217.

7. Bertha Spafford-Vester, *Our Jerusalem: An American Family in the Holy City, 1881–1949* (Jerusalem: Ariel, 1988), 273–74. The photograph has been reproduced in numerous publications, notably Walid Khalidi, *Avant leur diaspora: Une histoire des Palestiniens par la photographie, 1876–1948* (Paris: Revue d'études palestiniennes, 1986), 48.

8. Tom Segev, *One Palestine, Complete: Jews and Arabs under the Mandate,* trans. Haim Watzman (New York: Metropolitan Books, 2000), 54–55.

9. Henry Laurens, *La Question de Palestine* (Paris: Fayard, 1999–2015), 1:306–10.

10. See, e.g., https://upload.wikimedia.org/wikipedia/commons/8/8e /Balfour_declaration_unmarked.jpg.

11. "Proclamation of General Allenby," in *Source Records of the Great War,* ed. Charles F. Horne and Walter F. Austin, vol. 5, *1917* (United States of America: National Alumni, 1923), 417.

12. Segev, *One Palestine, Complete,* 127–44.

13. R. Storrs, Public Notice no. 34 (Jerusalem, 8th April 1918), in *Jerusalem, 1918–1920,* ed. C. R. Ashbee (London: John Murray, 1921), appendix 5, 77.

14. Catherine Nicault, *Une histoire de Jérusalem, 1850–1967* (Paris: CNRS, 2008), 207–8.

15. C. R. Ashbee, interview in *The Observer* (London), 1919, quoted by Annabel Wharton, "Jerusalem Remade," in *Modernism and the Middle East: Architecture*

and Politics in the Twentieth Century, ed. Sandy Isenstadt and Kishwar Rizvi (Seattle: University of Washington Press, 2008), 46.

16. Amos Reichman, "Jérusalem 1939–1945: Une ville en paix?" (master's thesis, École normale supérieure de Lyon / Université Paris-Est, 2012).

17. Imperial War Museum London, Private Papers of S Burr, 88/8/1, letter, February 23, 1940, quoted in René Wildangel, *Zwischen Achse und Mandatsmacht, Palästina und der Nationalsozialismus* (Berlin: Klaus Schwartz Verlag, 2007), 259–60, cited in Christian Destremau, *Le Moyen-Orient pendant la Seconde Guerre mondiale* (Paris: Perrin, 2011), 179.

18. Hala Sakakini, *Jerusalem and I: A Personal Record* (Amman: Economic Press, 1990), 68, 81.

19. Amos Oz, *A Tale of Love and Darkness,* trans. Nicholas de Lange (Orlando, FL: Harvest, 2005), 26.

20. Archives of the Ministère des Affaires étrangères (MAE), Nantes, Jérusalem, série B, carton 135.

21. Arthur Ruppin, *Memoirs, Diaries, Letters,* ed. Alex Bein, trans. Karen Gershon (Jerusalem: Weidenfeld and Nicolson, 1971), 301.

22. MAE, Nantes, Jérusalem, série C, carton 6.

23. Reichman, "Jérusalem 1939–1945."

24. Dan Bitan, "L'UNSCOP et l'internationalisation de Jérusalem en 1947: Un plan pour préserver l'hégémonie occidentale en Palestine?," in *De Balfour à Ben Gourion: Les Puissances européennes et la Palestine 1917–1948,* ed. Dominique Trimbur and Ran Aaronsohn (Paris: CNRS, 2008), 435–86.

25. Salim Tamari, ed., *Jerusalem, 1948: The Arab Neighbourhoods and Their Fate in the War* (Bethlehem: Institute of Jerusalem Studies, 1999).

26. "War in the Old City: The Diaries of Constantine Mavrides," trans. John N. Tleel, in Tamari, *Jerusalem, 1948,* appendix 1, 280, 281.

27. Sakakini, *Jerusalem and I,* 111.

28. Haganah Intelligence Service report, January 5, 1948, IDF Archives 2605-49-3, quoted in Benny Morris, *The Birth of the Palestinian Refugee Problem Revisited* (Cambridge: Cambridge University Press 2004), 124.

29. Meron Benvenisti, *City of Stone: The Hidden History of Jerusalem,* trans. Maxine Kaufman Nunn (Berkeley: University of California Press, 1996), 56–63.

30. Laurens, *La Question de Palestine,* 3:278–82.

31. He left to posterity one of the first great surveys of Jerusalem's history: 'Aref el-'Aref, *Tarikh al-Quds* [History of al-Quds] (Cairo: Dar al-Ma'arif, 1951).

32. Nasser Eddin Nashashibi, *Jerusalem's Other Voice: Ragheb Nashashibi and Moderation in Palestinian Politics, 1920–1948* (Exeter, UK: Ithaca, 1990), 219.

33. Meron Benvenisti, *Jérusalem, une histoire politique,* trans. Katherine Werchowski and Nicolas Weill (Paris: Actes Sud, 1996), 146.

34. Lemire, *La Soif de Jérusalem,* 551–69.

35. Private collection of Yussuf al-Budeiri, Brown Engineers International, *The Hashemite Kingdom of Jordan: Jerusalem, a Feasibility Report for the Supply of Water to Jerusalem from Ain Fashkha* (1960).

36. U. O. Schmelz, *Modern Jerusalem's Demographic Evolutions* (Jerusalem: Jerusalem Institute for Israel Studies, 1987).

37. Norman Bentwich, "Editor's Note," in *Hebrew University Garland: A Silver Jubilee Symposium*, ed. Norman Bentwich (London: Constellation Books, 1952), ix, quoted in Martin Gilbert, *Jerusalem in the Twentieth Century* (London: John Wiley and Sons, 1996), 249.

38. Alain Dieckhoff, *Les Espaces d'Israël* (Paris: Presses de Sciences Po, 1989), 128.

39. Laurens, *La Question de Palestine*, 4:36.

40. Resolutions and other official records may be accessed via the United Nations Digital Library (https://digitallibrary.un.org/) or the UN's Official Document System (https://documents.un.org/prod/ods.nsf/home.xsp).

41. "Basic Law: Jerusalem, Capital of Israel," The Knesset (website), https://www.knesset.gov.il/laws/special/eng/basic10_eng.htm.

42. Benvenisti, *City of Stone*, 64–65.

43. Benvenisti, *City of Stone*, 66–67.

44. "Live Bomb Placed Under Seat in Jerusalem Cinema," *Jewish Telegraphic Agency*, October 10, 1967.

45. Gideon Weigert, *Israel's Presence in East Jerusalem* (Jerusalem: Jerusalem Post Press, 1973), quoted in Gilbert, *Jerusalem in the Twentieth Century*, 309.

46. Gilbert, *Jerusalem in the Twentieth Century*, 314.

47. Jonathan Rokem, "The Power of Discourse in Urban Planning Conflict: Jerusalem and the Case of the Damascus Gate Area" (MSc diss., London School of Economics and Political Science, 2006), 21.

48. Yael Horowitz, *The "Seam" Area: Planning Guidelines* (Jerusalem: Town Planning Department, Policy Planning Section, 1981).

49. Dieckhoff, *Les Espaces d'Israël*, 130.

50. Jonathan Rokem, "What Does Green Really Mean? Towards Reframing Jerusalem's Planning Policy," in *Critical Cities: Ideas, Knowledge and Agitation from Emerging Urbanists*, ed. Deepa Naik and Trenton Oldfield, vol. 2 (London: Myrdle Court Press, 2010), 76–92.

51. Maya Choshen, "Demographic Processes in Polarized Cities: The Case of Jerusalem," in *Divided Cities in Transition: Challenges Facing Jerusalem and Berlin*, ed. Michèle Auga, Schlomo Hasson, Rami Nasrallah, and Stephan Stetter (Jerusalem: Friedrich Ebert Stiftung, International Peace and Cooperation Center, Jerusalem Institute for Israel Studies, 2005), 15.

52. Eric Silver, "Divided," *Jewish Chronicle* (London), June 2, 1989, quoted in Gilbert, *Jerusalem in the Twentieth Century*, 337.

53. Benvenisti reports this surprising statement in his memoir *Sons of the Cypresses: Memories, Reflections, and Regrets from a Political Life*, trans. Maxine Kaufman-Lacusta in consultation with Michael Kaufman-Lacusta (Berkeley: University of California Press, 2007), 85.

54. Rokem, "What Does Green Really Mean?"

CONCLUSION

Epigraph: Meron Benvenisti, *City of Stone: The Hidden History of Jerusalem*, trans. Maxine Kaufman Nunn (Berkeley: University of California Press, 1996), 3–4.

1. Vincent Lemire, "Le Manteau rapiécé des prophètes: Lieux saints partagés d'Israël-Palestine," in *Lieux saints partagés*, ed. Dionigi Albera, Isabelle Marquette, and Manoël Pénicaud (Arles: Actes Sud; Marseille: MuCEM, 2015), 60–65.

2. Halbwachs, *Topographie légendaire.*

3. The Open Jerusalem project, conducted from 2014 to 2019, focused on the period from the Ottoman reforms of the 1840s to the end of the British mandate a century later. See the website http://www.openjerusalem.org/.

4. Finkelstein and Silberman, *Bible Unearthed;* Galor and Bloedhorn, *Archaeology of Jerusalem.*

Bibliography

Abel, Felix-Marie. "Lettre d'un Templier trouvée récemment à Jérusalem."
     Revue biblique 35 (1926): 288–95.
Abu-Manneh, Butrus. "The Georgians in Jerusalem during the Mamluk
     Period." In *Egypt and Palestine: A Millennium of Association (868–1948)*,
     edited by Amnon Cohen and Gabriel Baer, 102–12. Jerusalem: Ben-Zvi
     Institute; New York: St. Martin's, 1984.
———. "The Rise of the Sanjak of Jerusalem in the Late 19th Century." In *The
     Palestinians and the Middle East Conflict*, edited by Gabriel Ben-Dor,
     21–34. Ramat Gan: Turtledove Press, 1978.
Adler, Elkan Nathan, ed. *Jewish Travellers*. London: Routledge and Sons, 1930.
Adomnán. *The Pilgrimage of Arculfus in the Holy Land (about the Year A.D.
     670)*. Translated by James Rose McPherson. London: Palestine Pilgrims'
     Text Society, 1895.
Alem, Jean-Pierre. *La Déclaration Balfour: Aux sources de l'État d'Israël*. Paris:
     Éditions Complexe, 1982.
Allenby, Sir Edmund. "Proclamation of General Allenby." In *1917*, 417. Vol. 5 of
     Source Records of the Great War, edited by Charles F. Horne and Walter F.
     Austin. United States of America: National Alumni, 1923.
Amir-Moezzi, Mohammad Ali, ed. *Dictionnaire du Coran*. Paris: Robert
     Laffont, 2007.
Amitai-Preiss, R. "Ṣafad." In *Encyclopaedia of Islam*, 2nd ed., edited by
     P. Bearman, Th. Bianquis, C. E. Bosworth, E. van Donzel, and W. Heinrichs.

Leiden: Brill, 2006–. http://dx.doi.org/10.1163/1573-3912_islam_SIM_ 6435.

Ammianus Marcellinus. *History*. Translated by John C. Rolfe. Vol. 2. Loeb Classical Library. Cambridge, MA: Harvard University Press, 2000.

Antébi, Élisabeth. *L'Homme du Sérail*. Paris: NiL, 1996.

'Aref, 'Aref el-. "The Closing Phase of Ottoman Rule in Jerusalem." In *Studies on Palestine during the Ottoman Period*, edited by Moshe Ma'oz, 334–40. Jerusalem: Magnes Press, Hebrew University, and Yad Izhak Ben-Zvi, 1975.

———. *Tarikh al-Quds*. Cairo: Dar al-Ma'arif, 1951.

Arnon, Adar. "The Quarters of Jerusalem in the Ottoman Period." *Middle Eastern Studies* 28, no. 1 (January 1992): 1–65.

Arnould, Caroline. *Les Arcs romains de Jérusalem: Architecture, décor et urbanisme*. Fribourg: Éditions universitaires de Fribourg; Göttingen: Vandenhoeck und Ruprecht, 1997.

Arnould-Béhar, Caroline, and André Lemaire, eds. *Jérusalem antique et médiévale: Mélanges en l'honneur d'Ernest-Marie Laperrousaz*. Paris: Peeters, 2011.

Asali, Kamil J., ed. *Jerusalem in History*. New York: Olive Branch, 1990.

———, ed. *Jerusalem in History: 3000 BC to the Present Day*. 2nd ed. London: Kegan Paul, 1997.

———. "Jerusalem under the Ottomans, 1516–1831 AD." In *Jerusalem in History: 3000 BC to the Present Day*, edited by Kamil J. Asali, 2nd ed., 200–227. London: Kegan Paul, 1997.

Aslanov, Cyril. *Le Français au Levant, jadis et naguère: À la recherche d'une langue perdue*. Paris: Champion, 2006.

Attias, Jean-Christophe, and Esther Benbassa. *Israël, la terre et le sacré*. Paris: Flammarion, 2001.

Auld, Sylvia, and Robert Hillenbrand, eds. *Ottoman Jerusalem: The Living City, 1517–1917*. 2 vols. London: Altajir World of Islam Trust, 2000.

Avci, Yasemin, and Vincent Lemire. "De la modernité administrative à la modernisation urbaine: Une réévaluation de la municipalité ottomane de Jérusalem (1867–1917)." In *Municipalités méditerranéennes: Les Réformes urbaines ottomanes au miroir d'une histoire comparée (Moyen-Orient, Maghreb, Europe méridionale)*, edited by Nora Lafi, 73–138. Berlin: K. Schwarz, 2005.

Avci, Yasemin, Vincent Lemire, and Falestin Naïli. "Publishing Jerusalem's Ottoman Municipal Archives (1892–1917): A Turning Point for the City's Historiography." *Jerusalem Quarterly* 60 (Autumn 2014): 110–19.

Babylonian Talmud. Translated by Michael L. Rodkinson as *New Edition of the Babylonian Talmud*. Vol. 5. Boston: Talmud Society, 1918.

Bahat, Dan. *The Illustrated Atlas of Jerusalem*. Jerusalem: Carta, 1996.

———. *The Jerusalem Western Wall Tunnel*. Jerusalem: Israel Exploration Society, 2013.

Balard, Michel. *Les Latins en Orient, XIᵉ–XVᵉ siècle*. Paris: Presses universitaires de France, 2006.

Ballanfat, Paul. "Jour du Jugement." In *Dictionnaire du Coran*, edited by Mohammad Ali Amir-Moezzi, 454–57. Paris: Robert Laffont, 2007.

———. "Résurrection." In *Dictionnaire du Coran*, edited by Mohammad Ali Amir-Moezzi, 747–49. Paris: Robert Laffont, 2007.

Baudelaire, Charles. *Les Fleurs du mal*. Translated by Richard Howard. Boston: David R. Godine, 2003.

Bearman, P., Th. Bianquis, C. E. Bosworth, E. van Donzel, and W. Heinrichs, eds. *Encyclopaedia of Islam*. 2nd ed. Leiden: Brill, 2006–.

Belayche, Nicole. "*Dimenticare . . . Gerusalemme:* Les Paganismes à Aelia Capitolina du IIᵉ au IVᵉ siècle de notre ère." *Revue des études juives* 158, nos. 3–4 (1999): 287–348.

———. "Du mont du Temple au Golgotha: Le Capitole de la colonie d'*Aelia Capitolina*." *Revue de l'histoire des religions* 214, no. 4 (1997): 387–413.

———. *Iudaea-Palaestina: The Pagan Cults in Roman Palestine (Second to Fourth Century)*. Tübingen: Mohr Siebeck, 2001.

Bell, H. I. "Translation of the Greek Aphrodito Papyri in the British Museum." *Der Islam* 2 (1911): 269–83, 372–84.

Ben-Arieh, Yehoshua. *Jerusalem in the 19th Century*. Translated by Gila Brand. 2 vols. Jerusalem: Yad Izhak Ben Zvi Institute, 1984–86.

Ben-Bassat, Yuval, and Eyal Ginio, eds. *Late Ottoman Palestine: The Period of Young Turk Rule*. London: I. B. Tauris, 2011.

Bentwich, Norman, ed. *Hebrew University Garland: A Silver Jubilee Symposium*. London: Constellation Books, 1952.

Benvenisti, Meron. *City of Stone: The Hidden History of Jerusalem*. Translated by Maxine Kaufman Nunn. Berkeley: University of California Press, 1996.

———. *Jérusalem, une histoire politique*. Translated by Katherine Werchowski and Nicolas Weill. Paris: Actes Sud, 1996.

———. *Sons of the Cypresses: Memories, Reflections, and Regrets from a Political Life*. Translated by Maxine Kaufman-Lacusta in consultation with Michael Kaufman-Lacusta. Berkeley: University of California Press, 2007.

Ben-Yehuda, Eliezer. *A Dream Come True*. Edited by George Mandel. Translated by T. Muraoka. Boulder, CO: Westview, 1993. Originally published as "Ha-Halom ve-Shivro," a series of articles in the Hebrew-language magazine *Ha-Toren* (New York, 1917–18).

Berceot, Florence. "Une escale dans la tempête: Des Juifs palestiniens en Corse (1915–1920)." *Archives Juives: Revue d'histoire des Juifs de France* 38, no. 1 (2005): 129–38. English abstract available at https://www.cairn-int.info /article-E_AJ_381_0129--any-port-in-a-storm-palestinian-jews.htm.

Berchem, Max van. *Matériaux pour un corpus inscriptionum arabicarum*, pt. 2, *Syrie du Sud*. Vol. 1, *Jérusalem "ville."* Mémoires publiés par les membres de l'Institut français d'archéologie orientale 43. Paris: E. Leroux, 1922. Vol. 2, *Jérusalem "ḥaram."* MIFAO 44. Cairo: Imprimerie de l'Institute français d'archéologie orientale du Caire, 1927. Vol. 3, *Jérusalem, Index général et planches.* MIFAO 45.1–2. Cairo: Imprimerie de l'Institute français d'archéologie orientale du Caire, 1949.

Bernstein, Deborah S. *Constructing Boundaries: Jewish and Arab Workers in Mandatory Palestine.* Albany: State University of New York Press, 2000.

Berthelot, Katell. "Les Liens étroits entre historiographie et récit de soi dans l'œuvre de Flavius Josèphe." In *Individu, récit, histoire,* edited by Maryline Crivello and Jean-Noël Pelen, 38–51. Aix-en-Provence: Presses universitaires de Provence, 2008.

———. "L'Israël moderne et les guerres de l'Antiquité, de Josué à Masada." *Anabasis* 1 (2005): 119–37.

Berthelot, Katell, Joseph E. David, and Marc Hirshman, eds. *The Gift of the Land and the Fate of the Canaanites in Jewish Thought.* New York: Oxford University Press, 2014.

Bickerman, Elias. *Der Gott der Makkabäer: Untersuchungen über Sinn und Ursprung der Makkabäischen Erhebung.* Berlin: Schocken, 1937. Translated by Horst Moehring as "The God of the Maccabees" (1978), reprinted in *Studies in Jewish and Christian History,* edited by Amram Tropper, vol. 2 (Leiden: Brill, 2007), 1025–149.

———. "La Charte séleucide de Jérusalem." *Revue des études juives* 100 (1935): 4–35.

———. "Une proclamation séleucide relative au temple de Jérusalem." *Syria* 25, no. 1 (1946): 67–85.

Bitan, Dan. "L'UNSCOP et l'internationalisation de Jérusalem en 1947: Un plan pour préserver l'hégémonie occidentale en Palestine?" In *De Balfour à Ben Gourion: Les Puissances européennes et la Palestine 1917–1948,* edited by Dominique Trimbur and Ran Aaronsohn, 435–86. Paris: CNRS, 2008.

Blenkinsopp, Joseph. "Temple and Society in Achaemenid Judah." In *Persian Period,* edited by Philip R. Davies, 22–53. Vol. 1 of *Second Temple Studies.* Sheffield: JSOT Press, 1991.

Boas, Adrian J. *Jerusalem in the Time of the Crusades: Society, Landscape and Art in the Holy City under Frankish Rule.* London: Routledge, 2001.

Bonnery, André, Mireille Mentré, and Guylène Hidrio. *Jérusalem, symboles et représentations dans l'Occident médiéval.* Paris: Grancher, 1998.

Bordeaux Pilgrim. *Itinerary from Bordeaux to Jerusalem: 'The Bordeaux Pilgrim' (333 A.D.).* Translated by Aubrey Stewart. London: Palestine Pilgrims' Text Society, 1887.

Bouquet, Olivier. *Les Pachas du Sultan: Essai prosopographique sur les agents supérieurs de l'État ottoman (1839–1909).* Leuven: Peeters, 2007.

Breger, Marshall J., Yitzhak Reiter, and Leonard Hammer, eds. *Holy Places in the Israeli-Palestinian Conflict: Confrontation and Co-existence.* Abingdon, UK: Routledge, 2010.

Breviary or Short Description of Jerusalem. In *The Epitome of S. Eucherius about Certain Holy Places (circ. A.D. 440), and The Breviary or Short Description of Jerusalem (circ. A.D. 530).* Translated by Aubrey Stewart. London: Palestine Pilgrims' Text Society, 1890.

Buresi, Pascal. "Les Conversions d'églises et de mosquées en Espagne aux XIe–XIIIe siècles." In *Religion et société urbaine au Moyen Âge: Études offertes à Jean-Louis Biget par ses élèves,* edited by Patrick Boucheron and Jacques Chiffoleau, 333–50. Paris: Publications de la Sorbonne, 2000.

Burgoyne, Michael H. "1187–1260: The Furthest Mosque (*al-Masjid al-Aqsa*) under Ayyubid Rule." In *Where Heaven and Earth Meet: Jerusalem's Sacred Esplanade,* edited by Oleg Grabar and Benjamin Z. Kedar, 150–75. Jerusalem: Yad Ben-Zvi Press; Austin: University of Texas Press, 2009.

———. *Mamluk Jerusalem: An Architectural Study.* With additional historical research by D. S. Richards. London: World of Islam Festival Trust, 1987.

Busse, Heribert. "Die 'Umar-Moschee im östlichen Atrium der Grabeskirche." *Zeitschrift des Deutschen Palästina-Vereins* 109 (1993): 73–82.

———. "Jerusalem in the Story of Muhammad's Night Journey and Ascension." *Jerusalem Studies in Arabic and Islam* 14 (1991): 1–40.

———. "'Omar's Image as the Conqueror of Jerusalem." *Jerusalem Studies in Arabic and Islam* 8 (1986): 149–68.

———. "The Tower of David / *Miḥrāb Dāwud:* Remarks on the History of a Sanctuary in Jerusalem in Christian and Islamic Times." *Jerusalem Studies in Arabic and Islam* 17 (1994): 142–65.

Büssow, Johann. *Hamidian Palestine: Politics and Society in the District of Jerusalem, 1872–1908.* Leiden: Brill, 2011.

Cahen, Claude, and Ibrahim Chabbouh. "Le Testament d'al-Malik aṣ-Ṣāliḥ Ayyūb." In "Mélanges offerts à Henri Laoust," vol. 1, 97–114. Special issue, *Bulletin d'études orientales* 29 (1977).

Campos, Michelle. *Ottomans Brothers: Muslims, Christians and Jews in Early Twentieth-Century Palestine.* Stanford, CA: Stanford University Press, 2011.

Canard, Marius. "La Destruction de l'Église de la Résurrection par le calife Ḥākim et l'histoire de la descente du feu sacré." *Byzantion* 35 (1965): 16–43. Reprinted in Canard, *Byzance et les musulmans du Proche-Orient.* London: Variorum Reprints, 1973.

Cassius Dio. *Roman History.* Translated by Earnest Cary. Vol. 8. Loeb Classical Library. Cambridge, MA: Harvard University Press, 1925.

Cerfaux, Lucien, and Julien Tondriaux. *Le Culte des souverains dans la civilisation gréco-romaine: Un concurrent du christianisme.* Paris: Desclée, 1956.

Charbit, Denis. *Sionismes, textes fondamentaux*. Paris: Albin Michel, 1998.

Chateaubriand, François-René de. *Itinéraire de Paris à Jérusalem*. Paris: Le Normant, 1811. Translated by F. Shoberl as *Travels in Greece, Palestine, Egypt, and Barbary, during the Years 1806 and 1807*. New York: Van Winkle and Wiley, 1814.

Choshen, Maya. "Demographic Processes in Polarized Cities: The Case of Jerusalem." In *Divided Cities in Transition: Challenges Facing Jerusalem and Berlin*, edited by Michèle Auga, Schlomo Hasson, Rami Nasrallah, and Stephan Stetter, 3–34. Jerusalem: Friedrich Ebert Stiftung, International Peace and Cooperation Center, Jerusalem Institute for Israel Studies, 2005.

Chronique d'Ernoul et de Bernard le Trésorier. Edited by L. de Mas Latrie. Paris: Libraire de la Société de l'histoire de France, 1871.

Cohen, Amnon. *Economic Life in Ottoman Jerusalem*. Cambridge: Cambridge University Press, 1989.

———. "The Expulsion of the Franciscans from Mount Zion." *Turcica* 18 (1986): 147–57.

———. *Juifs et musulmans en Palestine et Israël: Des origines à nos jours*. Paris: Tallandier, 2016.

———. "The Ottoman Approach to Christians and Christianity in Sixteenth-Century Jerusalem." *Islam and Christian-Muslim Relations* 7, no. 2 (1996): 205–12.

———. *Studies on Ottoman Palestine*. Farnham, UK: Ashgate, 2011.

———. "The Walls of Jerusalem." In *The Islamic World from Classical to Modern Times: Essays in Honor of Bernard Lewis*, edited by Clifford E. Bosworth, Charles Issawi, Roger Savory, and Abraham L. Udovitch, 467–78. Princeton, NJ: Darwin, 1989.

Cohen, Amnon, and Bernard Lewis. *Population and Revenue in the Towns of Palestine in the Sixteenth Century*. Princeton, NJ: Princeton University Press, 1978.

Corpus Inscriptionum Iudaeae/Palaestinae. Vol. 1, *Jerusalem*, pt. 1, *1–704*. Edited by Hannah M. Cotton, Leah Di Segni, Werner Eck, Benjamin Isaac, Alla Kushnir-Stein, Haggai Misgav, Jonathan Price, Israel Roll, and Ada Yardeni. Berlin: De Gruyter, 2010.

Creswell, K. A. C. *A Short Account of Early Muslim Architecture*. Harmondsworth: Penguin, 1958. Revised and supplemented by James W. Allan. Cairo: American University in Cairo Press, 1989.

Daʿādli, Tawfiq. "Mamlūk Epitaphs from Māmillā Cemetery." *Levant* 43, no. 1 (2011): 78–97.

Degeorge, Gérard, and Yves Porter. *L'Art de la céramique dans l'architecture musulmane*. Paris: Flammarion, 2001.

Delaborde, Henri-François. *Chartes de Terre sainte provenant de l'abbaye de N.-D. de Josaphat*. Paris: Ernest Thorin, 1880.

Der Matossian, Bedross. "The Young Turk Revolution: Its Impact on Religious Politics of Jerusalem (1908–1912)." *Jerusalem Quarterly File* 40 (2009): 18–33.

Déroche, Vincent. *Entre Rome et l'Islam, les chrétientés d'Orient (610–1054)*. Paris: SEDES, 1997.

Derogy, Jacques, and Hesi Carmel. *Bonaparte en Terre sainte*. Paris: Fayard, 1992.

Destremau, Christian. *Le Moyen-Orient pendant la Seconde Guerre mondiale*. Paris: Perrin, 2011.

Dieckhoff, Alain. *Les Espaces d'Israël*. Paris: Presses de Sciences Po, 1989.

Diodorus Siculus. *Historical Library*. Translated by Andrew Smith at "Diodorus Siculus: Historical Library." Attalus (website). http://www.attalus.org/info/diodorus.html.

Doumani, Beshara. "Palestinian Islamic Court Records: A Source for Socioeconomic History." *MESA Bulletin* 19 (1985): 155–72.

Dumper, Michael. *Jerusalem Unbound: Geography, History and the Future of the Holy City*. New York: Columbia University Press, 2014.

du Rozel, François-Charles. *Voyage de Jérusalem et autres lieux saincts effectué et décrit en 1644*. Edited by Émile Bonneserre de Saint-Denis. Paris: Dumoulin, 1864.

Eddé, Anne-Marie. *Saladin*. Translated by Jane Marie Todd. Cambridge, MA: Belknap Press of Harvard University Press, 2011.

Egeria. *The Pilgrimage of Etheria*. Translated by M. L. McClure and C. L. Feltoe. London: Society for Promoting Christian Knowledge, 1919.

Ekrem, Selma. "Jerusalem 1908: In the Household of the Ottoman Governor." *Jerusalem Quarterly* 50 (June 2012): 66–88.

Elad, Amikam. *Medieval Jerusalem and Islamic Worship: Holy Places, Ceremonies, Pilgrimage*. Leiden: Brill, 1995.

Eliav, Mordechai. *Britain and the Holy Land, 1838–1914: Selected Documents from the British Consulate in Jerusalem*. Jerusalem: Yad Izhak Ben-Zvi Press, 1997.

Elisséeff, Nikita. *Nur al-Din: Un grand prince musulman de Syrie au temps des croisades (511–569 H. / 1118–1174)*. Vol. 2. Damascus: Institut français de Damas, 1967.

Estat de la cité de Jherusalem. Translated by C. R. Conder as *The City of Jerusalem*. London: Palestine Pilgrims' Text Society, 1896.

Eucherius. *The Epitome of S. Eucherius about Certain Holy Places*. In *The Epitome of S. Eucherius about Certain Holy Places (circ. A.D. 440), and The Breviary or Short Description of Jerusalem (circ. A.D. 530)*. Translated by Aubrey Stewart. London: Palestine Pilgrims' Text Society, 1890.

Eusebius of Caesarea. *Ecclesiastical History*. Translated by Kirsopp Lake. Vol. 1. Loeb Classical Library. Cambridge, MA: Harvard University Press, 1961.

————. *Histoire ecclésiastique: Texte grec et traduction française.* Translated by Émile Grapin. Paris: Picard, 1905–13.

————. *Life of Constantine.* In *Eusebius: Church History, Life of Constantine, and Oration in Praise of Constantine the Great.* Translated by Ernest Cushing Richardson. Vol. 1 of *A Select Library of the Nicene and Post-Nicene Fathers of the Christian Church: Second Series,* edited by Philip Schaff and Henry Wace. New York: Christian Literature, 1890.

Faroqhi, Suraiya. *Approaching Ottoman History: An Introduction to the Sources.* New York: Cambridge University Press, 1999.

Faust, Avraham. "Did Eilat Mazar Find David's Palace?" *Biblical Archaeology Review* 38, no. 5 (2012): 47–52.

Finkelstein, Israel. "The Great Transformation: The 'Conquest' of the Highlands Frontiers and the Rise of the Territorial States." In *The Archaeology of Society in the Holy Land,* edited by Thomas E. Levy, 349–65. London: Leicester University Press, 1995.

————. "A Great United Monarchy? Archaeological and Historical Perspectives." In *One God, One Cult, One Nation: Archaeological and Biblical Perspectives,* edited by R. G. Kratz and H. Spieckermann, 3–28. Berlin: De Gruyter, 2010.

————. "Jerusalem in the Persian (and Early Hellenistic) Period and the Wall of Nehemiah." *Journal for the Study of the Old Testament* 32 (2008): 501–20.

Finkelstein, Israel, and Amihai Mazar. *The Quest for the Historical Israel: Debating Archaeology and the History of Early Israel.* Edited by Brian B. Schmidt. Leiden: Brill; Atlanta: Society of Biblical Literature, 2007.

Finkelstein, Israel, and Neil Asher Silberman. *The Bible Unearthed: Archaeology's New Vision of Ancient Israel and the Origin of Its Sacred Texts.* New York: Free Press, 2001. Translated by Patrice Ghirardi as *La Bible dévoilée: Les nouvelles révélations de l'archéologie* (Paris: Bayard, 2002).

————. *Les Rois sacrés de la Bible: À la recherche de David et Salomon.* Translated by Patrice Ghirardi. Paris: Bayard, 2006.

Flusin, Bernard. "L'Esplanade du Temple à l'arrivée des Arabes d'après deux récits byzantins." In *Abd al-Malik's Jerusalem,* edited by Julian Raby and Jeremy Johns, 17–31. Pt. 1 of *Bayt al-Maqdis.* Oxford Studies in Islamic Art 9. Oxford: Oxford University Press, 1992.

France, John. *Victory in the East: A Military History of the First Crusade.* Cambridge: Cambridge University Press, 1994.

Galor, Katharina, and Gideon Avni, eds. *Unearthing Jerusalem: 150 Years of Archaeological Research in the Holy City.* Winona Lake, IN: Eisenbrauns, 2011.

Galor, Katharina, and Hanswulf Bloedhorn. *The Archaeology of Jerusalem: From the Origins to the Ottomans.* New Haven, CT: Yale University Press, 2013.

Garfinkel, Yosef, Katharina Streit, Saar Ganor, and Michael G. Hasel. "State Formation in Judah: Biblical Tradition, Modern Historical Theories, and

Radiometric Dates at Khirbet Qeiyafa." *Radiocarbon* 54, nos. 3–4 (2012): 359–69.

Gat, Shimon. "The Seljuks in Jerusalem." In *Towns and Material Culture in the Medieval Middle East*, edited by Yaacov Lev, 1–39. Medieval Mediterranean 39. Leiden: Brill, 2002.

Geoltrain, Pierre, ed. *Aux origines du christianisme*. Paris: Gallimard, 2000.

Georgeon, François. *Abdulhamid II, le sultan calife (1876–1909)*. Paris: Fayard, 2003.

Géraud-Gomez, Christine. *Le Crépuscule du grand voyage: Les Récits de pèlerins à Jérusalem (1458–1612)*. Paris: Honoré Champion, 2000.

Gerber, Haim. *Ottoman Rule in Jerusalem, 1890–1914*. Berlin: Klaus Schwarz, 1985.

Geva, Hillel, and Dan Bahat. "Architectural and Chronological Aspects of the Ancient Damascus Gate Area." *Israel Exploration Journal* 48 (1998): 223–35.

Geva, Hillel, Benjamin Mazar, Yigal Shiloh, et al. "Jerusalem." In *The New Encyclopedia of Archaeological Excavations in the Holy Land*, edited by Ephraim Stern et al., vol. 2, 698–804. Jerusalem: Israel Exploration Society and Carta, 1993.

Ghosheh, Mohammad. "The Walls and Gates of Jerusalem before and after Sultan Süleymān's Rebuilding Project of 1538–40." In *Governing the Holy City: The Interaction of Social Groups in Jerusalem between the Fatimid and the Ottoman Period*, edited by Johannes Pahlitzsch and Lorenz Korn, 117–37. Wiesbaden, Reichert, 2004.

Gibson, Shimon, and David M. Jacobson. *Below the Temple Mount in Jerusalem: A Source Book on the Cisterns, Subterranean Chambers and Conduits of the Haram al Sharif*. BAR International Series 637. Oxford: Tempus Reparatum, 1996.

Gil, Moshe. "Dhimmi Donations and Foundations for Jerusalem (638–1099)." *Journal of the Economic and Social History of the Orient* 27 (1984): 156–74.

Gilbar, Gad. *Ottoman Palestine, 1800–1914: Studies on Economic and Social History*. Leiden: Brill, 1990.

Gilbert, Martin. *Jerusalem in the Twentieth Century*. London: John Wiley and Sons, 1996.

Gobillot, Geneviève. "Sceau des prophètes." In *Dictionnaire du Coran*, edited by Mohammad Ali Amir-Moezzi, 795–97. Paris: Robert Laffont, 2007.

Goitein, Shelomo D. "Contemporary Letters on the Capture of Jerusalem by the Crusaders." *Journal of Jewish Studies* 3 (1952): 162–77.

Goitein, S. D., and O. Grabar. "Al-Ḳuds." In *Encyclopaedia of Islam*, 2nd ed., edited by P. Bearman, Th. Bianquis, C. E. Bosworth, E. van Donzel, and W.

Heinrichs. Leiden: Brill, 2006–. http://dx.doi.org/10.1163/1573-3912_islam_COM_0535.

Goodman, Martin. *Rome and Jerusalem*. New York: Vintage, 2008.

Goren, Haim, ed. *Germany in the Middle East: Past, Present and Future.* Jerusalem: Magnes Press, 2003.

Grabar, Oleg. "A New Inscription from the Haram al-Sharif in Jerusalem: A Note on the Mediaeval Topography of Jerusalem." In *Studies in Islamic Art and Architecture: In Honour of Professor K. A. C. Creswell*, 72–83. Cairo: American University in Cairo Press, 1965.

———. "The Umayyad Dome of the Rock in Jerusalem." *Ars Orientalis* 3 (1959): 33–62.

Grabar, Oleg, and Benjamin Z. Kedar, eds. *Where Heaven and Earth Meet: Jerusalem's Sacred Esplanade.* Jerusalem: Yad Ben-Zvi Press; Austin: University of Texas Press, 2009.

Gribetz, Jonathan Marc. *Defining Neighbors: Religion, Race, and the Early Zionist-Arab Encounter.* Princeton, NJ: Princeton University Press, 2014.

Gutmann, Emanuel. "The Beginning of Local Government in Jerusalem." *Public Administration in Israel and Abroad* 8 (1968): 52–61.

Gutmann, Joseph, ed. *The Temple of Solomon: Archaeological Fact and Medieval Tradition in Christian, Islamic and Jewish Art.* Missoula, MT: Scholars Press, 1976.

Hadas-Lebel, Mireille. *Jérusalem contre Rome*. Paris: Cerf, 1990. Reprint, Paris: Tempus, 2012. Translated by Robyn Fréchet as *Jerusalem against Rome*. Leuven: Peeters, 2006.

Halbwachs, Maurice. *La Topographie légendaire des Évangiles en Terre sainte.* 1941. Reprint, Paris: Presses universitaires de France, 2008.

Halperin, Liora R. *Babel in Zion: Jews, Nationalism, and Language Diversity in Palestine, 1920–1948.* New Haven, CT: Yale University Press, 2014.

Hanssen, Jens, Thomas Philipp, and Stefan Weber, eds. *The Empire in the City: Arab Provincial Capitals in the Late Ottoman Empire.* Würzburg: Ergon in Kommission, 2002.

Harawī, al-. *Kitāb al-Ishārāt ilā Maʿrifat al-ziyārāt.* Translated by Josef W. Meri as *A Lonely Wayfarer's Guide to Pilgrimage*. Princeton, NJ: Darwin, 2004.

Heyd, Uriel. *Ottoman Documents on Palestine, 1552–1615: A Study of the Firman according to the Mühimme Defteri.* Oxford: Clarendon, 1960.

Hillenbrand, Robert, and Sylvia Auld. *Ayyubid Jerusalem: The Holy City in Context, 1187–1250.* London: Altajir Trust, 2009.

Hintlian, George. "Armenians of Jerusalem." *Jerusalem Quarterly* 2 (1998): 40–44.

Horowitz, Yael. *The "Seam" Area: Planning Guidelines.* Jerusalem: Town Planning Department, Policy Planning Section, 1981.

Ilbert, Robert. *Alexandrie 1830–1930: Histoire d'une communauté citadine.*
    Cairo: Institut français d'archéologie orientale, 1996.
———. "De Beyrouth à Alger: La Fin d'un ordre urbain." *Vingtième siècle: Revue
    d'histoire* 32 (octobre–décembre 1991): 15–24.
Jacobson, Abigail. *From Empire to Empire: Jerusalem from Ottoman to British
    Rule.* Syracuse, NY: Syracuse University Press, 2011.
Jawhariyyeh, Wasif. *Storyteller of Jerusalem: The Life and Times of Wasif
    Jawhariyyeh, 1904–1948.* Northampton MA: Olive Branch, 2013.
Jerome, Saint. Letter to Eustochium (404). Translated by Joan Ferrante. Episto-
    lae: Medieval Women's Letters (website), Columbia Center for New Media
    Teaching and Learning. https://epistolae.ctl.columbia.edu/letter/445.html.
Jerphagnon, Lucien. *Julien, dit l'Apostat: Histoire naturelle et sociale:* Paris:
    Tallandier, 1986.
John of Würzburg. *Descriptio terrae sanctae.* Translated by Aubrey Stewart as
    Description of the Holy Land by John of Würzburg (A.D. 1160–1170).
    London: Palestine Pilgrims' Text Society, 1890.
John Rufus. *Life of Peter the Iberian.* In *John Rufus: The "Lives" of Peter the
    Iberian, Theodosius of Jerusalem, and the Monk Romanus,* edited and
    translated by Cornelia B. Horn and Robert R. Phenix Jr. Atlanta: Society of
    Biblical Literature, 2008.
Josephus, Flavius. *Jewish Antiquities.* Translated by Ralph Marcus. Loeb
    Classical Library. Cambridge, MA: Harvard University Press, 1998. First
    published 1934.
———. *The Jewish War.* Translated by H. St. J. Thackeray. Vol. 3. Loeb Classical
    Library. London: William Heinemann; Cambridge, MA: Harvard University
    Press, 1961.
Kaplony, Andreas. "635/638–1099: The Mosque of Jerusalem (*Masjid Bayt
    al-Maqdis*)." In *Where Heaven and Earth Meet: Jerusalem's Sacred Espla-
    nade,* edited by Oleg Grabar and Benjamin Z. Kedar, 100–131. Jerusalem:
    Yad Ben-Zvi Press; Austin: University of Texas Press, 2009.
Kark, Ruth, and Michal Oren-Nordheim. *Jerusalem and Its Environs, Quar-
    ters, Neighborhoods, Villages, 1800–1948.* Jerusalem: Hebrew University
    Magnes Press, 2001.
Kedar. Benjamin Z. "The Battle of Hattin Revisited." In *The Horns of Hattin:
    Proceedings of the Second Conference of the Society for the Study of the
    Crusades and the Latin East, Jerusalem and Haifa, 2–6 July 1987,* edited by
    Benjamin Z. Kedar, 190–207. Jerusalem: Yad Izhak Ben-Zvi, 1992.
———. "The Jerusalem Massacre of July 1099 in the Western Historiography of
    the Crusades." *Crusades* 3 (2004): 15–75.
———. "A Twelfth-Century Description of the Jerusalem Hospital." In *Welfare
    and Warfare,* edited by Helen Nicholson, 3–26. Vol. 2 of *The Military
    Orders.* Aldershot: Ashgate, 1998.

Kedar, Benjamin Z., and Denys Pringle. "1099–1187: The Lord's Temple (*Templum Domini*) and Solomon's Palace (*Palatium Salomonis*)." In *Where Heaven and Earth Meet: Jerusalem's Sacred Esplanade*, edited by Oleg Grabar and Benjamin Z. Kedar, 133–49. Jerusalem: Yad Ben-Zvi Press; Austin: University of Texas Press, 2009.

Kessler, Christel. "'Abd al-Malik's Inscription in the Dome of the Rock: A Reconsideration." *Journal of the Royal Asiatic Society* 102 (1970): 2–14.

Khalidi, Rashid. *Palestinian Identity: The Construction of Modern National Consciousness*. New York: Columbia University Press, 1997. Translated by Joëlle Marelli as *L'Identité palestinienne: La Construction d'une conscience nationale moderne*. Paris: La Fabrique, 2003.

Khalidi, Walid. *Avant leur diaspora: Une histoire des Palestiniens par la photographie, 1876–1948*. Paris: Revue d'études palestiniennes, 1986.

Klein, Menachem. *Lives in Common: Arabs and Jews in Jerusalem, Jaffa and Hebron*. London: Hurst, 2014.

Korn, Lorenz. "The Structure of Architectural Patronage in Ayyubid Jerusalem." In *Governing the Holy City: The Interaction of Social Groups in Jerusalem between the Fatimid and the Ottoman Period*, edited by Johannes Pahlitzsch and Lorenz Korn, 71–89. Wiesbaden: Reichert, 2004.

Krämer, Gudrun. *A History of Palestine: From the Ottoman Conquest to the Founding of the State of Israel*. Princeton, NJ: Princeton University Press, 2008.

Kratz, R. G., and H. Spieckermann, eds. *One God, One Cult, One Nation: Archaeological and Biblical Perspectives*. Berlin: De Gruyter, 2010.

Küchler, Max. *Jerusalem: Ein Handbuch und Studienreiseführer zur Heiligen Stadt*. With contributions from Klaus Bieberstein, Damian Lazarek, Siegfried Ostermann, Ronny Reich, and Christoph Uehlinger. Göttingen: Vandenhoeck und Ruprecht, 2007.

Kushner, David, ed. *Palestine in the Late Ottoman Period: Political, Social and Economic Transformation*. Jerusalem: Yad Izhak Ben-Zvi, 1986.

———. *To Be Governor of Jerusalem: The City and District during the Time of Ali Ekrem Bey, 1906–1908*. Istanbul: Isis, 2005.

Laurens, Henry. *La Question de Palestine*. 5 vols. Paris: Fayard, 1999–2015.

———. "Le Projet d'État juif attribué à Bonaparte." *Revue d'études palestiniennes* 33 (Fall 1989): 69–83. Reprinted as "Le Projet d'État juif en Palestine attribué à Bonaparte" in Henry Laurens, *Orientales* (Paris: CNRS Éditions, 2007), 123–43.

Lemire, Vincent. "The Awakening of Palestinian Hydropolitical Consciousness: Jerusalem Water Conflict of 1925." *Jerusalem Quarterly* 48 (January 2012): 31–53.

———. *Jerusalem 1900: The Holy City in the Age of Possibilities*. Translated by Catherine Tihanyi and Lys Ann Weiss. Chicago: University of Chicago Press,

2017. Originally published as *Jérusalem 1900: La Ville sainte à l'âge des possibles* (Paris: Armand Colin, 2013).

———. *La Soif de Jérusalem: Essai d'hydrohistoire (1840–1948)*. Paris: Publications de la Sorbonne, 2010.

———. "Le Manteau rapiécé des prophètes: Lieux saints partagés d'Israël-Palestine." In *Lieux saints partagés*, edited by Dionigi Albera, Isabelle Marquette, and Manoël Pénicaud, 60–65. Arles: Actes Sud; Marseille: MuCEM, 2015.

———. "Zama bi-Yerushalayim: A-historya shel haair birei ashpakat ha-maim 1840–1948." [In Hebrew.] *Cathedra* 151 (2014): 133–58.

Letter of Aristeas. Translated by Moses Hadas as *Aristeas to Philocrates (Letter of Aristeas)*. Eugene, OR: Wipf and Stock, 2007. First published 1951 by Harper Brothers (New York).

Levine, Lee I. *Jerusalem: Portrait of the City in the Second Temple Period (538 B.C.E.–70 C.E.)*. Philadelphia: Jewish Publication Society of America, 2002.

Lipschits, Oded. "Between Archaeology and Text: A Reevaluation of the Development Process of Jerusalem in the Persian Period." In *Congress Volume Helsinki 2010*, edited by M. Nissinen, 145–65. Leiden: Brill, 2012.

Little, Donald P. *A Catalogue of the Islamic Documents from al-Ḥaram aš-Šarīf in Jerusalem*. Beiruter Texte und Studien 29. Beirut: Orient-Institut der Deutschen Morgenländischen Gesellschaft, 1984.

———. "Communal Strife in Late Mamlūk Jerusalem." *Islamic Law and Society* 6, no. 1 (1999): 69–96.

———. "The Governance of Jerusalem under Qāytbāy." In *The Mamluks in Egyptian and Syrian Politics and Society*, edited by Michael Winter and Amalia Levanoni, 143–62. Medieval Mediterranean 51. Leiden: Brill, 2004.

———. "Haram Documents Related to the Jews of Late Fourteenth Century Jerusalem." *Journal of Semitic Studies* 30, no. 2 (1985): 227–64.

———. "Jerusalem under the Ayyubids and Mamluks, 1187–1516 AD." In *Jerusalem in History: 3000 BC to the Present Day*, edited by Kamil J. Asali, 2nd ed., 177–99. London: Kegan Paul, 1997.

———. "Mujīr al-Dīn al-ʿUlaymī's Vision of Jerusalem in the Ninth/Fifteenth Century." *Journal of the American Oriental Society* 115 (1995): 237–47.

Loiseau, Julien. *Les Mamelouks (XIIIᵉ–XVIᵉ siècle): Une expérience du pouvoir dans l'Islam médiéval*. Paris: Seuil, 2014.

Lory, Pierre. "Abraham." In *Dictionnaire du Coran*, edited by Mohammad Ali Amir-Moezzi, 9–14. Paris: Robert Laffont, 2007.

Luckenbill, Daniel David. *The Annals of Sennacherib*. Oriental Institute Publications 2. Chicago: University of Chicago, 1924.

Lutfi, Huda. *Al-Quds al-Mamlûkiyya: A History of Mamlûk Jerusalem Based on the Ḥaram Documents*. Berlin: K. Schwarz, 1985.

Ma, John. "Relire les *Institutions des Séleucides* de Bikerman." In *Rome, a City and Its Empire in Perspective: The Impact of the Roman World through Fergus Millar's Research*, edited by S. Benoist, 59–84. Leiden: Brill, 2012.

Magness, Jodi. "Aelia Capitolina: A Review of Some Current Debates about Hadrianic Jerusalem." In *Unearthing Jerusalem: 150 Years of Archaeological Research in the Holy City*, edited by Katharina Galor and Gideon Avni, 313–24. Winona Lake, IN: Eisenbrauns, 2011.

Mango, Cyril. "The Temple Mount, AD 614–638." In *Abd al-Malik's Jerusalem*, edited by Julian Raby and Jeremy Johns, 1–16. Pt. 1 of *Bayt al-Maqdis*. Oxford Studies in Islamic Art 9. Oxford: Oxford University Press, 1992.

Mannâ, Adel. "Jérusalem sous les Ottomans." In *Jérusalem: Le Sacré et le politique*, edited by Farouk Mardam-Bey and Élias Sanbar, 191–217. Arles: Actes Sud, 2000.

Mantran, Robert. *Histoire de l'Empire ottoman*. Paris: Fayard, 1989.

Ma'oz, Moshe, ed. *Studies on Palestine during the Ottoman Period*. Jerusalem: Magnes Press, Hebrew University, and Yad Izhak Ben-Zvi, 1975.

Maraval, Pierre. *L'Empereur Justinien*. 1999. Reprint, Paris: Presses universitaires de France, 2012.

———. *Lieux saints et pèlerinages d'Orient*. Paris: Cerf, 1985. Reprint, Paris: CNRS, "Biblis," 2011.

———. *Récits des premiers pèlerins chrétiens au Proche-Orient*. Paris: Cerf, 2002.

Mardam-Bey, Farouk, and Élias Sanbar. *Jérusalem, le sacré et le politique*. Arles: Actes Sud, 2000.

Mattar, Philip, ed. *Encyclopedia of the Palestinians*. New York: Facts on File, 2000.

Mavrides, Constantine. "War in the Old City: The Diaries of Constantine Mavrides." Translated by John N. Tleel. In *Jerusalem, 1948: The Arab Neighbourhoods and Their Fate in the War*, edited by Salim Tamari, appendix 1, 272–93. Bethlehem: Institute of Jerusalem Studies, 1999.

Mazar, Amihai. "Archaeology and the Biblical Narrative: The Case of the United Monarchy." In *One God, One Cult, One Nation: Archaeological and Biblical Perspectives*, edited by R. G. Kratz and H. Spieckermann, 29–58. Berlin: De Gruyter, 2010.

———. *Archaeology of the Land of the Bible, 10,000–586 B.C.E.* New York: Doubleday, 1990.

Mazar, Eilat. "Did I Find King David's Palace?" *Biblical Archaeology Review* 32, no. 1 (2006): 16–27, 70.

———. *The Palace of King David: Excavations at the Summit of the City of David; Preliminary Report of Seasons 2005–2007*. Jerusalem: Shoham Academic Research and Publication, 2009.

Mazar, Eilat, Yuval Goren, Wayne Horowitz, and Takayoshi Oshima. "Jerusalem 2: A Fragment of a Cuneiform Tablet from the Ophel Excavations." *Israel
Exploration Journal* 64, no. 2 (2014): 129–39.

Mazar, Eilat, Wayne Horowitz, Takayoshi Oshima, and Yuval Goren. "A
Cuneiform Tablet from the Ophel in Jerusalem." *Israel Exploration Journal*
60, no. 1 (2010): 4–21.

Mazar, Eilat, and Orit Peleg. " 'The House of the Menorot' in the Temple Mount
Excavations: The Earliest Synagogue Discovered in Jerusalem." [In Hebrew;
includes an abstract in English.] *Cathedra* 94 (1999): 55–74.

Mazza, Roberto. *Jerusalem from the Ottomans to the British*. London: Tauris,
2009.

———. "Missing Voices in Rediscovering Late Ottoman and Early British
Jerusalem." *Jerusalem Quarterly* 53 (April 2013): 61–71.

Meddeb, Abdelwahab, ed. *Multiple Jérusalem*. Paris: Maisonneuve et Larose,
1996.

Miquel, André. *Ousâma: Un prince syrien face aux croisés*. Paris: Tallandier,
2007.

Montefiore, Moses. "A Narrative of a Forty Days' Sojourn in the Holy Land." In
An Open Letter Addressed to Sir Moses Montefiore ... , by Meyer Auerbach
and Samuel Salant, 2nd ed., 41–148. London: Wertheimer, Lea, 1877.

Morris, Benny. *The Birth of the Palestinian Refugee Problem Revisited*. Cambridge: Cambridge University Press, 2004.

Müller, Christian. *Der Kadi und seine Zeugen: Studie der mamlukischen
Haram-Dokumente aus Jerusalem*. Wiesbaden: Harrassowitz, 2013.

Muqaddasi, al-. *Aḥsanu-t-taqāsīm fī maʿrifati-l-aqālīm*. Translated by G. S. A.
Ranking and R. F. Azoo. Calcutta: Asiatic Society of Bengal, 1897.

Naʾaman, Nadav. "When and How Did Jerusalem Become a Great City? The
Rise of Jerusalem as Judah's Premier City in the Eighth–Seventh Centuries
B.C.E." *Bulletin of the American Schools of Oriental Research* 347 (2007):
21–56.

Nashashibi, Nasser Eddin. *Jerusalem's Other Voice: Ragheb Nashashibi and
Moderation in Palestinian Politics, 1920–1948*. Exeter, UK: Ithaca, 1990.

Netzer, Ehud. *The Architecture of Herod, the Great Builder*. Tübingen: Mohr
Siebeck, 2006.

Newman, Hillel. "The Temple Mount of Jerusalem and the Capitolium of Aelia
Capitolina." In *Knowledge and Wisdom: Archaeological and Historical
Essays in Honour of Leah Di Segni*, edited by Giovanni C. Bottini, L. Daniel
Chrupcała, and Joseph Patrich, 35–42. Milan: Terra Santa, 2014.

Nicault, Catherine. *Une histoire de Jérusalem, 1850–1967*. Paris: CNRS, 2008.

Orrieux, Claude, and Édouard Will. *Ioudaïsmos-Hellènismos: Essai sur le
judaïsme judéen à l'époque hellénistique*. Nancy: Presses Universitaires de
Nancy, 1986.

Oz, Amos. *A Tale of Love and Darkness*. Translated by Nicholas de Lange. Orlando, FL: Harvest, 2005.

Pahlitzsch, Johannes. "The Transformation of Latin Religious Institutions into Islamic Endowments by Saladin in Jerusalem." In *Governing the Holy City: The Interaction of Social Groups in Jerusalem between the Fatimid and the Ottoman Period*, edited by Johannes Pahlitzsch and Lorenz Korn, 47–69. Wiesbaden: Reichert, 2004.

Pahlitzsch, Johannes, and Lorenz Korn, eds. *Governing the Holy City: The Interaction of Social Groups in Jerusalem between the Fatimid and the Ottoman Period*. Wiesbaden: Reichert, 2004.

Panzac, Daniel, ed. *Les Villes dans l'Empire ottoman, activités et sociétés*. Paris: CNRS, 1994.

Patlagean, Evelyne. *Un Moyen Âge grec: Byzance, IXᵉ–XVᵉ siècle*. Paris: Albin Michel, 2007.

Piacenza Pilgrim. *Itinerarium*. In *Of the Holy Places Visited by Antoninus Martyr (circ. 530 A.D.)*. Translated by Aubrey Stewart. London: Palestine Pilgrims' Text Society, 1887.

Pliny the Elder. *Natural History*. Translated by H. Rackham. Loeb Classical Library. London: Heinemann; Cambridge, MA: Harvard University Press, 1952.

Potin, Yann. "Saint Louis l'Africain: Histoire d'une mémoire inversée." *Afrique et histoire* 1 (2003): 23–74.

Pouzet, Louis. "De la paix armée à la négociation et à ses ambiguïtés: L'Accord de Jaffa (1229/626) entre Frédéric II et al-Malik al-Kamil." In *Chrétiens et musulmans au temps des croisades: Entre l'affrontement et la rencontre*, edited by Louis Pouzet and Louis Boisset, 91–116. Beirut: Presses de l'Université Saint-Joseph, 2007.

Powers, David S. "Revenues of Public 'Waqfs' in Sixteenth-Century Jerusalem." *Archivum Ottomanicum* 9 (1984): 163–202.

Prawer, Joshua. *The History of the Jews in the Latin Kingdom of Jerusalem*. Oxford: Clarendon, 1988.

———. "The Settlement of the Latins in Jerusalem." *Speculum* 27 (1952): 490–503.

Prémare, Alfred-Louis de. *Les Fondations de l'islam: Entre écriture et histoire*. Paris: Seuil, 2002.

Pringle, Denys. *The City of Jerusalem*. Vol. 3 of *The Churches of the Crusader Kingdom of Jerusalem: A Corpus*. Cambridge: Cambridge University Press, 2007.

Puech, Vincent. *Constantin, le premier empereur chrétien*. Paris: Ellipse, 2011.

Purvis, James D. *Jerusalem, the Holy City: A Bibliography*. 2 vols. London: Scarecrow, 1991.

The Qur'an. Translated by M. A. S. Abdel Haleem. Oxford: Oxford University Press, 2004.

Rabbat, Nasser. "The Meaning of the Umayyad Dome of the Rock." *Muqarnas* 6 (1989): 12–21.

Rapoport, Yossef. *Marriage, Money and Divorce in Medieval Islamic Society*. Cambridge: Cambridge University Press, 2005.

Reich, Ronny. *Excavating the City of David: Where Jerusalem's History Began*. Jerusalem: Israel Exploration Society, Biblical Archaeology Society, 2011.

———. "A Fiscal Bulla from the City of David, Jerusalem." *Israel Exploration Journal* 62, no. 2 (2012): 200–205.

Reichman, Amos. "Jérusalem 1939–1945: Une ville en paix?" Master's thesis, École normale supérieure de Lyon / Université Paris-Est, 2012.

Richards, Donald S. "Saladin's Hospital in Jerusalem: Its Foundation and Some Later Archival Material." In *The Frankish Wars and Their Influence on Palestine: Selected Papers Presented at Birzeit University's International Academic Conference Held in Jerusalem, March 13–15, 1992*, edited by Khalil Athamina and Roger Heacock, 70–82. Beir Zeit: Birzeit University Publications, Mediterranean Studies Unit, 1994.

Robert the Monk. *Historia Hierosolymitana*. Excerpted in *Urban and the Crusaders*, translated by Dana Carleton Munro, 5–8. Vol. 1, no. 2 of *Translations and Reprints from the Original Sources of European History*. Philadelphia: University of Pennsylvania, 1895.

Rokem, Jonathan. "The Power of Discourse in Urban Planning Conflict: Jerusalem and the Case of the Damascus Gate Area." MSc diss., London School of Economics and Political Science, 2006.

———. "What Does Green Really Mean? Towards Reframing Jerusalem's Planning Policy." In *Critical Cities: Ideas, Knowledge and Agitation from Emerging Urbanists*, edited by Deepa Naik and Trenton Oldfield, vol. 2, 76–92. London: Myrdle Court Press, 2010.

Rosen-Ayalon, Myriam. "On Suleiman's *Sabīls* in Jerusalem." In *The Islamic World from Classical to Modern Times: Essays in Honor of Bernard Lewis*, edited by Clifford E. Bosworth, Charles Issawi, Roger Savory, and Abraham L. Udovitch, 589–607. Princeton, NJ: Darwin, 1989.

Rouxpetel, Camille. *L'Occident au miroir de l'Orient chrétien: Cilicie, Syrie, Palestine et Égypte (XIIᵉ–XIVᵉ siècle)*. Bibliothèque des Écoles françaises d'Athènes et de Rome 369. Rome: École française de Rome, 2015.

———. "Trois récits occidentaux de la descente du feu sacré au Saint-Sépulcre (Pâques 1101): Polyphonie chrétienne et stratégies discursives." *Mélanges de l'École française de Rome—Moyen Âge* 126-1 (2014): https://doi.org/10.4000/mefrm.1932.

Ruppin, Arthur. *Memoirs, Diaries, Letters*. Edited by Alex Bein. Translated by Karen Gershon. Jerusalem: Weidenfeld and Nicolson, 1971.

Sakakini, Hala. *Jerusalem and I: A Personal Record*. Amman: Economic Press, 1990.

Salenson, Irène. *Jérusalem: Bâtir deux villes en une*. Paris: Éditions de l'Aube, 2014.

Sanbar, Elias, ed. *Jérusalem et la Palestine: Le Fonds photographique de l'École biblique de Jérusalem*. Paris: Hazan, 2013.

Schmelz, U. O. *Modern Jerusalem's Demographic Evolutions*. Jerusalem: Jerusalem Institute for Israel Studies, 1987.

Schölch, Alexander. *Palestine in Transformation, 1856–1882*. Washington DC: Institute for Palestine Studies, 1993.

Sebag Montefiore, Simon. *Jerusalem: The Biography*. New York: Alfred A. Knopf, 2011.

Sebeos. *History*. In *The Armenian History Attributed to Sebeos*. Pt. 1, *Translation and Notes*. Translated by R. W. Thomson. Liverpool: Liverpool University Press, 1999.

Segev, Tom. *One Palestine, Complete: Jews and Arabs under the Mandate*. Translated by Haim Watzman. New York: Metropolitan Books, 2000.

Sharon, Moshe. "The Ayyubid Walls of Jerusalem: A New Inscription from the Time of al-Muʿaẓẓam ʿĪsā." In *Studies in Memory of Gaston Wiet*, edited by Miriam Rosen-Ayalon, 179–93. Jerusalem: Institute of Asian and African Studies, Hebrew University of Jerusalem, 1977.

Shiloh, Yigal. "Jérusalem ancienne: Une ville cananéenne et une capitale israélite." In *Archéologie, art et histoire de la Palestine*, edited by E.-M. Laperrousaz, 119–32. Paris: Cerf, 1988.

Sivan, Emmanuel. "The Beginnings of the 'Faḍāʾil al-Quds' Literature." *Der Islam* 48 (1971): 100–110.

———. "Le Caractère sacré de Jérusalem dans l'Islam aux XIIᵉ–XIIIᵉ siècles." *Studia Islamica* 27 (1967): 149–82.

Sluglett, Peter, ed. *The Urban Social History of the Middle East, 1750–1950*. New York: Syracuse University Press, 2008.

Socrates of Constantinople. *Ecclesiastical History*. Translated by A. C. Zenos in *Socrates, Sozomenus: Church Histories*, edited by Philip Schaff and Henry Wace, 1–178. Vol. 2 of *Nicene and Post-Nicene Fathers, Second Series*. Buffalo, NY: Christian Literature, 1890.

Spafford-Vester, Bertha. *Our Jerusalem: An American Family in the Holy City, 1881–1949*. Jerusalem: Ariel, 1988.

Sperber, Dan. *Roman Palestine, 200–400: The Land*. Ramat Gan: Bar-Ilan University, 1978.

Sroor, Musa. *Fondations pieuses en mouvement: De la transformation du statut de propriété des biens waqfs à Jérusalem (1858–1917)*. Aix-en-Provence: IREMAM; Damascus: IFPO, 2005.

Storrs, R. Public Notice no. 34 (Jerusalem, 8th April 1918). In *Jerusalem, 1918–1920*, edited by C. R. Ashbee, appendix 5, 77. London: John Murray, 1921.

Tamari, Salim, ed. *Jerusalem, 1948: The Arab Neighbourhoods and Their Fate in the War.* Bethlehem: Institute of Jerusalem Studies, 1999.

———. *Year of the Locust: A Soldier's Diary and the Erasure of Palestine's Ottoman Past.* Berkeley: University of California Press, 2011.

Tarchnišvili, Michael. *Le Grand Lectionnaire de l'Église de Jérusalem (V^e–VIIIe siècle).* Vol. 1, Corpus Scriptorum Christianorum Orientalium 188, Scriptores iberici, vol. 9, text; 189, Scriptores iberici, vol. 10, translation. Vol. 2, Corpus Scriptorum Christianorum Orientalium 204, Scriptores iberici, vol. 13, text; 205, Scriptores iberici, vol. 14, translation. Leuven: Peeters, 1959–60.

Thébert, Yvon. "À propos du 'triomphe du christianisme.'" *Dialogues d'histoire ancienne* 14 (1988): 277–345.

Theodosius. *On the Topography of the Holy Land.* In *Theodosius (A.D. 530).* Translated by J. H. Bernard. London: Palestine Pilgrims' Text Society, 1893.

Tillier, Mathieu. "ʿAbd al-Malik, Muḥammad et le Jugement dernier: Le Dôme du Rocher comme expression d'une orthodoxie islamique." In *Les Vivants et les morts dans les sociétés médiévales,* edited by Société des historiens médiévistes de l'Enseignement supérieur public, 341–65. Paris: Éditions de la Sorbonne, 2018.

Trimbur, Dominique, ed. *De Bonaparte à Balfour: La France, l'Europe occidentale et la Palestine (1779–1917).* Paris: CNRS, 2001.

———. *Une école française à Jérusalem: De l'École pratique d'études bibliques des Dominicains à l'École biblique et archéologique française de Jérusalem.* Paris: Cerf, 2002.

Tsafrir, Yoram. "70–638: The Temple-less Mountain." In *Where Heaven and Earth Meet: Jerusalem's Sacred Esplanade,* edited by Oleg Grabar and Benjamin Z. Kedar, 72–99. Jerusalem: Yad Ben-Zvi Press; Austin: University of Texas Press, 2009.

ʿUlaymī, Mujīr al-Dīn al-. *Al-Uns al-jalīl bi-taʾrīkh al-Quds wa l-Khalīl.* Vol. 2. Cairo: n.p., n.d.

———. *Histoire de Jérusalem et d'Hébron depuis Abraham jusqu'à la fin du XVe siècle de J.-C.: Fragments de la "Chronique" de Moudjîr-ed-dyn traduits sur le texte arabe.* Translated by Henri Sauvaire. Paris: Ernest Leroux, 1876.

Urvoy, Marie-Thérèse. "Jésus." In *Dictionnaire du Coran,* edited by Mohammad Ali Amir-Moezzi, 438–41. Paris: Robert Laffont, 2007.

Uziel, Joe, Esther Eshel, and Nahshon Szanton. "A Late Iron Age Inscribed Sherd from the City of David." *Israel Exploration Journal* 65, no. 2 (2015): 167–78.

Valensi, Lucette. "Anthropologie comparée des pratiques de dévotion: Le Pèlerinage en Terre sainte au temps des Ottomans." In *Urbanité arabe: Hommage à Bernard Lepetit,* edited by Dakhlia Jocelyne, 33–75. Arles: Sindbad–Actes Sud, 1998.

Vincent, Hugues, and Félix-Marie Abel. *Jérusalem nouvelle.* Vol. 2 of *Jérusalem: Recherches de topographie, d'archéologie et d'histoire.* Paris: Joseph Gabalda, 1914.

Volney, Constantin-François de. *Voyage en Syrie et en Égypte (1783–1785).* Paris: Dienne and Volland, 1787. Translated as *Travels through Syria and Egypt, in the Years 1783, 1784, and 1785.* Dublin: White, Byrne, W. Porter, Moore, Dornin, and Wm. Jones, 1793.

Weigert, Gideon. *Israel's Presence in East Jerusalem.* Jerusalem: Jerusalem Post Press, 1973.

Weinfeld, Moshe. "Jerusalem: A Political and Spiritual Capital." In *Capital Cities: Urban Planning and Spiritual Dimensions,* edited by J. Goodnick Westenholz, 15–40. Jerusalem: Bible Lands Museum, 1998.

Wharton, Annabel. "Jerusalem Remade." In *Modernism and the Middle East: Architecture and Politics in the Twentieth Century,* edited by Sandy Isenstadt and Kishwar Rizvi, 39–60. Seattle: University of Washington Press, 2008.

Wildangel, René. *Zwischen Achse und Mandatsmacht, Palästina und der Nationalsozialismus.* Berlin: Klaus Schwartz Verlag, 2007.

William of Tyre. *Historia rerum in partibus transmarinis gestarum.* Translated by Emily Atwater Babcock and A. C. Krey as *A History of Deeds Done beyond the Sea.* Vol. 1. New York: Columbia University Press, 1943.

Wood, Abigail. "Soundscapes of Pilgrimage: European and American Christians in Jerusalem's Old City." *Ethnomusicology Forum* 23 (2014): 285–305.

Young, George. *Corps de droit ottoman.* Vol. 1. Oxford: Clarendon, 1905.

Contributors

VINCENT LEMIRE is an associate professor (with habilitation) of contemporary history at the University of Paris-Est / Gustave Eiffel, a member of its "Analyse comparée des pouvoirs" research team, the director of the Open Jerusalem European Research Council project, and the current director of the French Research Centre in Jerusalem (Centre de recherche français à Jérusalem). His current work focuses on contemporary Jerusalem and the Middle East, environmental history, and the making of urban cultural heritage. Among other publications, he is the author of *La Soif de Jérusalem: Essai d'hydrohistoire (1840–1948)* (Publications de la Sorbonne, 2010) and *Jerusalem 1900: The Holy City in the Age of Possibilities* (translated by Catherine Tihanyi and Lys Ann Weiss for University of Chicago Press, 2017; originally published by Armand Colin, 2013).

KATELL BERTHELOT is a historian working on Jews and Judaism in the Hellenistic and Roman periods, and a professor at the French National Center for Scientific Research / Aix-Marseille University. From 2007 to 2011, she was appointed as a researcher at the French Research Centre in Jerusalem. She coedited the Bibliothèque de Qumrân series (Éditions du Cerf) from 2006 to 2018 and is the author of *In Search of the Promised Land? The Hasmonean Dynasty between Biblical Models and Hellenistic Diplomacy* (Vandenhoeck und Ruprecht, 2018) and *Jews and Their Roman Rivals: Pagan Rome's Challenge to Israel* (Princeton University Press, 2021).

JULIEN LOISEAU is a professor of the history of the medieval Islamic world at Aix-Marseille University and a former director of the French Research Centre in Jerusalem. A historian and an Arabist, he has devoted his research to Egypt, Palestine, and Ethiopia in the Middle Ages. He is the author of *Reconstruire la Maison du sultan: Ruine et recomposition de l'ordre urbain au Caire, 1350–1450* (IFAO, 2010) and *Les Mamelouks (XIIIᵉ-XVIᵉ siècle): Une expérience du pouvoir dans l'Islam médiéval* (Seuil, 2014), which won a prize from the Institut du Monde Arabe in 2015 and is forthcoming in English translation. He recently edited "Ethiopia and Nubia in Islamic Egypt: Connected Histories of Northeastern Africa," a special issue of *Northeastern African Studies* (vol. 19, no. 1 [2019]).

YANN POTIN, a historian and archivist, is a senior research fellow at the Archives nationales and a part-time associate professor of legal history in the Institut de droit public, sciences politiques et sociales at the Sorbonne Paris Nord University. As an associate researcher at the French Research Centre in Jerusalem, he has been a member of the European Research Council project Open Jerusalem's steering committee. He coedited, with Patrick Boucheron and others, *France in the World: A New Global History* (Other Press, 2019) and has recently published *Trésor, écrits, pouvoirs: Archives et bibliothèques d'État en France à la fin du Moyen Âge* (CNRS, 2020).

Index

Founded in 1893,
UNIVERSITY OF CALIFORNIA PRESS
publishes bold, progressive books and journals
on topics in the arts, humanities, social sciences,
and natural sciences—with a focus on social
justice issues—that inspire thought and action
among readers worldwide.

The UC PRESS FOUNDATION
raises funds to uphold the press's vital role
as an independent, nonprofit publisher, and
receives philanthropic support from a wide
range of individuals and institutions—and from
committed readers like you. To learn more, visit
ucpress.edu/supportus.

Printed in the USA
CPSIA information can be obtained
at www.ICGtesting.com
LVHW091046110224
771542LV00017B/104/J